T0044129

We Hope You
Find Your Trails

The Dayhiker's Guide to the National Parks, First Edition

ISBN 978-1-62128-079-8
Library of Congress Control Number (LCCN): 2023904621

Printed in the United States of America

Published by Stone Road Press
Author/Photographer/Trail Map Maker/Designer: Michael Joseph Oswald

This title is also published in electronic format. Content appearing in print may not be available electronically.

Corrections/Contact

This guidebook has been researched and written with the greatest attention to detail in order to provide you with the most accurate and pertinent information. Unfortunately, travel information is subject to change, and inadvertent errors and omissions do occur. Should you encounter a change, error, or omission while using this guidebook, write to corrections@stoneroadpress.com. Your contribution will help make future editions better than the last.

Find us online at StoneRoadPress.com, Facebook (facebook.com/thestoneroadpress), Twitter (@stoneroadpress), Instagram (@stoneroadpress), and Flickr (stoneroadpress).

Disclaimer

Your safety is important to us. If any activity is beyond your ability or threatened by forces outside your control, do not attempt it. It is also suggested to check with the park to confirm information (weather and trail/road conditions in particular) when it matters most.

The primary purpose of this guidebook is to enhance our readers' national park experiences, but the author and publisher cannot be held responsible for any experiences while traveling.

Cover and Introduction Photo Descriptions

Front cover: Cathedral Valley Overlook (Capitol Reef)
Introduction Pages: Castle (Badlands), Butterflies (Great Smoky Mountains), Boy Scout Trail (Joshua Tree)
About the Author: Druid Arch (Canyonlands)
Opposite Contents: Queen's Garden (Bryce Canyon)
Closing Pages: Bison (Wind Cave), Feral Horses (Theodore Roosevelt), Cracker Lake (Glacier), Grizzly Bears (Katmai)
Back Cover: Delta Lake (Grand Teton)

STONE ROAD PRESS

About me

Hi, I'm Mike. I've been fortunate to enjoy quite a bit of time in our magnificent parks. In an effort to share this joy, I've put in some work creating highly-useful tools to help national park explorers like you. I love watching prairie dogs, making natural tripods (for photos like this one), and sharing a smile with fellow park enthusiasts as they enjoy a beautiful day in a beautiful place.

Having worked in an office after college, I feel like I understand the value of vacation time and income. You don't want to waste either one. National Parks are often vast expanses of largely undeveloped land. To make the most of your National Park adventures, you need a good guide. I'm obviously biased, but I believe this book will guide you to some truly exceptional places.

Mesquite Flat Sand Dunes (Death Valley)

Supporting Park People

I'm Here to Help

One of the best things about this life path is meeting fellow National Park enthusiasts like you. A few of them are working on their own high-quality, National-Park-themed things.

Dan is awesome. We met in person through a mutual friend a few years back. Many of us were at the edge of our office chairs wondering when a 2023-model snowball he rolled would melt, but he also creates very clever National Park designs at Nine Day Weekend.

It's likely you already know about National Parks Traveler. Kurt's doing good work over there, spreading the National Park news.

If you are working on making positive contributions to the outdoors/National Park communities, tell me about it by writing to mike@stoneroadpress.com. I know (far too well) how difficult it is to run a business and I'm more than happy to help (if we share a similar purpose).

NATIONAL PARKS
TRAVELER

NationalParksTraveler.org

**Where more than 2 million readers and
listeners a year get their national park news**

ESSENTIAL COVERAGE FOR ESSENTIAL PLACES
News | Features | Editorials | Opinion | Podcasts | Webinars

CONTENTS

Hiking

Hello, fellow hiker! I'm really excited you're getting ready to explore the U.S. National Parks—some of our planet's most spectacular and diverse landscapes—on foot. It's not uncommon for people to think hiking is this extreme activity. It certainly can be, but in all hiking's forms, it always looks an awful lot like walking to me. It's walking with flare! Occasionally scrambling boulders. Climbing ladders. Slogging up/down mountains. Cruising through canyons. And sometimes, when it's least like walking, you just sit along the shore of a picturesque alpine lake, maybe dreaming about…what trail to hike next! Those tend to be my favorite moments. And I'm confident this book will get you out in the wilderness, where you can dream about what's next!

While hiking is walking, you really need to know your limits. Pay careful attention to trail distance, elevation gain, and elevation (all provided in these pages). If you find a dream trail but aren't sure you can do it, train. Exercise—on flat land at sea level or running hills at 10,000 feet—can prepare you for any of these trails. Well, maybe not climbing Mount Whitney. That's nearly impossible! The other thing you must prepare for are conditions (weather and trail). You don't want to be in a slot canyon when it's raining (sometimes even when it's raining miles away). But don't avoid the parks or stay in your tent/hotel because a little water is falling from the sky. Places with towering cliffs like Yosemite and Zion sprout ephemeral waterfalls during heavy rain and/or rapid snowmelt. Winter is often a magical (and uncrowded) time to explore your parks. Take advantage of it. But if trails are icy, be sure to have traction devices and maybe even hiking poles.

About the Trails

So, what's included? There are 198 trail maps, featuring 280 trails. They range from easy to extreme, and 0.3 to 30.0 miles. Extremely-long-distance trails are not the norm. Of the trails detailed within these pages, the average distance is 5.9 miles. The average difficulty lies between moderate and strenuous. 46 are considered easy (short and flat). 107 are moderate (short and steep or long and relatively flat). 119 are strenuous (long and/or lots of elevation gain). 8 are extreme (serious exposure and/or challenging obstacles). Most trails do not allow dogs but a few do and National Parks are becoming increasingly pet friendly. Check with the park, if you intend to bring your pooch. Basic data for each trail includes difficulty, distance, climbing, and type of trail (loop, point-to-point, lollipop, figure 8). Climbing refers to the total number of feet you ascend on the trail. For every trail beginning and ending at the same trailhead, you will descend an equal number of feet. Some trails are flat and you climb only a few feet. Other trails are Mount Whitney and you climb (and then descend) more than a mile.

No individual trail maps are included for Mammoth Cave, Congaree, Biscayne, Everglades, Dry Tortugas, Gateway Arch, Isle Royale, Voyageurs, Wind Cave, Hot Springs, Carlsbad Caverns, White Sands, Petrified Forest, Glacier Bay, Lake

Clark, Katmai, Gates of the Arctic, and Kobuk Valley. But you'll still find a park map and a brief discussion on their hiking trails. For example, White Sands has nine miles of trails. Alkali Flat is fantastic, but a trail map doesn't convey information any more efficiently than words. There are no trail junctions. The terrain is undulating dunes, barely showing up in shaded relief. It's staked the entire way, and most of the time you can follow footprints from start to finish. Or look at Isle Royale. It has a large network of trails but the island can only be reached by boat or plane, making it a backpacking/paddling destination. With that said, there are a few dayhiking possibilities and they're covered in the blurb beneath the park map.

Many of the parks are paradise for dayhikers. I have yet to meet a mile of trail I didn't enjoy at Glacier and Yosemite! It's bordering on information overload, but you'll also find "more trail" sections for most of the parks where dayhiking is covered in detail. Put simply, more trails warrant discussion. And, especially when visiting any of the ultra-popular destinations (Acadia, Great Smoky Mountains, Grand Teton, Yellowstone, Glacier, Rocky Mountain, Arches, Zion, Grand Canyon, Sequoia, Yosemite, Mount Rainier) during peak season, extra information doesn't hurt!

About the Trail Maps

I made the trail maps in Adobe Illustrator using data from the USGS National Map. Each map features a shaded relief background, depicting the area's terrain. You'll also find specific elevation data at prominent locations like trailheads, junctions, passes, and peaks. Elevation data combined with shaded relief provides considerable insight into the trail's difficulty. There are a few areas (like canyons) where elevation data is provided near the trail, so you have a better idea of your surroundings too. Tall walls make for dramatic scenery!

Trailheads and parking areas are clearly marked on each map. There's plenty of space in the parks, but it can get crowded. Crowdedness is directly proportional to the number of parking spaces. And there never seems to be enough of them between 9am and 3pm. I've listed the number of parking spaces at the trailheads. Some are an approximation (~), as many visitors get creative making their own parking space. When parking at popular destinations, especially early in the morning, it's a good idea to consider your surroundings. Just as it's no fun arriving at a trailhead with a full lot, it's kind of a bummer if you get back to your car and find it parked in by others who made their own spots. To alleviate the parking predicament, a couple parks run free shuttle services during peak season. Shuttle stops are also clearly identified on the trail maps.

A few of the maps have multiple trails or variants worth considering. Those variants and loops are highlighted on each map with a solid-colored path beneath the standard, green-dashed trail line. Trailheads for every trail covered in this book are clearly pinpointed on the trail maps as well as the park map at the beginning of each section.

Elevation data was sourced from Google Earth. If you'd like to find more places to explore, I highly recommend scrolling around Google Maps, Google Earth, and/or the USGS National Map Viewer. (Or wait for me to make another book!) The United States possesses an incredible amount of geographic diversity and about one-fifth of all land is federal. Excellent hiking (and camping) opportunities are everywhere, including other public land: Bureau of Land Management (BLM), United States Forest Service (USFS), as well as State Parks and other National Park Service (NPS) units. The BLM manages 245 million acres. USFS manages 193 million acres. NPS manage 85 million acres.

Below is a legend for all the trail maps.

Trail Map Legend

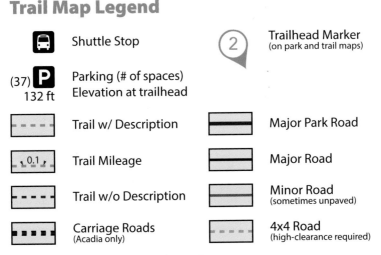

Shuttle Stop

Trailhead Marker
(on park and trail maps)

(37) Parking (# of spaces)
132 ft Elevation at trailhead

Trail w/ Description

Major Park Road

Trail Mileage

Major Road

Trail w/o Description

Minor Road
(sometimes unpaved)

Carriage Roads
(Acadia only)

4x4 Road
(high-clearance required)

Online Trailhead Location Map

This QR code leads to a Google Map with trailhead locations for all the trails detailed in this book. I'm planning on treating it as a living document, adding layers of information over the years. But, if you didn't know about them already, I also wanted to point you to custom Google Maps (or whatever map service has similar functionality). They can be a very useful trip-planning tool.

Make a custom map for each trip or keep one master document for all your adventures. Mark where you're staying, trails, outfitters, restaurants, maybe even places to avoid, whatever. You can add layers. Choose your own icons. Allow friends and/or family to add their own points of interest. It's an unbelievably useful tool. I do this a lot, and these maps greatly increase efficiency while exploring this great, big, beautiful country of ours. Maybe it'll help you too!

Best Dayhiking Parks

Acadia (Maine)
Great Smoky Mountains (TN/NC)
Grand Teton (Wyoming)
Yellowstone (Wyoming)
Glacier (Montana)
Big Bend (Texas)
Rocky Mountain (Colorado)
Arches (Utah)
Canyonlands (Utah)
Capitol Reef (Utah)
Bryce Canyon (Utah)
Zion (Utah)
Joshua Tree (California)
Death Valley (California)
Sequoia (California)
Yosemite (California)
Redwood (California)
Mount Rainier (Washington)
Olympic (Washington)
North Cascades (Washington)

Best Trails

Precipice (Acadia)
Beehive (Acadia)
Pemetic Northwest (Acadia)
Giant Slide (Acadia)
Old Rag (Shenandoah)
Long Point (New River Gorge)
Alum Cave/Mount LeConte (Great Smoky Mountains)
Charlie's Bunion (Smoky Mtns)
Notch (Badlands)
Castle (Badlands)
Delta Lake (Grand Teton)
Lake Solitude (Grand Teton)
Fairy Falls (Yellowstone)
Avalanche Peak (Yellowstone)
Union Falls (Yellowstone)
Swiftcurrent Pass (Glacier)
Grinnell Glacier (Glacier)
Hidden Lake (Glacier)
Highline (Glacier)
Sperry Chalet (Glacier)
Santa Elena Canyon (Big Bend)
South Rim (Big Bend)

Devil's Hall (Guadalupe Mtns)
Alkali Flat (White Sands)
Chasm Lake (Rocky Mountain)
Sky Pond (Rocky Mountain)
Black Lake (Rocky Mountain)
Emerald Lake (Rocky Mountain)
Odessa Lake (Rocky Mountain)
High Dune (Great Sand Dunes)
Delicate Arch (Arches)
Chesler Park/Joint (Canyonlands)
Spring Canyon (Capitol Reef)
Cassidy Arch (Capitol Reef)
Fairyland Loop (Bryce Canyon)
Navajo Loop (Bryce Canyon)
Angel's Landing (Zion)
Observation Point (Zion)
The Narrows (Zion)
South Kaibab (Grand Canyon)
Cape Royal (Grand Canyon)
Bristlecone (Great Basin)
Wheeler Peak (Great Basin)
Boy Scout/Willow Hole (Joshua Tree)
Bear Gulch/High Peaks (Pinnacles)
Golden Canyon (Death Valley)
Mesquite Flat Dunes (Death Valley)
Telescope Peak (Death Valley)
Lakes (Sequoia)
Sentinel Dome (Yosemite)
Mist/JMT/Half Dome (Yosemite)
Lassen Peak (Lassen Volcanic)
Cinder Cone (Lassen Volcanic)
Tall Trees (Redwood)
Fern Canyon (Redood)
Comet Falls (Mount Rainier)
Skyline (Mount Rainier)
Burroughs Mountains (Mt Rainier)
Tolmie Peak Lookout (Mt Rainier)
Lake/Mount Angeles (Olympic)
High Divide (Olympic)
Sahale Arm (North Cascades)
Hidden Lake Lookout (N Cascades)
Maple Pass (North Cascades)
Root Glacier (Wrangell–St. Elias)
Thorofare Ridge (Denali)
Harding Icefield (Kenai Fjords)
Sliding Sands (Haleakala)
Pipiwai (Haleakala)

*__Trail Name__ = Top 25 Trails

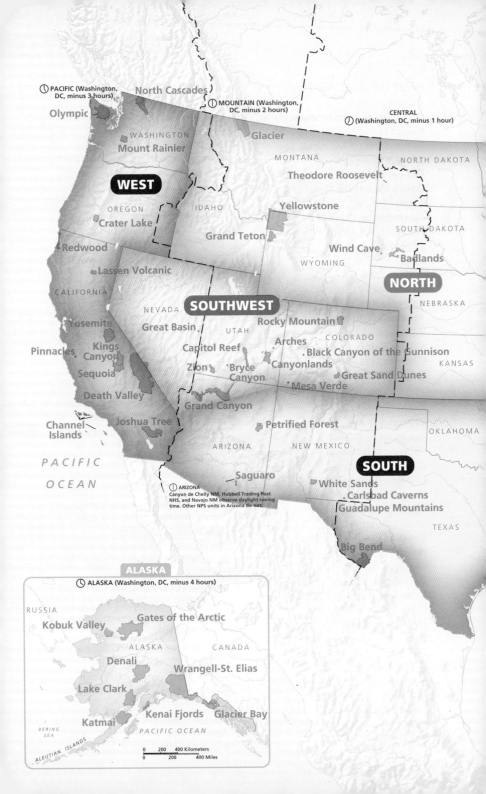

EASTERN (Washington, DC)

Voyageurs
Isle Royale
MINNESOTA
LAKE SUPERIOR
MAINE
Acadia
WISCONSIN
LAKE HURON
VT
NH
MA
RI
CT
MICHIGAN
LAKE ONTARIO
NEW YORK
IOWA
LAKE ERIE
PENNSYLVANIA
NJ
ATLANTIC
OCEAN
Indiana Dunes
Cuyahoga Valley
ILLINOIS
INDIANA
OHIO
MD
DE
Shenandoah
Gateway Arch
WEST
VIRGINIA
New River
Gorge NP
VIRGINIA
KENTUCKY
MISSOURI
Mammoth Cave
NORTH CAROLINA
TENNESSEE
Great Smoky Mountains
ARKANSAS
SOUTH
CAROLINA
Hot
Springs
Congaree
ALABAMA
GEORGIA
EAST
North

Scale for all areas except Alaska
0   100   200   300   400 Kilometers
0   100   200   300   400 Miles

MISSISSIPPI
LOUISIANA
FLORIDA

GULF OF MEXICO

Everglades
Biscayne
Dry Tortugas

REMOTE ISLANDS

HAWAII (Washington, DC, minus 5 hours;
minus 6 hours during daylight saving time)
KAUA'I
NI'IHAU
O'AHU
MOLOKA'I
Haleakala
MAUI
HAWAII
PACIFIC
OCEAN
HAWAI'I
Hawai'i Volcanoes

REMOTE ISLANDS

AMERICAN SAMOA (Washington,
DC, minus 5 hours; minus 6 hours
during daylight saving time)
American Samoa
TUTUILA   OFU   TA'Ū
AMERICAN SAMOA
PACIFIC OCEAN

REMOTE ISLANDS

PUERTO RICO and VIRGIN ISLANDS
(Washington, DC, plus 1 hour; same
time during daylight saving time)
VIRGIN ISLANDS
PUERTO RICO
Virgin
Islands

The East

North

EASTERN (Washington, DC)

0   100   200   300   400 Kilometers
0   100   200   300   400 Miles

NORTHEAST

BOSTON AREA
Adams NHP
Boston African American NHS
Boston Harbor Islands NRA
Boston NHP
Frederick Law Olmsted NHS
John Fitzgerald Kennedy NHS
Longfellow House-
  Washington's Headquarters NHS
Minute Man NHP
Salem Maritime NHS
Saugus Iron Works NHS

NEW YORK CITY AREA
African Burial Ground NM
Castle Clinton NM
Federal Hall N MEM
Gateway NRA (also NJ)
General Grant N MEM
Governors Island NM
Hamilton Grange N MEM
Saint Paul's Church NHS
Statue of Liberty NM
Stonewall NM
Theodore Roosevelt Birthplace NHS

PHILADELPHIA AREA
Edgar Allan Poe NHS
Hopewell Furnace NHS
Independence NHP
Thaddeus Kosciuszko N MEM
Valley Forge NHP

BALTIMORE AREA
Fort McHenry NM and
  Historic Shrine
Hampton NHS

NATIONAL CAPITAL

DISTRICT OF COLUMBIA
Belmont-Paul Women's
  Equality NM
Carter G. Woodson Home NHS
Constitution Gardens
Ford's Theatre NHS
Franklin Delano Roosevelt
  Memorial
Frederick Douglass NHS
Korean War Veterans Memorial
Lincoln Memorial
Lyndon Baines Johnson
  Memorial Grove
Martin Luther King, Jr.
  Memorial
Mary McLeod Bethune
  Council House NHS
National Capital Parks
National Mall
Pennsylvania Avenue NHS
Rock Creek Park
Theodore Roosevelt Island
Thomas Jefferson Memorial
Vietnam Veterans Memorial
Washington Monument
White House
World War I Memorial
World War II Memorial

MARYLAND
Antietam NB
Catoctin Mountain Park
Chesapeake and Ohio Canal
  NHP (also DC and WV)
Clara Barton NHS
Fort Washington Park
Greenbelt Park
Monocacy NB
Piscataway Park
Potomac Heritage NST
  (also PA, VA, and DC)

VIRGINIA
Arlington House,
  The Robert E. Lee Memorial
George Washington Memorial
  PKWY (also MD)
Manassas NBP
Prince William Forest Park
Wolf Trap National Park for the
  Performing Arts

Acadia
Hiking Trails: 150+ miles

Precipice

Beehive

Acadia Favorites

(1) **Bar Island**
Easy | 2.0 miles | 220 feet

(2) **Ladder**
Strenuous | 2.3 miles | 670 feet

(3) **Precipice**
Extreme | 2.2 miles | 950 feet

(4) **Beehive**
Extreme | 1.1 miles | 490 feet

(5) **Gorham Mountain**
Moderate | 2.8 miles | 480 feet

(6) **Jordan Cliffs**
Strenuous | 3.1 miles | 890 feet

(7) **Northwest Pemetic**
Strenuous | 1.6 miles | 785 feet

(8) **Cadillac Mountain**
Strenuous | 3.0 miles | 1,210 feet

(9) **Giant Slide**
Strenuous | 4.6 miles | 1,100 feet

(10) **Beech Cliff**
Strenuous | 2.1 miles | 460 feet

(11) **Perpendicular**
Strenuous | 2.4 miles | 850 feet

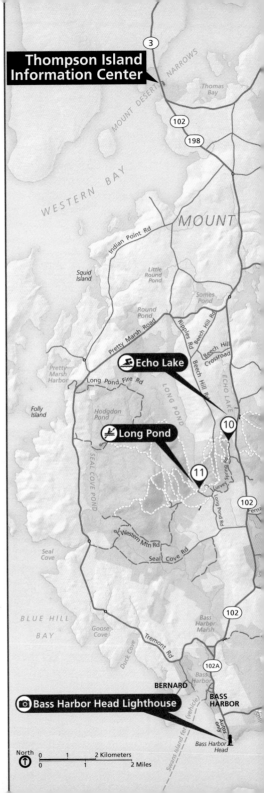

Thompson Island Information Center

3

102

198

MOUNT DESERT NARROWS

Thomas Bay

WESTERN BAY

MOUNT

Indian Point Rd

Squid Island

Little Round Pond

Somes Pond

Round Pond

Ripples Rd

Beech Hill Rd

Beech Hill Crossroad

Pretty Marsh Road

Echo Lake

ECHO LAKE

Pretty Marsh Harbor

Long Pond Fire Rd

LONG POND

Folly Island

Hodgdon Pond

Long Pond

10

11

Spring Rd

SEAL COVE POND

Curves

Long Pond Rd

102

Fern

Western Mtn Rd

Seal Cove

Seal Cove Rd

BLUE HILL BAY

Goose Cove

Bass Harbor Marsh

102

Tremont Rd

Duck Cove

102A

Bass Harbor

BERNARD

BASS HARBOR

Swans Island ferry (vehicle)

Autos only

📷 **Bass Harbor Head Lighthouse**

Bass Harbor Head

North

0   1   2 Kilometers
0   1   2 Miles

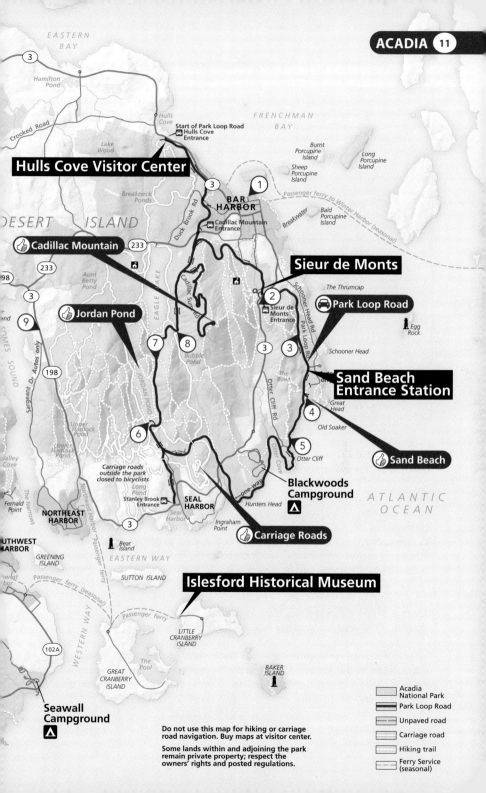

EASTERN
BAY

3

Hamilton
Pond

Crooked Road

Hulls
Cove

Lake
Wood

Start of Park Loop Road
Hulls Cove
Entrance

Hulls Cove Visitor Center

FRENCHMAN
BAY

Burnt
Porcupine
Island

Long
Porcupine
Island

Sheep
Porcupine
Island

Breakneck
Ponds

3

1

BAR
HARBOR

Cadillac Mountain
Entrance

Passenger ferry to Winter Harbor (seasonal)

Breakwater

Bald
Porcupine
Island

DESERT   ISLAND

👍 **Cadillac Mountain**

233

233

Aunt
Betty
Pond

98

3

👍 **Jordan Pond**

9

198

Duck Brook Rd

Cadillac Summit Rd

EAGLE LAKE

Bubble
Pond

Sieur de Monts

2

Sieur de
Monts Entrance

🚗 **Park Loop Road**

The Thrumcap

Schooner Head Rd

Park Loop Rd

3

3

Schooner Head

The Bowl

Egg
Rock

**Sand Beach
Entrance Station**

7

8

JORDAN POND

Upper
Hadlock
Pond

198

Lower
Hadlock
Pond

6

Otter Cliff Rd

Great
Head

Old Soaker

4

Otter Cove

5

Otter Cliff

👍 **Sand Beach**

Valley
Cove

Carriage roads
outside the park
closed to bicyclists

Stanley Brook
Entrance

Fernald
Point

The Narrows

NORTHEAST
HARBOR

Long
Pond

SEAL
HARBOR

one-way

Seal
Harbor

Hunters Head

**Blackwoods
Campground**
⛺

ATLANTIC
OCEAN

UTHWEST
HARBOR

3

Bear
Island

Ingraham
Point

👍 **Carriage Roads**

GREENING
ISLAND

EASTERN WAY

SUTTON ISLAND

Islesford Historical Museum

Passenger ferry (seasonal)

bor

Passenger ferry

LITTLE
CRANBERRY
ISLAND

102A

GREAT
CRANBERRY
ISLAND

The
Pool

BAKER
ISLAND

WESTERN WAY

**Seawall
Campground**
⛺

Do not use this map for hiking or carriage
road navigation. Buy maps at visitor center.

Some lands within and adjoining the park
remain private property; respect the
owners' rights and posted regulations.

Acadia
National Park

Park Loop Road

Unpaved road

Carriage road

Hiking trail

Ferry Service
(seasonal)

BAR ISLAND

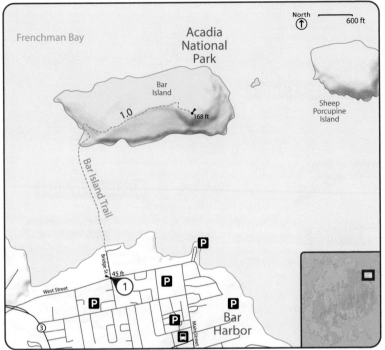

Bar Island | Easy | 2.0 miles | 220 feet | Out-and-back
Trailhead: Downtown Bar Harbor at Bridge Street & West Street (1)

Bar Island is fun—especially for families—thanks to the tides. Almost half the trail is crossing Mount Desert Narrows via a rocky land bridge that reveals itself around low tide. So, you need to check a tide table. The park suggests it's safe to cross within 90 minutes of low tide. Expect to get your feet wet near either end of that 3-hour window. Upon reaching Bar Island, continue hiking to the 168-foot summit and its rock pile for decent views back to Bar Harbor. You can also stroll along the coastline. Just don't lose track of time. If the tide strands you on the island, you're looking at a 9-hour wait until the next low tide or a $100+ water taxi ride back to Bar Harbor. Little Moose Island, over at Schoodic Peninsula is a similarly tidal hiking opportunity.

Bar Island is great for anyone staying in Bar Harbor. You should have no problem walking to the trailhead, located at the north end of Bridge Street. For everyone else, metered parking is available along West Street. There are also several parking lots nearby. Alternatively, Village Green, the Island Explorer Shuttle depot (exploreacadia.com) is only four blocks away. Parking is highly competitive in summer, and nearly impossible for the 4th of July. Arrive early or use the shuttle.

LADDER

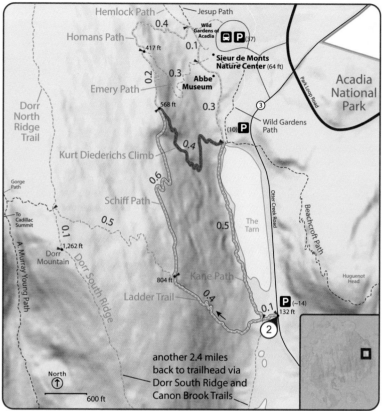

Hemlock Path — Jesup Path
Homans Path — 0.4
Wild Gardens of Acadia
417 ft
0.1
Sieur de Monts
Nature Center (64 ft)
0.2 0.3
Emery Path — Abbe Museum
Acadia National Park
568 ft 0.3
3
Dorr North Ridge Trail
(10) Wild Gardens Path
Kurt Diederichs Climb
0.4
Gorge Path
0.6
Schiff Path
To Cadillac Summit
0.5 The Tarn 0.5
Beachcroft Path
1,262 ft
Dorr Mountain
0.1
Huguenot Head
A. Murray Young Path
Dorr South Ridge
804 ft
Kane Path
Ladder Trail
0.4
0.1
132 ft
2
North
another 2.4 miles back to trailhead via Dorr South Ridge and Canon Brook Trails
600 ft

Ladder | Strenuous | 2.3 miles | 670 feet | Loop
Trailhead: Ladder, Otter Creek Road (2) or Sieur de Monts

Acadia is well-known for its ladder trails. Steel rungs and rails aid hikers ascending a few of Mount Desert Island's otherwise unapproachable rocky summits. Ladder isn't as extreme or as popular as Precipice and Beehive but there's a fair amount of exposure-induced thrills. The orange loop highlighted above is a quick way to check out the ladder section. You can also return via Homans Path (yellow loop), adding less than a mile. It's pretty neat (and highly recommended). Or consider continuing up to Dorr Mountain, where you can return to the trailhead via Dorr's North or South Ridge or keep going down the backside of Dorr Mountain and up to Cadillac Summit. The options are almost endless! Continuing to Cadillac isn't as scenic as the alternatives but it is a workout and a way to avoid the summertime Cadillac crowds/traffic.

You'll find roadside parking on Otter Creek Road (2) or parking lots at Sieur de Monts and just north of the Tarn. Sieur de Monts is a designated shuttle stop.

PRECIPICE

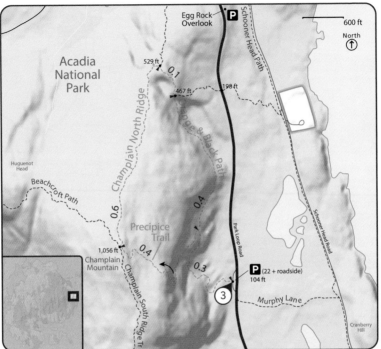

Precipice | Extreme | 2.2 miles | 950 feet | Loop
Trailhead: Precipice Trailhead, Park Loop Road (3)

Precipice is another ladder trail. It also has the most exposure, the greatest fear factor, and ... it's the most fun (if you aren't afraid of heights)! So, know you'll be walking along narrow cliff-faces, climbing steel ladders, and summitting Champlain Mountain via a trail that is more vertical than horizontal. It's just about as close to rock climbing as you can get without climbing any rock. The trail is straight forward. Go up Precipice. Proceed at your own pace and let faster hikers pass. Catch your breath and enjoy the views atop Champlain Mountain, and then take Champlain North Ridge (moderately steep but nothing compared to what you just did) to the Orange & Black Trail junction. Here, you have two choices. Take Orange & Black Trail south back to Precipice and the trailhead. Or walk east, which quickly intersects Park Loop Road, and then follow the road back to your vehicle. Precipice is fantastic, but it isn't for anyone afraid of heights. If you're not sure this hike is for you, bring binoculars or a long lens to the trailhead and watch hikers navigate the trail. You can get a pretty good idea what's in store from the parking area. One important note: The trail closes each summer to protect falcon habitat.

There's a moderately-sized parking lot at the trailhead on Park Loop Road. The lot fills early. While turnover is fairly rapid, an early start is a good idea.

BEEHIVE

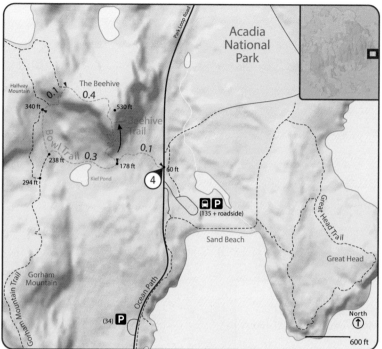

Beehive | Extreme | 1.1 miles | 490 feet | Lollipop
Trailhead: Bowl, Park Loop Road across from Sand Beach (4)

Beehive is another great ladder trail. It's about half as strenuous as Precipice. Bowl Trailhead is on the west side of Park Loop Road, just north of Sand Beach Parking Lot. Use the crosswalk. The trail is well-marked and easy to follow. Take Bowl to Beehive. Climb the hive using the rungs and rails and return via Bowl Trail. Alternatively, you could return via Gorham Mountain and Ocean Path. It's longer but considerably more interesting. Hike south to Gorham Mountain, scramble across Cadillac Cliffs, and then catch Ocean Path back to Sand Beach. Together, it's still less than four miles, and you'll walk right past Thunder Hole. And Otter Cliffs and Boulder Beach are on Ocean Path just south of Gorham Mountain Trailhead, if you'd like to make a quick out-and-back to have a look. Thunder Hole is typically most thunderous right between high and low tide (check the tides if you want the best chance of hearing some thunder).

Parking is at Sand Beach or the right lane of Park Loop Road (when permitted). Sand Beach is a shuttle stop and an extremely popular destination. Adding Gorham Mountain and Ocean Path to the hiking itinerary dramatically increases your parking choices, which is something you should be thinking about. Or use the shuttle.

GORHAM MOUNTAIN

Gorham Mountain |
Moderate | 2.8 miles | 480
feet | Loop
Trailhead: Gorham Mountain, Park Loop Rd (5)

Gorham Mountain and Cadillac Cliffs are worth a visit no matter what, but it's a particularly good sunset alternative (along with Ocean Path), if you strike out on securing a Cadillac Mountain permit. Like most Acadia trails, it's easy-to-follow. Hiking up Gorham Mountain, you'll reach a junction at the Bates Memorial (Bates helped establish many of the trails and the style of cairns you'll see throughout the park). Cadillac Cliffs is a little more strenuous with some rock scrambling. It's a good choice! Do Cadillac Cliffs on the way to Gorham Mountain and skip it on the way back for a 1.7-mile out-and-back. Better yet, continue beyond Gorham Mountain to Bowl Trail (add the Beehive if you're looking for some excitement) and loop back via Ocean Path for a 2.8-mile loop, passing Thunder Hole. The best chances for Thunder Hole bringing the thunder is typically between high and low tide. Plan accordingly. Ocean Path continues beyond Gorham Mountain Trailhead to Boulder Beach and Otter Cliffs. As a bonus, Gorham Mountain Trail is a hot spot for blueberry enthusiasts! Blueberry season usually begins in late July.

While Gorham Mountain Trailhead is less popular than Sand Beach or Thunder Hole, don't count on finding parking there (especially in summer). The road is one-way and you'd have to circle back around if the Gorham lot is full. In summer, begin looking for parking at Sand Beach and take a spot if you see one. Or use the Island Explorer Shuttle.

JORDAN CLIFFS

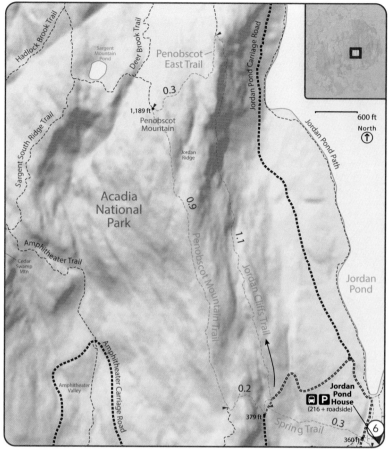

Jordan Cliffs | Strenuous | 3.1 miles | 890 feet | Lollipop
Trailhead: Jordan Pond House (6)

This ladder trail takes you high above Jordan Pond, with exceptional views of Pemetic Mountain, Cadillac Mountain, the Bubbles, and, once you reach Penobscot Mountain Trail, across Long Pond (not the quiet side Long Pond) to the Atlantic Ocean. While there's some exposure, the rungs and rails aren't as intimidating as you'll find at Beehive or Precipice. For more miles, add some summits (Sargent Mountain, Gilmore Peak, Parkman Mountain and/or Bald Peak), loop a lake or two (Jordan Pond, Bubble Pond, or Eagle Lake), or enjoy a leisurely stroll along the miles of crushed stone carriage roads. Once again, Acadia's nearly limitless hiking options are on display.

There are three large parking lots at the south end of Jordan Pond but it's also the busiest area of the park. Get an early start or take the shuttle.

PEMETIC NORTHWEST

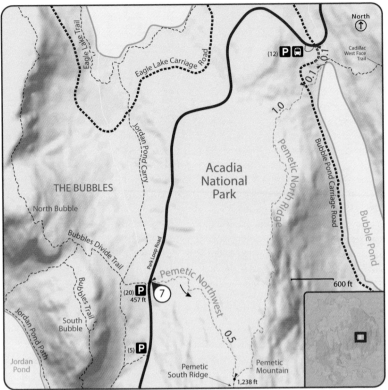

Pemetic Northwest | Strenuous | 1.6 miles | 785 feet | Point-to-point
Trailhead: Across Park Loop Road from Bubble Rock Parking Lot (7)

Several routes reach the summit of Pemetic Mountain, where you'll find fantastic 360-degree views of Mount Desert Island. The most fun is Pemetic Northwest. It ascends quickly and includes some scrambling and surprises. Hiking options are abundant. An out-and-back to Pemetic's summit is about one mile from the Bubble Rock parking lot. The point-to-point to Bubble Pond via Pemetic North Ridge is less than two miles, but you'll have to hike or shuttle back to Bubble Rock (or Jordan Pond). Bubble Pond is serene compared to Jordan Pond and you'll find an iconic carriage road bridge nearby. A more gradual return choice is Pemetic South Ridge, which leads back to Jordan Pond via Jordan Path. And then there's Pemetic East Cliff Trail. Rather than accessing it from a roadside trailhead, you must hike in via Day Mountain or the Triad. The short East Cliff trail intersects Pemetic South Ridge.

Parking lots at Bubble Rock and Bubble Pond are small but convenient (if you find space). Jordan Pond has way more parking and a proportionate increase in activity. Bubble Pond and Jordan Pond are Island Explorer Shuttle stops.

CADILLAC MOUNTAIN

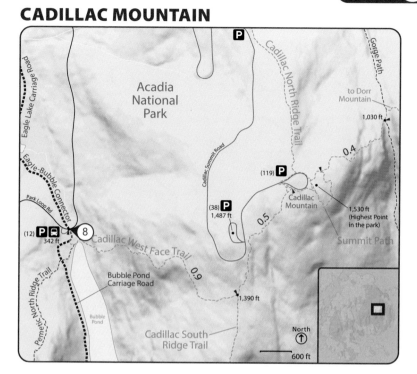

Cadillac Mountain | Strenuous | 3.0 miles | 1,210 feet | Out-and-back
Trailhead: Bubble Pond on Park Loop Road (8)

During peak season, driving to the top of Cadillac Mountain requires a permit (recreation.gov). Early birds bundle up and arrive in time to enjoy some of the East Coast's first rays of light. You can also hike to the summit. Trails converge from each direction. The most interesting is Cadillac West Face. It's steep and rocky, with a couple wooden ladders. Sunrise chasers without a permit might be tempted to choose this path to the top of Cadillac since it's the shortest, but its steep and rocky nature make for difficult trekking in the dark.

South Ridge, beginning at Blackwoods Campground, is a better early morning choice, but it's long by Acadia standards at 3.5 miles one way. For something uncommon, you could take Bubble Pond Carriage Road to Canon Brook Trail, which climbs to Cadillac South Ridge. North Ridge is the compromise. The trail begins on Park Loop Road from a small parking area shortly after the road becomes one way. From there, it's 2.2 miles to the summit, climbing roughly 1,260 feet. Ascending the Cadillac from the east isn't as scenic and to reach the trail you'll have to climb up and down Dorr Mountain or hike Gorge Path.

Shuttles do not reach Cadillac's summit. So, should you hike up, you'll have to find a ride or hike back down.

GIANT SLIDE

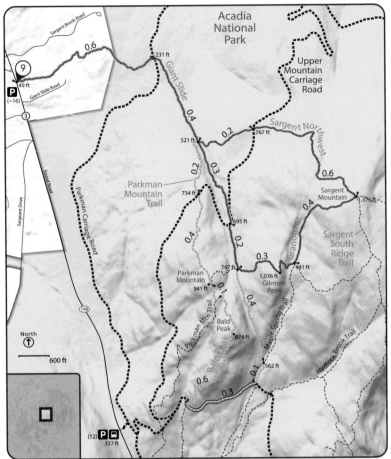

Giant Slide | Strenuous | 4.6 miles | 1,100 feet | Lollipop
Trailhead: Giant Slide, Sound Road (9)

Giant Slide begins on private property, and then crosses Parkman Carriage Road before following Sargent Brook through some fun (but often slippery) rock features. Most of the fun features are along Giant Slide between Parkman Mountain Trail and Upper Mountain Carriage Road. Once you reach Grandgent Trail, it's decision time. You can make a 4.1-mile loop over to the park's second highest peak, Sargent Mountain (1,373 feet). You'll walk across Gilmore Peak (1,036 feet) before summiting Sargent and returning down Giant Slide. An easier and longer (but still strenuous) alternative is to circle around to the south side of Bald Peak (974 feet), climb it, go down and up to Parkman Mountain (941 feet), and then return via Giant Slide.

BEECH CLIFF

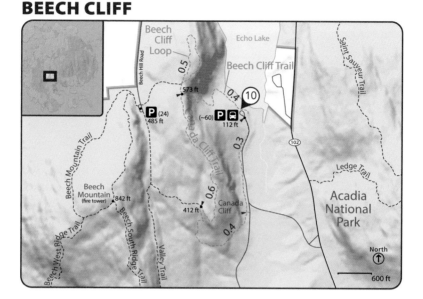

Parking is along the road at the trailhead. The Island Explorer Shuttle operates a route covering Sound Drive, with a designated stop at Parkman Mountain Trailhead (where there's a small lot and roadside parking). So, it isn't too inconvenient to hike up Giant Slide and down Parkman Mountain Trail (or Bald Peak) to Parkman Mountain Trailhead to catch the shuttle (or walk along Sound Drive or Parkman Carriage Road) back to where you started.

Beech Cliff | Strenuous | 2.1 miles | 460 feet | Loop
Trailhead: Echo Lake Beach Parking Area (10)

Beech Cliff isn't as exciting as Precipice or Beehive, but it's a quick climb beginning at one of the island's quiet side's top destinations, Echo Lake Beach. Steel ladders make the most precipitous trail sections possible and there's a half-mile Beech Cliff Loop providing views of Echo Lake. Return to the parking lot via Canada Cliff Trail. A nice ladder-less alternative is to park at the end of Beech Hill Road. You'll have a few loop options from the Beech Mountain Trailhead.

There's quite a bit of space at Echo Lake Beach Parking Area but it'll fill up in summer. It's also a shuttle stop. The Beech Mountain Trailhead parking area has room for about two dozen cars. It also fills in summer.

PERPENDICULAR

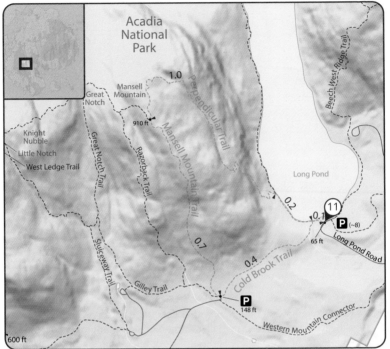

Perpendicular | Strenuous | 2.4 miles | 850 feet | Loop
Trailhead: Long Pond Road (11)

Perpendicular is considered one of the park's ladder trails, but it's more of a stone staircase with a handful of steel rungs. You'll have some views along the way, but the trail is heavily forested. Sights improve along Mansell Mountain Trail. Continue hiking down to Gilley Field and return to the parking area via Cold Brook Trail. Even though Long Pond is popular this is a wonderful area that lives up to the Quiet Side moniker. The dense trail network holds the potential for a variety of loop hikes on either side of Long Pond. I plan on checking them out next trip to Acadia. Maybe I'll see you there?

Parking is very limited and while not as popular as Echo Lake (or the other side of the island), it's frequented by plenty of paddlers and hikers. In summary, you better get an early start or cross your fingers.

MORE INFO

Regions

Acadia is more than Mount Desert Island (where all the described trails are located). A few miles of hiking trails are found at Schoodic Peninsula and Isle au Haut as well.

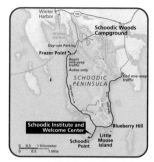

Visitation & Seasons

Acadia is extremely busy from June through October and quite quiet the rest of the year. Fall foliage typically peaks in early October. Even though very few visitors arrive in winter, it isn't a terrible time to explore.

Island Explorer Shuttle

Island Explorer (exploreacadia.com) is great! Shuttles operate during peak season. Routes run all over Mount Desert Island and to Schoodic Peninsula. There are designated stops, but drivers drop off/pick up at any safe spot along the way, so you can get creative with hiking itineraries. Nothing beats a good point-to-point hike. Look at a map and make your own!

Carriage Roads

There are about 45 miles of crushed-stone carriage roads, mostly concentrated around Jordan Pond. They serve as a more leisurely alternative to the park's often steep and rocky hiking trails.

Bar Island

Ladder Trails

Ladder trails feature steel rails and rungs to help climb near-vertical hills. You must be fairly comfortable with exposure and heights. If you think you might have issues, consider trying Perpendicular or Beech Cliff or Ladder before the more extreme Precipice Trail. It's also a good idea to go early, late, or in the shoulder seasons. These trails (Precipice and Beehive in particular) are popular, and crowds tend to increase exposure anxiety.

Jordan Cliffs

Pets

Acadia is fairly pet-friendly. Pets are allowed on many trails and on Island Explorer Shuttles (but not on the seats). You can't take your furry friends to Sand Beach (mid-June through mid-September), Echo Lake (mid-May through mid-September), into public buildings, on ranger programs, on ladder trails, or to Wild Gardens of Acadia.

Cuyahoga Valley
Hiking Trails: 180+ miles

Ledges

Cuyahoga Valley Favorites

① **Blue Hen & Buttermilk**
Moderate | 3.4 miles | 690 feet

② **Ledges**
Moderate | 2.2 miles | 200 feet

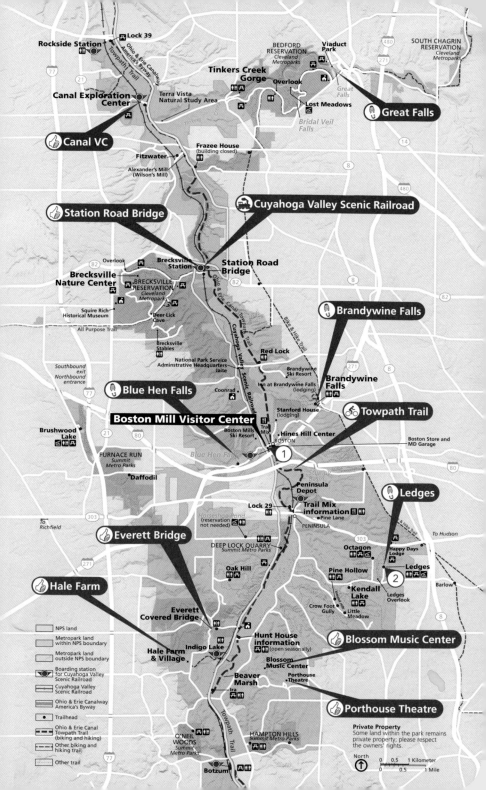

Lock 39
Rockside Station
Canal Exploration Center
👍 **Canal VC**
Terra Vista Natural Study Area
Fitzwater
Frazee House (building closed)
Alexander's Mill (Wilson's Mill)

Tinkers Creek Gorge
BEDFORD RESERVATION Cleveland Metroparks
Viaduct Park
Overlook
Lost Meadows
Bridal Veil Falls
🎤 **Great Falls**
Great Falls
SOUTH CHAGRIN RESERVATION Cleveland Metroparks

👍 **Station Road Bridge**
Overlook
Brecksville Station
Brecksville Nature Center
BRECKSVILLE RESERVATION Cleveland Metroparks
Squire Rich Historical Museum
Deer Lick Cave
All Purpose Trail
Brecksville Stables
National Park Service Adminstrative Headquarters-Jaite
Coonrad

🚂 **Cuyahoga Valley Scenic Railroad**
Station Road Bridge
Red Lock
🎤 **Brandywine Falls**
Brandywine Ski Resort
Inn at Brandywine Falls (lodging)
Brandywine Falls

🎤 **Blue Hen Falls**
Boston Mill Visitor Center
Brushwood Lake
FURNACE RUN Summit Metro Parks
Daffodil
Boston Mills Ski Resort
Blue Hen Falls
BOSTON
Stanford House (lodging)
Hines Hill Center
🚴 **Towpath Trail**
Boston Store and MD Garage

Southbound exit Northbound entrance
To Richfield

Peninsula Depot
Lock 29
🎤 **Ledges**
Trail Mix information
Pine Lane
PENINSULA
(reservation not needed)
Horseshoe Pond
👍 **Everett Bridge**
DEEP LOCK QUARRY Summit Metro Parks
Octagon
Happy Days Lodge
Oak Hill
Pine Hollow
Ledges
Ledges Overlook
Kendall Lake
Crow Foot Gully
Little Meadow
Barlow
To Hudson

👍 **Hale Farm**
Everett Covered Bridge
Indigo Lake
Hale Farm & Village
Hunt House information (open seasonally)
👍 **Blossom Music Center**
Blossom Music Center
Porthouse Theatre
Beaver Marsh
Ira
👍 **Porthouse Theatre**

NPS land
Metropark land within NPS boundary
Metropark land outside NPS boundary
Boarding station for Cuyahoga Valley Scenic Railroad
Cuyahoga Valley Scenic Railroad
Ohio & Erie Canalway America's Byway
Trailhead
Ohio & Erie Canal Towpath Trail (biking and hiking)
Other biking and hiking trail
Other trail

O'NEIL WOODS Summit Metro Parks
HAMPTON HILLS Summit Metro Parks

Private Property
Some land within the park remains private property; please respect the owners' rights.

North
0   0.5   1 Kilometer
0   0.5   1 Mile

Botzum

BLUE HEN & BUTTERMILK FALLS

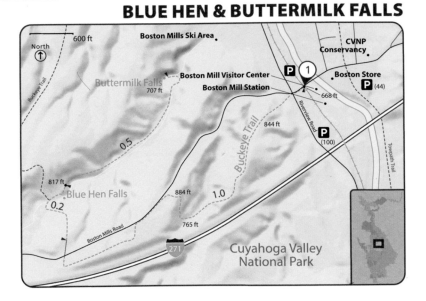

Blue Hen & Buttermilk Falls | Moderate | 3.4 miles | 690 feet | Out-and-back
Trailhead: Boston Mill Visitor Center (1)

Blue Hen is one of the park's most popular waterfalls. It's only 15 feet tall, but the setting is divine, especially in fall, when colorful leaves accent the (usually) two-pronged waterfall. Today, you park along the Cuyahoga River near Boston Mill Visitor Center (or at Towpath Trail's parking lot on the east side of the river). From there, it's uphill along Buckeye Trail for a mile to the Blue Hen trailhead. If conditions are safe, many visitors like to get a closer look walking along the creek bed near the base of the falls. And then you can chase another waterfall, continuing (mostly) along the north side of the stream down to Buttermilk Falls. Terrain and pathfinding become more difficult as you go.

There used to be parking near the Blue Hen Trailhead on Boston Mills Road. Today, you park near Boston Mill Visitor Center or Towpath Trail.

Ledges | Moderate | 2.2 miles | 200 feet | Loop
Trailhead: Ledges, Kendall Park Road (2)

Ledges is about cool rocks. Most are found at the north end, but completing the loop is a good idea (check out the overlook, too). Ice Box Cave may sound exciting, but it's been closed as long as I've been exploring our parks due to white-nose syndrome (a bat disease). So don't get the kids' hopes up about a "cave." But there's still plenty of rocky fun to get excited about, particularly a narrow hallway near the main path. You can look into it from above and you can walk through it from below. While you're walking through the stone walls, take a closer look at a few sculptures carved into the rock (but please don't leave your mark). There's also a shelter, picnic area, and large grassy field.

LEDGES

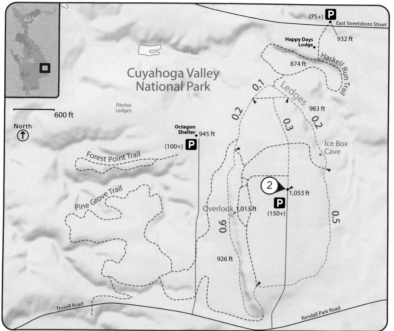

The main Ledges parking area is large, but it fills up (especially on summer/holiday weekends). Fortunately, turnover is fairly rapid. You can also reach the Ledges circuit from the parking area at Octagon or Happy Days Lodge (decent options if you'd like to hike a little farther).

You can ride the Cuyahoga Valley Scenic Railroad (cvsr.com), which provides a fun change of pace while exploring the park by foot or bike or kayak (the Explorer Program lets you bring bikes and kayaks aboard). There are two ski hills (Boston Mills and Brandywine), several cultural exhibits (including Hale Farm and Village), an outdoor amphitheater (Blossom Music Center), and an outdoor theater (Porthouse Theatre).

Uniquely Cuyahoga Valley

More Trails

There are quite a few other trails worth checking out. The short walk to the overlooks at Brandywine Falls should not be skipped. Towpath Trail is great for biking (especially in conjunction with Cuyahoga Valley Scenic Railroad) but hiking is nice too. I really enjoyed the areas around Station Road Bridge, Boston, and Ira.

There are also several excellent trails outside the park's boundaries. Sagamore Creek Loop begins at Frazee House or Alexander Road Trailhead. It requires a couple stream crossings and some route finding but you're rewarded with a waterfall (from above). Great Falls is a short walk from a confusing-to-reach parking area in Viaduct Park near the north end of the national park. And Gorge Metro Park at the park's southern end is worth visiting.

Shenandoah
Hiking Trails: 500+ miles

Riprap

Shenandoah Favorites

(1) **Compton Peak**
Moderate | 2.3 miles | 770 feet

(2) **Little Devil's Stairs**
Strenuous | 7.0 miles | 1,720 feet

(3) **Overall Run Falls**
Strenuous | 5.9 miles | 860 feet

(4-5) **Stony Man**
Moderate | 3.4 miles | 790 feet

(6-7) **Hawksbill Mountain**
Moderate | 1.6–2.8 miles | 680 feet

(8) **Blackrock**
Easy | 1.1–1.6 miles | 200 feet

(9-10) **Riprap/Wildcat Ridge**
Strenuous | 9.0 miles | 2,000 feet

(11) **Old Rag**
Extreme | 5.4–9.2 miles | 1,760+ ft

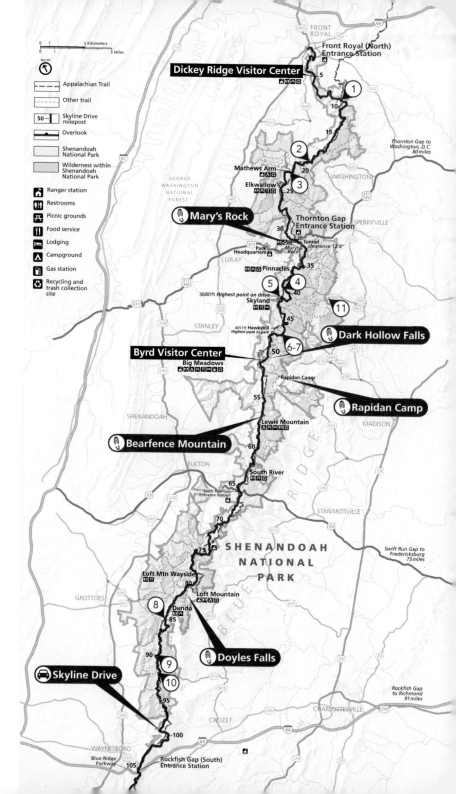

COMPTON PEAK

Compton Peak | Moderate | 2.3 miles | 770 feet | Out-and-back
Trailhead: Compton Gap, Skyline Drive Mile 10.4 (1)

Compton Peak delivers mountain views and strange rocks. From the parking area, cross Skyline Drive and hike along the Appalachian Trail until you reach an intersection. Right (north) leads to a scenic overlook. Left (south) leads to a great example of columnar jointing. It's the same type of geologic formation found at more well-known sites like Devil's Tower in Wyoming, Sheepeater Cliffs at Yellowstone, Devil's Postpile in California, and Mount Rainier. Columnar jointing is found all around the globe. This rockpile is a nice specimen and something of a Blue Ridge Mountains anomaly. As a bonus, Lands Run Falls Trailhead is just to the north on Skyline Drive.

Compton Gap isn't a particularly popular parking area on Skyline Drive. It's also reasonably sized, but expect the lot to be full through summer (especially on weekends). Fortunately, if the lot's full, there are many hiking alternatives nearby (like Lands Run Falls and the next two entries).

Little Devil's Stairs | Strenuous | 7.0 miles | 1,720 feet | Lollipop
Trailhead: Keyser Run Road, Skyline Drive Mile 19.4 (2)

Little Devil's Stairs is a fun journey, with a wide variety of features. Beginning at Keyser Run Road (Mile 19.4 of Skyline Drive) you'll take a nice casual walk downhill along Keyser Run Fire Road (sometimes called Jinney Gray Road). In less than one mile, you'll reach an intersection with Little Devil's Stairs and Pole Bridge Link. Here's your first decision. I prefer hiking up wet, potentially-slippery terrain so I chose to stay on Keyser Run Road all the way to the

LITTLE DEVIL'S STAIRS

bottom of Little Devil's Stairs. Along the way you'll pass a small cemetery. Take a respectful look around this interesting graveyard. At the bottom you'll find the Little Devil's Stairs Trailhead, a small parking area, and (usually) a handful of walking sticks. This parking area (confusingly on Keyser Run Road) is a good option for anyone arriving from the east. From here, Little Devil's Stairs is almost entirely uphill, with a few stream crossings. They're typically nothing more than hopping rocks to the other side but could be difficult during periods of intense rain/snowmelt. Enjoy the hike. After about two miles you'll be back at the Keyser Run Road/Pole Bridge Link Intersection. Turn right onto Keyser Run Road to return to your vehicle.

Overall Run Falls | Strenuous | 5.9 miles | 860 feet | Out-and-back
Trailhead: Mathews Arm Campground, Skyline Drive Mile 22.1 (3)

At 93 feet, Overall Run is the tallest waterfall in the park. There are several options to reach it. You can make the shorter hike up from Thompson Hollow Trailhead or the longer hike down from a parking area along Skyline Drive (Mile 21.1), but the most convenient choice for many is to reach these

OVERALL RUN FALLS

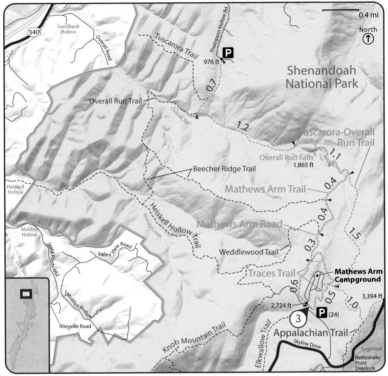

wonderful waterfalls from Mathews Arm Campground (Mile 22.1). Not into camping? No problem. You can also use the large parking area near the campground checkpoint. It provides access to Traces Trail, a short loop departing from either end of the lot. Traces intersects Mathews Arm Road. Beginning on Traces or the campground's north end, take Mathews Arm Road to Mathews Arm Trail, and then continue downhill on Tuscarora-Overall Run Trail to a viewpoint of a beautiful 29-foot waterfall. There's an overlook and you can hike down to its base. Continue along the main trail to see 93-foot Overall Run Falls. Most of this hike is a pleasant walk in the woods and the conclusion is worth the effort. (Consider the Thompson Hollow Trailhead if you're arriving from the west.)

Stony Man | Moderate | 3.4 miles | 790 feet | Loop
Trailhead: Little Stony Man, Mile 39.1 (4) or Stony Man, Mile 41.7 (5)

As the name suggests, you're going to encounter some stones. If you have the time, hike the full loop. No time to spare, hike up to Stony Man from Skyland and Little Stony Man from Skyline Drive (in whatever order makes more sense). For the loop, begin at Stony Man Trailhead near the entrance

STONY MAN

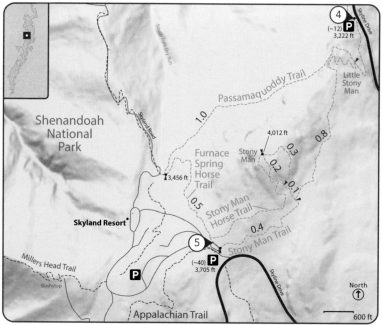

to Skyland. Walk to the far end of the lot to start on Furnace Spring Trail, which is the least interesting stretch and hardest to follow. It's a wide, rocky, somewhat undefined path frequented by horses. It's also easy to walk past Passamaquoddy. Passamaquoddy is mostly level. You'll pass below power lines and end with some interesting rocks. Rocks become even more interesting at Little Stony Man. Complete the loop by heading up to Stony Man (via the Appalachian Trail) for exceptional Shenandoah views. While Stony Man is a pretty good spot for sunset, it's also nice in the morning when the wide-open expanse to the west receives its first rays of light. The small network of short trails atop Stony Man isn't anything to worry about. Even if you find yourself on the horse trail, you should notice the Stony Man parking area long before an errant return to the Skyland Resort area. (There is a stable at Skyland Resort, if you'd rather explore this area on the back of a horse. This is also where rock climbing classes are offered. For more information on either activity, visit goshenandoah.com.)

Hawksbill Mtn | Moderate | 1.6–2.8 miles | 420–680 feet | Out-and-back or Loop
Trailhead: Hawksbill Gap, Mile 45.5 (6) or Upper Hawksbill, Mile 46.5 (7)

Hawksbill (4,051 feet) is the tallest point in the park, offering commanding views and serving as a popular sunset destination (bring a headlamp or go on the night of a full moon). Like with many popular destinations, there are a few

HAWKSBILL MOUNTAIN

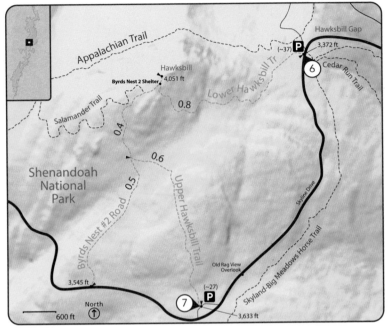

options to reach the panorama-providing peak. An out-and-back along Lower Hawksbill Trail (Mile 45.5) is the steepest (690 ft) and shortest (1.6 miles) choice. An out-and-back along Upper Hawksbill (Mile 46.5) is slightly more gradual (520 feet) and longer (2.0 miles). You could also make a 2.8-mile loop (860 feet) from Hawksbill Gap by taking the short connector to the Appalachian Trail and winding your way up Hawksbill Mountain via Salamander Trail, finally returning to the trailhead via Lower Hawksbill. Regardless of what route you choose, make sure you do not get to Byrds Nest 2 Shelter and turn around. The viewpoint is just beyond the shelter.

Last time I was there, I noticed a large group of people congregating at Upper Hawksbill in an open space on the far side of Skyline Drive. Using the Sky-land–Big Meadows Horse Trail may open another loop option, connecting Upper and Lower Hawksbill, but I'm not 100% sure. It's also close to the Cedar Run–Whiteoak Canyon Circuit (which is good but less compelling and more popular than Little Devil's Stairs).

Blackrock | Easy | 1.1–1.6 miles | 200 feet | Loop
Trailhead: Blackrock Summit Parking, Skyline Drive Mile 84.8 (8)

If you're entering the park at Rockfish Gap (south end) and need a quick stretch before finishing the drive to your overnight accommodations, Blackrock is a fantastic choice (really, any time you're passing by, Blackrock is a good choice

BLACKROCK

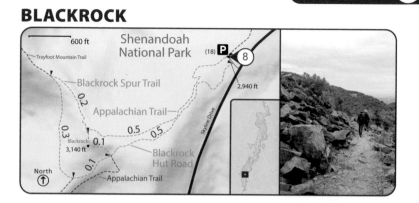

for a quick stop). Both loop options are easy, although you can scramble about the massive pile of rocks (slightly enhancing your views while greatly increasing the difficulty). Scientists believe the rocks you find here were once the seabed of the Iapetus Ocean. Obviously, that's long before the Appalachian Mountains. Beyond ancient ocean rocks and views to the north of Rockytop/Austin Mountain, this is a lovely walk in the woods. On such a short trail, you wouldn't think there's room for confusion but there is a tiny bit. You'll have your choice of taking the Appalachian Trail or Blackrock Hut Road/Trayfoot Mountain Trail to/from the parking area. Knowing that fact is all you need to eliminate any confusion. Shenandoah's unique trail markers are located right where they ought to be, pointing you back in the direction of the Summit Parking area.

Riprap & Wildcat Ridge | Strenuous | 9.0 miles | 2,000 feet | Loop
Trailhead: Riprap, Mile 90 (9) or Wildcat Ridge, Mile 92.1 (10)

This is one of the better loops. The highlights are rocky views (Calvary Rocks and Chimney Rocks), a small waterfall, and a refreshing swimming hole (just beyond the old Riprap Shelter). Trailhead and direction aren't especially important for this trek. Choose clockwise and you'll have the more gradual climb up Riprap Trail to return to the trailhead. Counterclockwise leaves you with the steeper Wildcat Ridge. The other thing to consider is when you want to explore Chimney Rock and Calvary Rocks. Counterclockwise brings you there sooner, when you'll likely have more energy to scramble around a bit. Clockwise gets you there later, when you might have less energy but will have better lighting. I enjoy gradual climbs and adhere to a "best for last" mentality, so my preference is to park at Riprap and go clockwise. This way the swimming hole and scenic rocks are closer to the conclusion. But, again, it doesn't matter much. No wrong answer on this one. You could simply hike out to Chimney Rock from Riprap as an out-and-back if you're short on time or uninterested in a longer hike.

Expect the parking areas to fill during summer and holiday weekends. If you'd like to take it easy, this is a nice backpacking area too.

RIPRAP/WILDCAT RIDGE

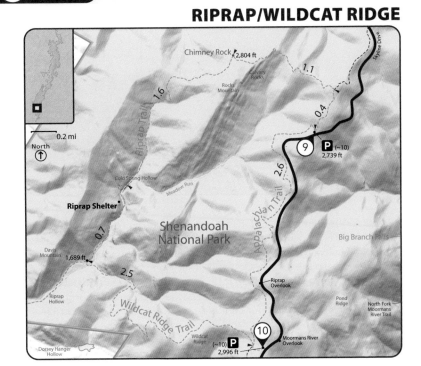

Old Rag | Extreme | 5.4–9.2 miles | 1,760–2,348 feet | Out-and-back or Loop
Trailhead: Old Rag Parking Area, Route 600 (11) or Berry Hollow

Old Rag is an iconic Shenandoah hike. The 9.2-mile circuit from the Old Rag Parking Area features a fun scramble up a rocky slope to Old Rag and its oft-Instagrammed rocks. The return trip is a bit of a boring slog, following Weakley Hollow Fire Road all the way back to the parking area. For the loop, it's important to spot the sign directing you onto Weakly Hollow Fire Road (and the Old Rag Parking Area). The short alternative is to park at Berry Hollow Road and hike to Old Rag summit (bypassing the fun rock scramble) as an out-and-back. You can also access the popular Cedar Run–Whiteoak Canyon loop from Berry Hollow Road. This is something to consider when choosing where to stay and for how long. Exploring Shenandoah from the bottom up can be a refreshing approach compared to always hiking down and back up, beginning your hikes from Skyline Drive.

Old Rag is extremely popular. In 2022, the park instituted a pilot program requiring all hikers to have a ticket (recreation.gov) from March through November. When we went to print, that remained the situation. 800 tickets are available each day. 400 are available 30 days in advance of the reservation date. The remaining 400 are released five days ahead.

OLD RAG

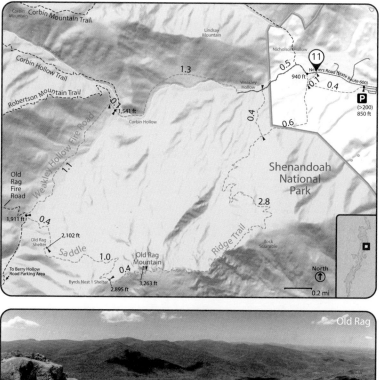

Old Rag

Trails are marked with paint blazes on trees. White blazes mark the Appalachian Trail. Blue blazes mark hiking trails. And yellow blazes mark hiking/horseback riding trails. Watch for them to know you're on the right path.

Trail Blazes

More Trails

There's a lot of great hiking to be enjoyed at Shenandoah. Dark Hollow Falls (moderate, 1.4 miles) is a short, relatively easy hike to a waterfall Thomas Jefferson used to frequent. Continuing the presidential theme, you could also take Mill Prong (moderate, 4.0 miles) to Rapidan Camp (President Hoover's 'Brown House'). If you're looking for a leisurely stroll, Big Meadows is the place. Bearfence Mountain (moderate, 0.8 mile) is good. Mary's Rock (moderate, 2.8 miles) is a fine viewpoint. Cedar Run–Whiteoak Circuit is quite popular, but I don't feel like it's as enjoyable as Little Devil's Stairs or Old Rag. And then there are things I plan to do on my next visit. For example, I've hiked to Upper and Lower Doyles Falls (very nice) but I did them as an out-and-back. I really should've made a loop with Jones Run Trail, using the Appalachian Trail to connect them. Rockytop, Brown Mountain, and Big Run are worth looking into.

New River Gorge
Hiking Trails: 90+ miles

Long Point

New River Gorge Favorites

① **Long Point**
Easy | 3.0 miles | 320 feet

② **Kaymoor Miner's**
Strenuous | 1.2 miles | 1,020 feet

③ **Butcher Branch**
Moderate | 1.1 miles | 400 feet

④-⑤ **Endless Wall**
Moderate | 2.7 miles | 300 feet

⑥ **Grandview Rim**
Moderate | 2.9 miles | 260 feet

⑦ **Castle Rock**
Moderate | 0.9 mile | 170 feet

⑧ **Tunnel**
Easy | 0.4 mile | 100 feet

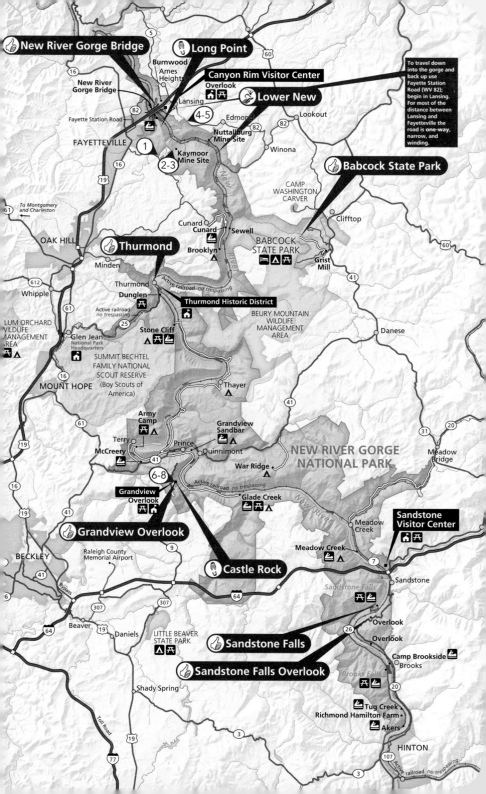

NEW RIVER GORGE BRIDGE AREA

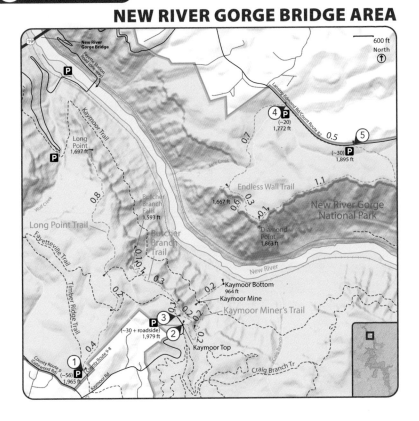

Long Point | Easy | 3.0 miles | 320 feet | Out-and-back
Trailhead: County Route 9-8/Newton Road (1)

Long Point Trail is fairly short and mostly flat, while serving up some of the best views you can find of New River Gorge Bridge. It's definitely all about the destination as the journey is a gentle, predominantly forested walk. From Long Point, the bridge is almost due north, so lighting is usually good all day, especially from fall through spring when the sun is further south. Still, the bridge and rock outcropping look best in the soft morning/evening light (and peak when leaves have changed color, usually mid- to late October). Bicycles are allowed on all but the final 0.2 mile, where you'll find a "no bicycles beyond this point" sign and a bike rack. The trailhead's parking lot is large, but it fills up regularly, especially on weekends. Do not park alongside the road (you'll probably get ticketed). There's a little extra space at the Gatewood Road inter-section. Otherwise you can park at the end of Kaymoor Road and get to Long Point via Fayetteville Trail.

Kaymoor Miner's | Strenuous | 1.2 miles | 1,020 feet | Out-and-back
Trailhead: Kaymoor Top, end of Kaymoor Road (2)

A fair amount of people love Kaymoor Miner's Trail. Perhaps because of its coal-mining history. Perhaps because of the trickling waterfall you'll pass near the top. But I think people love it because it's a serious workout. It shouldn't come as a surprise that the trail is all downhill. You are walking from Kaymoor Top to Kaymoor Bottom. We aren't living in opposite world. But what isn't obvious is the fact it includes 821 stairs from the mine to the bottom. If you like stairs, you'll love this trail. Closed-off coal-mining ruins where coal was sorted, processed, and loaded onto railroad cars are a bonus. So, the ruins and history are interesting, and the stairmaster will turn your buns to steel, but I'd steer clear of this trail if you aren't interested in a steep out-and-back (especially if it's muddy). If what you want is mining history and ruins, Kaymoor is interesting, but I preferred Nuttallburg, located on the other side of the New River. You can drive or hike to Nuttallburg (the hike is steep but also quite neat, walking beneath the mine's conveyor).

Butcher Branch | Moderate | 1.1 miles | 400 feet | Out-and-back
Trailhead: Fayetteville, end of Kaymoor Road (3)

From the Fayetteville Trailhead, Butcher Branch quickly diverges from Fayetteville Trail (leading to Long Point). Butcher Branch features nearly continuous fun features, including rock walls and a cascading waterfall. You can also access Butcher Branch from Kaymoor Top (last time I was there, you really had to look for the trail junction—they were in the process of making trail improvements so it may be better when you visit). Extend the hike some more by snaking up to Long Point via Fayetteville Trail.

Both Kaymoor Miner's and Butcher Branch trails begin at the end of Kaymoor Road. There's a small parking area (maybe room for two dozen vehicles). Kaymoor Miner's begins at the south end of the lot. Butcher Branch/Fayetteville begins at the north end. The lot doesn't fill nearly as often as Long Point's and there's additional parking alongside the road, but it does get busy.

Endless Wall | Moderate | 2.7 miles | 300 feet | Loop
Trailhead: Fern Creek (4) or Nuttall (5), Lansing-Edmond Road

The star of the east side of New River Gorge is Endless Wall. It's a great hike but there are a couple things to know. 1). For a complete loop, you'll have to walk a half-mile along the road between Fern Creek and Nuttall parking areas. 2). The primary loop runs along the rim of the gorge, but there's also a lower segment accessed via two tricky steel ladders. The section of trail beneath the rim is frequented by rock climbers, but if using the ladders isn't an immediate "nope," check it out. 3). Both ladders are not marked or obvious from the rim. 4). If you do the lower section, be sure to backtrack to Diamond Point (it's marked well), adding about a mile to the loop. 5). You can save a little time and distance by doing a 2.3-mile lollipop of the rim and lower ladder section departing from Fern Creek Trailhead. With that said, there are a few nice viewpoints looking upstream (south) in between the south ladder and Nuttall parking area. And 6). There's no better or worse trailhead or loop direction for the full loop. Park where you find space and proceed in either direction.

Grandview Rim | Moderate | 2.9 miles | 260 feet | Out-and-back
Trailhead: Grandview Main Overlook (6)

With only five parking spaces at Turkey Spur Rock, you might want to consider walking Grandview Rim instead of driving. There are several decent vistas along the way, but it's even better if you fold Castle Trail into the mix. With just a few gentle hills, this trail is moderately difficult due to its length.

Castle Rock | Moderate | 0.9 mile | 170 feet | Loop
Trailhead: Grandview Main Overlook (7)

Whether you're hiking or not, Grandview should be on your shortlist of sites to see at New River Gorge. As a bonus, there are some exceptional trails. Castle Rock Trail begins near Grandview Main Overlook. It travels north below the rim for roughly a half-mile, passing by very impressive rock formations. The trail isn't difficult, but there are some ups and downs and quite a bit of uneven terrain. While you can do an out-and-back, I'd recommend looping it with Rim Trail. The view from North Overlook is great (and much more peaceful than Grandview Overlook).

Tunnel | Easy | 0.4 mile | 100 feet | Loop
Trailhead: Grandview Main Overlook (8)

While the namesake Tunnel has been closed all three times I've been there (and still was when this title went to print), it's a nice, shady trail worth the short amount of time and effort required for the loop. It's easy, but you will need to climb/descend quite a few stairs along the way. The scenery is similar to Castle Rock but with less impressive rocks. So, if it's one or the other and you don't mind a moderately difficult trail, head to Castle Rock first.

More Trails

There's a boardwalk (easy, 0.2 mile) at Sandstone Falls. Nearby you'll find a steep (and often muddy) waterfall hike, Big Branch (strenuous, 2.0 miles). If you're looking to backpack, Glade Creek (moderate, 11.2 miles) has a few campsites. It also has two trailheads. One is near Grandview. It's only accessible with a 4x4. The other is down by the river (about an hour away by car). It's a good hike, featuring swimming holes and a short spur to Kate's Falls. The waterfall spur trail is about a mile from the

Big Branch

GRANDVIEW AREA

600 ft
North
Turkey Spur Rock 🅿 (5)
2,322 ft
1.0
Grandview
Rim Trail
0.1
North Overlook
2,479 ft
Castle Rock Trail
0.3
0.5
Grandview
⑦ Overlook
2,493 ft
(~160) 🅿
⑥ ⑧
**Grandview
Visitor Center**
2,504 ft
0.4
Tunnel Trail
New River Gorge
National Park
Castle Rock

4x4 trailhead. Coming from the other direction, a landslide wiped out a portion of the trail before Kate's Falls, but it was not impassable (use common sense and you'll be fine). Still a good idea to always check in on trail conditions. I enjoyed Headhouse (moderate, 0.7 mile), Conveyor (strenuous, 0.8 mile), and Tipple (easy, 0.6 mile) trails, exploring Nuttallburg mine site. You can also drive to Nuttallburg.

More Activities

The New and Gauley rivers provide some of the best commercially operated whitewater in the country. Upper New is your family-friendly run. Upper Gauley is the wildest of the bunch. Lower New has a few class V rapids, and the thrills crank up a level in spring. Lower Gauley is a wild ride too. There are a bunch of river outfitters, many offer camping and other activity packages. Mountain biking and rock climbing are popular as well. New River Gorge Bridge viewing locations include Canyon Rim Visitor Center, Fayette Station Road Bridge, and Long Point. Bridge walking tours are offered for a fee.

Mammoth Cave
Hiking Trails: 80+ miles

A turtle at Turnhole Bend

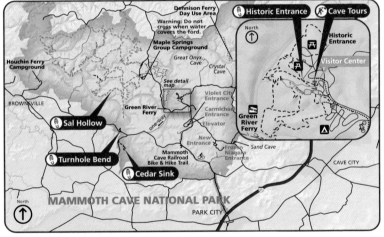

Hiking Mammoth Cave

Mammoth Cave is about what's under the earth's surface, not above it. But there are a few worthwhile hikes. If you don't do a cave tour entering/exiting through the Historic Entrance, hike the short, paved, moderately-steep path to the cave's natural entrance. It begins behind the visitor center. You can continue past the entrance to take a look at where River Styx exits the cave system into the Green River and then return up Heritage Hill, where you'll find the grave of Stephen Bishop (a slave and early tour guide/explorer) in the Old Guide's Cemetery. Green River Bluffs is also decent and a fairly easy walk. Beyond the Visitor Center area, the short walks along Cedar Sink (lollipop), Turnhole Bend Nature Trail (loop), and Sand Cave (out-and-back) are nice and shady with a few interesting sites. For longer options, you can make a variety of loops from Maple Springs Trailhead departing on Sal Hollow Trail. The northern half of the park is largely unvisited aside from horseback riders.

Great Smoky Mountains
Hiking Trails: 800+ miles

Appalachian Trail

Great Smoky Mountains Favorites

1 Grotto Falls
Moderate | 2.6 miles | 540 feet

2 Chimney Tops
Strenuous | 3.8 miles | 1,270 feet

3 Alum Cave/Mount LeConte
Strenuous | 10.1 miles | 2,760 feet

4 Charlie's Bunion
Moderate | 8.6 miles | 1,600 feet

5 Andrew's Bald
Moderate | 3.5 miles | 980 feet

6 Rocky Top
Strenuous | 12.4 miles | 3,500 ft

7-8 Gregory Bald
Strenuous | 9.8–11.7 mi | 3,000 ft

9 Ramsey Cascade
Moderate | 7.7 miles | 2,240 feet

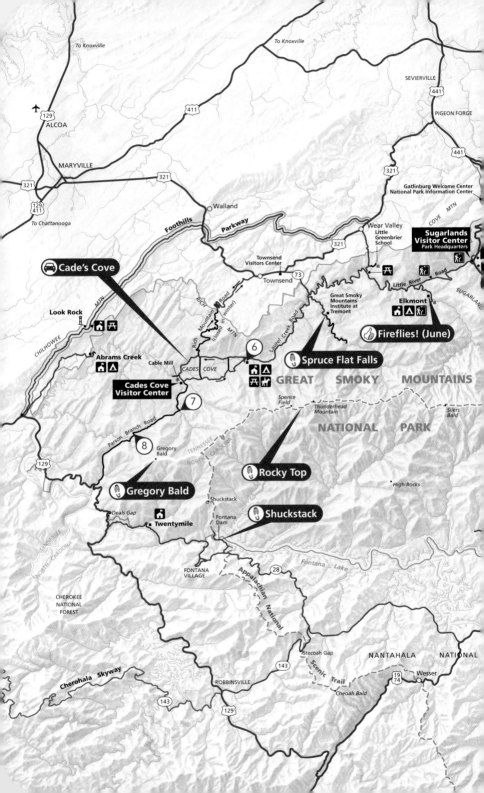

To Knoxville

To Knoxville

SEVIERVILLE

411

441

PIGEON FORGE

129

ALCOA

321

Walland

441

MARYVILLE

321

Gatlinburg Welcome Center
National Park Information Center

321

Foothills   Parkway

Wear Valley
Little
Greenbrier
School

COVE MTN

Sugarlands
Visitor Center
Park Headquarters

321

Little River
Road

129

411

To Chattanooga

Townsend
Visitors Center

73

Townsend

SUGARLAND

🚗 Cade's Cove

Look Rock

CHILHOWEE MTN

RICH MOUNTAIN ROAD
(closed in winter)

RICH MTN

Great Smoky
Mountains
Institute at
Tremont

Laurel Creek Road

Elkmont

Abrams Creek

Cable Mill

CADES COVE

6

🎙 Spruce Flat Falls

👍 Fireflies! (June)

Cades Cove
Visitor Center

7

GREAT   SMOKY   MOUNTAINS

Spence
Field

Thunderhead
Mountain

Silers
Bald

Parson Branch Road

8

Gregory
Bald

TENNESSEE
NORTH CAROLINA

🎙 Rocky Top

NATIONAL   PARK

High Rocks

129

🎙 Gregory Bald

Deals Gap

Shuckstack

🥾 Shuckstack

Twentymile

Fontana
Dam

TENNESSEE
NORTH CAROLINA

FONTANA
VILLAGE

Appalachian   National

Fontana   Lake

28

CHEROKEE
NATIONAL
FOREST

STECOAH GAP

NANTAHALA   NATIONAL

Cherohala   Skyway

143

Scenic   Trail

19
74

Wesser

ROBBINSVILLE

143

129

Cheoah Bald

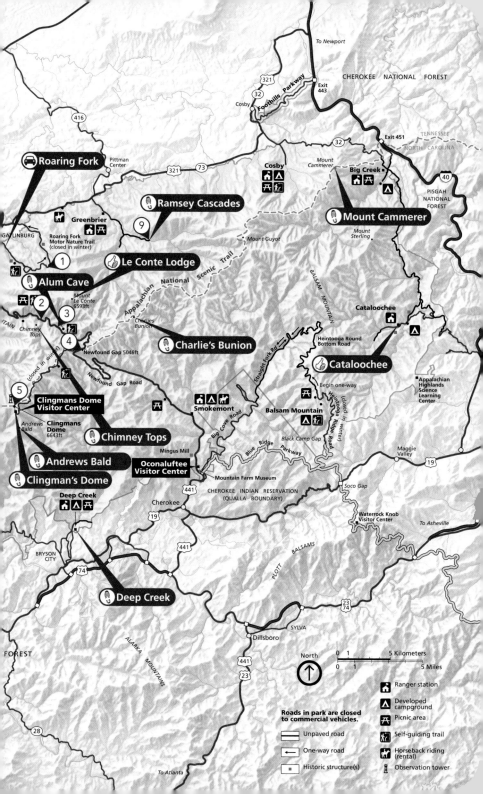

Roaring Fork

To Newport

CHEROKEE NATIONAL FOREST

Exit 443

Foothills Parkway

Cosby

321
32

Mount Cammerer

Exit 451

TENNESSEE
NORTH CAROLINA

32

Big Creek

PISGAH NATIONAL FOREST

40

416

Pittman Center

Mount Sterling

Ramsey Cascades

Mount Cammerer

Greenbrier

Roaring Fork Motor Nature Trail (closed in winter)

GATLINBURG

9

321   73

Cosby

Mount Guyot

Mount Cammerer

Le Conte Lodge

1

Appalachian National Scenic Trail

Balsam Mountain

Cataloochee

Alum Cave

Mount Le Conte 6593ft

2

3

Charlies Bunion

Heintooga Round Bottom Road

Cataloochee

4

Chimney Tops

Newfound Gap 5046ft

Charlie's Bunion

Straight Fork Rd

Appalachian Highlands Science Learning Center

(closed in winter)

Newfound Gap Road

Begin one-way

5

Clingmans Dome Visitor Center

Smokemont

Balsam Mountain

Maggie Valley

Andrews Bald

Clingmans Dome 6643ft

Big Cove Road

Black Camp Gap

(closed in winter)

19

Chimney Tops

Mingus Mill

Blue Ridge Parkway

Soco Gap

Andrews Bald

Oconaluftee Visitor Center

Mountain Farm Museum

Waterrock Knob Visitor Center

Clingman's Dome

CHEROKEE INDIAN RESERVATION (QUALLA BOUNDARY)

To Asheville

Deep Creek

441

Cherokee

BRYSON CITY

19

74

441

PLOTT BALSAMS

23
74

Deep Creek

23
74

SYLVA

ALARKA MOUNTAINS

Dillsboro

North

0   1   5 Kilometers

0   1   5 Miles

FOREST

441

23

28

Roads in park are closed to commercial vehicles.

Unpaved road

One-way road

Historic structure(s)

Ranger station

Developed campground

Picnic area

Self-guiding trail

Horseback riding (rental)

Observation tower

To Atlanta

GROTTO FALLS

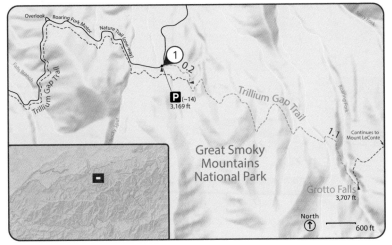

Grotto Falls | Moderate | 2.6 miles | 540 feet | Out-and-back
Trailhead: Roaring Fork Motor Nature Trail Stop #5 (1)

Grotto Falls isn't the tallest or prettiest waterfall in the Smokies, but it is one you can walk behind (just be careful on the slippery rocks). It's also a short and straightforward trail, not far from Gatlinburg. The trailhead, located on the opposite side of the parking area, leads you along a short access path to Trillium Gap Trail. From there it's a gradual ascent to the popular waterfall. In spring you'll be treated to a swollen stream and an abundance of wildflowers. Energy and time permitting, you can continue hiking to Trillium Gap, where you'll find a spur trail to the top of Brushy Mountain (4,900 feet). Summiting Brushy Mountain adds about four more miles to the hiking total. Another alternative is to take Trillium Gap Trail all the way to the summit of Mount LeConte (and LeConte Lodge). That adds a little more than five miles (one-way). From there, you could spend the night (backpacking or at the lodge—reservations required about a year in advance), return the way you came (about 6.8 miles from LeConte Summit), or complete a point-to-point trek using Alum Cave (see next) or Boulevard (about 8 miles to Newfound Gap via the Appalachian Trail) if you can arrange a ride. You could also return where you started via Bullhead or Rainbow Falls trails. Either of those options results in roughly a 14-mile loop, with major elevation gain (~3,400 feet).

Roaring Fork Motor Nature Trail closes for winter, but you can still reach Grotto Falls by beginning at Rainbow Falls Trailhead (Cherokee Orchard Loop Road), which adds more than three miles to the hike. Another thing to note is the popularity of Roaring Fork Motor Nature Trail. You'll want to arrive early during peak season. Pack your patience if you're arriving mid-day in summer or fall when leaves have changed color.

CHIMNEY TOPS/ALUM CAVE

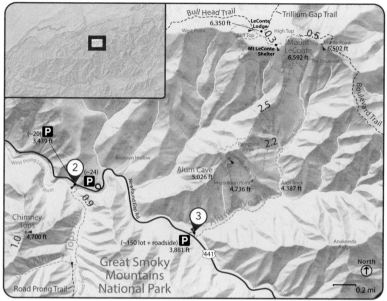

Chimney Tops | Strenuous | 3.8 miles | 1,270 feet | Out-and-back
Trailhead: Chimney Tops, Newfound Gap Road (2)

Chimney Tops highlight used to be its conclusion, a rocky scramble to its summit and outstanding panoramic views. A few years ago, the park put up a "closed" sign a quarter-mile from the peak, citing unstable terrain due to a recent devastating fire. Prior to the fire, the journey (a steep climb, and lots of stone stairs) wasn't exactly worth the effort without the fun finish. Although views improve dramatically after trees drop their leaves. The fire and work from the park's non-profit, including establishment of a new observation point, make the journey worthwhile once more. Views toward Mount LeConte are enjoyable (but still not the same). The park says it will reevaluate trail stability. That's something worth looking into before heading to the Smokies.

Alum Cave/Mt LeConte | Strenuous | 10.1 miles | 2,760 feet | Out-and-back
Trailhead: Alum Cave Bluffs, Newfound Gap Road (3)

Alum Cave is about the journey just as much as the final destination, well, as long as you don't mind a hard, (often) sweaty uphill climb. Along your way to the park's third tallest peak, you'll cross log bridges, walk through Arch Rock, and gain sweeping views to a nearby knife-edge ridgeline (Little Duck Hawk) and its unique rock feature called Eye of the Needle from Alum Cave (which is really more cove than cave). Of course, views are superior from the summit and Myrtle Point. From Alum Cave, it's about three more miles toiling uphill to the top of Mount LeConte and LeConte Lodge.

CHARLIE'S BUNION

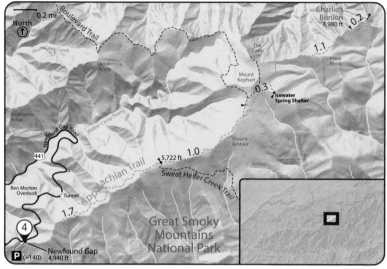

Not a fan of long, continuous climbs? There are alternative Mount LeConte options. A good choice for a point-to-point Mount LeConte hike is to go up via Appalachian and Boulevard trails from Newfound Gap, spend the night, and then hike down Alum Cave (if you arrange a ride, cache a car, or hitch). You can also reach Mount LeConte from Trillium Gap or Bull Head trails from Roaring Fork Motor Nature Trail (but those have a lot of elevation gain too).

There's a large parking area at the trailhead, with a smaller roadside lot and ample room alongside Newfound Gap Road. It's a good idea to get an early start for this hike. If you're passing through in the afternoon and aren't real keen on parking along the road, you'll want to have a few backups ready (like Chimney Tops, Charlie's Bunion, or Clingman's Dome).

Charlie's Bunion | Moderate | 8.6 miles | 1,600 feet | Out-and-back
Trailhead: Newfound Gap, Newfound Gap Road (4)

This is probably my favorite trail along Newfound Gap Road. The journey isn't great (there are only a few sweeping views) but it's relatively flat, there's a shelter along the way, and what's not to like about a bunion? The bunion is a rocky outcropping. Dayhikers will almost certainly be there, enjoying lunch with a view, but it's quite peaceful, especially compared to the crowds at Rockefeller Memorial (the only request made by John D. Rockefeller, Jr. when he donated $5 million to help establish the park) or Clingman's Dome. The trail is well-marked and easy-to-follow. The most confusing part is making sure you get on the spur to Charlie's Bunion. Pay attention and you should notice the rocky bunion in the distance long before the spur. Along the way you'll notice

ANDREW'S BALD

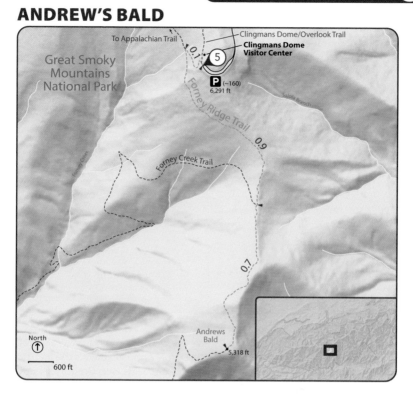

markers to a fun-sounding destination called "The Jump-Off." While there are views to the east and Charlie's Bunion, you're better off redirecting the extra time and mileage to another Smoky Mountain trail.

There's been a lot of talk about Mount LeConte already. Look at Boulevard Trail on the Charlie's Bunion Map. That's the route to Mount LeConte with the least elevation gain. And it's the quickest route to Myrtle Point.

Newfound Gap offers a large parking area with pretty rapid turnover thanks to most people only stopping to take in the roadside views and Rockefeller Memorial. It's one of the easier popular destinations to find a parking space during peak season.

Andrew's Bald | Moderate | 3.5 miles | 980 feet | Out-and-back
Trailhead: Clingman's Dome (5)

For most visitors, a stop at Clingman's Dome, the highest point in the park, is obligatory. It's great for sunrise or sunset, and the short, paved path with a steady grade to the lookout provides the ultimate 360-degree view. On your

ROCKY TOP

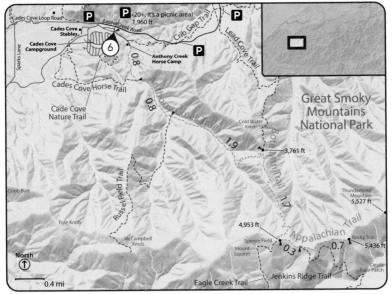

Great Smoky
Mountains
National Park

Cades Cove Loop Road

P 1,960 ft

P (20+, it's a picnic area)

P

Laurel Creek Road

Crib Gap Trail

Lead Cove Trail

Cades Cove Stables

Cades Cove Campground

6

Anthony Creek Horse Camp

P

Sparks Lane

Cades Cove Horse Trail

Cade Cove Nature Trail

Cold Water Knob

Anthony Creek Trail

1.9

3,761 ft

Cobb Butt

Russell Field Trail

Thunderhead Mountain 5,527 ft

Bote Mountain Trail

1.7

Pole Knob

McCampbell Knob

4,953 ft

Spence Field

Appalachian Trail

Rocky Top 5,436 ft

North

Mount Squires

0.3

0.7

Devils Race Patch

0.4 mi

Eagle Creek Trail

Jenkins Ridge Trail

visit, you might feel compelled to escape the crowd by going on a hike. You have two realistic options near Clingman's Dome. Andrew's Bald is the first. I'm not sure I'd pick it as the winner of a Battle of the Balds with Gregory's, but it requires considerably less effort and time. Andrew's also holds the distinction of the highest bald in the park, and, like Gregory's, features annual rhododendron and flame azalea blooms (late spring/early summer). The trail is not easy, but it's been improved with stone steps and drainage. Alternatively, you could head down Forney Creek Trail to Forney Creek Cascade (and backcountry campsite). Or do both! A side trip to Forney Creek Cascade adds about five more miles to the roundtrip distance.

The parking area at Clingman's Dome is large and popular. Like Newfound Gap, it turns over pretty quickly as most visitors only go up to the lookout (which is something you should do too).

Rocky Top | Strenuous | 12.4 miles | 3,500 feet | Out-and-back
Trailhead: Anthony Creek, Cades Cove Picnic Area (6)

A lot of people wish they were on ol' Rocky Top. But let me tell you, it isn't for everyone. This is a strenuous hike. It's non-stop up, and views don't develop until you reach Spence Field on the Appalachian Trail. And even there, you're somewhat hemmed in by trees. At Spence Field, you won't find any telephone bills, corn, or penned up ducks, but the climb isn't over. You have about another 500 feet of elevation left to gain on the way to Rocky Top. And, if you're going all that way, you might as well continue another 0.6 mile (one-way) to

GREGORY BALD

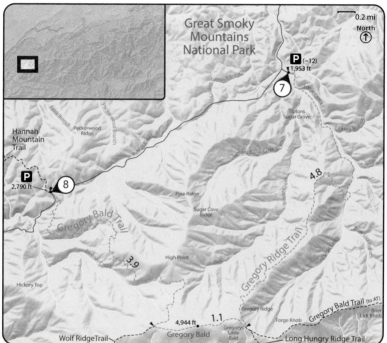

Thunderhead Mountain. You could also turn this into a lollipop by following the Appalachian Trail west to Russell Field Trail, and back to Cades Cove Picnic Area. Going the lollipop route adds an extra two miles.

The trailhead is located at the southeast corner of Cades Cove Picnic Area. There's a fair amount of parking and it's a relatively quiet spot, especially compared to nearby Cades Cove.

Gregory Ridge/Bald | Strenuous | 11.7/9.8 miles | 3,000/2,150 feet | Out-and-back (Point-to-point is possible)
Trailhead: Gregory Ridge (7) or Gregory Bald (8), Parson Branch Road

When most people talk about Gregory Bald it's usually to discuss the stunning display of flame azaleas (late spring/early summer). Be warned, it gets hot in June. So come prepared to sweat as it's a steady climb to the nearly 5,000-ft bald. During cooler months, the trek still has its redeeming qualities. From Gregory Bald, you can look down on Cades Cove. To reach it you take Gregory Ridge (11.7 miles, 3,000 feet elevation gain) or Gregory Bald (9.8 miles, 2,150 feet elevation gain) trails. With a cached car or arranged ride, you could do a point-to-point. (Parsons Branch Road was closed beyond Gregory Ridge Trailhead, but it should be opening again in 2023—something to keep an eye on.)

RAMSEY CASCADES

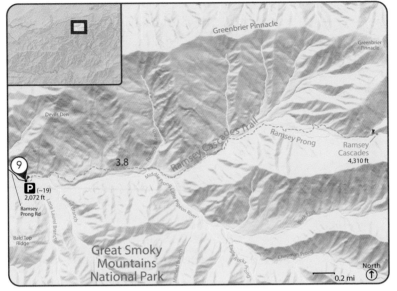

Parking areas are small, and during peak season, it'll be difficult to find a spot after morning. And you better arrive early when the azaleas are in bloom (to beat the heat and the crowds). The park reopened Parson Branch Road in 2023, so you should be able to drive out/in from US-129 (a highway that is also worth checking out if you like twisting, winding roads, with a bunch of sports cars/motorbikes zooming up and down it). Cades Cove Road, at the other end of Parson Branch Road, closes overnight and it regularly closes to motorists, allowing guests to enjoy it on foot or bicycle without a constant string of cars to negotiate. Check with the park for a current schedule of Cades Cove Road before arriving.

Ramsey Cascades | Moderate | 7.7 miles | 2,240 feet | Out-and-back
Trailhead: Greenbrier (9)

The journey is an enjoyable walk through old-growth forest, crossing a stream, and finally making an increasingly rugged ascent to the reason people complete this nearly 8-mile hike ... the park's tallest waterfall. Along the way to 100-foot Ramsey Cascades, you'll gain quite a bit of elevation, but it's a mostly gradual climb. And in the beginning you'll follow an old gravel road. One of the nice things about Ramsey Cascades is there's very little potential for confusion. It's out-and-back. No trail intersections. No decisions to make. No tempting spur trails (aside from the old, overgrown, and unmaintained path up to Greenbrier Pinnacle, where a fire tower used to reside). No obvious and erratic social trails. Just a straight shot to the falls and back. Although some people do like to hop in the creek for a refreshing dip.

MORE INFO

Parking Fee

While the park doesn't have an entrance fee, they introduced a parking permit in 2023. You must have a permit to park for more than 15 minutes. Day/week permits are available from recreation.gov. Annual permits are available from Great Smoky Mountains Association.

Baby owl on Gregory Ridge Trail

Charlie's Bunion

More Trails

Spruce Flat Falls is a short (less than two miles), relatively easy walk to a picturesque waterfall. It begins at the Lumber Ridge Trailhead near Great Smoky Mountains Institute at Tremont. The trailhead parking area only has room for a few cars, so you'll need luck or an early start. Follow Buckeye Trail to the south to reach the waterfall. Otherwise, nearby Laurel Falls is probably the most popular easy waterfall hike (and it offers more parking availability). I recommend camping at Deep Creek. Summertime visitors have a blast floating the river in innertubes, and you have direct access to Tom Branch, Indian Creek, and Juney Whank Falls. The Cataloochee Area is probably better known to horseback riders, but there are some good hiking options here. Next time out there I plan on making a big loop (~18 miles) to Mount Sterling via Palmer Creek, Little Cataloochee, Long Bunk, Mount Sterling, and Pretty Hollow Gap trails. There are waterfalls and swimming holes at Big Creek. Hike beyond the trails listed here and, who knows, you might end up in the park's exclusive 900-mile club, probably hiking your last miles deep in the Smokies interior at a place like Bone Valley.

Crowds

Every year Great Smoky Mountains is the most visited National Park. I'm not exactly sure what constitutes a visit, considering there are many non-recreational motorists and no entrance stations, but arrive in summer or for fall foliage and you won't question the data. Fortunately for you, the best way to escape the crowds is to go on a hike. Whether it's Newfound Gap, Cades Cove, Clingmans Dome, or any other popular destination, you only need to walk a mile or two until the buzz of traffic gets lost in the trees. With that said, don't expect to have any of these trails to yourself (unless you're hiking off-season with an early start).

Grotto Falls

Congaree
Hiking Trails: 20+ miles

River Trail

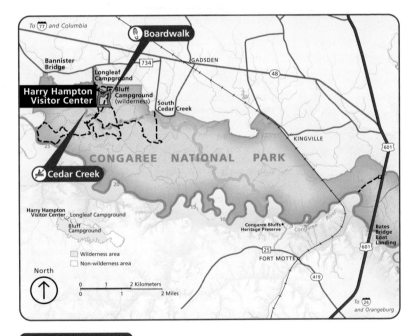

To (77) and Columbia

Boardwalk

Bannister Bridge

GADSDEN

734

48

Longleaf Campground

Harry Hampton Visitor Center

Bluff Campground (wilderness)

South Cedar Creek

KINGVILLE

601

CONGAREE NATIONAL PARK

Cedar Creek

Harry Hampton Visitor Center

Longleaf Campground

Bluff Campground

25

20

15

10

Congaree Bluffs Heritage Preserve

Congaree River

Bates Bridge Boat Landing

FORT MOTTE

25

419

601

Wilderness area

Non-wilderness area

North

0   1   2 Kilometers
0   1   2 Miles

To (26) and Orangeburg

Hiking Congaree

I find hiking around Congaree quite enjoyable. There are big trees and primeval swampland. But it's not exactly the unbelievable scenery you'll find in our western parks. Still, that's not to say you shouldn't pop in and take a walk if you're in the area. Record breaking trees and cypress knees protruding from the floodplain create a fairytale-like environment and the boardwalk lets you explore it any time of year (unless the floodplain is extremely flooded). I haven't been particularly lucky spotting wildlife at Congaree yet (no snakes or owls) but I have stumbled across feral hogs on River and Kingsnake trails and those encounters were surprisingly exciting. The trails here are straightforward, well-marked, and, if you're ambitious, you could do them all in one long day. Also, fireflies put on a show in spring.

Biscayne
Hiking Trails: <10 miles

Jetty Trail to Convoy Point

Hiking Biscayne

Biscayne is 95% water. There are a total of five trails found on the nearby keys. The longest of which is the 7-mile Spite Highway (AKA Elliott Key Boulevard), running the length of Elliott Key. And then there are very short loops on Boca Chita and Adams keys. Back on the mainland, you'll find a short (0.25-mile) trail to Convoy Point near Dante Fascell Visitor Center. Biscayne is about water and what's beneath its surface, not land. Arrive here expecting great hiking and you'll likely leave disappointed. Boat tours are great!

KENDALL

SOUTH MIAMI

MATHESON HAMMOCK PARK
(Miami-Dade County)

KEY BISCAYNE

BILL BAGGS
CAPE FLORIDA STATE PARK

Boundary marker

STILTSVILLE

Stiltsville

👍 **Bill Baggs State Park**

PARK BOUNDARY

SOLDIER KEY

FOWEY ROCKS
Arratoon Apcar
wreck

BLACK POINT PARK
(Miami-Dade County)

BISCAYNE   NATIONAL   PARK

🚂 **Boca Chita Key**

harbor • Boca Chita Key

SANDS KEY

Restricted
Area

Triumph Reef

🚂 **Boat Tours**

BISCAYNE BAY

**Dante Fascell
Visitor Center**
Convoy Point
Park Headquarters

👣 **Elliott Key Blvd**

Elliott Key Harbor

👍 **Mandalay Wreck**

Lugano wreck
Mandalay wreck

Elliott Key

E
L
L
I
O
T
T

K
E
Y

HOMESTEAD BAYFRONT PARK
Herbert Hoover Marina
(Miami-Dade County)

Erl King wreck

Alicia wreck

🦩 **Jones Lagoon**

Adams Key
Day-use area

19th-century
wooden sailing
vessel wreck

Anniversary Reef

O
T
T
E
N

K
E
Y

O
L
D

R
H
O
D
E
S

K
E
Y

Pacific Reef

PARK BOUNDARY

Elkhorn
Coral Reef   The Drop

INTRACOASTAL WATERWAY

K
E
Y

L
A
R
G
O

Rocky Reef

Ball Buoy Reef

Park's eastern boundary extends to 60ft (18m) depth

SANCTUARY BOUNDARY

PARK BOUNDARY

JOHN PENNEKAMP
CORAL REEF
STATE PARK
(protected area)

**Do Not Use This Map
For Navigation**
Zones and regulations are
subject to change. For safe
boating, National Ocean
Survey charts are
indispensable. Use chart
11451 (purchase at visitor
center) or charts 11462,
11463, and 11465.

Everglades
Hiking Trails: 50+ miles

Baby gators (Shark Loop Road)

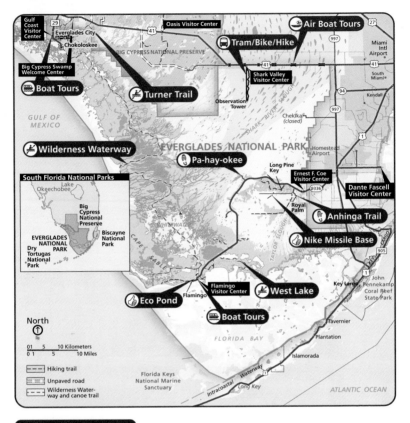

Hiking Everglades

Everglades has an awful lot to offer, hiking just isn't one of those things. While most hikers aren't looking to gain 3,000 feet of elevation on every hike, things are usually more interesting with a good amount of topography. Everglades is a massive, flat, river of grass. The highest point in the park measures slightly taller than the average man can reach ... a measly eight feet. On the other hand, this might be refreshing. Hiking is easy (unless you're slogging through a slough). The only must-do trails are Anhinga (easy, 0.8 mile), located at the end of Royal Palm Road, and Shark Valley (moderate, 15 miles), situated along the park's northern boundary. Both are reliably good places for gator watching. Shark Valley's Tram Road is also open to bikes (rentals available) and trams (fee). If you're going to walk it, it's a good idea to go counterclockwise. There's more shade, providing a bit of a reprieve from the Florida heat. There's also more water on this side, which makes for excellent gator and bird spotting. Look carefully. Baby gators can be difficult to identify. Walking the full loop might not be worth the sweat equity, but biking or tramming to the observation tower will give you a bird's eye view of the river of grass.

Speaking of river of grass. Boat tours, paddling, and airboat tours are all great ideas. There are some awfully fun mangrove-lined waterways.

Dry Tortugas
Hiking Trails: 1 mile

Fort Jefferson from Bush Key

0   1 Kilometer
0   1 Statute Mile
0   1 Nautical Mile

North

This map is an orientation aid for visitors to Dry Tortugas National Park. It should not be used in place of National Ocean Survey chart 11438, which is indispensable for safe boating on these waters.

Pulaski Shoal

GOOD SCUBA DIVING

Northkey Harbor

Texas Rock

TORTUGAS ECOLOGICAL RESERVE
TORTUGAS NORTH
PARK BOUNDARY

RESEARCH NATURAL AREA BOUNDARY

Brilliant Shoal

DRY TORTUGAS NATIONAL PARK

East Key
(closed to public)

Loggerhead Key

Hospital Key
(closed to public)

Middle Ground

Middle Key
(closed to public)

Loggerhead Key

Fort Jefferson
on Garden Key
(see inset below right)

DRY
TORTUGAS

Windjammer wreck

White Shoal

Loggerhead Reef

FLORIDA KEYS
NATIONAL MARINE
SANCTUARY

RESEARCH NATURAL AREA

RESEARCH NATURAL AREA BOUNDARY

Fort Jefferson

Inset scale
0   0.5 Kilometer
0   0.5 Statute Mile
0   0.5 Nautical Mile

Iowa Rock

Bird Key

Fort Jefferson
on Garden Key

Bush Key

Long Key
(closed to public)

GOOD
SNORKELING

Nurse Shark Special
Protection Zone
(closed to public June
through October)

Coral Special
Protection Zone
(closed to public)

GARDEN
KEY

Good snorkeling

Good snorkeling

MOAT

North
coaling
dock ruins

Good snorkeling

Visitor
Center

Seaplane
beach

Swimming
area

Dinghy
beach

South coaling
dock ruins

Good snorkeling

North

Fort Jefferson

Hiking Dry Tortugas

Florida! Lots of fun water activities and theme parks. Limited hiking. A short trail follows the shore of Bush Key (closes when sooty turns nest). You could count exploring Fort Jefferson as a hike. Walking between the upper and lower levels is a workout and don't forget about strolling (and snorkeling) around the former naval base's moat!

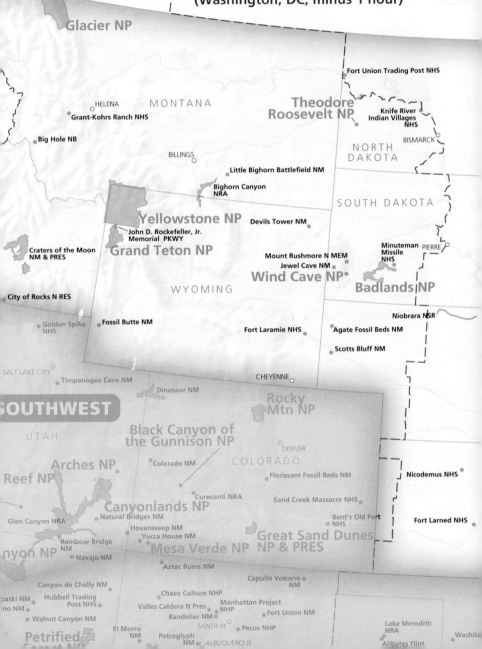

MOUNTAIN (Washington, DC, minus 2 hours)

CENTRAL (Washington, DC, minus 1 hour)

Glacier NP

Fort Union Trading Post NHS

MONTANA

Theodore Roosevelt NP

Knife River Indian Villages NHS

HELENA

Grant-Kohrs Ranch NHS

NORTH DAKOTA

BISMARCK

Big Hole NB

BILLINGS

SOUTH DAKOTA

Little Bighorn Battlefield NM

Bighorn Canyon NRA

Yellowstone NP

Devils Tower NM

John D. Rockefeller, Jr. Memorial PKWY

Craters of the Moon NM & PRES

Grand Teton NP

Mount Rushmore N MEM

Jewel Cave NM

Minuteman Missile NHS

PIERRE

City of Rocks N RES

WYOMING

Wind Cave NP

Badlands NP

Golden Spike NHS

Fossil Butte NM

Niobrara NSR

Fort Laramie NHS

Agate Fossil Beds NM

Scotts Bluff NM

SALT LAKE CITY

Timpanogos Cave NM

CHEYENNE

SOUTHWEST

Dinosaur NM

Rocky Mtn NP

UTAH

Black Canyon of the Gunnison NP

DENVER

COLORADO

Arches NP

Colorado NM

Florissant Fossil Beds NM

Nicodemus NHS

Reef NP

Curecanti NRA

Sand Creek Massacre NHS

Canyonlands NP

Natural Bridges NM

Bent's Old Fort NHS

Fort Larned NHS

Glen Canyon NRA

Hovenweep NM

Yucca House NM

Rainbow Bridge NM

Mesa Verde NP

Great Sand Dunes NP & PRES

nyon NP

Navajo NM

Aztec Ruins NM

Capulin Volcano NM

satki NM

Hubbell Trading Post NHS

Chaco Culture NHP

Valles Caldera N Pres

Manhattan Project NHP

Fort Union NM

no NM

Walnut Canyon NM

Bandelier NM

SANTA FE

Lake Meredith NRA

El Morro NM

Pecos NHP

Petrified

Petroglyph NM

ALBUQUERQUE

Washita

Alibates Flint

The North

Voyageurs NP

Isle Royale NP

Grand Portage NM

LAKE SUPERIOR

Apostle
Islands
NL

Keweenaw NHP

FARGO

Pictured Rocks
NL

MINNESOTA

Saint Croix NSR

WISCONSIN

Sleeping Bear Dunes
NL

Mississippi NRRA
ST PAUL
MINNEAPOLIS

Pipestone NM

MICHIGAN

LAKE MICHIGAN

Effigy Mounds NM

MADISON

MILWAUKEE

LAN

Missouri NRR

IOWA

River Rai

NEBRASKA

DES MOINES

Herbert Hoover NHS

CHICAGO

Pullman NM

Indiana
Dunes NP

OMAHA

LINCOLN

NORTH

Homestead NM
of America

INDIANA

Av
He

ILLINOIS

INDIANAPOLIS

SPRINGFIELD
Lincoln Home NHS

Gateway Arch NP

KANSAS CITY

George Rogers
Clark NHP

TOPEKA

Harry S Truman NHS

Brown v. Board
of Education NHS

ST LOUIS

JEFFERSON CITY

KANSAS

Tallgrass Prairie
N PRES

Ulysses S.
Grant NHS

LOUISVILLE

Lincoln Boyhood N MEM

Abraha
NHP

WICHITA

Fort Scott NHS

MISSOURI

Mammoth
Cave NP

Wilson's Creek
NB

Ozark NSR

Big South Fork N

George Washington Carver NM

Fort Donelson NB

Obed WS

NASHVILLE

Stones River N

Pea Ridge NMP

TENNESSEE

Buffalo NR

Great Smoky M

lefield NHS

TULSA

OKLAHOMA CITY

Indiana Dunes
Hiking Trails: 50+ miles
Lakefront views

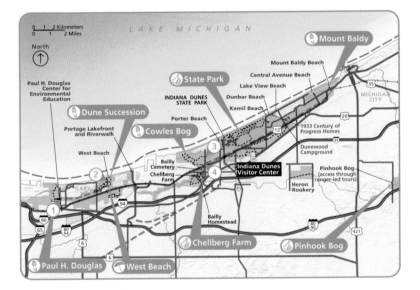

Indiana Dunes Favorites

① **Paul H. Douglas**
Moderate | 3.5 miles | 120 feet

② **Dune Succession**
Moderate | 0.9 miles | 100 feet

③-④ **Cowle's Bog**
Moderate | 4.7 miles | 200 feet

Paul H. Douglas | Moderate | 3.5 miles | 120 feet | Out-and-back
Trailhead: Paul H. Douglas Center for Environmental Education (1)

Paul H. Douglas (formerly Miller Woods) is one of the more scenic trails found along Indiana's Lake Michigan Coast. It explores a variety of ecosystems,

PAUL H. DOUGLAS

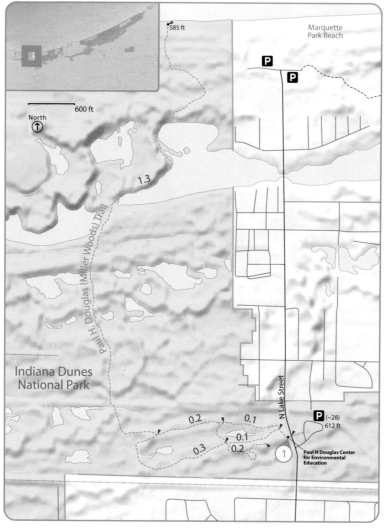

beginning in a black oak savanna, leading up to open dunes, and concluding at Lake Michigan's sandy shoreline. From the beach, it is possible to walk all the way to West Beach (and beyond), but most visitors take a short stroll and return the way they came. This is a great destination for groups with varied interests and/or abilities, as you'll have the option to explore the Education Center (check the operating hours), hike either of the short loops (about one mile), or hike the entire trail to Lake Michigan. There's quite a bit of parking in the lot across the street from the Paul H. Douglas Center.

DUNE SUCCESSION

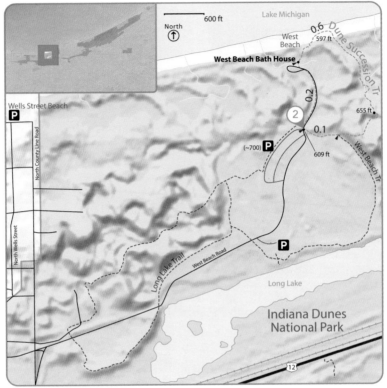

Dune Succession | Moderate | 0.9 miles | 100 feet | Loop
Trailhead: West Beach Parking Area (2)

After a recent rebranding effort, Dune Succession trail is now known as the Diana Dunes Dare. They're probably trying to keep up with the popular 3 Dunes Challenge just down the road at Indiana Dunes State Park (which is also worth visiting while you're in the area). Aliterative names aside, no one should need to dare you to complete this short hike (unless you're stair-averse—there are more than 250 of those). After a sign near the trailhead tells you about Diana, you'll find educational displays discussing the four stages of dune development. And then the trail drops you off on West Beach, which is a great place to get comfortable and enjoy the lake and/or distant Chicago skyline.

West Beach offers a huge parking area, but it fills in summer. It's about a quarter mile from the parking area to West Beach and the bath house, but there is a drop-off area for visitors and their beach gear.

COWLE'S BOG

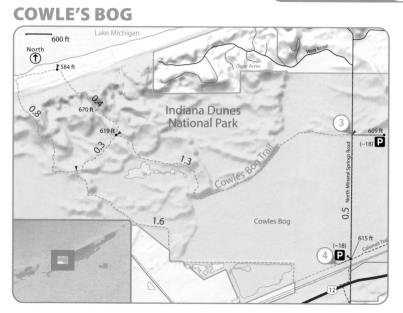

Lake Michigan

600 ft

North

584 ft

0.8

0.4

670 ft

619 ft

0.3

Dune Acres

West Road

Indiana Dunes
National Park

1.3

Cowles Bog Trail

3

609 ft

(~18) P

North Mineral Springs Road

0.5

1.6

Cowles Bog

615 ft

(~18)

4 P

Calumet Trail

12

Cowle's Bog | Moderate | 4.7 miles | 200 feet | Loop
Trailhead: Main Lot (3) or Greenbelt Lot (4), North Mineral Springs Road

Cowle's Bog is similar to Paul H. Douglas. The main differences being Cowle's Bog is a loop and slightly more secluded. But there's a catch. The whole park has an industrial vibe, but it's particularly heavy around Cowle's Bog. Steel mills, power plants, railroads, and power lines are almost perpetually present. Loop direction isn't important, but I'd recommend beginning with the walk along the road (regardless which trailhead you park at). Bisecting the bog, Mineral Springs Road is actually quite scenic but who wants to end a nice trail with a half-mile roadside walk as motorists pass you by? Both parking areas have quite a bit of space, but things fill up on beautiful weekends.

More Trails

Mount Baldy and Pinhook Bog are two more trails worth mentioning. Pinhook Bog can only be accessed with a ranger. You can hike near Mount Baldy on your own, but to hike onto it, that'll require a ranger, too. I also enjoyed the walk around Chelberg Farm and hike to Bailly Homestead and Cemetery. They're more cultural than natural, but sometimes that's a pleasant change of pace.

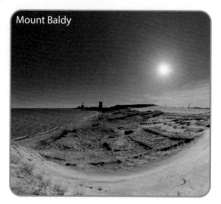

Mount Baldy

Gateway Arch
Hiking Trails: <2 miles
Kiener Plaza Park

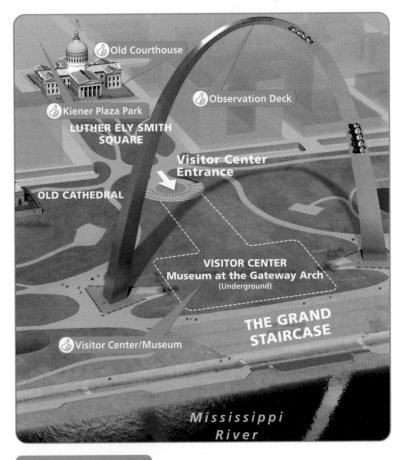

Hiking Gateway Arch

National Park enthusiasts are constantly criticizing the decision to redesignate Jefferson National Expansion Memorial as Gateway Arch. The criticism is warranted but, if you think about its symbolism as a monument to the west and exploration (and all the "real" National Parks we love), it works quite nicely. Regardless how you see it, it's not a hiking destination. You'll find less than two miles of paved paths connecting 4th street, Museum, Arch, and Mississippi River. Gateway Arch may not be everyone's idea of a National Park, but you'd be hard pressed to find more interesting photographic opportunities along any two miles of trail in the entire collection of National Parks than you'll find circling this steel monument—it's incredibly photogenic!

Isle of Moose

Isle Royale
Hiking Trails: 160+miles

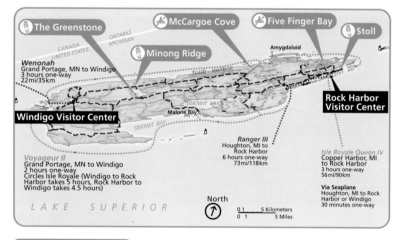

The Greenstone

McCargoe Cove

Five Finger Bay

Stoll

Minong Ridge

ONTARIO
MICHIGAN

CANADA
UNITED STATES

Amygdaloid

Wenonah
Grand Portage, MN to Windigo
3 hours one-way
22mi/35km

TODD HARBOR

Windigo Visitor Center

SISKIWIT LAKE

Malone Bay

SISKIWIT BAY

**Rock Harbor
Visitor Center**

Voyageur II
Grand Portage, MN to Windigo
2 hours one-way
Circles Isle Royale (Windigo to Rock
Harbor takes 5 hours, Rock Harbor to
Windigo takes 4.5 hours)

Ranger III
Houghton, MI to
Rock Harbor
6 hours one-way
73mi/118km

Isle Royale Queen IV
Copper Harbor, MI
to Rock Harbor
3 hours one-way
56mi/90km

Via Seaplane
Houghton, MI to Rock
Harbor or Windigo
30 minutes one-way

LAKE   SUPERIOR

North

0 1   5 Kilometers
0 1   5 Miles

Hiking Isle Royale

Only accessible by boat and seaplane, Isle Royale is primarily a backpacking destination. However, dayhiking and daytrips are possible, taking the *Queen Royale IV* (Copper Harbor, MI) or the *Seahunter III* (Grand Portage, MN). Both options leave you with more time on a boat than on land, but if you aren't into camping/backpacking or couldn't make lodging accommodations work out, it's an option. Arriving at Rock Harbor aboard the *Queen Royale IV*, you'd probably only have time to walk a portion of Stoll Memorial Trail. Arriving at Windigo aboard the *Seahunter III*, you could do the Windigo Nature Walk. In short, day trips aren't a great idea. It's a little better idea if you take a seaplane out of Houghton, MI, but still not great. Bring your backpack and spend a few days with the moose!

Voyageurs is about the water, not the land (Grassy Bay Cliff)

Voyageurs
Hiking Trails: 100+ miles

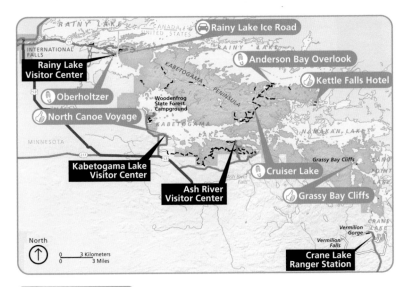

- Rainy Lake Ice Road
- **Rainy Lake Visitor Center**
- Anderson Bay Overlook
- Kettle Falls Hotel
- Oberholtzer
- Woodenfrog State Forest Campground
- North Canoe Voyage
- **Kabetogama Lake Visitor Center**
- **Ash River Visitor Center**
- Cruiser Lake
- Grassy Bay Cliffs
- Grassy Bay Cliffs
- Vermilion Gorge
- Vermilion Falls
- **Crane Lake Ranger Station**

INTERNATIONAL FALLS

RAINY LAKE

CANADA / UNITED STATES

KABETOGAMA PENINSULA

KABETOGAMA LAKE

NAMAKAN LAKE

MINNESOTA

North

0   3 Kilometers
0   3 Miles

Hiking Voyageurs

It makes sense that the Land of 10,000 Lakes' National Park is all about boating! What doesn't make sense is coming here excited about easily-accessible hiking trails. With that said, a handful can be reached by car. Oberholtzer (easy, 1.7 miles) up at Rainy Lake is okay. Blind Ash Bay (moderate, 3.3 miles), beginning near Kabetogama Lake is pleasant. But if you want to have a great time at Voyageurs, hiking should be an afterthought (unless you're backpacking the interior lakes via Cruiser Lake Trail). If you haven't done it before, camping by boat or canoe is pretty darn fun! Houseboat rentals are also available.

Badlands
Hiking Trails: 10 miles   Castle

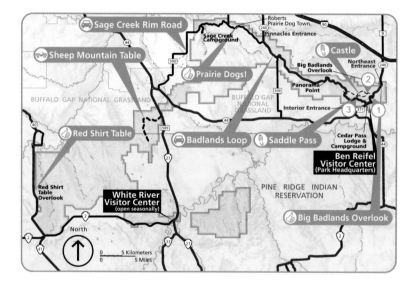

Badlands Favorites

① **Notch**
Moderate | 1.2 miles | 120 feet

③ **Saddle Pass**
Strenuous | 0.7 miles | 275 feet

② **Castle–Medicine Root**
Moderate | 6.3 miles | 220 feet

Notch | Moderate | 1.2 miles | 120 feet | Out-and-back
Trailhead: Badlands Loop Road (1)

Badlands may not have a huge network of maintained hiking trails, but the few miles it has are interesting. Notch Trail begins at a large parking area serving Door, Window, and Notch trailheads. A lot of kids don't even go on the trails. They simply run off to play on the rocks. Not a bad approach. A better one is to take Notch Trail. While short and relatively easy, Notch isn't for everyone.

BEN REIFEL VISITOR CENTER AREA

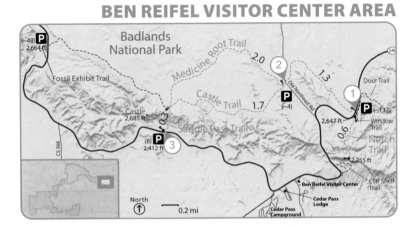

There's a wooden-rung ladder and a short stretch of exposed trail. If that has you second-guessing the hike, it's such a short walk to the ladder, stroll over and decide on the spot. As for the Notch. The view overlooks Cliff Shelf Trail and the lodge, campground, etc. It's good but you'll find better views along Badlands Loop Road, so Notch is more about the journey than the destination.

Castle–Medicine Root | Moderate | 6.3 miles | 220 feet | Loop
Trailhead: Badlands Loop Road (1) or Old Northeast Road (2)

The Castle–Medicine Loop presents a few options. You can begin from the Door/Notch/Window parking lot. The trailhead is just on the other side of Badlands Loop Road. Or, if you'd like to shorten the trek a bit, park at the trailhead on unpaved Old Northeast Road. You'd miss out on some cool rock formations between Badlands Loop Road and Old Northeast roads, and last time I saw sheep navigating delicate ridgelines in this area, but it's shorter. And shorter might be exactly what you're looking for, especially during the scorching summer. There are plenty of pretty rocks along Castle and Medicine Root, but the highlight is undoubtedly the viewpoint from a rocky pinnacle (Castle) near the convergence of Castle, Medicine Root, and Saddle Pass trails. After enjoying the view, return via the Medicine Root/Castle Loop or continue to Fossil Exhibit Trail (also neat).

Saddle Pass | Strenuous | 0.7 mile | 275 feet | Out-and-back
Trailhead: Badlands Loop Road (3)

If you want to reach Castle viewpoint mentioned above even quicker, you can climb Saddle Pass Trail. There's a large parking area at the trailhead on Badlands Loop Road. It's short but very steep, covering tricky terrain. The main point is to hike up to the Castle (also accessed via Castle/Medicine Root), where you'll have sweeping Badlands views.

Where the bison roam

Wind Cave
Hiking Trails: 30+ miles

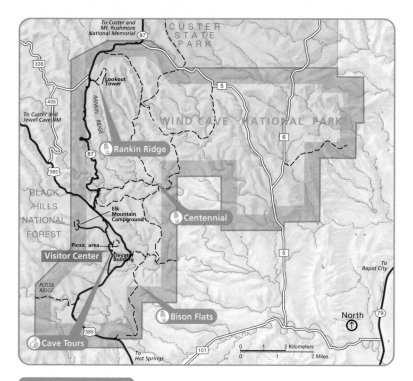

Hiking Wind Cave

If you'd like to see prairie dogs and bison in person, Wind Cave is exceptional. Hiking is okay. Cold Brook Canyon (easy, 2.8 miles), Wind Cave Canyon (easy, 3.6 miles), and Boland Ridge (strenuous, 5.4 miles) trails felt similar. Although Cold Brook Canyon is the only one with a prairie dog town. That's a huge plus! Love those little critters! Boland Ridge is slightly more scenic with some rolling hills (and I picked up poison ivy on this one). Rankin Ridge (easy, 1.0 mile) is a short loop with a lookout tower. You can make a loop of Lookout Point and Centennial trails (moderate, 4.4 miles). You'll see prairie dogs on Lookout Point. I'd recommend going counterclockwise. That way you'll end with the dogs, and avoid a false trail just before the final stretch back up to the parking area. For better hiking, check out nearby Custer State Park.

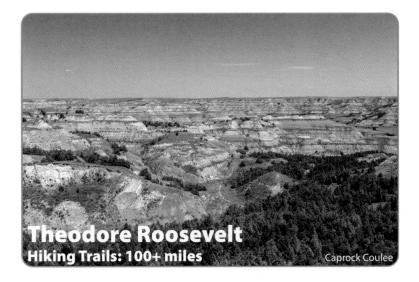

Theodore Roosevelt
Hiking Trails: 100+ miles

Caprock Coulee

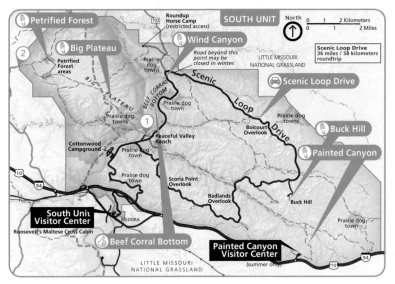

Theodore Roosevelt Favorites

1 **Big Plateau (South)**
Moderate | 5.2 miles | 560 feet

3 **Caprock Coulee (North)**
Moderate | 3.8 miles | 550 feet

2 **Petrified Forest (South)**
Strenuous | 10.2 miles | 800 feet

S. UNIT/BIG PLATEAU/PETRIFIED FOREST

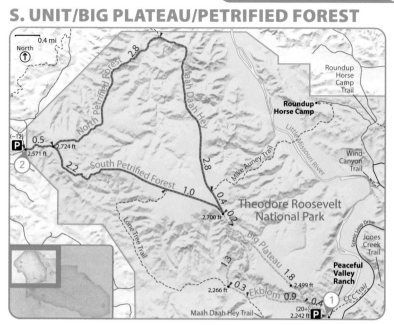

Big Plateau | Moderate | 5.2 miles | 560 feet | Loop
Trailhead: Peaceful Valley Ranch (1)

Big Plateau is probably my favorite hike in the park. There's a small dirt lot on the west side of the access road just before Peaceful Valley Ranch, where you'll find Ekblom Trailhead, the start of this journey. There's additional parking just down the road at the ranch. The trail is clearly marked at the far end of the dirt lot. Starting the hike along Ekblom Trail, it won't be long and you'll reach the Little Missouri River. You must cross it. This is rarely a problem, but it's good to know to bring water-friendly footwear and a towel (water level varies, turn around if you aren't comfortable with it). If you're hiking in the morning, I'd beeline for the steep climb up to Big Plateau to enjoy morning light on its vast grassy expanse. This is a great place for wildlife viewing. You'll likely see bison and a prairie dog or two (just kidding—they're everywhere). Return via Maah Daah Hey and Ekblom. Before you know it, you'll be back at the Little Mo, taking off your shoes to cross its muddy water, the last obstacle before returning to Peaceful Valley Ranch.

Petrified Forest Loop | Strenuous | 10.2 miles | 800 feet | Loop
Trailhead: West Park Boundary (2)

Petrified Forest Loop is another good hike. The trailhead is located on the South Unit's western boundary, about a 30-minute drive from Cottonwood Campground, including unpaved (but well-maintained) roads. If you have no interest in petrified wood, this trail is still worth considering thanks to colorful

Big Plateau

badlands, wildlife opportunities, and pleasant prairies. If you are a petrified wood afficionado, you're in the right place. Theodore Roosevelt National Park possesses the third highest concentration of petrified wood in the United States. You can do an out-and-back on either South or North Petrified Forest trail. It's roughly 1.5 miles (one-way) in either direction until you begin to see petrified wood specimens. The full loop is long and somewhat monotonous. If you're into the wood, you'll probably spend quite a bit of time off trail checking things out. Potential bison and pronghorn sightings spice things up a bit.

Reaching the trailhead is a little bit of a chore. You take exit 23 on I-94, and then head north along Forest Service Road 730, following the signs. There should be "Petrified Forest" signs all the way to the trailhead.

Figure 8 | Strenuous | 14.8 miles | 1,340 feet | Figure 8
Trailhead: Peaceful Valley Ranch (1) or West Park Boundary (2)

If you're looking for a real serious hike, combine the Big Plateau and Petrified Forest loops into one massive Figure 8. To me, the highlight is wildlife watching (and panoramic-view-enjoying) on the Big Plateau, but others will be all about those petrified trees or maybe the river crossing. Spend the day and enjoy them all!

NORTH UNIT/CAPROCK COULEE

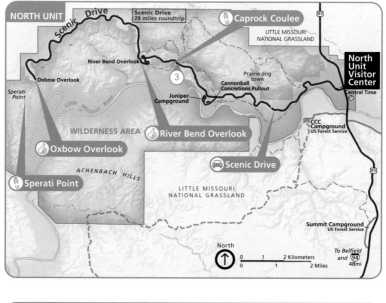

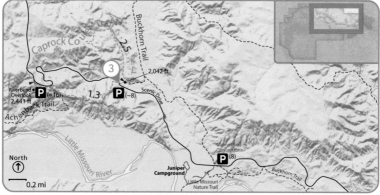

Caprock Coulee | Moderate | 3.8 miles | 550 feet | Out-and-back
Trailhead: Caprock Coulee Nature Trail (3) or River Bend Overlook

Start at Caprock Coulee Trailhead on Scenic Drive and you'll find the short and easy nature trail portion with signage explaining what you'll see (and that a coulee is a steep, narrow valley). Coulees are cool but the most compelling portion is the ridge from River Bend Overlook back to Caprock Coulee Trailhead, which is high above colorful/bentonite badlands and the Little Missouri River. However, do the full loop. You won't have any regrets. In addition to a pleasant hike, River Bend Overlook is a fantastic sunset site.

Park Units

Theodore Roosevelt is three distinct units. The South Unit is easiest to access, with I-94 running along its southern boundary. But it still has some complications, like four separate entry points. Painted Canyon Visitor Center is accessed from I-94, exit 32. Scenic Loop Drive and the south unit's visitor center are accessed from I-94, exits 27 and 34. And unpaved roads lead to Petrified Forest Trailhead and Roundup Horsecamp from the west and north, respectively. The North Unit is about an hour drive from South Unit Visitor Center. It's more remote but also more straightforward, with one road entering the park from the east. Finally, there's Elkhorn Ranch, a former property of Theodore Roosevelt. It's a long drive on dirt roads to reach ruins of his ranch in a grassy setting alongside the Little Missouri River.

Petrified Forest

Buck Hill

More Trails

Theodore Roosevelt presents an abundance of short and rewarding hikes. Wind Canyon, Boicourt Overlook, Buck Hill, and Coal Vein trails, all beginning from the South Unit's Scenic Loop Drive, have decent returns for minimal time/energy investment. Painted Canyon is a great area to be for sunrise/sunset, and Painted Canyon Trail is nice. And there's a big figure 8 through the park's interior formed by Paddock Creek (Upper and Lower) and Talkington (Upper and Lower) trails. The entire figure 8 is more than 20 miles. The North Unit is somewhat similar. There's a large figure 8 formed by two loops (Buckhorn and Achenbach trails). Sperati Point is another short trail delivering some outstanding badlands views.

Visitation

Crowds are never overwhelming at Theodore Roosevelt. Weather can be erratic, but visiting the park in spring to watch the bison or fall to enjoy the colors can be a very peaceful holiday.

Prairie Dogs!

Wildlife

This is a pretty good wildlife park, especially for prairie dog enthusiasts like me. Prairie dogs are everywhere. Hundreds of them! Bison are usually easy to find. The South Unit has a healthy population of feral horses (although conversations are ongoing about removing them). Both are good, but the South Unit is superior when it comes to wildlife sightings. The bison herd is twice as big and it's more developed, making animals more accustomed to humans and humans having easier access to park land. Remember to give animals their space.

Delta Lake

Grand Teton
Hiking Trails: 50+ miles

Grand Teton Favorites

(1) Lake Solitude
Strenuous | 18.2 miles | 4,000 feet

(2) Delta Lake
Strenuous | 7.1 miles | 2,400 ft

(2) Surprise/Amphitheater Lakes
Strenuous | 9.6 miles | 3,000 feet

(3-4) Phelps Lake
Moderate | 6.6 miles | 500 feet

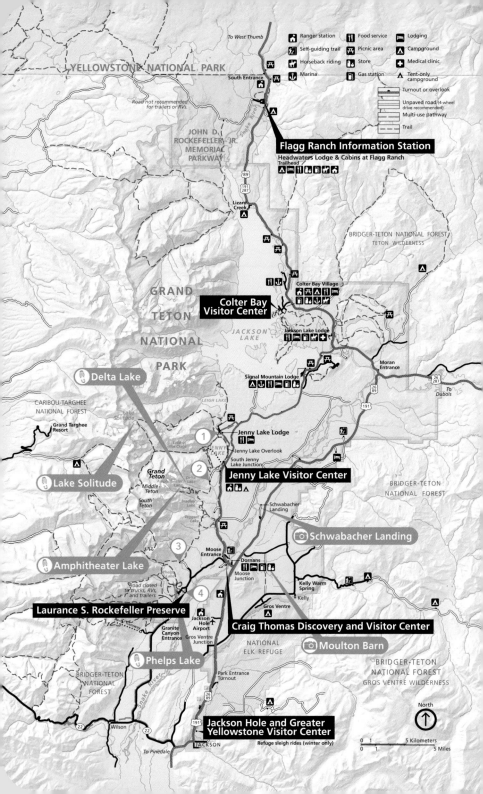

To West Thumb

Ranger station
Self-guiding trail
Horseback riding
Marina
Food service
Picnic area
Store
Gas station
Lodging
Campground
Medical clinic
Tent-only campground

Turnout or overlook
Unpaved road (4-wheel drive recommended)
Multi-use pathway
Trail

YELLOWSTONE NATIONAL PARK

South Entrance

Road not recommended for trailers or RVs.

JOHN D.
ROCKEFELLER, JR.
MEMORIAL
PARKWAY

Flagg Ranch Information Station
Headwaters Lodge & Cabins at Flagg Ranch
Trailhead

89
191
287

Lizard Creek

BRIDGER-TETON NATIONAL FOREST
TETON WILDERNESS

GRAND

Colter Bay Village

Colter Bay Visitor Center

TETON

JACKSON LAKE

Jackson Lake Lodge

NATIONAL

Moran Entrance

To Dubois

PARK

26
287

Signal Mountain Lodge

26
191

Delta Lake

CARIBOU-TARGHEE NATIONAL FOREST

LEIGH LAKE

Lake Solitude

Grand Targhee Resort

Jenny Lake Lodge

Lake Solitude

1

Jenny Lake Overlook

South Jenny Lake Junction

Grand Teton

JENNY LAKE

2

Jenny Lake Visitor Center

BRIDGER-TETON NATIONAL FOREST

Middle Teton

Bradley Lake

South Teton

Schwabacher Landing

Taggart Lake

Amphitheater Lake

3

Moose Entrance

Schwabacher Landing

Road closed to trucks, RVs, and trailers

Dornans

Moose Junction

Kelly Warm Spring

Laurance S. Rockefeller Preserve

4

Kelly

Jackson Hole Airport

Gros Ventre

Granite Canyon Entrance

Gros Ventre Junction

Craig Thomas Discovery and Visitor Center

Phelps Lake

NATIONAL ELK REFUGE

Moulton Barn

BRIDGER-TETON NATIONAL FOREST
GROS VENTRE WILDERNESS

BRIDGER-TETON NATIONAL FOREST

Park Entrance Turnout

North

26
89

22

Wilson

22

Jackson Hole and Greater Yellowstone Visitor Center

191

JACKSON

Refuge sleigh rides (winter only)

To Pinedale

0   1   5 Kilometers
0   1   5 Miles

LAKE SOLITUDE

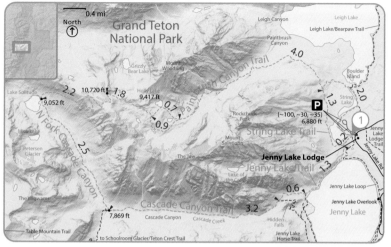

Lake Solitude | Strenuous | 18.2 miles | 4,000 feet | Loop
Trailhead: String Lake (1)

Few trails shower hikers with ever-changing mountain views like the Cascade Canyon–Paintbrush Canyon Loop, stopping at Lake Solitude. It's absolutely wonderful. It seems like most people prefer to go clockwise. However, even though Paintbrush Canyon is steeper, it's also prettier, so my preference is to do the prettier part in the morning light. Beginning with Paintbrush also gets you to Lake Solitude sooner (as long as you power your way up to Paintbrush Divide). Another positive to a counterclockwise approach is Hidden Falls and Inspiration Point will be near the end of your hike, and then it'll be easier to decide whether you have enough time and energy left for them. (I'd rather take a break at Holly Lake on Paintbrush Canyon, than at Inspiration Point, but that's just me.) The hike is long, but you'll enjoy several blissful hours walking among these sublime mountains. And there's very little to be confused about (aside from getting to Hidden Falls, which should be expected since it's hidden).

This is a popular backpacking destination (and something to consider, especially if you aren't sure about being able to dayhike it). Another great backpacking option is to hike behind Grand, Middle and South Teton by taking Paintbrush Canyon to Lake Solitude, but instead of returning via Cascade Canyon, take Teton Crest Trail (past Schoolroom Glacier) and loop back via Death Canyon Trail. You can take the Jenny Lake shuttle (first trip at 7am) but it doesn't shorten the trek and that's a little bit of a late start. I'd stick with beginning at the String Lake Trailhead, located near Jenny Lake Lodge. Snow sticks around Paintbrush Canyon well into summer, so it's important to check trail conditions with the park or stop in at Jenny Lake Ranger Station.

SURPRISE, AMPHITHEATER, DELTA LAKES

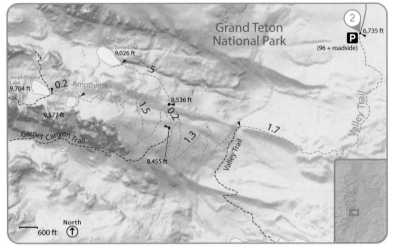

Grand Teton
National Park

6,735 ft
P (96 + roadside)

Delta Lake
9,026 ft

Amphitheater Lake
9,704 ft

Amphitheater Lake

Surprise Lake
9,577 ft

0.2

8,536 ft

Garnet Canyon Trail

1.5

0.2

1.3

8,455 ft

1.7

Valley Trail

Valley Trail

North

600 ft

Surprise/Amphitheater Lakes | Strenuous | 9.6 miles | 3,000 feet | Out-and-back
Delta Lake | Strenuous | 7.1 miles | 2,400 feet | Out-and-back
Trailhead: Lupine Meadows (2)

Surprise and Amphitheater Lakes are small but picturesque alpine lakes nestled within the jagged peaks of the Teton Range. The views are tremendous, but they are earned, not given. After an easy first mile or so, it's a long steady climb to Surprise and then Amphitheater lakes. You'll pass a few spur trails. Garnet Canyon Trail is the primary route for climbing Grand Teton, and, even if you aren't after a summit, it serves up nice views of Middle Teton. There's also an unmarked and most-likely unseen spur trail to Delta Lake. If you're up for some scrambling and a bit of an adventure, don't skip it.

Delta Lake, with Grand Teton looming in the background, is the stuff of your outdoor adventuring dreams. To get there, you'll have to do a little rock scrambling and shuffle up a steep (and sandy) escarpment, but boy is it worth it. As an out-and-back from Lupine Meadows, it's a little more than seven miles. Tacking it onto a Surprise and Amphitheater lakes itinerary only adds another mile. Other than its relative increased difficulty, the main thing you need to know is the spur trail is unmarked (in fact, it's more hidden than Hidden Falls). Occasionally good-intentioned hikers build a cairn at the junction, but they inevitably are removed (by if you know, you know-type hikers). With that said, if you know to look for the trail at the back of a switchback, you should spot it with ease. Miss it. No problem. Catch it on the way back from Amphitheater Lake. It is much easier to spot coming down.

Lupine Meadows is a very popular trailhead. It will be crowded in summer but there always seems to be enough room thanks to additional parking along

PHELPS LAKE

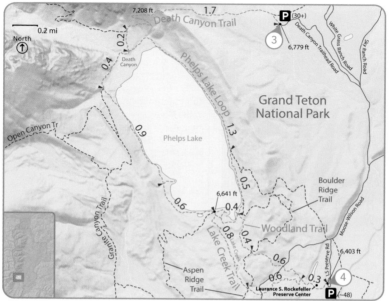

Phelps Lake | Moderate | 6.6 miles | 500 feet | Loop
Trailhead: Death Canyon (3) or Laurance S. Rockefeller Preserve (4)

Lupine Meadows Road. An early start is still a good idea. Late arrivals will not only have less daylight, but you could add a mile or more walking to the trailhead. Plus, morning light is best at each lake.

Phelps Lake is the best Grand Teton trail that doesn't penetrate the spectacular mountain range's interior. It's relatively flat with an abundance of scenic views looking toward Death Canyon. With that said, the loop can leave you wanting some changing scenery. For a short trek, simply walk to the south end of the lake and back. Or lengthen it and shake up the scenery by taking Aspen Ridge or Boulder Ridge Trails. I took Aspen Ridge last time there. It added an element of solitude, but the scenery was better by the lake. In fall, I imagine it'd be fantastic. As for the loop around Phelps Lake, the big attraction is a large rock on the lake's northeast shoreline. Visitors have a lot of fun cannonballing off it.

Parking at the Laurance S. Rockefeller Preserve lot is about as competitive as it gets. During peak season, they'll be letting one car in as one car leaves for most of the day. So, it's a good idea to arrive early. An alternative is to hike in via Death Canyon Trail. (Hiking into Death Canyon is a good idea too. Backpackers should think about taking Alaska Basin Trail to Schoolroom Glacier, and then Lake Solitude.) You may have an easier time finding a parking spot. You'll get better views of Death Canyon. The tradeoff is the hiking is tougher, which isn't necessarily a bad thing.

Death Canyon at the back of Phelps Lake

More Trails

Grand Teton is a relatively small park but there are more trails. The primary omissions are Death Canyon and Table Mountain (strenuous, 12.0 miles). Death Canyon is visible from Phelps Lake, and, like all great Grand Teton trails, it leads into the Tetons. Table Mountain is unique in that the trailhead is located on the west side of the range. The path goes directly toward the back side of Grand Teton. Of all the easy trails, String Lake (3.7 miles) and Jenny Lake (7.1 miles) are probably the best, but there are several fun historic sites too!

More Activities

Visitation is vigorous in summer. One of the better ways to avoid crowds is to book an outfitter-led tour. Horseback riding, Snake River floats, rock climbing, and fly fishing are popular. And many outfitters are available for each one. I still think waking up early and exploring the mountains on your own is the better choice, but outfitters always find a way to keep things exciting (and you're already at an exciting destination). Boat rentals are available at Jackson Lake. Bring your own watercraft (even an SUP), and you'll need a permit and Aquatic Invasive Species inspection (fees).

Watch for wildlife!

Cunningham Cabin

More Attractions

Grand Teton National Park is a favorite of photographers. Moulton Barns and Schwabacher Landing are the two most popular destinations, but Menor's Ferry Historic District (Chapel of the Transfiguration) and Cunningham Cabin are fun places to peruse as well. And then there's Mount Moran, the sentinel looming at the southwest corner of Jackson Lake. Jackson Lake itself is fun to explore on a boat tour (or rent a boat and cruise on your own). And then, of course, the big attraction is Yellowstone National Park, directly to the north.

Yellowstone
Hiking Trails: 1,000+ miles

Old Faithful

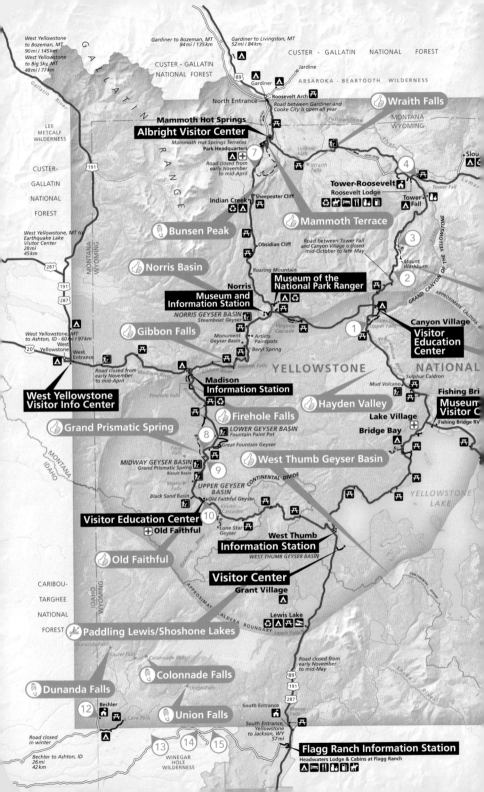

A B S A R O K A

Beartooth Highway
closed from mid-
October to late May

Road between Gardiner and
Cooke City is open all year

Cooke
City

Silver
Gate

Northeast Entrance

212

Northeast Entrance
to Red Lodge, MT
69mi / 111 km

reek

Pebble Creek

5   6

NORTH
ABSAROKA
WILDERNESS

SHOSHONE

NATIONAL

FOREST

RANGE

River

PARK

👍 Lamar Valley

👍 Backpacking/Pack Trips - Cache Creek

👢 Mount Washburn

👍 Grand Canyon of the Yellowstone

👢 Avalanche Peak

NORTH   ABSAROKA
WILDERNESS

East Entrance

20

Road closed from
early November
to early May

14
16

East Entrance
to Cody, WY
53 mi
85 km

d
er

11

A B S A R O K A

SHOSHONE NATIONAL FOREST

WASHAKIE WILDERNESS

Eagle Peak
11358ft
Highest point
in the park

👢 Backpacking the Thorofare

BRIDGER - TETON
NATIONAL FOREST

TETON   WILDERNESS

R A N G E

Yellowstone
River

North

↑

0   5   10 Kilometers
0   5   10 Miles

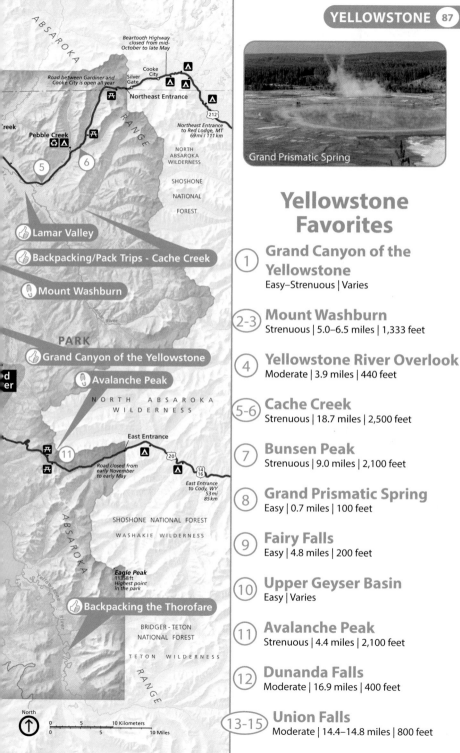

Grand Prismatic Spring

Yellowstone Favorites

1 **Grand Canyon of the Yellowstone**
Easy–Strenuous | Varies

2-3 **Mount Washburn**
Strenuous | 5.0–6.5 miles | 1,333 feet

4 **Yellowstone River Overlook**
Moderate | 3.9 miles | 440 feet

5-6 **Cache Creek**
Strenuous | 18.7 miles | 2,500 feet

7 **Bunsen Peak**
Strenuous | 9.0 miles | 2,100 feet

8 **Grand Prismatic Spring**
Easy | 0.7 miles | 100 feet

9 **Fairy Falls**
Easy | 4.8 miles | 200 feet

10 **Upper Geyser Basin**
Easy | Varies

11 **Avalanche Peak**
Strenuous | 4.4 miles | 2,100 feet

12 **Dunanda Falls**
Moderate | 16.9 miles | 400 feet

13-15 **Union Falls**
Moderate | 14.4–14.8 miles | 800 feet

GRAND CANYON OF THE YELLOWSTONE

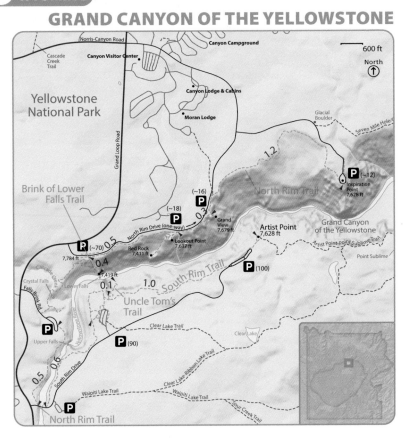

Grand Canyon of the Yellowstone | Varies
Trailhead: Multiple Parking Areas along South and North Rim Drives (1)

Grand Canyon of the Yellowstone is one of the park's iconic locations. While it isn't exactly a true hiking destination, you can easily log a few miles walking along the north and south rims of this one-of-a-kind canyon. Both sides have their merits. Artist Point is my favorite spot to simply enjoy the view and Uncle Tom's Trail (stairs) provides the best up-close experience. They're both on the South Rim. One of the nicest things about the North Rim is it's a short walk from the lodges and campground at Canyon Village. The views from Red Rock Point and Lookout Point are tremendous, and Brink of Lower Falls Trail leads you down a steep grade directly to the top of Lower Falls. Most guests' eyeballs are glued to Lower Falls, but Upper Falls is no slouch and having a look comes with considerably smaller crowds.

There are two reasons to get an early start at Grand Canyon of the Yellowstone. 1). Both waterfalls face east, making them most appealing in the morning light. And 2). Parking will be less competitive before 9am, which is only highly

MOUNT WASHBURN

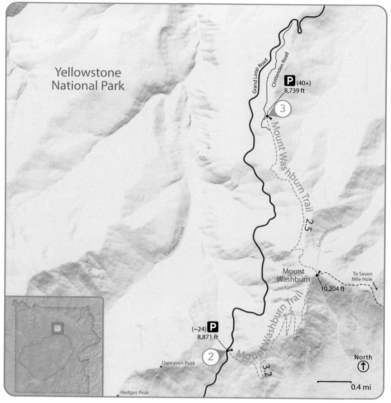

competitive in summer. South Rim Drive is two-way traffic for its entire length and there are large parking areas near Upper Falls View/Uncle Tom's Trail and the end of the road at Artist Point. North Rim Drive is one-way, with parking on either side of the road at Brink of Lower Falls Trail, Red Rock/Lookout Point, and Grand View, to go along with frequent pullouts and a fair amount of space at Inspiration Point (two-way traffic). In summer, it's best to park and walk or, better yet, stay overnight at Canyon Village. Late spring and fall are very manageable in a vehicle. And then, if you'd like an even more unique experience, consider visiting in winter when snowcoaches reach this stunning canyon.

Mount Washburn | Strenuous | 5–6.5 miles | 1,333 feet | Out-and-back or Point-to-point | **Trailhead:** Dunraven Pass (2) or Chittenden Road (3)

Mount Washburn is a classic Yellowstone hike. You can approach the summit and its lookout tower from the north, parking at the end of Chittenden Road. This trail is shorter, wider, and steeper. It's also open to bicyclists. On the southern slope of the mountain, you can hike up from Dunraven Pass Trailhead,

YELLOWSTONE RIVER OVERLOOK

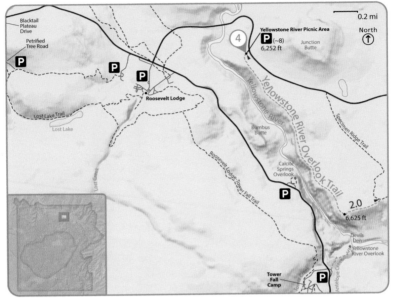

located on Grand Loop Road about 4.5 miles north of Canyon Village. This route is a bit longer but also better for hiking. You could also arrange a ride and do it as a point-to-point. Washburn's summit is a great place to be on a clear day, thanks to distant views of the mountainous terrain to the east.

Yellowstone River Overlook | Moderate | 3.9 miles | 440 feet | Out-and-back
Trailhead: Yellowstone River Picnic Area (4)

The effort-to-views ratio is pretty darn high for this trail. After the initial climb from the picnic area, you're greeted with stunning views above the Yellowstone River. Yes, it's similar to what you'll see at Grand Canyon of the Yellowstone, but without the crowds (and no Upper and Lower Yellowstone Falls).

Cache Creek | Strenuous | 18.7 miles | 2,500 feet | Point-to-point
Trailhead: Lamar River (5) and Thunderer (6)

A lot of visitors expecting stunning mountain vistas leave Yellowstone woefully unimpressed. Mount Washburn is nice, but things don't get serious until you reach the Absaroka Range running the length of the park's eastern boundary. Cache Creek leads hikers (primarily backpackers) into some of the more impressive mountains. But this loop is a bad dayhike idea (requiring a great deal of route finding to cross Thunderer). It's included to make you aware, high elevation is everywhere at Yellowstone, prominent peaks are not. This is the opposite of Grand Teton, just to the south, which spoils motorists with unlimited mountain landscapes from the road. The main motorist-

CACHE CREEK

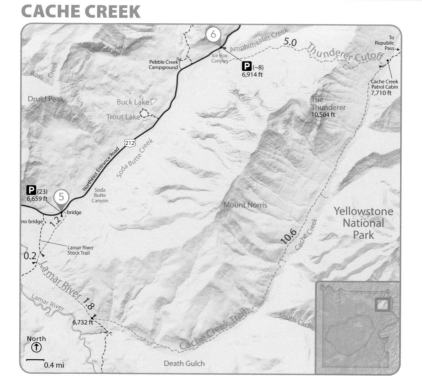

friendly features at Yellowstone are waterfalls and geothermal features (which are awesome!). With that said, breathtaking mountain scenery exists. And if you really want to get off the beaten path, it's a good idea to look beyond the national park in this corner of Wyoming and Montana. For example, begin this trail outside the park by crossing Republic Pass and exiting at Lamar River.

Bunsen Peak/Osprey Falls | Strenuous | 9.0 miles | 2,100 feet | Loop
Trailhead: Bunsen Peak (7)

First, a little fun trivia: the summit is named for German chemist Robert Bunsen who invented the Bunsen Burner. He also studied geysers. This loop, especially when combined with the 2.3-mile (roundtrip) spur to Osprey Falls, packs a lot of variety. You'll pass through forests and meadows. You'll walk down to a 150-ft waterfall, crashing over ancient volcanic rocks. And then you'll be treated to 360-degree views atop Bunsen Peak before hiking down the mountain back to the trailhead. It's a moderately popular trail and there's only room for about twenty vehicles at the trailhead, with another pullout just to the south. The service road is a bit of a slog through a downed-tree wasteland, but Osprey Falls is a very nice reward for your effort.

BUNSEN PEAK/OSPREY FALLS

Snow Pass Trail

Terrace
Mountain

89

Yellowstone
National Park

Grand Loop Road

Joffe Lake Road

Gardner River

Osprey Falls Trail

Sheepeater
Canyon

Howard Eaton/Mammoth Golden Gate Trail

Fawn
Pass
Trail

Cathedral
Rock

Bunsen Peak Trail

1.9

1.7

1.2

(~20) **P**
7,261 ft

7

Bunsen Peak
8,551 ft

1.4

6,425 ft

Osprey
Falls

1.7

Service Road

Swan
Lake

North

0.2 mile

Grand Prismatic Spring | Easy | 0.7 mile | 100 feet | Lollipop
Trailhead: Grand Prismatic Spring Parking Lot (8)

Grand Prismatic Spring loop is one of the park's busiest areas. Coach buses stop here, along with pretty much everyone else on their way to Upper Geyser Basin from West Yellowstone. Still, it's worth a quick visit. But just so you know, an eye-level view of Grand Prismatic Spring doesn't produce the results many visitors expect. The spring's colors only 'pop' when viewed from above while the sun is high in the sky. For that you'll need to book a helicopter tour or make the short walk to an overlook on the other side of the spring (described in the next entry for Fairy Falls). Regardless of the spring's color saturation, walking around this boardwalk has something of a fairytale feel to it. Steam rises from the springs. Some bubble continuously. It's cool, and, quite frankly, made better by the steady stream of visitors who come to enjoy it. Still, West Yellowstone to Old Faithful is the busiest area of the park.

FAIRY FALLS/GRAND PRISMATIC SPRING

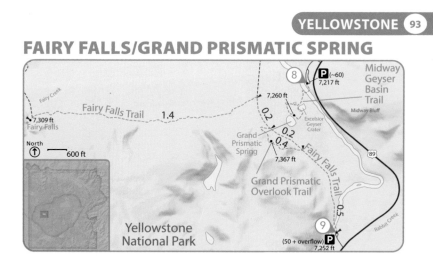

Fairy Falls/Grand Prismatic Spring Overlook | Easy | 4.8 miles | 200 feet | Out-and-back | **Trailhead:** Fairy Falls (9)

The journey to reach Fairy Falls and Grand Prismatic Overlook is ordinary for Yellowstone standards but the trickle of a fall—all 200 feet of it—and scenic overlook are two destinations you do not want to skip. It bears repeating that Grand Prismatic will not have the same colorful pop in the early morning and late evening. It needs some direct sunlight. So, if you arrive in the morning, catch the overlook on the return trip. In the evening, stop at it first. The overlook is one of the park's more recent improvements. Before its construction, people trudged up the hill, making a ton of social paths. Some visitors still scurry higher up the hillside, much to the chagrin of park rangers, I imagine.

Fairy Falls Trailhead has one of the biggest parking areas at Yellowstone. But it fills to capacity in summer. Fortunately, parking turns over regularly as most motorists are only stopping for the overlook. If you'd like to avoid large and competitive parking lots, you can also hike to Fairy Falls from the trailhead at the end of Fountain Flat Drive. It's not the best use of valuable Yellowstone time, adding nearly five miles to the hike.

Upper Geyser Basin | Easy–Strenuous | Varies | Out-and-back
Trailhead: Old Faithful Area (10)

Old Faithful is the busiest area in the park and yet I feel like it's also the most misunderstood and underappreciated. This is because most guests hustle down here, check the Old Faithful schedule, wait in the bleachers for an eruption, and return to their car to head to the next destination. Bad idea. There's so much more to see. Old Faithful isn't the only reliable geyser. The park posts (online and at each geyser) eruption predictions for Castle, Grand, Daisy, Riverside, and Great Fountain, too! Every one of those except Great Fountain is located at Upper Geyser Basin. But there's a lot more. Beehive

UPPER GEYSER BASIN/OLD FAITHFUL

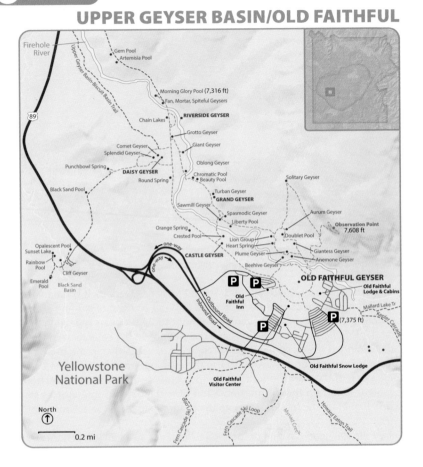

Firehole River

Gem Pool
Artemisia Pool

Morning Glory Pool (7,316 ft)

Fan, Mortar, Spiteful Geysers

RIVERSIDE GEYSER

Chain Lakes

Grotto Geyser

Giant Geyser

Comet Geyser
Splendid Geyser

Oblong Geyser

Punchbowl Spring

DAISY GEYSER

Chromatic Pool
Beauty Pool

Solitary Geyser

Round Spring

Black Sand Pool

Turban Geyser

GRAND GEYSER

Sawmill Geyser

Aurum Geyser

Spasmodic Geyser

Observation Point
7,608 ft

Orange Spring

Liberty Pool

Crested Pool

Lion Group
Heart Spring

Doublet Pool

Opalescent Pool
Sunset Lake

one-way

Giantess Geyser

Rainbow
Pool

one-way

CASTLE GEYSER

Plume Geyser

Anemone Geyser

Emerald
Pool

Cliff Geyser

Beehive Geyser

Black Sand
Basin

OLD FAITHFUL GEYSER

Old Faithful
Lodge & Cabins

Outbound Road

Inbound Road

Old
Faithful
Inn

Mallard Lake Tr

(7,375 ft)

**Yellowstone
National Park**

Old Faithful Snow Lodge

Old Faithful
Visitor Center

North

0.2 mi

erupts most days. Observation Point provides an alternative view of Old Faithful. Chromatic Pool, Punchbowl Spring, Grotto Geyser, and Morning Glory Pool are all interesting. There's a lot to see. And hear. And smell. Geyser basins are experiences for more senses than sight. Please do not stop for Old Faithful and carry on your way. There is one caveat, you need to have some patience. Most eruptions last a few minutes, so you could see any of them going off in the distance with enough time to catch the show but, in my opinion, it's better to be there from start to finish. And, of course, spouting columns of scalding-hot water aren't for everyone. If some people in your group aren't in to sitting around, they could hike Mallard Lake Trail or Howard Eaton Trail (which leads to Lone Star Geyser—it erupts about every three hours). In a park filled with so much biological diversity, the diversity of geothermal areas is equally impressive. Each one features wildly different sights, sounds, and smells.

AVALANCHE PEAK

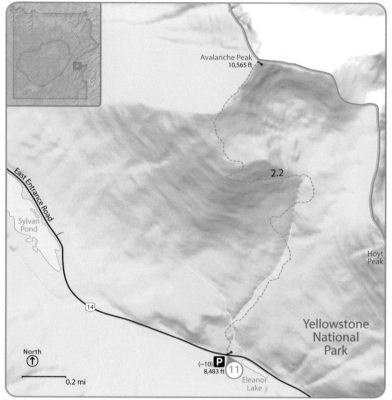

Avalanche Peak | Strenuous | 4.4 miles | 2,100 feet | Out-and-back
Trailhead: Avalanche Peak/Eleanor Lake, East Entrance Road (11)

Along with Mount Washburn, Avalanche Peak is one of the easier ways to get decent mountain views at Yellowstone, and views across Yellowstone Lake are a bonus. But it's a steep, strenuous climb to get there. The trail is relentless in its incline and there's little-to-no protection from the sun and wind. Avalanche Peak's summit is beyond the end of the marked trail at the park boundary.

Dunanda Falls | Moderate | 16.9 miles | 400 feet | Out-and-back
Trailhead: Bechler Ranger Station (12)

It's nearly impossible to argue Yellowstone's Cascade Corner is better for dayhiking than backpacking. And backpacking gets even better if you can arrange a ride to do a point-to-point backpacking trip. For example, you can through hike from Old Faithful to Bechler via Howard Eaton and Bechler River trails, passing many waterfalls (like Ouzel and Colonnade) and geothermal features along the way. However, there are a few things you can do as (long) day hikes. Dunanda Falls is one of the best options. Aside from a couple stream

DUNANDA FALLS

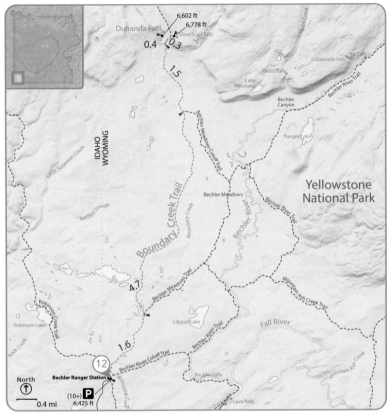

crossings, the journey is easy and unspectacular. This trail is often traversed by horses and its design has them in mind. At each ford, the trail usually intersects a wide stretch of stream. Look off to the side of the main trail and you'll often find an easier crossing for humans. With that said, even if you must take off your shoes, the streams are not a major obstacle late in the summer season. The stretch of Boundary Creek Trail is long, and, quite frankly, a little boring for most hiker's taste. If you enjoy tranquility, then it's perfect. I feel like it's a good idea to make the short (but steep) ascent to view Silver Scarf Falls before heading down to Dunanda. For starters, it's a pretty waterfall, but it will also help get bearings on Dunanda as you can look down on it from the trail. It's also easy to lose track of time soaking in Dunanda's pools that you might feel rushed enough to skip the nearby attractions even after hiking all this way. The access trail to Dunanda is not marked or particularly easy to find. It's located at the back of site 9A3 (which is marked and easy to find and a highly desirable site among backpackers). From the site, with the recent acquisition of Dunanda Falls bearings, you should be able to find the steep trail down to Boundary Creek. Follow the creek up to the waterfall and enjoy, just be careful as there are several hot springs running into the river here. And they are hot.

UNION FALLS

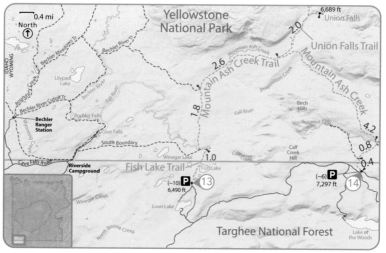

The trailhead is located near Bechler Ranger Station. It takes considerable commitment to reach but it's worth it, especially if you plan a few other stops. The backside of the Tetons can be a fun place to play, and this is a sparsely populated and less-commercialized part of the country, so you won't have all the hullabaloo found in and around Jackson, WY.

Union Falls | Moderate | 14.4–14.8 miles | 400–800 feet | Out-and-back
Trailhead: Fish Lake (13), Cascade Creek (14), Grassy Lake (15)

At 250 feet, Union is the second tallest waterfall in the park. The tallest is Lower Falls of the Yellowstone River. A few million visitors see Lower Falls each year. A tiny fraction of that have the privilege of seeing Union Falls, and it's nearly as incredible. I guess that's the kind of difference a 15-mile hike creates. To be one of the few who reach Union Falls, you have a few options. You can set out from the Bechler/Cave Falls area, but those are backpacking trips, not dayhiking, clocking in at 20+ miles. However, Cave Falls/Bechler is a nice area to visit (where you can hike up to Dunanda, Colonnade, and Ouzel falls, as well as a few shorter options). The other three trailheads are a long, slow drive from Bechler/Cave Falls. It usually takes at least an hour and a half to get from Cave Falls to Fish Lake Trailhead on mostly unpaved roads. Fish Lake, Cascade Creek and Grassy Lake trailheads can also be accessed from Grand Teton National Park via Grassy Lake Road (Ashton–Flagg Ranch Road). Grassy Lake Trailhead is a little less than two hours from Jackson Lake Lodge at Grand Teton. And it's about a forty-minute drive between Grassy Lake and Fish Lake Trailheads. As for the hikes, Grassy Lake Trailhead provides the most direct route to Union Falls, at roughly 14.4 miles. From Cascade Creek, it's about 14.8 miles and you'll be tempted to take the short spur near the trailhead, which leads to Terraced Falls. It's about 14.7 miles from Fish Lake Trailhead. All of them require fording a river (come prepared). If you'd like to slow down and enjoy the area more, there are two backpacking sites (permit required) near Union Falls and four more along the trails. Slowing down and enjoying this remote corner of the park is a good idea, but dayhiking is possible.

With more than 1,000 miles of trails at Yellowstone, this list barely scratches the surface of your hiking opportunities. If you're looking for a long, strenuous hike to one of the park's tallest summits, check out Electric Peak (extreme, 18.0 miles) in the park's northwest corner. It even concludes with a scramble. Another option near Bunsen Peak is to hike to the remains of a lookout tower atop Mount Holmes. It also pushes dayhiking to its limits (20 miles), but it's another solid choice if you have the stamina. For short and easy, consider Wraith Falls (1 mile) near Mammoth or Trout Lake (1.2 miles) near Lamar Valley. But there are many more.

More Trails

Safety

Yellowstone is a park you should explore with a considerable amount of caution.

Grizzlies: They probably receive the most headlines, but I feel like they're the least of your concerns. First, in 2019 interested parties estimated there's about 150 bears with home ranges wholly or partially inside the park. Walking among two million acres of wilderness, it's unlikely you'll come across a grizzly. If you'd like to, the best places to look are Hayden and Lamar valleys, Mount Washburn, and from Fishing Bridge to the East Entrance. Whatever you're doing, it's still a good idea to take a few grizzly precautions. Hiking in a group. Carry bear spray. If you do see one, keep your distance (at least 100 yards).

Other Wildlife: Bison might be the most dangerous animals in the park. Do not approach them. Do not pose for photos with them. Always stay at least 25 yards away from them. They're big (the largest land mammal in North America) and they're fast (can run up to 35 mph). Upset one and you (or your vehicle) are in trouble.

Geothermal Features: Stay on the boardwalks!

Time Management

Plan at least three days.

Staying in the park is well worth the premium and planning.

If you'd like to set up an in-park basecamp, the most convenient campgrounds are Norris and Canyon. They're as centrally located as you can get.

Of the Cascade Corner waterfalls, Union Falls is the easiest to do as a daytrip from Yellowstone or Grand Teton, plus there's a fair amount of camping available along Grassy Lake Road. Reaching Bechler is a good idea, but it's also a bigger commitment.

If you're traveling a great distance to get here and likely won't return for some time (if ever), do not return home without going down to Grand Teton (and treat it as more than a quick daytrip). The Tetons will spice up your scenery with aggressive mountain peaks.

Glacier
Hiking Trails: 600+ miles

Grinnell Glacier Overlook (Highline Trail)

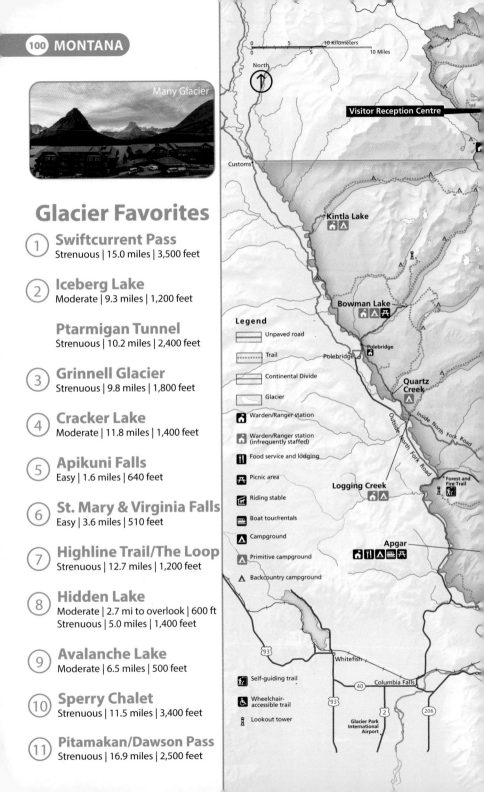

Many Glacier

Glacier Favorites

(1) Swiftcurrent Pass
Strenuous | 15.0 miles | 3,500 feet

(2) Iceberg Lake
Moderate | 9.3 miles | 1,200 feet

Ptarmigan Tunnel
Strenuous | 10.2 miles | 2,400 feet

(3) Grinnell Glacier
Strenuous | 9.8 miles | 1,800 feet

(4) Cracker Lake
Moderate | 11.8 miles | 1,400 feet

(5) Apikuni Falls
Easy | 1.6 miles | 640 feet

(6) St. Mary & Virginia Falls
Easy | 3.6 miles | 510 feet

(7) Highline Trail/The Loop
Strenuous | 12.7 miles | 1,200 feet

(8) Hidden Lake
Moderate | 2.7 mi to overlook | 600 ft
Strenuous | 5.0 miles | 1,400 feet

(9) Avalanche Lake
Moderate | 6.5 miles | 500 feet

(10) Sperry Chalet
Strenuous | 11.5 miles | 3,400 feet

(11) Pitamakan/Dawson Pass
Strenuous | 16.9 miles | 2,500 feet

Visitor Reception Centre

Customs

Kintla Lake

Bowman Lake

Polebridge

Quartz Creek

Outside North Fork Road

Inside North Fork Road

Logging Creek

Forest and Fire Trail

Apgar

Whitefish

Columbia Falls

Glacier Park International Airport

Legend

Unpaved road

Trail

Continental Divide

Glacier

Warden/Ranger station

Warden/Ranger station (infrequently staffed)

Food service and lodging

Picnic area

Riding stable

Boat tour/rentals

Campground

Primitive campground

Backcountry campground

Self-guiding trail

Wheelchair-accessible trail

Lookout tower

10 Kilometers

10 Miles

North

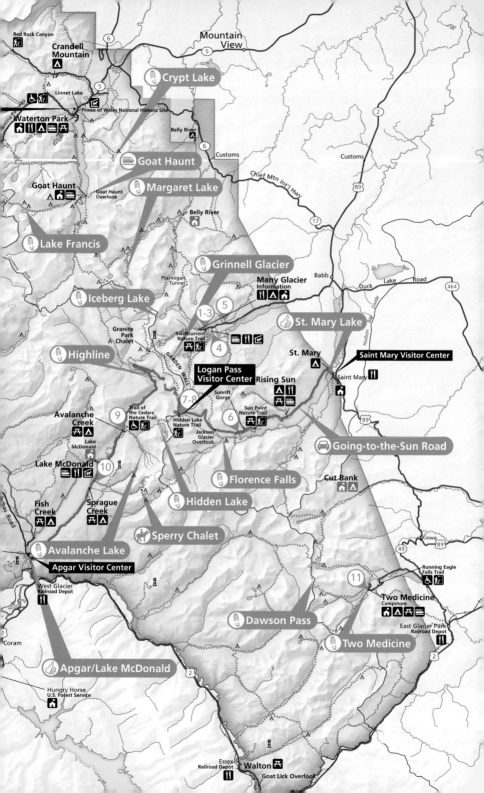

SWIFTCURRENT/GRINNELL GLACIER/CRACKER

Swiftcurrent Pass | Strenuous | 15.0 miles | 3,500 feet | Out-and-back
Trailhead: Swiftcurrent, Many Glacier (1)

This is one of the more challenging hikes at Glacier but don't feel too intimidated by it. It's a go-as-far-as-you-like trail, with highly rewarding easy, moderate, and strenuous lengths. From the trailhead, a short walk leads to a spur to Fishercap Lake. Nice and easy. If you want some more, it's about a mile further across mostly-flat terrain to Redrock Lake. Another two miles and you'll reach Bullhead Lake, only gaining a few hundred feet in elevation. Continue to the back of the valley, where you'll find a stunning amphitheater. Turning around at this point is a good idea for most. It's a highly-enjoyable 7.8-mile out-and-back. Those of you looking for punishment, carry on to the pass (and lookout tower). This is where things get serious. It's steep, sometimes exposed switchbacks leading up to Swiftcurrent Pass and the spur trail to the lookout tower atop Swiftcurrent Mountain (the highest maintained trail in the park). It doesn't take too long until you gain a clear look back at Swiftcurrent Valley. Expect wind at the pass and lookout tower. Yes, the grade can be challenging, but the rewards earned along the way are considerable. Time and energy permitting, consider hiking to the south along Highline Trail to do another climb up to Grinnell Glacier Overlook, one of the best viewpoints in the park. This route takes you past Granite Park Chalet (book a night if you can!). There's a backcountry camp nearby too. The dayhiking point-to-point alternative is to get dropped off at Logan Pass, hike Highline Trail (tacking on Grinnell Glacier Overlook), and then hike out to Many Glacier via Swiftcurrent Pass (adding the spur to Swiftcurrent Lookout). It'd be an absolute dream if you can score overnight accommodations in Many Glacier. Another thing to note is Highline Trail continues north of Swiftcurrent Pass (past a social trail leading to a photogenic rocky point high above Iceberg Lake) all the way to Goat Haunt.

ICEBERG LAKE/PTARMIGAN/APIKUNI FALLS

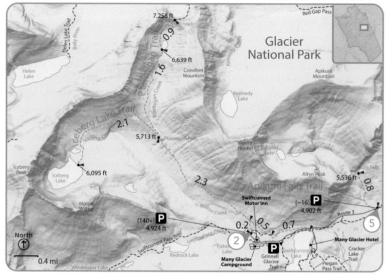

The trailhead is located at the west end of Swiftcurrent Motor Inn's parking area. With the inn and two popular trailheads, this is a busy area.

Iceberg Lake | Moderate | 9.3 miles | 1,200 feet | Out-and-back
Ptarmigan Tunnel | Strenuous | 10.2 miles | 2,400 feet | Out-and-back
Trailhead: Iceberg-Ptarmigan, Many Glacier (2)

Iceberg Lake and Ptarmigan Tunnel share a trailhead, beginning at roughly 5,000 feet elevation. Either choice features an easy grade for Glacier standards, however things get serious from Ptarmigan Lake to Ptarmigan Tunnel. Along the way you'll experience a mix of dense forest and mountain vistas. You'll also walk above Ptarmigan Falls with somewhat obstructed views of the waterfall below. Near the waterfall, you'll come to an intersection. Left leads to Iceberg Lake, resting at 6,095 feet in a very dramatic setting. Right leads to Ptarmigan Lake. From Ptarmigan Lake, switchbacks climb steeply up Ptarmigan Wall to Ptarmigan Tunnel (7,200 feet elevation). The tunnel doors typically open in mid-July. On the other side you're treated to views of Belly River Valley (an exceptional backpacking area).

Iceberg-Ptarmigan Trailhead is located in Many Glacier just north of Swiftcurrent Motor Inn's cabins. Parking is very limited. Your best choice is to stay at Swiftcurrent Motor Inn or Many Glacier Campground, but those aren't easy reservations to make. If you're competing for parking space, be sure to get an early start if your visit is outside the timed-entry permit requirement window (which started in 2023 for Many Glacier).

Grinnell Glacier | Strenuous | 9.8 miles | 1,800 feet | Out-and-back
Trailhead: Grinnell Glacier, Many Glacier (3)

Grinnell Glacier is one of the finest hiking experiences in all our precious parks. The trailhead is located at a picnic area, and the trail begins with a forested walk. You'll cross Swiftcurrent Creek, stroll along Swiftcurrent Lake, and then reach the shore of Lake Josephine after one mile. The trail follows the entire north shore of Lake Josephine. At the end of the lake, you'll find a trail junction. Down leads to Grinnell Lake (6.8 miles roundtrip from the parking lot). Up leads to Upper Grinnell Lake, residing at the foot of the imposing Garden Wall, where Grinnell and Salamander Glaciers cling to its cliffs. There's some exposure along the way, but nothing to concern yourself with unless you have a particularly acute fear of heights. Grade increases the closer you get to Upper Grinnell Lake (6,519 feet), but there's room to sit or stand and take a break, as the tireless hikers continue onward and upward. The views and climb are equally breathtaking. This is one of those hikes where the journey stacks up respectably to the destination, and the destination is wonderful (as long as it isn't socked in with fog). From Upper Grinnell Lake/Glacier, enjoy a lunch, watch for other hikers above you at Grinnell Glacier Overlook (via Highline Trail), or sit and soak in nature's perfection.

There are a few things to know before you go. 1). The trail usually opens fully in mid-July. You'll want to monitor status at the park's website (nps.gov/glac) or socials. 2). The view back to Garden Wall is very nice from Grinnell Glacier Lookout (ranger-guided hikes end here before the trail fully opens), but it's also pretty similar to what you get from the road leading into Many Glacier. And a trip to the lookout point stops short of the trail's most fun portions. What I'm saying is, if you can't hike all the way, there are better options, many of them nearby. 3). You can shave 3.4 miles off the hike, motoring across Swiftcurrent Lake and Lake Josephine with Glacier Boat Co. (glacierparkboats.com). I've done both and I preferred the boat trip (plus, if you're visiting during the timed-entry period, reserving a boat ride will get you a permit to Many Glacier). 4). It warrants a bit more contemplation, but don't immediately disregard a Glacier (or Many Glacier) trip if Grinnell Glacier Trail isn't fully open. With camping and lodging reservations being in incredibly high demand, you must consider taking what you can get and making the most of it. In June, or earlier, there's still plenty of hikes to enjoy, and the park's east side remains accessible thanks to Highway 2. Late-opening trails like Grinnell Glacier and Hidden Lake/Highline incentivize coming back another time :)

Grinnell Glacier Trailhead is located less than a half mile east of Many Glacier Campground and less than one mile from Many Glacier Hotel. There's a small, paved loop around a picnic area with parking but, when the trail is open, parking overflows to the road's gravel shoulder and beyond.

Cracker Lake

Cracker Lake | Moderate | 11.8 miles | 1,400 feet | Out-and-back
Trailhead: Many Glacier Hotel, Many Glacier (4)

Park enthusiasts might know Cracker Lake better from aerial images taken at the summit of Mount Siyeh (a trail that isn't listed because the summit trail is an unofficial social path and Siyeh Trail is pretty good but not great without it). With that said, hiking to Cracker's shore for an up-close look at its turquoise water ... will probably have you wanting to get up on top of Mount Siyeh). The trail's moderately long, and the first half isn't particularly exciting. Once you come around the bend and into a mountain-lined canyon, the view quality increases dramatically. Don't walk to the lake's northeastern tip and turn around. The trail continues all the way to the far end of the lake. (If you're looking for a one-night backpacking trip, look no further than Cracker Lake. There's one solitary campsite at the lake.) Expect to encounter a few horses along the way (which is an alternative transportation method if you're comfortable on a horse and have some spare cash).

The trail begins at the southwest corner of the large parking lot behind Many Glacier Hotel.

Apikuni Falls | Easy | 1.6 miles | 640 feet | Out-and-back
Trailhead: Poia Lake, Many Glacier (5)

It's a short but very rewarding trail. You'll begin with a short flat stretch before ascending about 500 feet to the towering waterfall. At most parks, this probably wouldn't be considered an easy hike. The grade is steady, and it gets rocky near the waterfall.

Poia Lake Trailhead is located roughly 1.1 miles east of Many Glacier Hotel.

ST. MARY & VIRGINIA FALLS

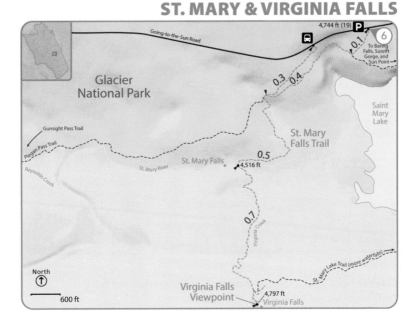

St. Mary & Virginia Falls | Easy | 3.6 miles | 510 feet | Out-and-back
Trailhead: Sunrift Gorge, Going-to-the-Sun Road (6)

The easiest and shortest route to St. Mary Falls is to take the boat ride from Rising Sun (glacierparkboats.com). It'll be less than two miles. However, it's a good idea to hike in from Going-to-the-Sun Road to explore the area at your leisure. There's an awful lot to see and it's nice to not be rushed at the water-falls even if they are popular. There's a bit of up and down, and a few gradual steps, but it's a very doable trail for most visitors. You'll find some other water-falls in the area as well, and, if you're looking to stretch this hike out, consider hopping on Gunsight Pass Trail to Florence Falls, adding about ten miles to the hike.

There's a medium-sized parking area on the south side of Going-to-the-Sun Road, west of Sunrift Gorge. There's also a shuttle stop. Taking the shuttle saves about a half mile of hiking.

Highline/The Loop | Strenuous | 12.7 miles | 1,200–3,500 feet | Point-to-point
Trailhead: Logan Pass, Going-to-the-Sun Road (7)

Highline Trail receives an awful lot of fanfare. Beginning at Logan Pass Visi-tor Center, you immediately cross Going-to-the-Sun Road, and then follow a wide path with a steep drop-off to the west as you contour Garden Wall. High-line parallels the Continental Divide (and Garden Wall) all the way to Granite Park Chalet (graniteparkchalet.com). You'll pass through grassy prairies, often

HIGHLINE/THE LOOP

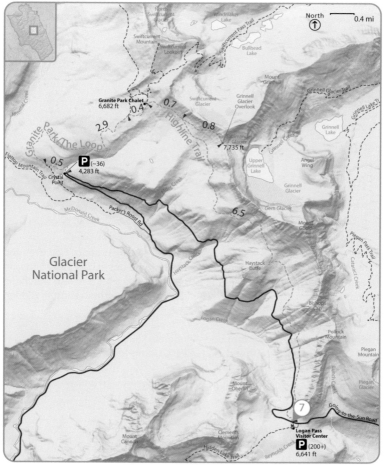

accented with wildflowers and remnants of winter's snowfall. The highlight isn't the trail itself, it's a steep spur to Grinnell Glacier Overlook, where you look down on Upper Grinnell Lake, and hikers enjoying Grinnell Glacier Trail. The fanfare is warranted. There isn't much to complain about, but if I'm picking nits, there are a few. Highline parallels Going-to-the-Sun Road, so views from the trail aren't too dissimilar to those from your car. Of course, you can't reach Grinnell Glacier Overlook in your car! The other quibble is most people do this as a loop with the aptly named The Loop trail, which you pick up at Granite Park Chalet. It works, but it's all ordinary scenery (by Glacier standards) back to Going-to-the-Sun Road (Crystal Point), where you'll need to catch a shuttle back to Logan Pass. A better, but more complicated, option is the one mentioned in the Swiftcurrent Pass writeup, hiking Highline as a point-to-point to Many Glacier. The difficulty is arranging a ride, caching a vehicle, and/or

HIDDEN LAKE OVERLOOK

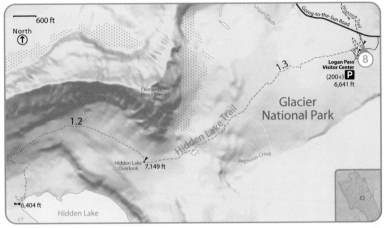

600 ft

North
⬆

Logan Creek

Going-to-the-Sun Road

Highline Trail

1.3

Logan Pass
Visitor Center
(200+) 🅿
6,641 ft

8

Clements
Mountain

Glacier
National Park

1.2

Hidden Lake Trail

Hidden Lake
Overlook 7,149 ft

Reynolds Creek

6,404 ft

Hidden Lake

securing reservations in Many Glacier (which is a great idea). However you do it, it's unlikely you'll have any regrets, unless you get up to Grinnell Glacier Overlook and have zero-foot visibility. That would be a bummer, so watch the forecast and plan accordingly. If you're looking for something shorter, Hidden Lake Overlook is wondrous!

Hidden Lake/Overlook | Strenuous/Moderate | 5.0/2.7 miles | 1,400/600 feet | Out-and-back | **Trailhead:** Logan Pass, Going-to-the-Sun Road (8)

Hidden Lake Overlook is one of the finest spots to enjoy a morning at Glacier National Park. The hardest parts of this scenic walk are a few sets of stairs near the visitor center. The beginning is paved. Pavement gives way to boardwalk, which soon becomes dirt. Overall, it's a relatively flat walk to what is undeniably one of the park's finest views, overlooking Hidden Lake, Bearhat Mountain looming in the background. It's perfectly fine if you enjoy the view and return to the visitor center but there is more. An unmarked but obvious social trail often referred to as "The Dragon's Tail" contours Reynolds Mountain, south of the overlook. The park doesn't mention it but

Hidden Lake Overlook

AVALANCHE LAKE

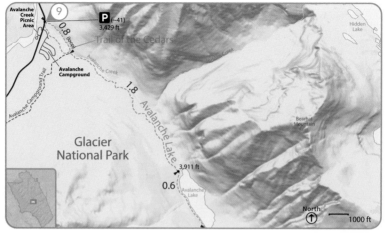

it's something worth knowing for your visit. I'd recommend extending the hike by staying on the main trail down to Hidden Lake. It's just 2.5 miles of extra hiking down to the northwest shore of the lake and back (and it'll really get your heart racing). Remember Logan Pass is the highest point on Going-to-the-Sun Road. Snow will be present into summer.

The trailhead is located near the entrance to Logan Pass Visitor Center. Parking fills, so it's a good idea to get an early start or take the shuttle. Early is better, as Bearhat looks best in the morning light! Highline looks better in the afternoon/evening light (just make sure you have time to complete the loop).

Avalanche Lake | Moderate | 6.5 miles | 500 feet | Out-and-back
Trailhead: Avalanche Lake, Going-to-the-Sun Road (9)

By Glacier standards, the walk to Avalanche Lake is more of an easy hike than a moderate one, but it is on the long side, with a steady grade. If you're looking for a short and easy trail, go for Trail of the Cedars. It's fun, just not nearly as spectacular a setting as Avalanche Lake. It's a little less than three miles to reach the scenic lake's shore. Beyond Trail of the Cedars, you're looking at a relatively leisurely forest hike. Avalanche Lake is quite special and it's no secret. Parking at the trailhead is extremely competitive, perhaps the most competitive in the park (even with Going-to-the-Sun Road reservation requirements). In a perfect world, you'd be camping at Avalanche. If not, you're going to want to have an early wakeup call or use the shuttle. Crossing your fingers hoping for a space isn't a bad idea as long as you have a backup plan. There are many great choices if you don't mind more miles and way more elevation gain. Sperry Chalet (and the surrounding area) is fantastic! Or you could head to less-popular sites like Lincoln Lake (17+ miles) or Mount Brown Lookout (9+ miles).

SPERRY CHALET

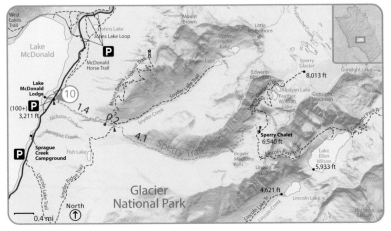

Sperry Chalet | Strenuous | 11.5 miles | 3,400 feet | Out-and-back
Trailhead: Sperry, Going-to-the-Sun Road (10)

If it's within your budget, a night at Sperry Chalet (sperrychalet.com) is one of the best ideas you can have. There's much to see in the area surrounding the chalet and it's a little bit of a stretch to do it in a day. Plus, you'll be treated to dinner and breakfast, as well as a trail lunch for the return trek. From the chalet you can walk over to Lincoln Pass for a tremendous view of Lake Ellen Wilson and Lincoln Lake. Lake Ellen Wilson rests about 1,300 feet above Lincoln Lake (this is the "gunsight"). It's also a good idea to head up Sperry Glacier Trail, where people have all kinds of fun. The key takeaway is this hike really isn't about the chalet, it's about the surroundings. If you are able to make the strenuous dayhike (or are fortunate enough to get a night at the chalet), the area around Sperry Chalet has some of the most breathtaking sights Glacier has to offer. Dayhikers can catch lunch at the chalet. Dinner and/or breakfast require reservations (if you're backpacking). A considerable amount of this area burned in 2017. In many ways it's even more beautiful today, opening views, and allowing new plantlife to take root. The chalet suffered damage too. It closed for reconstruction and reopened in 2020.

Pitamakan/Dawson Pass | Strenuous | 16.9 miles | 2,500 feet | Loop
Trailhead: North Shore, Two Medicine Campground (12)

More outstanding Glacier scenery! Colorful Panoramic views. Prominent peaks. Picturesque passes. Sublime lakes. This long and arduous loop checks all the boxes for a truly once-in-a-lifetime-level Glacier hiking experience. For long loops like this, I'm generally thinking about how to maximize the morning light. In that regard, it doesn't matter much. While the whole loop is awfully pretty, all the big vistas are at the back of the loop between the

DAWSON PASS–PITAMAKAN PASS

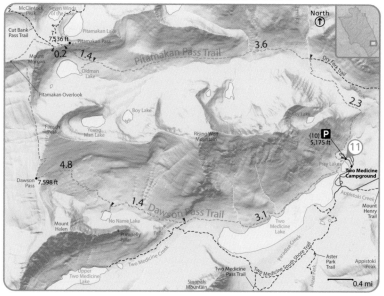

two passes, and you have a couple hours of hiking to even begin the ascent to each one. However, there is a unique advantage to a counterclockwise approach that's worth mentioning. You can shave a few miles off the trip by catching a boat (glacierparkboats.com) across Two Medicine Lake. Tempting, but it's probably more effort than it's worth. 1). You must get tickets for the 5pm tour. 2). The dock is near the mouth of Two Medicine Creek, so you'd have to deviate from the loop highlighted above. And 3). There's a pretty good chance you'll spend a lot of hiking time thinking about whether you're going to make it to the dock in time. And, if you miss it, now you're on the wrong side of Two Medicine Lake and you must choose whether to backtrack to the North Shore or suck it up and hike the South Shore Trail back. And if you're early, you're sitting at the dock. On the positive side, you'd get to see Twin Falls, which isn't bad. Personally, the biggest pro to counterclockwise is, if you're cruising and have plenty of time, you can detour to Upper Two Medicine Lake, adding a solid three miles to the journey. Regardless which direction you choose, the profile is somewhat similar. Long, relatively flat, often-forested trail, until you hit a backcountry lake (No Name Lake for Dawson, Oldman Lake for Pitamakan) where the intensity ratchets up a bit. One thing to know is, while you'll be hiking along the Continental Divide Trail between Two Medicine Campground and Pitamakan Pass, the actual Continental Divide follows the ridge between Pitamakan and Dawson (where it's often windy—pack a windbreaker!). It's great! But Pitamakan has some serious exposure.

Glacier truly is heaven for hikers. You have some of the best dayhiking choices listed already but there's much more. At Two Medicine, you'll find Running Eagle Falls (easy, 0.5 mile). It's also called Trick Falls because at high-water level, a second waterfall flows directly over the lower fall. In spring or after/during a heavy rain, Running Eagle is a good place to be. Also at Two Medicine, you can take the boat cruise (glacierparkboats.com) across Upper Two Medicine Lake and do the short walk to Twin Falls (easy, 1.8 miles with boat ride). There's a wealth of hiking opportunities in the Lake McDonnald/Apgar area (which is another good reason you don't need to wait for Going-to-the-Sun Road to fully open to visit). Lincoln Lake (moderate, 16.0 miles), Apgar Lookout (moderate, 7.2 miles). Unfortunately, most of the best trails are also serious workouts. If you're looking for something easier, consider walking along the shore of Lake McDonald (from Fish Creek). Logging Lake Trail runs all the way to Grace Lake. It's flat but long (more than 12 miles one-way). A better option might be to slow down to truly enjoy the unbelievable scenery by backpacking (permit required). Permits are available through recreation.gov. Belly River, Gunsight Pass, Bowman Lake, Cut Bank, Two Medicine, Many Glacier. They're all great backpacking areas. And Goat Haunt is a backpacking hub. Many trails converge here. But you can also reach it by boat (watertoncruise.com). If you're just stopping out on the boat, you could get up to Goat Haunt Overlook (easy, 2.0 miles). Lake Francis, a stunning setting similar to Avalanche Lake, is about six miles to the west. If you're desperate to find some less-popular trails, look at the trailheads along US-2.

More Trails

More Activities

Hiking isn't the only A+ activity at Glacier. Horseback riding (Many Glacier and Lake McDonald), paddling, whitewater rafting, and boating are all exceptional. There are guided boat tours (glacierparkboats.com or watertoncruise.com). There are narrated driving tours aboard historic red jammers (glaciernationalparklodges.com). The more time exploring Glacier the better, but to truly get to know it, you must hike into its interior.

Timed-Entry Permits

Timed-Entry Permits are required seasonally for Going-to-the-Sun Road, North Fork Road, Many Glacier, and Two Medicine. Find all the current details at recreation.gov. Yes, it's an extra complication, but due to overwhelming popularity, reservations have become a necessity to improve the overall visitor/staff experience.

When to Visit

Going-to-the-Sun Road fully opens on Mother Nature's (and the plow operator's) schedule, usually by late June/early July. Trails like Grinnell Glacier and Ptarmigan Tunnel don't fully open until mid-July. Most visitors arrive in July and August but spring and fall can be great too. Come hike lower elevation trails. Weather, although temperamental, is often pleasant by April (and into November). Waterfalls are charged up in spring. Colors change in fall. Plus, you can still get around the park via US-2.

Shuttles

Free shuttles run along Going-to-the-Sun Road from when it fully opens (late June/mid-July) until early September. It's a great feature and makes a few point-to-point hikes possible like Highline/Loop Trail.

Grinnell Glacier Trail

Canyon NP

Glen Canyon NRA

Curecanti NRA

Sand Creek Massacre NH

Canyonlands NP

Natural Bridges NM

Bent's NHS

Hovenweep NM

Yucca House NM

Rainbow Bridge NM

Navajo NM

Mesa Verde NP

Great Sand Du NP & PRES

anyon NP

Aztec Ruins NM

Capulin Volcano NM

Canyon de Chelly NM

Chaco Culture NHP

upatki NM

Hubbell Trading Post NHS

ano NM

Valles Caldera N Pres

Manhattan Project NHP

Walnut Canyon NM

Bandelier NM

Fort Union NM

Petrified Forest NP

El Morro NM

SANTA FE

Pecos NHP

Petroglyph NM

ALBUQUERQUE

NM

El Malpais NM

A

NEW MEXICO

Tonto NM

Salinas Pueblo Missions NM

Casa Grande Ruins NM

tus

Gila Cliff Dwellings NM

Saguaro NP

White Sands NP

Fort Bowie NHS

Chiricahua NM

Carlsbad Caverns NP

Tumacacori NHP

Coronado N MEM

EL PASO

Chamizal N MEM

Guadalupe Mountains NP

⊕ **MOUNTAIN (Washington, DC, minus 2 hours)**

Fort Davis NHS

⊕ ARIZONA

Canyon de Chelly NM, Hubbell Trading Post NHS, and Navajo NM observe daylight saving time. Other NPS units in Arizona do not.

Rio Grande WSR

Big Bend NP

The South

KANSAS

Brown v. Board
of Education NHS

Fort Larned NHS

Tallgrass Prairie
N PRES

JEFFERSON CITY

MISSO

Fort

WICHITA

Fort Scott NHS

Wilson's Cre
NB

George Washington C

Pea Ridge NMP

TULSA

Buffalo N

Lake Meredith
NRA

Washita Battlefield NHS

OKLAHOMA CITY

Fort Smith NHS

Alibates Flint
Quarries NM

OKLAHOMA

ARKAN

Hot Springs NP

L
Li
H

Chickasaw NRA

Arkansas P

SOUTH

President W
Jefferson Cli
Birthplace H

FT WORTH

DALLAS

Pover

TEXAS

Waco Mammoth NM

Cane
Creol

Lyndon B. Johnson NHP

AUSTIN

Big Thicket
N PRES

LOUI

HOUSTON

Amistad NRA

SAN ANTONIO
San Antonio Missions NHP

CENTRAL
(Washington, DC, minus 1 hour)

Padre Island
NS

GULF OF MEXICO

Palo Alto Battlefield
NHP

Hot Springs
Hiking Trails: 20+ miles

Grand Promenade

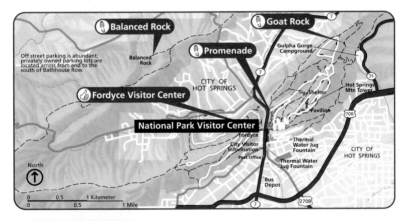

Hiking Hot Springs

Hot Springs doesn't fit most park enthusiast's idea of a National Park. The primary attraction is a bunch of manmade bathhouses, plumbed with water from nearby hot springs. The bathhouses are interesting and two are operational. And there are just enough trails to warrant a post-hike massage. The red-brick Promenade runs directly behind Bathhouse Row. It's short and easy, with the feel of a typical urban greenspace. Sunset Trail (moderate, 10+ miles) connects North, Hot Springs, West, Music, and Sugarloaf mountains. Hike the whole thing or choose a shorter section like walking to Balanced Rock from Cedar Glades Road or the area near Gulpha Gorge Campground is quite nice. Sticking with rock sightings, Goat Rock Trail (moderate, 1.1 miles) is also enjoyable. And the visitor center just got all new exhibits! And there's a lookout tower (fee) atop Hot Springs Mountain. No more ands. That's about it.

Santa Elena Canyon

Big Bend
Hiking Trails: 150+ miles

Big Bend Favorites

(1) **Santa Elena Canyon**
Moderate | 1.4 miles | 200 feet

(2) **Ward Spring**
Easy | 2.6 miles | 500 feet

(3) **Grapevine Hills**
Moderate | 2.0 miles | 250 feet

(4) **Lost Mine**
Moderate | 4.3 miles | 1,100 feet

(5) **Window**
Moderate | 3.9 miles | 700 feet

(6) **South Rim**
Strenuous | 12.9 miles | 2,000 feet

(7) **Dog Canyon**
Moderate | 4.4 miles | 120 feet

Devil's Den
Moderate | 6.6 miles | 350 feet

(8) **Mariscal Canyon Rim**
Strenuous | 7.4 miles | 1,200 feet

(9) **Hot Springs**
Easy | 1.2 miles | 350 feet

(10) **Ernst Tinaja**
Easy | 1.4 miles | 130 feet

(11) **Boquillas Canyon**
Moderate | 1.3 miles | 150 feet

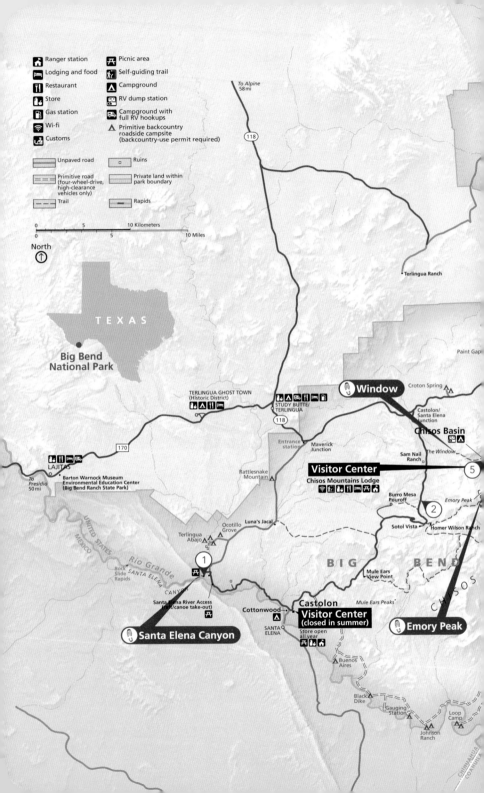

Legend

Ranger station
Lodging and food
Restaurant
Store
Gas station
Wi-fi
Customs

Picnic area
Self-guiding trail
Campground
RV dump station
Campground with full RV hookups
Primitive backcountry roadside campsite (backcountry-use permit required)

Unpaved road
Primitive road (four-wheel-drive, high-clearance vehicles only)
Trail

Ruins
Private land within park boundary
Rapids

0   5   10 Kilometers
0   5   10 Miles

North

TEXAS

Big Bend National Park

To Alpine 58 mi

118

Terlingua Ranch

TERLINGUA GHOST TOWN (Historic District)

STUDY BUTTE/ TERLINGUA

118

170

LAJITAS

To Presidio 50 mi

Barton Warnock Museum Environmental Education Center (Big Bend Ranch State Park)

Paint Gap

Window

Croton Spring

Castolon/ Santa Elena Junction

Chisos Basin

Sam Nail Ranch   The Window

Visitor Center
Chisos Mountains Lodge

Entrance station

Maverick Junction

Rattlesnake Mountain

5

Burro Mesa Pouroff

Emory Peak

2

Sotol Vista   Homer Wilson Ranch

Ocotillo Grove   Luna's Jacal

Terlingua Abajo

UNITED STATES

MEXICO

Rio Grande

Rock Slide Rapids

SANTA ELENA CANYON

Santa Elena Canyon

Santa Elena River Access (raft/canoe take-out)

Cottonwood

Castolon
Visitor Center
(closed in summer)
Store open all year

SANTA ELENA

B I G   **B E N D**

Mule Ears View Point

Mule Ears Peaks

Emory Peak

C H I S O S

Buenos Aires

Black Dike

Gauging Station

Loop Camp

Johnson Ranch

CHIHUAHUA
COAHUILA

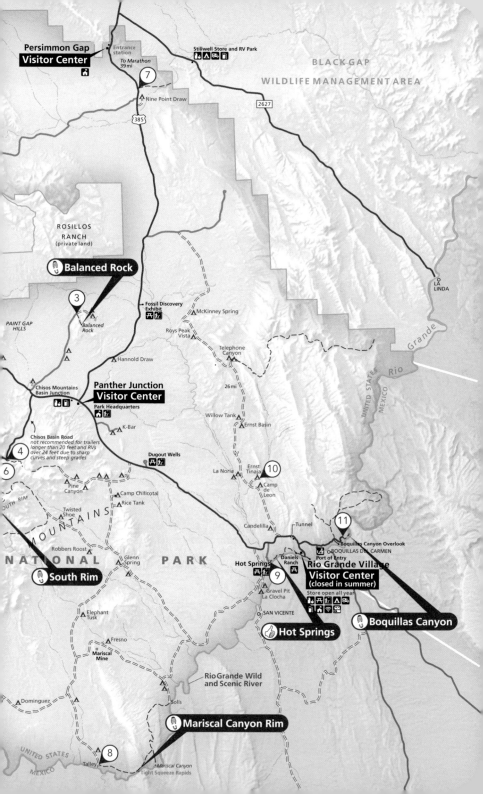

Persimmon Gap
Visitor Center

To Marathon 39 mi

Entrance station

Stillwell Store and RV Park

BLACK GAP

WILDLIFE MANAGEMENT AREA

⑦

Nine Point Draw

385

2627

ROSILLOS
RANCH
(private land)

LA LINDA

Rio Grande

👢 **Balanced Rock**

③

Balanced
Rock

PAINT GAP
HILLS

Fossil Discovery
Exhibit

McKinney Spring

Roys Peak
Vista

Telephone
Canyon

Hannold Draw

26 mi

UNITED STATES

Rio Grande

MEXICO

Chisos Mountains
Basin Junction

Panther Junction
Visitor Center

Park Headquarters

Willow Tank

Ernst Basin

Chisos Basin Road
not recommended for trailers
longer than 20 feet and RVs
over 24 feet due to sharp
curves and steep grades

④

K-Bar

Dugout Wells

La Noria

Ernst
Tinaja

⑩

Camp
de Leon

⑥

Pine
Canyon

Camp Chilicotal

Rice Tank

Candelilla

Tunnel

⑪

Boquillas Canyon Overlook

BOQUILLAS DEL CARMEN

Twisted
Shoe

MOUNTAINS

Robbers Roost

Glenn
Spring

Hot Springs

Daniels
Ranch

Port of Entry

Rio Grande Village
Visitor Center
(closed in summer)

👢 **South Rim**

SOUTH RIM

NATIONAL   **PARK**

Elephant
Tusk

Fresno

Mariscal
Mine

Gravel Pit
La Clocha

SAN VICENTE

Store open all year

👍 **Hot Springs**

⑨

👢 **Boquillas Canyon**

Dominguez

Solis

Rio Grande Wild
and Scenic River

👢 **Mariscal Canyon Rim**

UNITED STATES

MEXICO

Talley

⑧

Mariscal Canyon
Tight Squeeze Rapids

SANTA ELENA CANYON

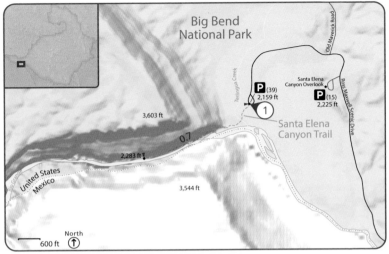

Santa Elena Canyon | Moderate | 1.4 miles | 200 feet | Out-and-back
Trailhead: The end of Ross Maxwell Scenic Drive (1)

Santa Elena Canyon is one of several must-stop destinations at Big Bend. In addition to imposing rock walls, canyon hikes like Santa Elena possess a highly desirable feature: it's nearly impossible to get lost. It's up, then down as you enter the canyon, but most of the short trail is an easy walk among precipitous rock walls. Be sure to stroll along (or in) the Rio Grande near the canyon's mouth. Many visitors like to walk into Mexico for a second or two. There's a fair amount of parking at the trailhead but it can get congested, especially during holidays and spring break. You may get muddy/wet crossing Terlingua Creek, and the trail can be impassable when it floods. Even if you can't hike the trail, the drive to Santa Elena Canyon is worth the time. It's also a popular place to paddle up into the canyon (but difficult during low water levels).

Ward Spring | Easy | 2.6 miles | 500 feet | Out-and-back
Trailhead: Ross Maxwell Scenic Drive (2)

Ward Spring is not a popular trail but in the evening light, it offers wondrous views of the Chisos Mountains, and the trail concludes at an interesting volcanic dike, which a few hikers like to explore. While there's much to see and do at Big Bend, it's unlikely you'll regret spending an hour or two hiking this trail. Parking is limited to a small pullout along Ross Maxwell Scenic Drive.

Ward Spring

WARD SPRING   GRAPEVINE HILLS

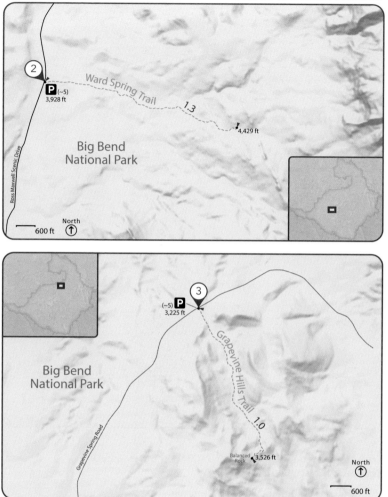

Grapevine Hills | Moderate | 2.0 miles | 250 feet | Out-and-back
Trailhead: Grapevine Hills Road (3)

Another super-fun short hike! If not for some rock scrambling it would be rated easy. With the scrambling, being agile will help as you step carefully through the jumble of rocks. The highlight is a balanced rock. And, if I'm being opinionated, it's one of the better balanced rocks found on NPS land. Morning light is better but it's a fun little trek any time of day (assuming pleasant weather). Grapevine Hills Road is unpaved. The park website says a sturdy, high-clearance vehicle is required. Last time I was there, the road wasn't bad with all types of vehicles at the trailhead. But this is the way with unpaved roads, always inquire about conditions before going out on them.

CHISOS MOUNTAINS

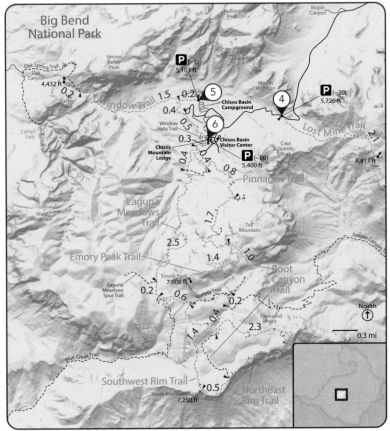

Lost Mine | Moderate | 4.3 miles | 1,100 feet | Out-and-back
Trailhead: Chisos Basin Road (4)

Lost Mine is a decent trail, but if you're prioritizing Chisos Mountains hikes, South Rim should be at the top of the list, then Window, then Lost Mine. Lost Mine starts with a steady climb, before flattening out to sweeping desert views. Again, it's nice but you can do better nearby.

Window | Moderate | 3.9 miles | 700 feet | Out-and-back
Trailhead: Chisos Basin Campground (5)

Window is unique in that it follows a precious desert molecule, H_2O, through Oak Creek Canyon to a rock window facing west toward Sam Nail Ranch. Unfortunately, rocks obstruct the window's view. It's still cool. However, there's something that might be even cooler, as long as the water's flowing and you don't mind working up a sweat going down and up a pretty serious grade. Oak Springs Trail (you pass the intersection along the way to the window) leads down to the desert floor, where you can continue to a hidden oasis and Cattail Falls (a true desert rarity). It's about another 2.5 miles one-way to add Cattail Falls to your itinerary and the journey is quite strenuous. (You can also reach Cattail Falls via a mostly flat road/trail beginning near Sam Nail Ranch.) Some campground guests like to head down to the window for sunset, but you're better off staying up at Chisos Basin, where you'll have a broader view of the horizon should you be lucky enough to catch an eruption of color. Beginning from Chisos Basin Visitor Center instead of the campground adds nearly two miles to the trek.

South Rim | Strenuous | 12.9 miles | 2,000 feet | Loop
Trailhead: Chisos Mountain Lodge (6)

If you have 13 miles in you, this is the trail to do. There are some switchbacks, and it's a pretty long, steady climb to the rim regardless which direction you choose, but the elevation gain is fairly modest for a mountainous trail of this length. Which way to go? Counterclockwise offers considerable pros. You'll get to the rim sooner and you'll arrive at the Emory Peak (highest point in the park) spur trail later. Emory Peak adds almost three miles, 800 feet of elevation gain, and some rock scrambling to the journey. While it's good, you're better off enjoying your time along the rim if this is an either-or situation. If you get an early start (or you're backpacking—it's a great place to backpack, with several sites along the rim), it'd be nice to walk the rim in a clockwise direction when the sun is still low in the eastern sky. Regardless which direction you go, be sure to walk out to South Rim Viewpoint, which is found at the end of an obvious-but-unmarked trail beginning directly behind a trail sign. It's labelled on the map. Another thing to know is that a large portion of the rim typically closes each year for nesting peregrine falcons (usually from February through May). During this time, you can still hike Southwest Rim Trail and loop back via Boot Canyon Trail. With that said, it's still a good idea to check in with the park about trail closures (especially if you're visiting during this period).

Chisos Mountains

The Chisos Mountains are the primary destination for most Big Bend visitors. Expect traffic to back up on Chisos Basin Road and camping/lodging reservations to book quickly for fall/winter holidays and spring break. If you're headed into the Chisos Mountains for a day of hiking, plan to get an early start. I'd strongly recommend spending at least one night up at Chisos Basin. The summer heat is hard to handle at Big Bend, but if you're looking for a quiet time to explore the Chisos Mountains, temperatures are usually 20 degrees cooler at elevation, with average daytime highs in the 80s. Bearable, indeed.

The Window

DOG CANYON/DEVIL'S DEN

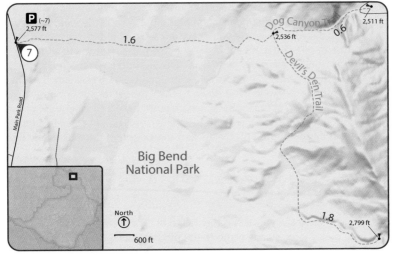

Dog Canyon | Moderate | 4.4 miles | 120 feet | Out-and-back
Devil's Den | Moderate | 6.6 miles | 350 feet | Out-and-back
Trailhead: Main Park Road (7)

Dog isn't nearly as impressive as the park's other canyons (Mariscal, Santa Elena, Boquillas, or even Tuff), but it's a decent hike. If you're entering from the north, stop a while and stretch your legs. The trail leads to a sandy wash, where you'll hit the Devil's Den intersection. The wash continues east into Dog Canyon and exits with open views reaching well beyond the park boundary. It's enjoyable but the real gem is Devil's Den.

Devil's Den shares the same access trail with Dog Canyon, you simply turn right at the wash, following it to the south. There should be a trail sign at the intersection, starting you on the correct path. It's cairn-spotting from that point on. Note, you will climb out of the wash and onto a flat-ish mesa, where you can investigate the Devil's Den from above. It's a really fun spot.

Devil's Den and Dog Canyon share a trailhead. It's located on Main Park Road, 3.5 miles south of Persimmon Gap Visitor Center. These are very quiet trails as parking is limited to a small roadside pullout.

Mariscal Canyon Rim | Strenuous | 7.4 miles | 1,200 feet | Out-and-back
Trailhead: Talley Road (8)

As you might imagine, it takes some work to reach the top of a 1,400-foot cliff, high above the Rio Grande. Whether you're floating the Rio Grande or walking its Rim, Mariscal Canyon is a dramatic setting. The effort expended to reach this lofty perch earns substantial rewards. Mariscal is taller and steeper

Devil's Den

MARISCAL CANYON RIM

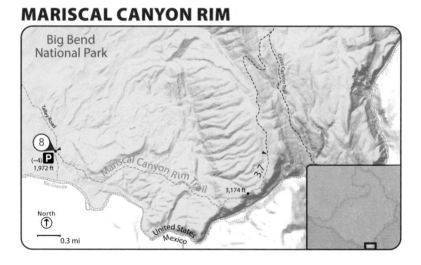

Big Bend National Park

Talley Road

8
(~4) P
1,972 ft

Mariscal Canyon Rim Trail

Rio Grande

Cross Canyon Trail

3.7

3,174 ft

North
0.3 mi

United States
Mexico

than Santa Elena and Boquillas canyons. Reaching the trailhead at the end of Talley Road requires a high-clearance 4x4 (and it's about two hours from the nearest pavement). River Road was pretty gnarly in this area when I was out there (be sure to check with the park about conditions). Thanks to its remote nature, there's a good chance you'll have the trail to yourself. That said, the park advises not to have valuables in your car specifically for this location. And when I arrived, a group of guys at a Talley campsite looked as if they were staking out the Mariscal Trailhead. Was it recency bias from the backcountry site reservation conversation? Were they just curious who was out in this remote corner? I don't know. What I do know is, nothing bad happened. You can also hike in from Solis. The trailhead is closer to pavement, but you'll still need a high-clearance 4x4 to reach it, and the hike is a little longer to the rim.

HOT SPRINGS

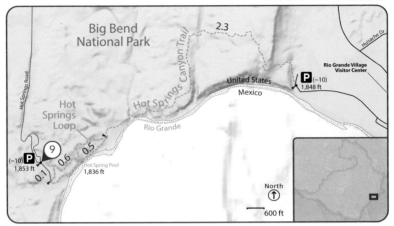

Hot Springs | Easy | 1.2 miles | 350 feet | Loop
Trailhead: Hot Springs Road (9)

A manmade pool along the shore of the Rio Grande is a very popular Big Bend destination. Bring your swimwear and join in the fun. There are two access options. The easiest is to drive to the end of Hot Springs Road (unpaved), where there's a large-ish parking area. The hike passes a dilapidated resort and you'll be at the spring in no time at all. Once you're finished soaking and socializing, continue the loop back to the parking area, totaling just over one mile. The longer option is to hike in from Daniel's Ranch (over by Rio Grande Village). It's about six miles roundtrip to Hot Springs, featuring a variety of Rio Grande views and passing some of the park's best birdwatching territory.

ERNST TINAJA

Ernst Tinaja | Easy | 1.4 miles | 130 feet | Out-and-back
Trailhead: Ernst Tinaja Camp, Old Ore Road (10)

Ernst Tinaja is a real nice treat found near the Ernst Tinaja primitive roadside campsite. To get there, you'll need a high-clearance 4x4. Access Old Ore Road from the south. It's a long, slow, and very rugged drive from the north. From the south, it's just five miles of increasingly uneven road. Once you're there, it's a short walk to a limestone canyon with some striking layered rock formations. Tinaja is Spanish for "large earthen jar," and you'll find natural water holes too. With the right vehicle, be sure to check this spot out. There's a small parking lot at the trailhead.

BOQUILLAS CANYON

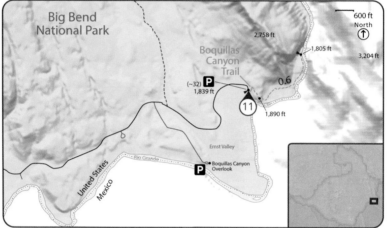

Boquillas Canyon | Moderate | 1.3 miles | 150 feet | Out-and-back
Trailhead: End of Boquillas Canyon Road (11)

From the trailhead it's a pretty steep climb to the top of a bluff with Rio Grande views. After descending, it's an easier but sandier walk to the canyon's mouth. The trail continues into the canyon to a very abrupt and kind of uneventful conclusion. Still worth a look though.

More Trails

There are a few more trails. Chimneys (moderate, 4.8 miles one-way) leads to weird rocks and ancient petroglyphs between Ross Maxwell Scenic Drive and Old Maverick Road (unpaved but accessible to regular cars). Tuff Canyon is a quick roadside attraction on Ross Maxwell Scenic Drive. Smoky Creek Trail leads past the Mule Ears and offers nice backpacking opportunities or long-distance, point-to-point hikes (combined with Dodson Trail). Marufo Vega (strenuous, 12.0 miles) is one of the few loops in the park. It begins near Boquillas Canyon Overlook. If you want to be way out there and on your own, check out Telephone Canyon. There are two primitive campsites near the trailhead. They're near the middle of Old Ore Road, an unpaved road requiring a high-clearance 4x4. It was quite treacherous out there, last time I visited.

Guadalupe Mountains
Hiking Trails: 80+ miles

Devil's Hall

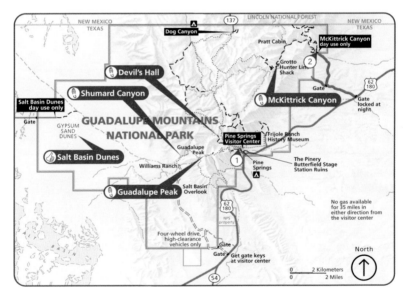

Guadalupe Mountains Favorites

(1) **Guadalupe Peak**
Strenuous | 8.0 miles | 3,000 feet

(2) **McKittrick Canyon**
Moderate | 6.8 miles | 330 feet

Devil's Hall
Moderate | 3.8 miles | 700 feet

Permian Reef
Strenuous | 6.1 miles | 2,100 feet

GUADALUPE PEAK/DEVIL'S HALL

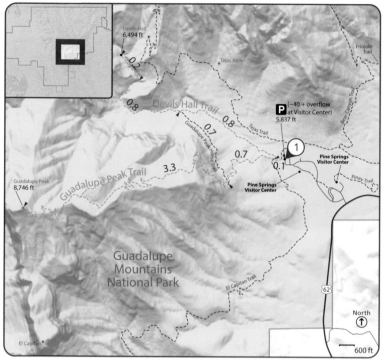

Guadalupe Peak | Strenuous | 8.0 miles | 3,000 feet | Out-and-back
Devil's Hall | Moderate | 3.8 miles | 700 feet | Out-and-back
Trailhead: Pine Springs Campground (1)

Guadalupe Peak (8,746 ft) is the highest point in Texas. That fact alone is enough for many visitors to put this arduous trek at the top of their hiking wish lists. It is tough, with plenty of switchbacks and often a whole lot of wind. But the views aren't too shabby. Before reaching the peak, you'll have panoramic views to the south overlooking El Capitan. At the summit, you'll be able to peer far across the flat salt basin. It's quite the contrast compared to Texas's tallest peak! Return the way you came. A horse trail connects Guadalupe Peak with Devil's Hall. Combining the two hikes saves about one mile.

Devil's Hall is great. Most of the trail follows a desert wash, but you'll encounter two truly spectacular features. The first is a rocky staircase. Although it's fun negotiating your way up and down the staircase, this isn't its most impressive feature. What's stunning are the rocks bookending the stairs. Without knowing what Devil's Hall looks like, you could mistakenly think the stairwy is it. It isn't. After enjoying a photo-op with the stairs, carefully choose the best way up them for you and continue less than a quarter mile to Devil's Hall, a a long rock hallway. Having read this (and seeing the photo), you'll know it when you

Pratt Cabin (McKittrick Canyon)

see it. While the elevation gain to Devil's Hall is reasonable, hiking in a sandy wash takes more effort than walking along firm ground. Your calves might be a little sore in the morning after this one.

The trailhead is conveniently located near Pine Springs Campground. Parking fills up in the fall and spring, especially during spring break. Arrive early if you'd like a parking space at the trailhead. Overflow parking is available at the visitor center.

McKittrick Canyon | Moderate | 6.8 miles | 330 feet | Out-and-back
Permian Reef | Strenuous | 6.1 miles | 2,100 feet | Out-and-back
Trailhead: McKittrick Canyon (2)

McKittrick Canyon is a gentle walk through a beautiful, sandy canyon. Come in fall when the leaves have changed for maximum beauty. There are several notable features along the way. Pratt Cabin, the original summer home of Wallace Pratt (an oil geologist), is the first major waypoint. Today it's a picnic/rest area as well as an interpretive site. The Pratts donated considerable land, along with this cabin and their other vacation home, Ship on the Desert, to the National Park Service. The Grotto is next, featuring a small cave with some whacky rock formations and another picnic area. Just beyond the Grotto is Hunter Line Shack. The trail continues beyond this point, and the elevation gain becomes serious. McKittrick Ridge Trail is often called the "toughest

MCKITTRICK CANYON/PERMIAN REEF

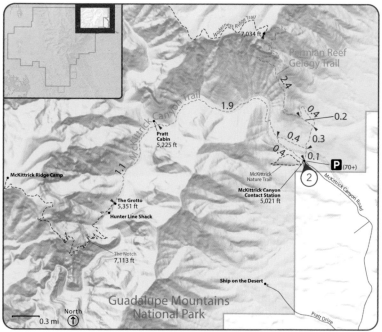

Wilderness Ridge Trail

7,034 ft

Permian Reef
Gelogy Trail

2.4

1.9

McKittrick Canyon Trail

0.4
0.2

Pratt
Cabin
5,225 ft

0.4
0.3

0.4

0.4
0.1

McKittrick Ridge Camp

1.1

P (70+)

McKittrick
Nature Trail

McKittrick Canyon Road

2

The Grotto
5,351 ft

**McKittrick Canyon
Contact Station**
5,021 ft

Hunter Line Shack

The Notch
7,113 ft

Ship on the Desert

Guadalupe Mountains
National Park

North

Pratt Drive

0.3 mi

trail in Texas." It's one more very strenuous mile to "The Notch," where you're rewarded with excellent views of McKittrick Canyon. Another 3.1 miles up the steep ridge you'll find a backcountry campsite (if you're thinking about backpacking, it's a good choice).

McKittrick Canyon is a popular trail. Permian Reef is not. Escaping the crowds can be its own reward but Permian Reef has much more to offer than that. There are plenty of interesting rocks to walk among, and the views, looking down on the crowd in McKittrick Canyon are awfully good. If you're trying to choose between the two, Permian Reef is the way to go, as long as you don't mind all the elevation gain.

McKittrick Canyon is a day-use area, with visiting hours from 8am until 5pm. The entrance gate is locked the rest of the day.

More Trails

There are a few more fun trails to check out, but they take some effort to reach. At the west side of the park, you'll find Salt Basin Dunes (day-use area). With a high-clearance 4x4, you can reach Williams Ranch, where you can hike up Shumard Canyon. The road isn't anything too undriveable but it's extremely rugged. There's also a gate at the start of the road. You'll need to stop in at the visitor center to get the key. There's a small network of trails in the park's interior, where backpackers like to explore. You can also get a feel of the park's interior from Dog Canyon at the park's northern boundary, but it's a somewhat low pay-off for a long drive to the trailhead.

Carlsbad Caverns
Hiking Trails: 50+ miles

Slaughter Canyon

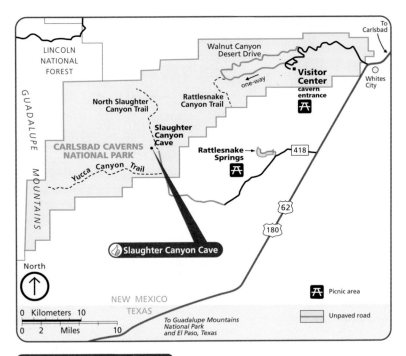

To
Carlsbad

LINCOLN
NATIONAL
FOREST

Walnut Canyon
Desert Drive

one-way

**Visitor
Center**
cavern
entrance

Whites
City

G U A D A L U P E

North Slaughter
Canyon Trail

Rattlesnake
Canyon Trail

**Slaughter
Canyon
Cave**

**Rattlesnake
Springs**

418

CARLSBAD CAVERNS
NATIONAL PARK

Yucca Canyon Trail

M O U N T A I N S

62

180

Slaughter Canyon Cave

North

NEW MEXICO

TEXAS

0 Kilometers 10

0   2   Miles   10

To Guadalupe Mountains
National Park
and El Paso, Texas

Picnic area

Unpaved road

Hiking Carlsbad Caverns

Unsurprisingly, hiking is a forgotten activity at Carlsbad Caverns. The scenery is similar to Guadalupe Mountains, but the trails here aren't quite as exciting. Rattlesnake Canyon is pretty good, but it requires a steep initial descent into the canyon. On the plus side, it's convenient, beginning on Walnut Canyon Drive, not far from the Visitor Center. It's a good idea to do the Slaughter Canyon Cave Tour, and while you're over there (you drive yourself to the trailhead for the tour) stick around to hike up Slaughter Canyon Trail. Still, the best hike you can do is entering the main cave's Natural Entrance and continuing all the way to the Big Room.

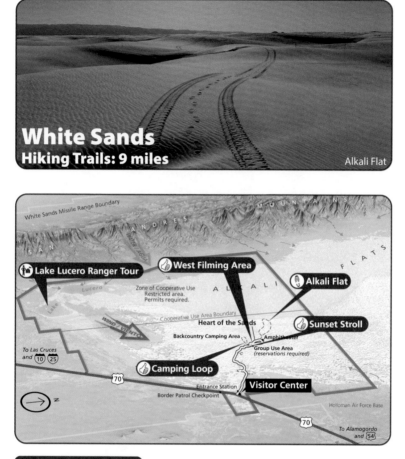

White Sands
Hiking Trails: 9 miles

Alkali Flat

Map labels:
- White Sands Missile Range Boundary
- SAN ANDRES MOUNTAINS
- ALKALI FLATS
- Lake Lucero Ranger Tour
- West Filming Area
- Alkali Flat
- Lucero
- Zone of Cooperative Use Restricted area. Permits required.
- Cooperative Use Area Boundary
- WIND VIENTO
- Heart of the Sands
- Sunset Stroll
- Backcountry Camping Area
- Amphitheater
- Group Use Area (reservations required)
- To Las Cruces and 10 25
- Camping Loop
- 70
- Entrance Station
- Border Patrol Checkpoint
- Visitor Center
- Holloman Air Force Base
- N
- 70
- To Alamogordo and 54

Hiking White Sands

As long as you aren't visiting in the middle of a heat wave, windstorm or missile testing, it shouldn't be a problem hiking all nine miles of trail in a day. The best of the bunch is Alkali Flat (moderate, 4.9 miles). Posts pounded into the sand mark the way, but they can be difficult to follow as shifting sand occasionally buries a marker or two. Shortly after sunrise, you should be able to follow footprints, although wind also tends to clear the sandy slate. The loop extends to the cooperative use area boundary, and, aside from the missile testing warning sign, this is the least exciting stretch. Another fun trail is the 2.2-mile loop around the backcountry camping area. You don't need to camp to hike it. Of the short trails (Playa, Dune Life, and Interdune Boardwalk), Dune Life is my favorite. But since they aren't a huge time commitment, you may as well do them yourself and see what you think. While it's a good idea to follow the trails, that isn't exactly what White Sands is about. It's about exploring the gypsum dunes. Explore freely through the Heart of the Dunes, just make sure you don't get lost. It can get unbelievably hot out there in summer.

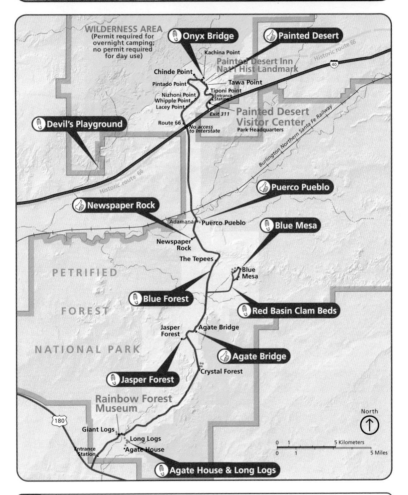

Petrified Forest
Hiking Trails: 7+ miles

Long Logs

Map labels:

WILDERNESS AREA
(Permit required for overnight camping; no permit required for day use)

Onyx Bridge

Painted Desert

Kachina Point

Painted Desert Inn
Nat'l Hist Landmark

Historic route 66

40

Chinde Point

Pintado Point

Tawa Point

Tiponi Point
Entrance
Station

Nizhoni Point
Whipple Point
Lacey Point

Exit 311

Painted Desert
Visitor Center

Devil's Playground

Route 66
No access
to Interstate

Park Headquarters

Burlington Northern Santa Fe Railway

Historic route 66

Puerco Pueblo

Newspaper Rock

Adamana

Puerco Pueblo

Blue Mesa

Newspaper
Rock

The Tepees

Blue
Mesa

PETRIFIED

Blue Forest

FOREST

Red Basin Clam Beds

Jasper
Forest

Agate Bridge

NATIONAL PARK

Agate Bridge

Crystal Forest

Jasper Forest

Rainbow Forest
Museum

North

180

Giant Logs

Long Logs

0   1   5 Kilometers

Entrance
Station

Agate House

0   1   5 Miles

Agate House & Long Logs

Hiking

There's just seven miles of maintained trails as well as a few longer "off-the-beaten-path" routes. Painted Desert Rim (easy, 1.0 mile), Blue Mesa (moderate, 1.0 mile), Crystal Forest (easy, 0.8 mile), Long Logs (easy, 1.6 miles), Agate House (easy, 2.0 miles), and Giant Logs (easy, 0.4 mile) are worth a look. It's pretty easy to do all of those in a day. Onyx Bridge (moderate, 4.0 miles), Blue Forest (moderate, 3.0 miles), Red Basin Clam Beds (moderate, 8.5 miles), and Devil's Playground (permit required) are great off-the-beaten-path choices. The park website (nps.gov/pefo) has detailed pdfs on each "off-the-beaten-path" hike.

Saguaro
Hiking Trails: 160+ miles
Wasson Peak

Vehicles over 25 feet not recommended. Weight limit 12,000 lbs. Use Avra Valley Road to enter park from the north.

State land

10

Cam-Boh

Saguaro West
Tucson Mountain District

State land

Signal Hill Petroglyphs

Ez-Kim-In-Zin

two-way

③ Hugh Norris

Many park trails are not shown on this map. Obtain detailed hiking maps at visitor centers.

Bajada Scenic Loop
Unpaved road
No oversize vehicles

②

Valley View Overlook Trail

①

Sus

Wasson Peak

TUCSON MOUNTAINS

Wasson Peak

Desert Station University of Arizona

Red Hills Visitor Center

Mam-A-Gah

④

King Canyon

Arizona-Sonora Desert Museum

Gates Pass Road

To 10 exit 257

TUCSON MOUNTAIN PARK

Unpaved road
Park land
Wilderness area
State land
Private property within park land (no public access)
Trail
The Arizona Trail

Gilbert Ray

Old Tucson Studios

To 86 and 19 exit 99

Vehicles over 25 feet not recommended. Weight limit 12,000 lbs. Use Avra Valley Road to enter park from the north.

0   1   2 Kilometers
0   1   2 Miles

North
↑

To 86

Saguaro West Routes to Wasson Peak

① Hugh Norris
Strenuous | 9.3 miles | 2,200 feet

③ Sweetwater
Strenuous | 8.9 miles | 2,100 feet

② Sendero Esperanza
Moderate | 7.6 miles | 1,700 feet

④ King Canyon
Strenuous | 6.7 miles | 1,800 feet

WASSON PEAK

Saguaro
National Park

Cactus
Wren Trail
Signal Hill
Signal Hill Trail
Signal Hill Road

Ez-Kim-In-Zin
Picnic Area

2

P (~17)
2,795 ft

3

Encinas Trail

N Sandario Road

Golden Gate Road

Wild Dog Trail

Apache
Peak

Dobe Wash Trail

Valley
View Trail

Bajada
Wash Trail

P (~10)
2,598 ft

2.5

Hohokam Rd

1

P (13+)
2,987 ft

Sendero
Esperanza
Trail

Wasson Peak
4,671 ft ♦ 0.3

Hugh Norris Tr.

0.7

0.9

Amole Peak

1.8

0.8

Sweetwater Tr. 3.1

Discovery
Trail

Kinney Road

Red Hills
Visitor Center

Red
Hills

W Mile Wide Road

4

Mam-A-Gah
Picnic Area

1.4

King Canyon
Trail

Gould Mine Tr.

0.9

0.8

P (50+)
2,909 ft

North ↑

0.3 mi

Hugh Norris | Strenuous | 9.3 miles | 2,200 feet | Out-and-back
Trailhead: Bajada Loop Drive (1)

Sendero Esperanza | Moderate | 7.6 miles | 1,700 feet | Out-and-back
Trailhead: Golden Gate Road (2)

Sweetwater | Strenuous | 8.9 miles | 2,100 feet | Out-and-back
Trailhead: Camino del Cerro (3)

King Canyon | Strenuous | 6.7 miles | 1,800 feet | Out-and-back
Trailhead: Kinney Road (4)

All four of these trails lead into the Tucson Mountains, providing access to
Wasson Peak. King Canyon is the most strenuous, but it shares an intense
stretch with Sweetwater Trail. Hugh Norris gains some serious elevation but
it's a mostly gradual climb after the initial ascent. The obvious question is,
which one do you choose? My first choice is Hugh Norris. It features lots of
Saguaro and interesting rocks, and the views down toward Red Hills Visitor
Center are quite nice. If you can cache a car or arrange a pick-up, I'd go up the
steep King Canyon Trail and down Hugh Norris (but I prefer steep climbs over
descents). And you could make a few funky loops thanks to other trails. The
Yellow Loop above is about 6.4 miles, of course you'll want to extend the trip
to Wasson Peak, adding another 4.2 miles. The Orange Loop above is 6.8 miles
(with another 0.6 to get to Wasson Peak. Better yet, combine them for a mega-
hike figure 8! King Canyon has the largest parking area, and it's also the most
popular trailhead. At King Canyon, you'll notice two parallel trails leading to
Mam-A-Gah Picnic Area. The one to the north leads through a fun wash and
requires climbing a few rock obstacles. Do that one!

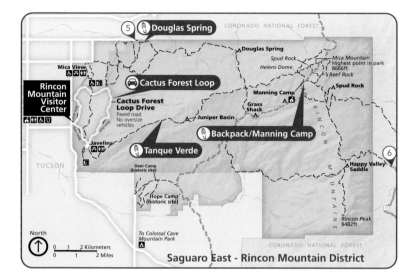

Saguaro East - Rincon Mountain District

Saguaro East Favorites

(5) **Douglas Spring**
Moderate | 6.8 miles | 1,600 feet

(6) **Rincon Peak**
Strenuous | 14.2 miles | 4,300 feet

Douglas Spring | Moderate | 6.8 miles | 1,600 feet | Out-and-back
Trailhead: Speedway Boulevard (5)

The trailhead is located along Saguaro East's northern boundary (about a ten-minute drive from Rincon Mountain Visitor Center. The trail is noteworthy for a couple ephemeral waterfalls. To reach both, Bridal Wreath and Ernie's Falls, you'll walk about seven miles. Along the way, you'll pass all the desert staples: saguaro, cholla, and plenty of scrubland. For some people the scenery may be a tad monotonous. Douglas Spring is also a good choice for backpackers. Continuing into the mountains, you'll hit Douglas Spring Camp after six miles (one-way). From there, you can continue to the popular Manning Camp via Cow Head Saddle or Manning Camp Trail. Due to the trailhead's location, the park does not recommend leaving valuables in your car.

Rincon Peak | Strenuous | 14.2 miles | 4,300 feet | Out-and-back
Trailhead: Miller Creek (6)

The road to Miller Creek is unpaved (and pretty darn rough), but most vehicles should be able to make it with some careful maneuvering. Miller Creek Trail crosses into the National Park, working its way up to Happy Valley Saddle. This is not an easy trail to follow. It isn't heavily used or well-marked, so come prepared to hunt cairns and possibly do a bit of backtracking. The terrain is

DOUGLAS SPRING

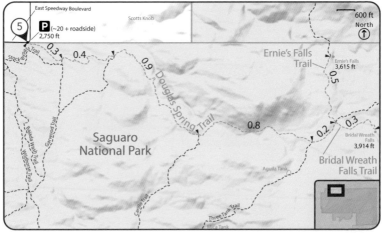

East Speedway Boulevard

Scotts Knob

5 P (~20 + roadside)
2,750 ft

600 ft
North

Stock Tr...ail
Garwood Trail
Wildhorse Trail
Ladino Web Trail
Carrillo Trail

0.3 0.4
0.9 Douglas Spring Trail

Saguaro
National Park

Ernie's Falls
Trail
Ernie's Falls
3,615 ft
0.5

0.8

0.2 0.3
Bridal Wreath
Falls
3,914 ft

Bridal Wreath
Falls Trail

Aguila Tank

Three Tank Trail
Mica Tank

rugged and rocky, gaining elevation quickly as you go. Things briefly flatten out at Happy Valley, but soon you'll be working your way up and across the western flank of the Rincon Mountains, with a significant grade up to the peak. Enjoy the views and return as you came. It's all downhill from here. Come prepared for a workout and don't forget water and sunscreen (although there is some shade along the way).

Tanque Verde

More Trails

At Tucson Mountain District (Saguaro West), Cactus Garden (easy, 0.1 mile) is short and easy to access, being located at Red Hills Visitor Center. Red Hills Visitor Center is a must-stop destination, as the setting displays big mountains and massive cactus. Desert Discovery (easy, 0.5 mile) is a self-guided loop. Signal Hill (easy, 0.5 mile) leads to a bunch of petroglyphs, and you can continue onto Cactus Wren Trail (easy, 3.0 miles), which features pleasant desert scenery. You'll also find a dense network of trails over at Cam-Boh Picnic Area on Pictured Rocks Road.

Over on the other side of Tucson, you'll find a similar trail network at Rincon Mountain District (Saguaro East). However, there's also a network of backcountry trails emanating from Manning Camp (7,941-feet elevation). Desert Ecology (easy, 0.3 mile) is a paved path. Cactus Forest Trail (easy, 5.2 miles) is near Desert Ecology. It bisects Cactus Forest Loop Drive. Freeman Homestead (easy, 1.0 mile) is a self-guided loop. And then there's a network of trails between the north end of Cactus Forest Loop and Speedway Boulevard. Tanque Verde is long, with relentless climbing and little shade, but there are a few fun sites. Both units close overnight.

RINCON PEAK

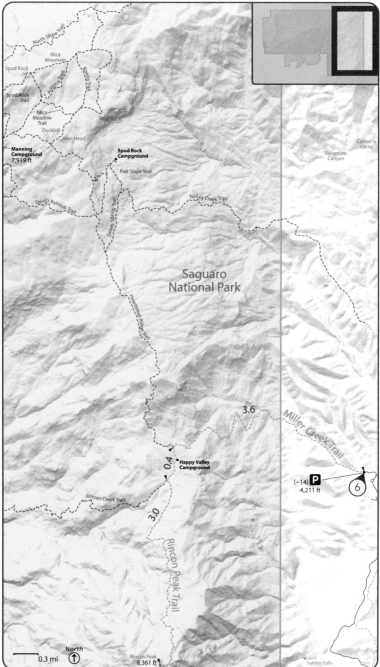

North Slope Trail

Mica
Mountain

Spud Rock

Spud Rock
Trail

Mica
Meadow
Trail

Duckbill

Man Head

Arizona Trail

Bonita Trail

Reef Rock

Manning
Campground
7,919 ft

Spud Rock
Campground

Fast Slope Trail

Devil's Bathtub Trail

Death Spring Trail

Turkey Creek Trail

Saguaro
National Park

Heartbreak Ridge Trail

3.6

Canon la
Carne

Sycamore
Canyon

Miller Creek Trail

0.4

Happy Valley
Campground

(~14) P
4,211 ft

6

Rincon Creek Trail

3.0

Rincon Peak Trail

North

0.3 mi

Rincon Peak
8,361 ft

Soldier Falls

Pacific NM

Hagerman Fossil
Beds NM

Craters of the Moon
NM & PRES

Minidoka NHS

City of Rocks N RES

Golden Spike NHS

SALT LAKE CITY
Timpanogos Cave NM

NEVADA

UTAH

Great Basin NP

SOUTHWEST

Bryce
Canyon NP

Capitol Reef NP

Cedar Breaks NM

pile NM

NP

zanar NHS

Zion NP

Glen Canyon NRA

Tule Springs
Fossil Beds
NM

Pipe Spring NM

Rainbow Bridge NM

LAS
VEGAS

Grand Canyon NP

Valley NP

Navajo NM

Castle Mountains NM

Lake Mead NRA

Canyon de

Mojave
N PRES

onica
ns NRA

Wupatki NM

Hubbell T
Po

Sunset Crater Volcano NM

OS ANGELES

Walnut Canyon N

Tuzigoot NM

Joshua
Tree NP

Montezuma Castle NM

Petrified
Forest N

The Southwest

ARIZONA

EGO

PHOENIX

Tonto NM

M

John D. Rockefeller, Jr.
Memorial PKWY

Grand Teton NP

Mount Rushmore N MEM

Jewel Cave NM

Wind Cave NP

WYOMING

Badla

Fossil Butte NM

Fort Laramie NHS

Agate Fossil Beds

Scotts Bluff NM

CHEYENNE

Dinosaur NM

Rocky
Mtn NP

Black Canyon of
the Gunnison NP

DENVER

Colorado NM

COLORADO

Arches NP

Florissant Fossil Beds NM

Curecanti NRA

Sand Creek
Massacre NHS

Canyonlands NP

Natural Bridges NM

Bent's Old
Fort NHS

ovenweep NM

Mesa
Verde NP

Great Sand
Dunes NP & PRES

Yucca House NM

Aztec Ruins NM

Capulin Volcano
NM

elly NM

Chaco Culture NHP

ng

Valles Caldera N Pres

Manhattan Project
NHP

HS

Bandelier NM

Fort Union NM

El Morro
NM

SANTA FE

Pecos NHP

Petroglyph
NM

ALBUQUERQUE

El Malpais
NM

NEW MEXICO

Salinas Pueblo Missions NM

Rocky Mountain Favorites

(1) Longs Peak
Extreme | 13.8 miles | 4,900 feet

Chasm Lake
Strenuous | 8.3 miles | 2,600 feet

(2) Sky Pond
Strenuous | 8.6 miles | 1,800 feet

Black Lake
Strenuous | 9.4 miles | 1,500 feet

(3) Bear Lake
Easy | 0.7 mile | 20 feet

Emerald Lake
Moderate | 3.3 miles | 700 feet

Hallett Peak
Strenuous | 9.6 miles | 3,300 feet

(3, 4, 6) Odessa/Fern Lake
Moderate | 11.5–13.9 mi | 3,300 ft

(5) Sprague Lake
Easy | 1.0 mile | 20 feet

(7) Ypsilon Lake
Strenuous | 8.5 miles | 2,900 feet

Lawn/Crystal Lake
Strenuous | 14.9 miles | 3,000 feet

(8) Lake of the Clouds
Strenuous | 12.6 miles | 2,600 feet

Skeleton Gulch
Moderate | 13.0 miles | 1,900 feet

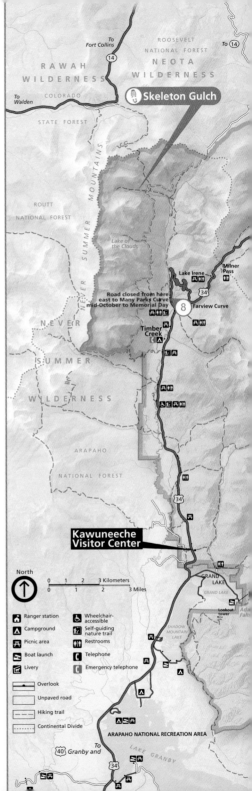

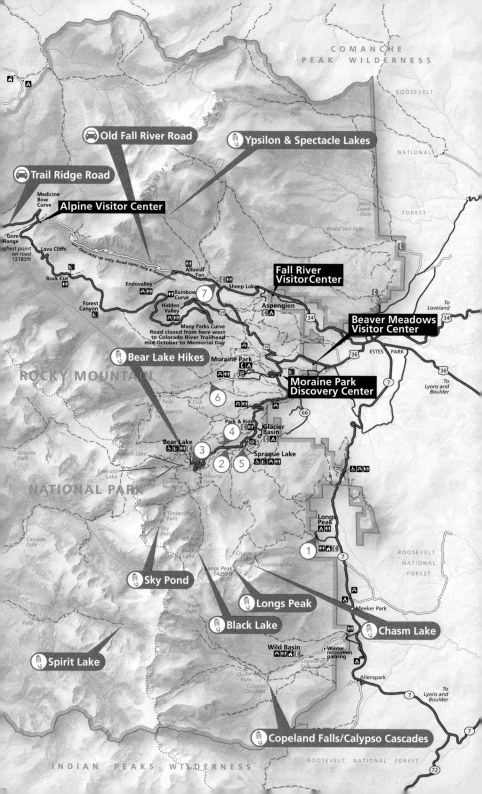

Old Fall River Road

Ypsilon & Spectacle Lakes

Trail Ridge Road

Alpine Visitor Center

Fall River Visitor Center

Beaver Meadows Visitor Center

Bear Lake Hikes

Moraine Park Discovery Center

Sky Pond

Longs Peak

Black Lake

Chasm Lake

Spirit Lake

Copeland Falls/Calypso Cascades

COMANCHE PEAK WILDERNESS

ROOSEVELT

NATIONAL

FOREST

Medicine Bow Curve

Gore Range
ghest point on road 12183ft

Lava Cliffs

Rock Cut

One-way up only. Road open July 4–September.

Forest Canyon

Endovalley

Rainbow Curve

Hidden Valley

Many Parks Curve
Road closed from here west to Colorado River Trailhead mid-October to Memorial Day

Alluvial Fan

Sheep Lake

Aspenglen

ROCKY MOUNTAIN

Moraine Park

NATIONAL PARK

Bear Lake

Nymph Lake

Emerald Lake

Dream Lake

Glacier Basin

Park & Ride

Sprague Lake

ESTES PARK

To Loveland

To Lyons and Boulder

Longs Peak

Longs Peak 14259ft

Columbine Falls

Meeker Park

Wild Basin

Winter recreation parking

Allenspark

ROOSEVELT NATIONAL FOREST

To Lyons and Boulder

INDIAN PEAKS WILDERNESS

ROOSEVELT NATIONAL FOREST

West Creek Falls

Bridal Veil Falls

Lost Falls

1
2
3
4
5
6
7

Rocky Mountain
Hiking Trails: 350+ miles

Sky Pond

LONGS PEAK/CHASM LAKE

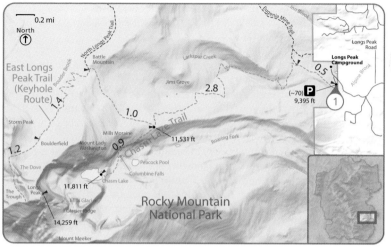

Longs Peak | Extreme | 13.8 miles | 4,900 feet | Out-and-back
Chasm Lake | Strenuous | 8.3 miles | 2,600 feet | Out-and-back
Trailhead: Longs Peak (1)

Many people dayhike Longs Peak, the highest peak and only 14er in the park, but it's a serious undertaking. If you're going to attempt it, you'll want to make sure you're acclimated to the elevation and start before sunrise (the parking lot fills ahead of sunrise on the busiest days!). It's better suited for an overnight, but, again, it's far from impossible to do in a day. The Keyhole Route to Longs Peaks features narrow ledges, loose rocks, and steep cliffs. It's an awful lot of scrambling. Making things even more difficult, snow persists well into summer. With proper preparation and experience as well as favorable weather, this climbing route is achievable, but for most it's fun to know people are making it to the top of Longs Peak on a regular basis. That knowledge is the same reason lots of us like to give it a try. Roughly half turn back long before the summit. If you're going to try to dayhike it, you better be prepared to turn around as well. Be honest with yourself. If you think it's out of your league, leave it for another time and head to Chasm Lake instead. You will not be disappointed.

Chasm Lake is great. The elevation gain is, well, let's say reasonable, and you'll need to do some light scrambling and a bit of route finding as you're closing in on the majestic setting, but huge rewards are found along the way. It's easily one of the best hikes in the park.

Back to parking, there's additional parking alongside the road but that fills up rapidly too. Arrive very early (especially on summer weekends), get dropped off, or cross your fingers.

Sky Pond | Strenuous | 8.6 miles | 1,800 feet | Out-and-back
Black Lake | Strenuous | 9.4 miles | 1,500 feet | Out-and-back
Trailhead: Glacier Gorge (2)

Sky Pond is a hike with a really fun journey, and then the destination is so incredible it'll make you forget about all the fun you just had along the way. As long as you're up for the elevation and can handle scrambling a brief but rocky (and often wet) obstacle, you'll have an absolute blast on this trail. Waterfalls! Alpine Lakes! Wild rocks! What's not to like? Alberta Falls is a nice treat within the first mile. From the falls, you'll reach the next trail junction after another mile. If anyone in your group is leery of scrambling some rocks, this is a good place to split up. Black Lake is also fantastic! But I'd put Sky Pond just above it for all the fun features along the way. Continue to The Loch, Timberline Falls, Lake of Glass, and Sky Pond. The trail is fairly obvious, and in all likelihood, you'll have plenty of company. But there are two things to note. You can walk right up to Timberline Falls. If there isn't a bottleneck at the rocky/waterfall-y scramble just before Lake of Glass (it's often slick), keep hiking and catch Timberline on the way down. If the scramble's backed up, walk on over for a look at Timberline. (Take your time at the scramble and allow everyone else to go at their own pace.) The second thing is the short rock scramble basically deposits you at Lake of Glass. Don't turn around here thinking it's Sky Pond. Sky Pond is another half-mile away over mostly flat terrain. Enjoy! On the way back, if you have the time and energy, take the spur up to Andrews Glacier and/or return via Lake Haiyaha and Emerald/Dream/Nymph lakes. This area is filled with all kinds of natural wonders.

To reach Black Lake, you follow the route to Sky Pond but head south past Mills Lake, through Glacier Gorge, and on to Ribbon Falls, just before arriving at the wonderful setting that is Black Lake. Black Lake is surrounded by towering peaks: McHenry's Peak (13,327 ft), Chief's Head Peak (13,579 ft), Pagoda Mountain (13,497 ft), Longs Peak (14,259 ft), and Storm Peak (13,326 ft). Bring your curiosity with you. There are social trails to a few smaller lakes in the vicinity. It's a similarly stunning setting to Sky Pond with less elevation gain and you don't have to scramble up a tricky little waterfall.

Parking is relatively limited at Glacier Gorge Trailhead, and it will fill up early. Alternatives are Bear Lake Trailhead (adding 0.4 mile roundtrip) or take the shuttle. Bear Lake has way more parking, but it fills too, early on summer weekends. Getting an early start remedies this dilemma, and you'll be happy you did, especially for the trek to Black Lake, where the views are exceptional to the west, south (and east). At Sky Pond, the best views are to the north, meaning lighting will be nice most of the day, as long as the sun is out. But the best argument for an early start is they're relatively long hikes, and you do not want to feel rushed.

SKY POND/BLACK, EMERALD, DREAM LAKE

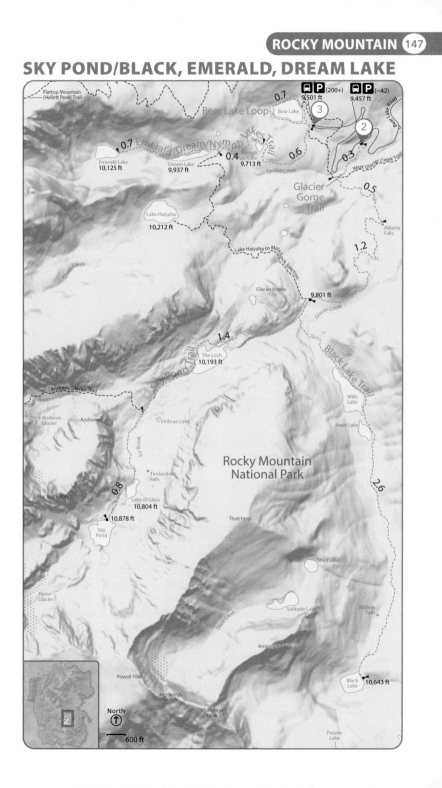

Flattop Mountain (Hallett Peak) Trail

P 9,501 ft (200+)
P 9,457 ft (~42)

3

2

0.7

Bear Lake Loop

Bear Lake

Lakes Trail

0.7 Emerald/Dream/Nymph

0.4

Nymph Lake 9,713 ft

0.6

0.3

Bear Lake Road

Emerald Lake 10,125 ft

Dream Lake 9,937 ft

Tyndall Creek

West Glacier Creek Trail

0.5

Glacier Gorge Trail

Lake Haiyaha 10,212 ft

Alberta Falls

Lake Haiyaha to Mills Lake Junction

1.2

Glacier Knobs

9,801 ft

Glacier Creek

Cross Creek

1.4

Sky Pond Trail

The Loch 10,193 ft

Black Lake Trail

Andrews Glacier Trail

Mills Lake

Andrews Creek

Andrews Glacier

Andrews Pass

Icy Brook

Embryo Lake

Jewel Lake

Rocky Mountain National Park

The Sharkstooth

0.8

Timberline Falls

Lake of Glass 10,804 ft

2.6

10,878 ft

Sky Pond

Thatchtop

Shelf Lake

Taylor Glacier

Ribbon Falls

Shelf Creek

Solitude Lake

Arrowhead

Powell Peak

Black Lake 10,643 ft

McHenrys Notch

McHenrys Peak

North
↑
600 ft

Frozen Lake

HALLETT PEAK/ODESSA LAKE

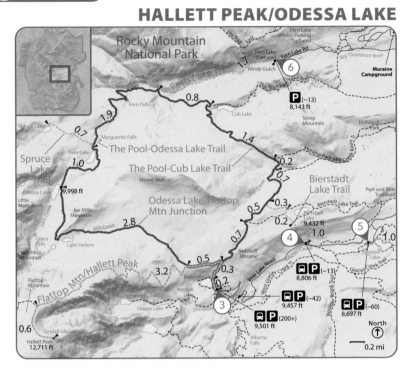

Bear Lake | Easy | 0.7 miles | 20 feet | Loop
Nymph, Dream, and Emerald Lakes | Moderate | 3.3 miles | 700 feet | Out-and-back
Hallett Peak | Strenuous | 9.6 miles | 3,300 feet | Out-and-back
Trailhead: Bear Lake (3)

Bear Lake is a short and flat loop around a nice lake. Check it out but stick around to get deeper into the park.

Walking to Nymph, Dream, and Emerald Lakes probably returns the most bang for your effort. The journey becomes a little more difficult from each successive lake but it's never a daunting task. Dream Lake is the location you'll most frequently see on Rocky Mountain marketing materials. With that said, don't take a look at it and turn around. Continue to Emerald. As a high-reward/low-effort trail, it's the most popular destination in the park, making it a good one to do in the off-season (even winter!). If you have more energy, walk over to Lake Haiyaha. An avalanche turned its alpine water green in 2022! Green, blue, or anything else in the visible spectrum, it's another pretty place.

The shores of Dream and Emerald Lakes are essential Rocky Mountain National Park destinations but how about hiking to the top of the peak standing prominently behind them? That's Hallett Peak and it's one heck of a hike! The grade increases one mile in, when you turn onto Flattop Mountain Trail. Don't worry, in less than a mile you'll come to a viewpoint directly above Dream Lake. Catch your breath and enjoy peering all the way to Longs Peak. By the time you reach the Emerald Lake Overlook, you'll have climbed above the tree line and soon you'll find the type of vast rocky terrain for which this mountain range is named.

All these trails begin at the ultra-popular Bear Lake Trailhead. There's a huge parking lot, but it fills up all the time in summer and popular weekends (taking the shuttle is a good idea during peak season).

Odessa/Fern Lake | Strenuous | 11.5–13.9 miles | 3,300 feet | Loop
Trailhead: Bear Lake (3), Bierstadt Lake (4), Fern Lake (6)

Looking for a loop? Yeah, I know, we all are. Rocky Mountain has those too! This trek to Odessa and Fern Lakes is about as good as it gets. It's a little on the long side but with regular rewards found along the way, you'll likely enjoy every moment. Loop direction doesn't matter much. My typical goal is to end with the best scenery, so it'd be counterclockwise from Bear Lake Trailhead or Clockwise from Fern Lake Trailhead. Choosing a trailhead is about more than just parking. Difference in mileage and elevation gain is not a trivial matter here. The highlighted loop is about 11.5 miles beginning at Bear Lake. It's more like 13 miles from Bierstadt Lake. And it stretches out to 14 miles from Fern Lake Trailhead (unpaved access road). You can also reach the loop from Hollowell Park Trailhead. With an abundance of waterfalls, this area is spectacular after a nice heavy rain (although you'll have mud to contend with). This is also a trail you must be prepared for snow and ice hanging around. But it's also one of your better options to escape the peak-season Bear Lake crowds, while still enjoying Bear Lake-level scenery. Regardless of season or trailhead, be sure to keep your eyes open for an unmarked trail near Lake Helene. It's difficult to argue anything other than Odessa Lake with Little Matterhorn towering in the background as the finest scenery along this loop, but Lake Helene is not too shabby (and you'd likely walk right by if you aren't looking). With an abundance of exceptional hiking choices, this is one of the best.

Sprague Lake | Easy | 1.0 mile | 20 feet | Loop
Trailhead: Sprague Lake (5)

This short, easy, packed-gravel loop around Sprague Lake is a popular sunrise and sunset destination, not only because it's beautiful but also because the lake is next to the parking area and Estes Park is about twenty minutes away.

YPSILON LAKE/LAWN LAKE

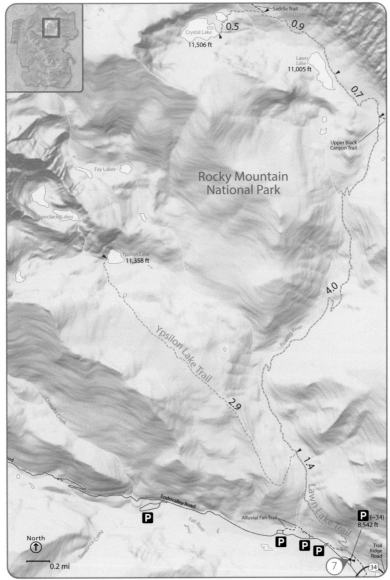

Ypsilon Lake | Strenuous | 8.5 miles | 2,900 feet | Out-and-back
Lawn/Crystal Lake | Strenuous | 14.9 miles | 3,000 feet | Out-and-back
Trailhead: Lawn Lake (7)

These trails begin by climbing above an alluvial fan, an eroded ravine formed in 1982 when the upstream Lawn Lake Dam burst releasing 30 million

LAKE OF THE CLOUDS/SKELETON GULCH

cubic feet of water, killing three people, and causing millions of dollars in damage. That'll give you something to think about as you make the almost continuous climb to either destination. And the destinations are similar in that more compelling scenery exists beyond them. From Ypsilon Lake, some adventurous hikers scramble up to Spectacle Lakes. (Don't do anything that makes you uncomfortable.) And Crystal Lake is nestled in the Rockies about a mile-and-a-half beyond Lawn Lake. These lakes aren't quite as stunning as those found in the Bear Lake area, but the lighter foot traffic is sure to be refreshing on a summer weekend.

Lake of the Clouds | Strenuous | 12.6 miles | 2,600 feet | Out-and-back
Skeleton Gulch | Moderate | 13.0 miles | 1,900 feet | Out-and-back
Trailhead: Colorado River (8)

At an incredibly popular park like Rocky Mountain, it's nice to have a few unpopular choices. Lake of the Clouds and Skeleton Gulch are near the top of that list. They're long. They're kind of tough. They share a strange feature, Grand Ditch, a non-public road running all the way to Little Yellowstone. And they also offer tranquility. Lake of the Clouds has a prettier conclusion.

Skeleton Gulch is mostly easy walking, except for a steep climb to Grand Ditch. It's also a good choice for a backpacking trip with a lone camp site nestled in the gulch. In a long day, a determined hiker could loop the two destinations together (17 miles), spending a lot of time walking Grand Ditch, which is considerably easier travel than most Rocky Mountain trails.

Young moose near Little Yellowstone

Shuttle

Free shuttles provide access to Bear Lake Road during peak season. Catch them at Beaver Meadows Visitor Center, Moraine Park or Glacier Basin Campground, and Estes Park Visitor Center. Get an early start or use the shuttle.

Timed Entry

A timed-entry system for Trail Ridge Road and Bear Lake Road has been in place since 2021. You can find current information at recreation.gov. Chances are, you'll need a permit May through mid-October, entering between 9am and 3pm. Earlier or later, no permit required.

More Trails

With over 350 miles of trails, there are many enjoyable options. Tundra Communities (easy, 1.0 mile) is a pleasant place to stretch your legs along Trail Ridge Road. Ute Trail near the Alpine Visitor Center is a good spot for sunset photos looking toward the Never Summer Mountains. And there are many more miles at Wild Basin, Lumpy Ridge, Cow Creek, East Inlet, and North Inlet trailheads.

Great Sand Dunes
Hiking Trails: 50+ miles

Sand dunes have ridges

Great Sand Dunes Favorites

1 **High Dune**
Strenuous | 3.1 miles | 650 feet

2 **Dunes Overlook**
Moderate | 1.9 miles | 450 feet

3 **Medano Lake**
Strenuous | 6.7 miles | 2,000 feet

4 **Sand Creek Lakes**
Strenuous | 9.5 miles | 2,000 feet

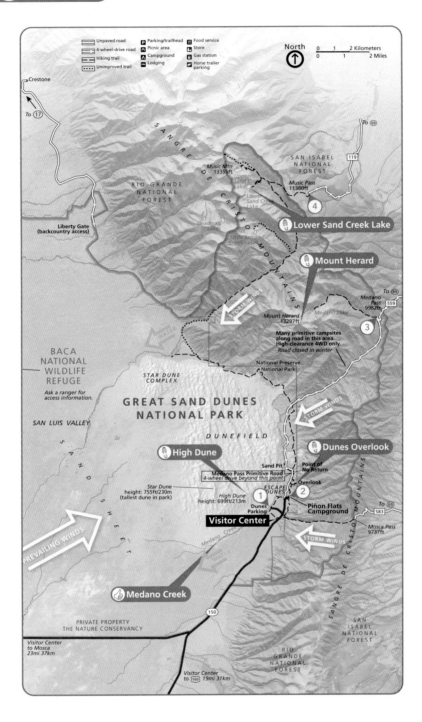

North

Unpaved road	P Parking/trailhead	¶ Food service
4-wheel-drive road	A Picnic area	Store
Hiking trail	A Campground	Gas station
Unimproved trail	Lodging	Horse trailer parking

0 1 2 Kilometers
0 1 2 Miles

To 17

Crestone

SANGRE DE CRISTO MOUNTAINS

RIO GRANDE NATIONAL FOREST

Music Mtn 13355ft

Upper Sand Creek Lake

Lower Sand Creek Lake

Deadman Lake

Little Sand Creek Lake

Liberty Gate (backcountry access)

To 69

SAN ISABEL NATIONAL FOREST

119

Music Pass 11380ft

4

Lower Sand Creek Lake

Mount Herard

To 69

Medano Pass 9982ft

559

Mount Herard 13297ft

Medano Lake

3

STORM WINDS

WATER

Many primitive campsites along road in this area. High-clearance 4WD only. Road closed in winter

BACA NATIONAL WILDLIFE REFUGE

Ask a ranger for access information.

SAN LUIS VALLEY

STAR DUNE COMPLEX

National Preserve
National Park

GREAT SAND DUNES NATIONAL PARK

DUNEFIELD

STORM WINDS

High Dune

Dunes Overlook

Sand Pit

Point of No Return

Medano Pass Primitive Road 4-wheel drive beyond this point

Overlook

ESCAPE DUNES

2

Star Dune height: 755ft/230m (tallest dune in park)

High Dune height: 699ft/213m

1

Dunes Parking

Piñon Flats Campground

To 69

583

Visitor Center

Mosca Pass 9737ft

PREVAILING WINDS

Medano Creek

STORM WINDS

SAND SHEET

Medano Creek

150

PRIVATE PROPERTY THE NATURE CONSERVANCY

SANGRE DE CRISTO MOUNTAINS

SAN ISABEL NATIONAL FOREST

Visitor Center to Mosca 23mi 37km

Visitor Center to 160 19mi 31km

RIO GRANDE NATIONAL FOREST

HIGH DUNE/DUNES OVERLOOK

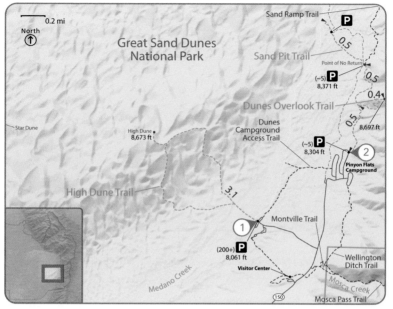

High Dune | Strenuous | 3.1 miles | 650 feet | Lollipop
Trailhead: Dunes Parking Lot (1)

High Dune isn't the tallest dune in the park, but it is the tallest visible dune from Dunes Parking Lot, making it the park's most popular "hike." Since the surface is a giant sand box, there's no marked path telling you where to go. There's also no right or wrong way to get there. Just hard and harder. The "easy" way is to follow the ridgelines. From Dunes Parking Lot, cross Medano Creek (you may need to take off your shoes) and continue directly to the dunefield. To your right (north), follow the most prominent ridgeline (likely featuring many footprints). Follow it up to a long, respectably-wide ridge running mostly east and west. High Dune will once again be a prominent landmark to the west. At this point, there shouldn't be any confusion about what route to take. It involves a short, relatively steep climb before the ridge tapers off and stretches into the distance (some visitors like to enjoy the sunset from this perch). Bounding down giant sand dunes is one of life's great joys. So, I'd suggest choosing your own path back and have all the fun frolicking among the dunes. If not, you can return as you came or there's another set of fairly-easy-to-follow ridges heading south near the short, steep climb up to the back of High Dune. It's slightly steeper than the way you came.

While hiking the dunes barefoot is ideal, the sand gets unbearably hot on warm sunny days. Choose your shoes carefully. Ones that will easily allow sand to sneak into them will be nearly as annoying as walking barefoot across sole-scorching sand.

MEDANO LAKE

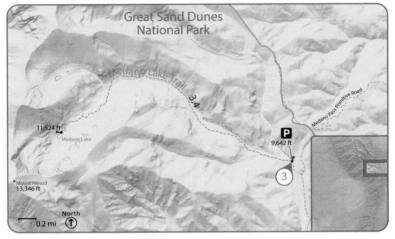

Great Sand Dunes
National Park

Medano Lake Trail

3.4

Medano Creek

11,524 ft

Medano Lake

Medano Pass Primitive Road

P
9,642 ft

③

• Mount Herard
13,346 ft

0.2 mi North ↑

Dunes Overlook | Moderate | 1.9 miles | 450 feet | Out-and-back
Trailhead: Pinon Flats Campground (2)

Not a must-hike, but Dunes Overlook is often a peaceful escape from the crowds congregating near Dunes Parking Lot. You can reach the trail directly from the back of Loop 2 at Pinon Flats Campground or drive down Medano Pass Primitive Road and park at Point of No Return, where you'll find another trailhead. Most vehicles should be able to make it to Point of No Return, no problem. Beyond that, things typically get a little sandier, but most vehicles should also be able to make it to Sand Pit, which is another fun, more peaceful area of the park. You can also hike to Sand Pit from Point of No Return. If you're really looking to get away from things, consider heading out on Sand Ramp Trail (22 miles roundtrip) from Point of No Return. It follows the edge of the dunefield all the way to the foot of Star Dune Complex (the highest elevation dunes in the park). There are backcountry campsites along the way.

Medano Lake | Strenuous | 6.7 miles | 2,000 feet | Out-and-back
Trailhead: Medano Pass (3)

First thing to know is that you'll need a 4x4 to reach the trailhead. You can access the trailhead from either direction on Medano Pass Primitive Road. If you're coming from the dunefield, it's a long, slow slog up, crossing Medano Creek several times along the way. And the road near the dunefield can be challenging for another reason … sand. It's a good idea to lower your air pressure. If you don't carry a pump, there's one near the RV dump station next to Pinon Flats Campground. Of course, that only helps if you're traveling Medano Pass Primitive Road from east to west (which is the recommended direction). As for the trail. It's less than four miles to a beautiful (but small) alpine lake. The lake is worth visiting on its own merit, but many hikers like to take things

SAND CREEK LAKES

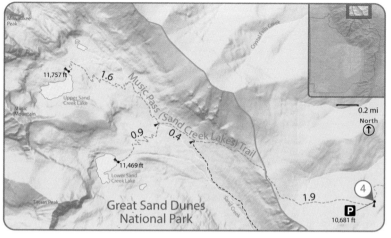

Milwaukee Peak

11,757 ft

1.6

Music Pass (Sand Creek Lakes) Trail

Crystal Falls Creek

0.2 mi

North

Upper Sand Creek Lake

Music Mountain

0.9

0.4

11,469 ft

Lower Sand Creek Lake

Tijeras Peak

Great Sand Dunes National Park

Sand Creek

1.9

4

P

10,681 ft

a step further, hiking roughly another mile-and-a-half (one-way) to the top of Mount Herard, where you can enjoy an aerial view of the massive dunefield. What you want to do is look for cairns leading up the slope on the righthand side (north) of the lake. About halfway there, you'll reach a ridgeline. Follow it (past a false summit) to the open mountaintop. Like with all 4x4 roads and high-elevation trails, it's a good idea to contact the park and ask about current conditions. Snow hangs around up here well into summer.

Sand Creek Lakes | Strenuous | 9.5 miles | 2,000 feet | Out-and-back
Trailhead: Music Pass (4)

A high-clearance 4x4 unlocks some more stunning scenery. It'll take a bit of rocking and rolling to get up here, but once you do, you've got all day to walk to (and enjoy) two picturesque alpine lakes. Hiking both lakes measures about ten miles. If for some reason you only have time for one, go with Lower. Rumor has it, this is also popular cutthroat trout country. So, if you enjoy fishing, bring your rod and tackle (obeying all regulations, of course).

More Info

The park is quite pleasant outside the busy summer tourist season. Yes, snow hangs around in the mountains, and it can begin falling as early as September in the high elevations, but daytime highs regularly reach the 50s (and occasionally higher) in November/December. That's great hiking weather, and who wouldn't love to see these undulating dunes blanketed in a fresh sheet of snow? Just come prepared for it. The 'low' flats surrounding the dunefield are still above 7,000 feet. No matter when you visit, spend at least one night. Playful light crossing the sand's undulating ridges is very fun to observe.

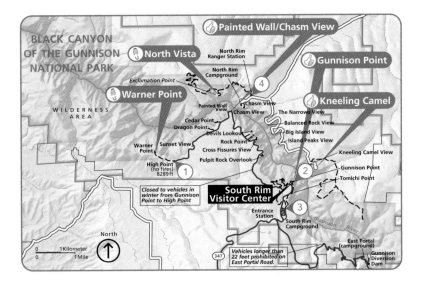

Narrows View (North Rim)

Black Canyon of the Gunnison
Hiking Trails: 20+ miles

Map Labels

BLACK CANYON OF THE GUNNISON NATIONAL PARK

WILDERNESS AREA

Painted Wall/Chasm View

North Vista

North Rim Ranger Station

North Rim Campground

Exclamation Point

Gunnison Point

Warner Point

Kneeling Camel

Painted Wall View

Chasm View

Chasm View

The Narrows View

Cedar Point

Balanced Rock View

Dragon Point

Big Island View

Devils Lookout

Island Peaks View

Rock Point

Warner Point

Sunset View

Cross Fissures View

Kneeling Camel View

Pulpit Rock Overlook

Gunnison Point

High Point (no fires) 8289ft

Tomichi Point

Closed to vehicles in winter from Gunnison Point to High Point

South Rim Visitor Center

Entrance Station

South Rim Campground

Gunnison River

East Portal (campground)

Gunnison Diversion Dam

North

0 1 Kilometer
0 1 Mile

347

Vehicles longer than 22 feet prohibited on East Portal Road.

Black Canyon of the Gunnison Favorites

① **Warner Point**
Moderate | 1.5 miles | 150 feet

④ **North Vista**
Strenuous | 6.7 miles | 1,100 feet

②-③ **Rim Rock/Oak Flat**
Strenuous | 3.3 miles | 800 feet

WARNER POINT

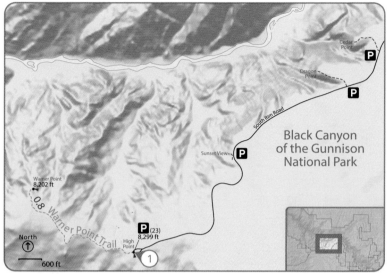

Warner Point | Moderate | 1.5 miles | 150 feet | Out-and-back
Trailhead: High Point, South Rim (1)

Most of the South Rim views come with very little effort. Park, walk a few hundred feet, and then you're staring into the depths of Black Canyon. Warner Point takes slightly more effort. The reward is peering down at the Gunnison River as it runs through the deepest section of canyon. But how deep is it? Well, it's 2,722 feet deep. That's so deep the tip of Burj Kalifa—a preposterously tall building—would just reach the canyon's rim. You'd need to stack ten Statues of Liberty on top of each other until the tenth Lady Liberty's eyes caught sight of the distant horizon. The trail is mostly flat and easy to follow, with the opportunity to scramble around at its conclusion (or continue to the canyon floor via the steep and strenuous Warner Route).

The trailhead is located at the end of South Rim Road. This is one of the park's most popular trails and there's only parking for about twenty vehicles. The normal thing would be to suggest an early start, but the view is to the east toward Serpent Point. Yes, it's a pretty good sunrise location, but if you want to see the canyon's impressive depth in the most flattering light, show up in the evening. Better yet, do both!

Warner Point

RIM ROCK/OAK FLAT/UPLANDS

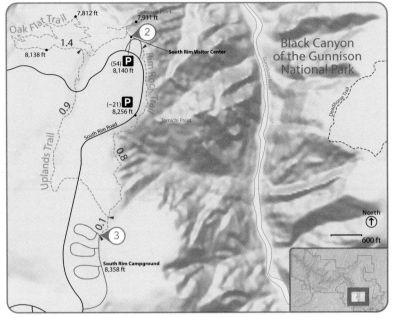

Rim Rock/Oak Flat/Uplands | Strenuous | 3.3 miles | 800 feet | Figure 8
Trailhead: South Rim Visitor Center (2), Tomichi Point, or South Rim Campground (3)

Warner Point is the deepest section of canyon. Painted Wall is the most marketed chunk of rock. It's awesome, but, in my opinion, the canyon around Gunnison Point and Oak Flat (and Kneeling Camel on the North Rim) is the most striking. Hiking this loop in its entirety isn't a huge undertaking, but Uplands (the only section open to pets) is less exciting than the rest. Rim Rock is an easy walk above the Rim, and Oak Flat takes you beneath it. To access Gunnison Point and Oak Flat, follow the stairs behind the visitor center.

More Trails

Deadhorse Trail (moderate, 5.0 miles) is mentioned briefly and its loop appears on the Rim Rock map above. If you're spending more than the typical "day in a park", check it out. You'll walk over to seldom-visited viewpoints, looking back at some of the most compelling canyon sections. Not all trails stay above the canyon's rim. There are seven inner canyon routes and they're no joke. Very steep (sometimes aided by chains). Strenuous. Often walking atop loose rock. Gunnison Route (3.0 miles), beginning near South Rim Visitor Center, is a good first choice. S.O.B. Draw (3.5 miles), beginning near the Ranger Station is the easiest North Rim option. Long Draw (2.0 miles) provides access to the narrowest section of canyon (about 40 feet wide). Slide Draw (2.0 miles) is a good choice if you're looking for more difficulty. Tomichi (2.0 miles) is the steepest route on the South Rim. Finally, the longest and easiest route into the canyon is Red Rock Canyon. The trail is easier because the canyon isn't as imposing. But, because the trail crosses private land, a permit is required (via lottery).

NORTH VISTA

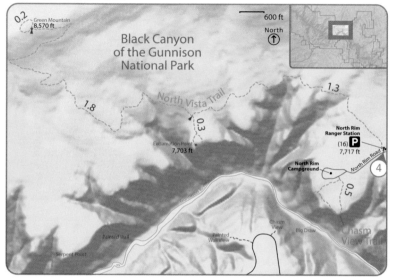

Green Mountain
8,570 ft

600 ft

North
↑

Black Canyon
of the Gunnison
National Park

1.3

1.8

North Vista Trail

0.3

North Rim
Ranger Station
(16) P
7,717 ft

Exclamation Point
7,703 ft

North Rim
Campground

North Rim Road

4

0.5

Chasm
View

Big Draw

Chasm
View Trail

Painted Wall

Painted
Wall View

Serpent Point

North Vista | Strenuous | 6.7 miles | 1,100 feet | Out-and-back
Trailhead: North Rim Ranger Station (4)

North Rim visitation is light. The unpaved access road is well-maintained and suitable for any vehicle, but it closes in winter. The primary rim-top hike on this side of the Gunnison is North Vista. But, while the view from Exclamation Point is good, views along the road (or Chasm View Trail) are just as nice or better (especially at sites like The Narrows and Kneeling Camel). Still, it's a decent trail to enjoy the peace and quiet, along with a couple canyon vistas. Walking to Exclamation Point Loop is easy, with a few modest ups and downs. Watch for the sign at the trail junction. It's out in the open but you could easily miss it if you're staring at your feet or carrying on a conversation. Continuing on, views from the top of Green Mountain are considerably less inspiring and the trail becomes more strenuous. There's a short loop at the summit but things are most interesting looking south from the steps leading up to the loop. If time is limited and you're trying to prioritize, I'd go to Exclamation Point and return to the Ranger Station, and then hike Chasm View and/or Deadhorse trails.

Exclamation Point

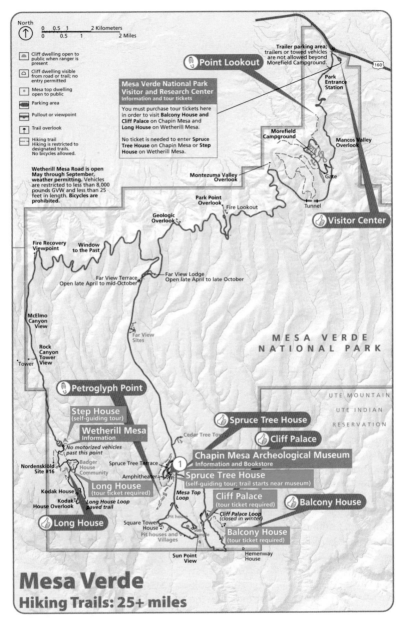

North

| 0 | 0.5 | 1 | 2 Kilometers |
| 0 | 0.5 | 1 | 2 Miles |

Cliff dwelling open to public when ranger is present

Cliff dwelling visible from road or trail; no entry permitted

Mesa top dwelling open to public

Parking area

Pullout or viewpoint

Trail overlook

Hiking trail
Hiking is restricted to designated trails. No bicycles allowed.

Wetherill Mesa Road is open May through September, weather permitting. Vehicles are restricted to less than 8,000 pounds GVW and less than 25 feet in length. Bicycles are prohibited.

Point Lookout

Trailer parking area; trailers or towed vehicles are not allowed beyond Morefield Campground.

Park Entrance Station

160

Mesa Verde National Park Visitor and Research Center
Information and tour tickets

You must purchase tour tickets here in order to visit Balcony House and Cliff Palace on Chapin Mesa and Long House on Wetherill Mesa.

No ticket is needed to enter Spruce Tree House on Chapin Mesa or Step House on Wetherill Mesa.

Morefield Campground

Mancos Valley Overlook

Gate

Montezuma Valley Overlook

Park Point Overlook
Fire Lookout

Tunnel

Visitor Center

Geologic Overlook

Fire Recovery Viewpoint
Window to the Past

Far View Lodge
Open late April to late October

Far View Terrace
Open late April to mid-October

McElmo Canyon View

Far View Sites

MESA VERDE NATIONAL PARK

Rock Canyon Tower View

Tower

Petroglyph Point

UTE MOUNTAIN

UTE INDIAN

RESERVATION

Step House
(self-guiding tour)

Spruce Tree House

Wetherill Mesa
Information

Cedar Tree Tower

Cliff Palace

Chapin Mesa Archeological Museum
Information and Bookstore

No motorized vehicles past this point

Spruce Tree Terrace

Nordenskiöld Site #16

Badger House Community

Amphitheater

Spruce Tree House
(self-guiding tour; trail starts near museum)

Kodak House

Long House
(tour ticket required)

Mesa Top Loop

Cliff Palace
(tour ticket required)

Kodak House Overlook

Long House Loop paved trail

Cliff Palace Loop
(closed in winter)

Balcony House

Long House

Square Tower House

Pit houses and Villages

Pit house

Balcony House
(tour ticket required)

Sun Point View

Hemenway House

Mesa Verde
Hiking Trails: 25+ miles

Mesa Verde Favorite

① **Petroglyph Point**
Moderate | 2.6 miles | 400 feet

PETROGLYPH POINT

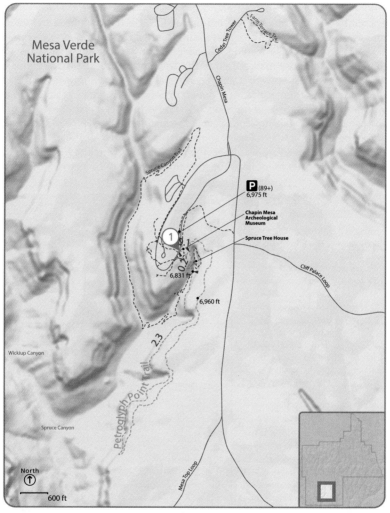

Petroglyph Point | Moderate | 2.6 miles | 400 feet | Loop
Trailhead: Chapin Mesa Archeological Museum (1)

Petroglyph Point is a pleasant surprise. It's short but there are a few things you need to know. The trailhead is gated. If you plan on arriving early, be sure to check online for when the gate opens. With that said, you can usually start in a clockwise direction and by the time you reach the gate near Spruce Tree House, it'll be open. Or vice versa, start late at the gate and you must complete the loop to return to your vehicle. Hikers are expected to register at the trailhead. The hike is not easy. You descend into Spruce Canyon, then work your way back up, contouring the western cliff. Along the way you'll encounter stone stairs (some very narrow) and a tight squeeze between massive boulders. Overall, it's pretty fun. The trail was intended to be done in a counterclockwise fashion (based on a now out-of-print trail guide matching numbered markers along the way), but it doesn't matter which way you go (unless you are starting early or late, of course!). However, if you do it clockwise, there isn't a sign directing you onto the trail, resulting in a well-worn false path leading hikers astray. No big deal, just know to hug the canyon's rim, walking around (and above) Spruce Tree House. Clockwise would be my choice, as it leaves some fun rock features for the end of your hike. Spruce Tree House would be the coolest thing you'll see in this area, but it's been closed for quite some time due to stability concerns.

Cliff Dwellings

Mesa Verde is unique among National Parks as its main attraction isn't all about nature. It's about culture. More exactly, it's about cliff dwellings left behind by Ancestral Puebloans. There are many. You used to be able to tour Spruce Tree House on your own, but it's been closed for several years due to stability concerns. Step House (Wetherill Mesa) is now the only cliff dwelling open to self-guided tours. Cliff Palace, Balcony House, and Long House can be seen on ranger-guided tours for about half the year. Tickets can be reserved at recreation.gov or stop at the visitor center near the entrance when you arrive. They also offer infrequent tours to five other cliff dwellings as well as sunrise (Balcony House) and twilight (Cliff Palace) tours. Those tickets are also sold through recreation.gov.

Petroglyph Point

More Trails

There are a few more trails. Point Lookout (strenuous, 2.2 miles) is a great option, especially if you're staying at the campground. Knife Edge (easy, 2.0 miles) and Prater Ridge (strenuous, 7.8 miles) provide views looking back to Cortez. You can also get a similar view by making the extremely short hike up to Montezuma Valley Overlook, which is a very good idea. Even though there aren't many trails here, expect to do quite a bit of walking exploring all the cultural sites. They're the real highlight!

Arches
Hiking Trails: 15+ miles

Delicate Arch (sunrise)

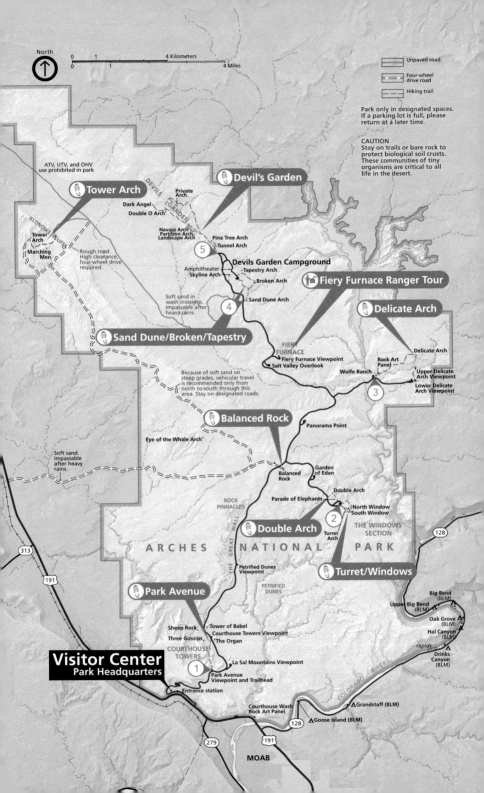

Arches Favorites

1 **Park Avenue**
Moderate | 1.9 miles | 300 feet

2 **The Windows**
Easy | 2.2 miles | 200 feet

3 **Delicate Arch**
Moderate | 3.2 miles | 700 feet

4 **Broken Arch**
Moderate | 2.6 miles | 200 feet

5 **Devil's Garden**
Strenuous | 7.8 miles | 1,100 feet

PARK AVENUE

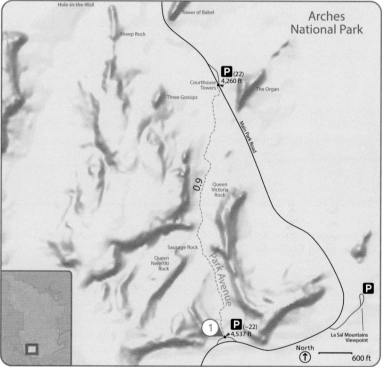

Park Avenue | Moderate | 1.9 miles | 300 feet | Out-and-back
Trailhead: Park Avenue (1)

Park Avenue is most visitor's introduction to Arches. But you won't find a single arch along the trail. Even without them, it's very cool. You'll be treated to towering sandstone spires and red rock fins (which in a few hundred thousand or so years might become arches too). The trail is only a mile long (one-way), and if you have a person or two in your group who aren't interested in the downhill walk, they can stop at La Sal Mountains Viewpoint and pick up the hikers by Courthouse Towers. Otherwise, return as you came.

WINDOWS/TURRET/DOUBLE ARCH

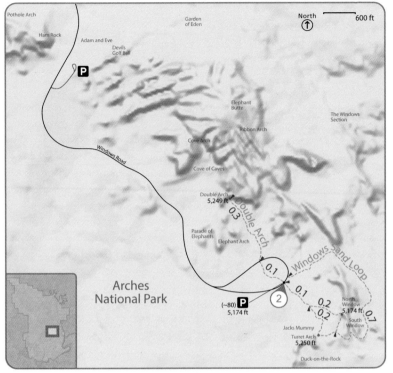

The Windows/Turret Arch/Double Arch | Easy | 2.2 miles | 200 feet | Loop & Out-and-back | **Trailhead:** The Windows (2)

Windows is a perfect example of what Arches is all about … low effort, high reward nature at its finest! Windows is a very popular sunrise/sunset destination. As you might imagine, the sun (and the moon) are often seen poking through the massive sandstone windows. But there's more. Do not go here, look through (and stand in) a Window or two and get back on the road. You have to check out the other arches. Turret Arch is nearby. And my favorite arch of this collection, Double Arch, is a short walk to the northwest. Two Windows, two arches (one a double!), all enjoyed in a little more than two miles of low-intensity walking. Jackpot!

Delicate Arch | Moderate | 3.2 miles | 700 feet | Out-and-back
Trailhead: Wolfe Ranch (3)

This is a great trail! Many guests curse the not-too-steep-but-kind-of-relentless hill that kicks things off (and a few turn back, especially in summer when afternoon highs regularly hit triple digits), but once you've crested that massive

DELICATE ARCH

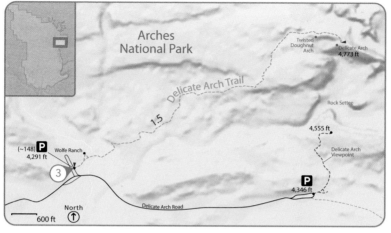

red rock, it's all pretty easy walking to one of the most dramatic settings in all the parks. Just as you're coming to Twisted Doughnut Arch (watch for it up and to your right), the trail narrows and the north side drops off. It's cliff-like but don't worry, the fear factor is low. If there are a lot of people on the trail and you don't want to walk near the cliff, just step to the side and let them pass. From there, it's one last big step up into the bowl where Delicate Arch resides. It is an incredibly special place and everyone knows it. The parking area is large but it's still a good idea to go in the morning or evening, for smaller crowds and better lighting.

If you're thinking about skipping Delicate Arch Trail in favor of Upper Delicate Arch Viewpoint. Don't. You can get a good view of Delicate Arch from the viewpoint with a long lens or binoculars, but with the naked eye, it looks tiny. And it's quite the climb (220 feet) to reach the upper viewpoint, where you'll have a half-way decent vantage point. So, if it's one or the other, go with Delicate Arch Trail. Both trails require a similar level of effort but the rewards are nowhere near the same. If you want to do both? Go for it!

Sand Dune Arch/Broken Arch/Tapestry Arch | Moderate | 2.6 miles | 200 feet | Out-and-back | **Trailhead:** Sand Dune Arch (4)

Another thing about Arches hikes is … they're really fun! This one is no exception. You can start from Sand Dune Arch Parking Area or Devil's Garden Campground (a wonderful convenience if you scored a campsite!). Departing from Sand Dune Arch, the trailhead's namesake arch is right around the corner. I'd take a peek and see how many people are in front of you, heading into the rock jumble where the arch resides. If it's a bunch, walk on by. If it's a few, go on in. Note that it is a little sandy walking between the sandstone walls that guide you to this secluded arch. The next destination is Broken Arch. The trail

SAND DUNE/BROKEN/TAPESTRY ARCHES

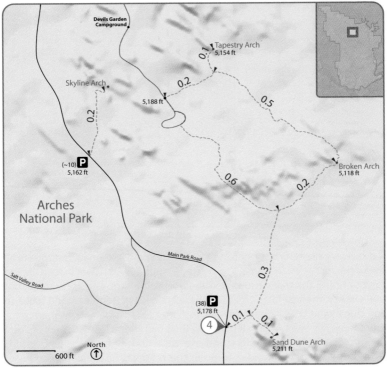

passes through it! Signs lead to Tapestry Arch, the least visited (but no less spectacular) arch of this trifecta. Now you might be tempted to return the way you came, thinking "who wants to walk through a campground?" That's the wrong train of thought. 1). Devil's Garden is one of the better campgrounds in the park system. It's not real high on privacy (like most) but the setting is exceptional, and that's what you'll enjoy hiking back to the trailhead.

Skyline Arch is also worth a quick stop. It's just a half-mile walk to the arch and back, and there are some rocks to fool around on near its base.

Devil's Garden | Strenuous | 7.8 miles | 1,100 feet | Loop
Trailhead: Devil's Garden (5)

Devil's Garden is the longest and most difficult of Arches' maintained trails. If you're evn the least bit hesitant about doing a little scrambling, do the loop clockwise. Beyond Landscape Arch, things get more rugged (actually the most rugged of the entire loop), providing a good early indicator if you'll be comfortable on this trail. It's nothing crazy, just traversing some rocks. Overall, the trail is well-marked and a good use of your park time. Hitting up all the spurs, you're looking at right around eight miles.

DEVIL'S GARDEN

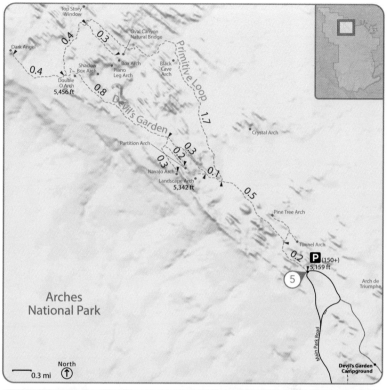

Top Story Window

Dark Angel

0.4

0.3

Oval Canyon Natural Bridge

Primitive Loop

0.4

Shadow Box Arch

Box Arch

Piano Leg Arch

Black Cave Arch

Double O Arch
5,456 ft

0.8

Devil's Garden

1.7

Crystal Arch

Partition Arch

0.3

0.2

0.3

Navajo Arch

Landscape Arch
5,342 ft

0.1

0.5

Pine Tree Arch

Tunnel Arch

0.2

P (150+)
5,159 ft

5

Arch de Triumphe

Arches
National Park

Main Park Road

Devil's Garden Campground

North
0.3 mi

Popularity & Ticketed Entry

Arches is a small park that receives huge crowds. Before the ticketed entry program, visitors could spend a lot of time waiting in their vehicles just to enter the park. That is not what anyone wants to be doing on their vacation. If the park is busy, you can enter via Salt Valley Road (unpaved) or Willow Flats Road (the park suggests 4x4) from US-191. It's also a good idea to check out other public land in the area. This corner of the country is home to some of the planet's finest scenery (including Canyonlands and Capitol Reef featured in the next two sections!).

Due to overwhelming popularity, the park implemented a ticketed entry program. Find all the details at recreation.gov.

More Trails

There are only a few more trails. Balanced Rock (easy, 0.3 mile) is a very short nature trail. It's impossible to miss Balanced Rock. The park road goes right by it. While the trail is nice, you can get a better view of Balanced Rock with the La Sal Mountains in the background by heading over to the picnic area on Willow Flats Road just to the west of the Main Park Road (evening light is best). And then there's Tower Arch (strenuous, 2.6 miles) on Salt Valley Road (an alternative park entry point from the north). It's another short, fun hike! You can almost drive directly to Tower Arch using a 4x4 road. However, I checked it out and gave it an immediate "nope." But I'm almost always on my own and play things a bit conservatively, especially when it comes to off-roading.

Fiery Furnace

Try to reserve space on a Fiery Furnace Ranger tour (recreation.gov). The park suggests joining a ranger tour your first time through the furnace. Do that and then you can explore it on your own (permit required). On your own or with a ranger, you'll love it!

Double Arch (Arches)

Canyonlands
Hiking Trails: 200+ miles

Joint Trail

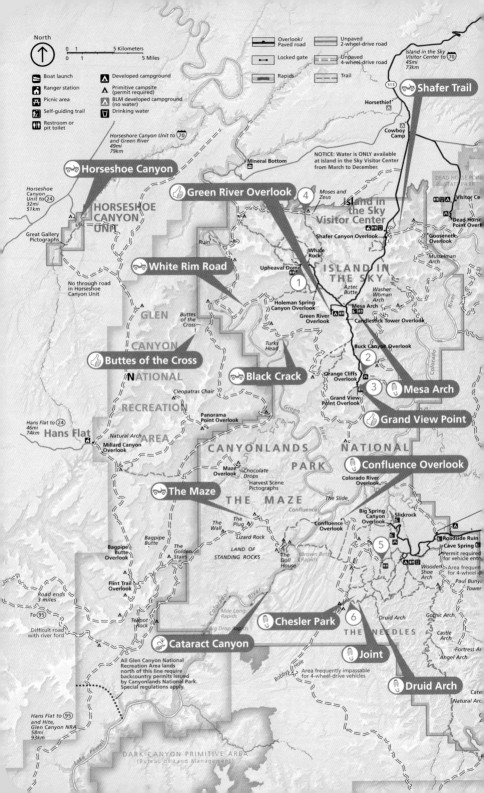

North

0   1   5 Kilometers
0   1   5 Miles

🚣 Boat launch
🏠 Ranger station
🏞 Picnic area
🥾 Self-guiding trail
🚻 Restroom or pit toilet

▲ Developed campground
△ Primitive campsite (permit required)
⧊ BLM developed campground (no water)
🚰 Drinking water

▭ Overlook/Paved road
⊶ Locked gate
▬ Rapids

▭ Unpaved 2-wheel-drive road
▭ Unpaved 4-wheel-drive road
▭ Trail

Horseshoe Canyon Unit to 70
49mi
79km

NOTICE: Water is ONLY available at Island in the Sky Visitor Center from March to December.

Island in the Sky Visitor Center to 70
45mi
73km

🚙 Shafer Trail

Horsethief

Cowboy Camp

🚙 Horseshoe Canyon

Mineral Bottom

Horseshoe Canyon Unit to 24
32mi
51km

HORSESHOE CANYON UNIT

👍 Green River Overlook   ④

Moses and Zeus

Island in the Sky Visitor Center

313

DEAD HORSE POINT STATE PARK

Visitor Ce

Dead Horse Point Overl

Great Gallery Pictographs

Shafer Canyon Overlook

Gooseneck Overlook

Musselman Arch

🚗 White Rim Road

Ruin

Whale Rock

ISLAND IN THE SKY

Upheaval Dome   ①

Aztec Butte

Washer Woman Arch

No through road in Horseshoe Canyon Unit

GLEN

Holeman Spring Canyon Overlook

Green River Overlook

Mesa Arch

Candlestick Tower Overlook

Colorado River

Buttes of the Cross

CANYON

Turks Head

Buck Canyon Overlook   ②

👍 Buttes of the Cross

NATIONAL

🚗 Black Crack

Orange Cliffs Overlook

🥾 Mesa Arch

Hans Flat to 24
46mi
74km

Hans Flat

RECREATION

Cleopatras Chair

Natural Arch
Millard Canyon Overlook

Panorama Point Overlook

Grand View Point Overlook   ③

👍 Grand View Point

AREA

CANYONLANDS   NATIONAL

🥾 Confluence Overlook

🚗 The Maze

Maze Overlook

Chocolate Drops

Harvest Scene Pictographs

PARK

Colorado River Overlook

THE   MAZE

The Slide

Confluence

Big Spring Canyon Overlook

Slickrock

Bagpipe Butte Overlook

Bagpipe Butte

The Plug

The Wall

Lizard Rock

LAND OF STANDING ROCKS

Confluence Overlook   ⑤

Roadside Ruin

Cave Spring

Permit required for vehicle access

Flint Trail Overlook

The Golden Stairs

The Doll House

Brown Betty Rapids

Wooden Shoe Arch

Area frequently used for 4-wheel-d

Paul Bunyan Tower

Road ends 3 miles

To 95

Difficult road with river ford

Teapot Rock

Colorado River

Mile Long Rapids

Big Drop Rapids

🥾 Chesler Park   ⑥

Druid Arch

Gothic Arch

Castle Arch

THE   NEEDLES

Fortress Ar

Angel Arch

🚣 Cataract Canyon

All Glen Canyon National Recreation Area lands north of this line require backcountry permits issued by Canyonlands National Park. Special regulations apply.

🥾 Joint

Bobby Jo Hole

Area frequently impassable for 4-wheel-drive vehicles

🥾 Druid Arch

Cate

Natural Arc

Hans Flat to 95 and Hite, Glen Canyon NRA
58mi
93km

DARK CANYON PRIMITIVE AREA
(Bureau of Land Management)

Lake Powell

Moab to
30mi
48km

ARCHES
NATIONAL PARK

Moab
Grandstaff

Goose Island

Moab
Information
Center

Gold Bar

Jaycee Park

Petroglyphs

Kings Bottom

Moonflower

Williams
Bottom

Moab to Monticello
53mi
85km

Corona Arch

Anticline
Overlook

Potash

Hatch Point

The Needles
Visitor Center

Hamburger Rock

Needles Overlook to 191
22mi
35km

Creek
Pasture

Superbowl

Permit required
for vehicle entry

Needles
Visitor
Center
35mi
56km

Newspaper Rock
Petroglyphs

Moses & Zeus

Canyonlands Favorites

(1) Syncline Loop
Strenuous | 13.0 miles | 2,700 feet

(2) White Rim Overlook
Easy | 1.7 miles | 550 feet

(3) Grand View Point
Easy | 1.7 miles | 150 feet

(4) Moses & Zeus
Easy | 1.5 miles | 600 feet

(5) Chesler Park/Joint
Strenuous | 10.2 miles | 1,600 feet

Druid Arch
Strenuous | 10.0 miles | 1,300 feet

(6) Joint
Moderate | 1.4 miles | 600 feet

SYNCLINE LOOP/UPHEAVAL DOME

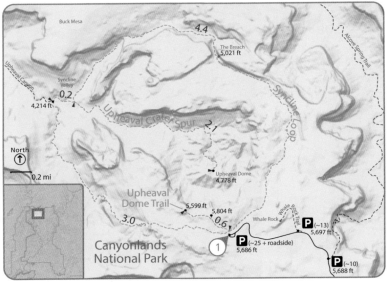

Syncline Loop/Upheaval Dome | Strenuous | 13.0 miles | 2,700 feet | Loop
Trailhead: Upheaval Dome (1)

If you're looking for a long hike at Island in the Sky, this is probably the one to do. The other choice would be Wilhite (12.2 miles, strenuous) which leads through some interesting terrain to White Rim Road. Syncline circles Upheaval Dome, an anomalous rock formation. There's been much speculation about the peculiar rock's origin. Speculating isn't my thing. But I can confirm, it looks pretty neat. No speculation required. Including the spurs to the Upheaval Dome Overlooks and dome itself, it's about 13 miles. That's a full-day hike for most. Considering how much fun stuff there is in this part of the country (in addition to better trails in Needles District), you'll want to research other activities before committing a day for Syncline Loop.

White Rim Overlook | Easy | 1.7 miles | 550 feet | Out-and-back
Trailhead: White Rim Overlook (2)

White Rim Overlook is a great alternative for two ultra-popular destinations. Mesa Arch is an unbelievably popular sunrise location. White Rim Overlook is great too! No arch, but that's okay. Bring a headlamp and get out to the overlook before the sun peeks out from the La Sal Mountains. It's also a great alternative if the parking area is full at Grand View Point. Full lot or not, stop at White Rim Overlook for a short walk and wonderful views any time of day as it's fairly centrally located above Monument Basin (the same funky rocks you look at from Grand View Point).

GRAND VIEW POINT

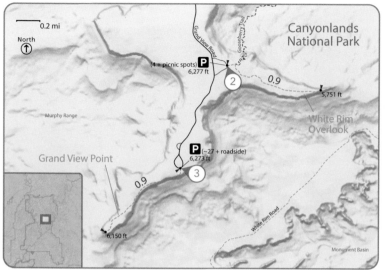

Grand View Point | Easy | 1.7 miles | 150 feet | Out-and-back
Trailhead: Grand View Point (3)

Grand View Point is well known for providing some of Canyonlands' most breathtaking vistas. This popular trail extends west to a rocky promontory, where a handful of visitors like to sit and enjoy the sunset each night. There aren't any guardrails protecting you from the cliff's edge, but, if you follow the cairns, you won't walk too close to it anyway. Personally, I feel like the views are better to the east. You can walk along the rim to the east as well (there isn't an official trail), and you'll enjoy some amazing views of Monument Basin below. (Or hike to White Rim Overlook!)

More Regions

Needles is the best region for long (10-mile and longer) hikes. Island in the Sky is best for short hikes. But there's more at Canyonlands. The Maze (4x4 required) is something of a "choose your own adventure" environment. As the name implies, orientation and navigation can be difficult, but it's not like you have to go far from your vehicle. The network of 4x4 roads is robust. And then there's Horseshoe Canyon, where you'll find ancient rock art. You can walk in from the north, east or south. All access roads are unpaved, and the north route is the only one that does not require a 4x4.

More Activities

Canyonlands is one of the most fun parks to explore with some curiosity. There are tons of wacky rocks and indescribable views, making it highly enjoyable to see the park from every angle. Hiking is the slow way to see what Canyonlands has to offer. Alternatively, Mountain biking, off-roading, and whitewater rafting are more expedient methods worth looking into.

MOSES & ZEUS

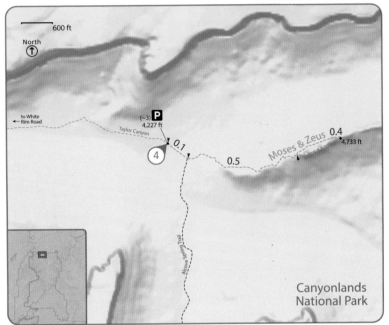

Moses & Zeus | Easy | 1.5 miles | 600 feet | Lollipop
Trailhead: Taylor (4)

Moses & Zeus is mentioned to draw your eyes to White Rim Road (4x4 required). This end of the 100-mile road isn't nearly as rugged as the east side and Lathrop Canyon (and you won't have wetness from the potash ponds to deal with). As a bonus, there's a solitary campsite in Taylor Canyon, which can be reserved through recreation.gov. The trail is short and sweet, meandering about some funky rocks, but the real treat is the drive down to the Green River.

Chesler Park/Joint | Strenuous | 10.2 miles | 1,600 feet | Lollipop
Trailhead: Elephant Hill (5)

This is truly fantastic hiking country. The Chesler Park lollipop highlighted in yellow gives you a great taste of the region. Plenty of Needles. Joint Trail, which is awesome! And, if you're feeling ambitious, adding Druid Arch onto it isn't a bad idea. The trail is well-marked and there aren't many points of confusion. There's a short spur to a lookout at the east end of Joint Trail. And at the west end of Joint Trail, you'll be hiking on a 4x4 road. The distance makes this trail strenuous, and you'll have to negotiate some uneven terrain, but nothing's extreme and the elevation change is modest compared to the total distance. Take your time and enjoy this beautiful place. Last time there, I made a little bigger loop, going up to Devil's Kitchen, back down through Devil's Pocket,

CHESLER PARK/JOINT/DRUID ARCH

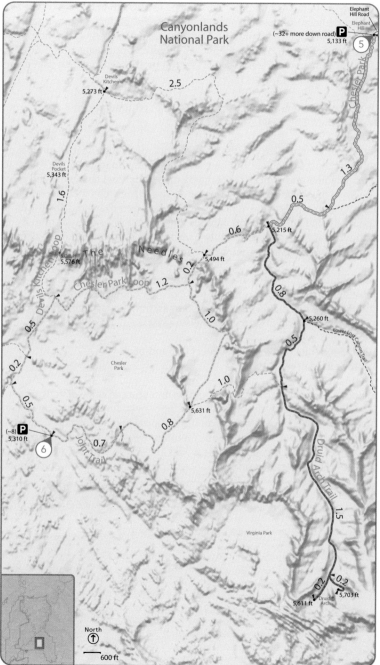

Canyonlands
National Park

Elephant
Hill Road

(~32+ more down road)
5,133 ft

Elephant
Hill

5

Chesler Park

Devils
Kitchen
5,273 ft

2.5

1.3

Devils
Pocket
5,343 ft

0.5

1.6

5,215 ft

0.6

Devils Kitchen Loop

S.O.B. Hill
5,576 ft

The   Needles

5,494 ft

0.8

0.2

Chesler Park Loop

1.2

5,260 ft

Lower Lost Canyon Trail

1.0

0.5

0.5

Chesler
Park

0.2

1.0

0.5

5,631 ft

Druid Arch Trail

(~8)
5,310 ft

P

6

0.8

Joint Trail

0.7

1.5

Virginia Park

0.2   0.2

5,703 ft

5,611 ft   Druid
Arch

North
↑

600 ft

and then onto the 4x4 road to Joint. Adding Druid Arch to it, I was on the trail just about from sunrise to sunset on a short (but perfect) October day. The only thing tricky about that route is to catch the unmarked (but obvious) trail up to Devil's Kitchen near an Elephant Canyon campsite (site EC1). S.O.B. Hill offers up some sweet views of Devil's Pocket to the north and Chesler Park to the south. All around, great hiking!

Druid Arch | Strenuous | 10.0 miles | 1,300 feet | Out-and-back
Trailhead: Elephant Hill (5)

Druid is a massive arch. The final viewpoint looks south, so the sun will be behind it most of the year, but it's still a sight to see. To reach it, you'll have to climb a ladder and a rocky chute. If you miss (or ignore) the unmarked junction up to the viewpoint, you will come around to the arch's south face. It's not a great view but worth the minimal effort to walk over there (missing the junction is a happy little accident). Most of the walk is following a wash, so it can be boring (at least relative to other Canyonlands scenery) and more difficult than it's elevation gain suggests, but interest-level picks up the closer you get.

The road to Elephant Hill Trailhead is unpaved but usually accessible to all vehicles. You can also access this trail network (along with other excellent choices like Lost Canyon and Peekaboo trails) from Squaw Flat Campground, which is an amazing place to spend a few nights.

Joint | Moderate | 1.4 miles | 600 feet | Out-and-back
Trailhead: Joint (6)

Hiking in from the north is a great option, but you can drive directly to Joint Trailhead with a high-clearance 4x4. I'll be honest, I have yet to drive over there (comments about how the road is technical and frequently impassable intimidated me, but I've seen people/vehicles over there that have me thinking it's not as treacherous as some would like you to believe). I'll do it next time, send me a message (mike@stoneroadpress.com) if you'd like an update.

More Trails

And there are a few more trails. Wilhite (12.2 miles), Gooseberry (5.4 miles), Lathrop (13.6 miles), and Murphy (10.8 lollipop) are strenuous hikes from Island in the Sky down to White Rim Road. Mesa Arch (easy, 0.5 mile) is an extremely popular sunrise destination. Murphy Point (easy, 3.6 miles) offers sweeping views across Green River to the Maze. Whale Rock (moderate, 1.0 mile) includes a steep and steady climb to the top of a massive red rock. False Kiva is cool but when we went to print it was closed due to vandalism (ask a ranger about current status and location). Fort Bottom Ruin (moderate, 3.0 miles) begins on White Rim Road and leads to a somewhat unimpressive rock ruin (access is a little tricky).

Grand View Point

Capitol Reef
Hiking Trails: 80+ miles

On the way to Spring Canyon

Capitol Reef Favorites

(1) **Chimney Rock**
Moderate | 3.5 mi | 700 ft

Spring Canyon
Moderate | 9.5 mi | 300 ft

(2) **Hickman Bridge**
Moderate | 1.7 mi | 360 ft

Navajo Knobs
Strenuous | 8.9 mi | 2,900 ft

(3) **Cohab Canyon**
Moderate | 3.1 mi | 500 ft

(4-5) **Grand Wash**
Easy | 4.5 miles | 220 feet

(4) **Cassidy Arch**
Strenuous | 3.1 miles | 800 feet

(6) **Capitol Gorge**
Easy | 1.9 miles | 200 feet

Golden Throne
Moderate | 3.6 miles | 720 feet

(7) **Lower Cathedral Valley**
Moderate | 2.4 miles | 310 feet

(8) **Burro Wash**
Strenuous | 6.5 miles | 600 feet

(9) **Halls Creek Narrows**
Strenuous | 23.1 miles | 1,400 feet

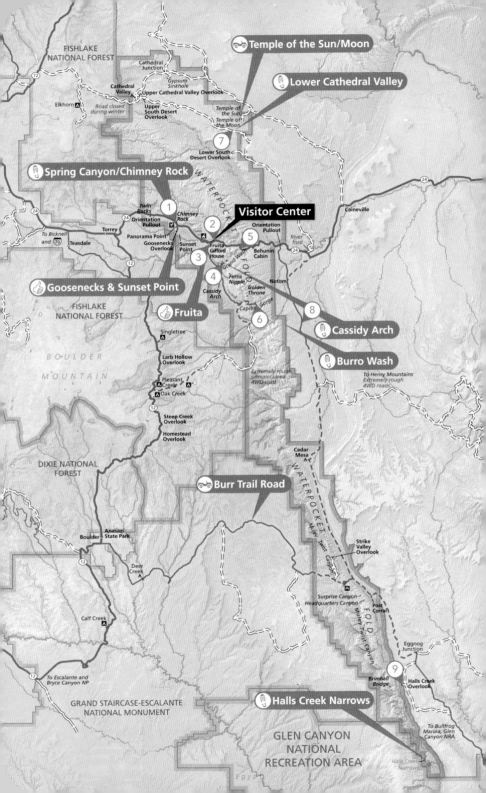

FISHLAKE
NATIONAL FOREST

Cathedral
Junction

Gypsum
Sinkhole

Cathedral
Valley

Upper Cathedral Valley Overlook

Elkhorn ▲

Road closed
during winter

Upper
South Desert
Overlook

🚙 **Temple of the Sun/Moon**

Temple of
the Sun;
Temple of
the Moon

📷 **Lower Cathedral Valley**

⑦

Lower South
Desert Overlook

24

72

📷 **Spring Canyon/Chimney Rock**

Twin
Rocks

①

Chimney
Rock

②

Caineville

24

24

Orientation
Pullout

Torrey

Teasdale

12

To Bicknell
and 70

Panorama Point

Goosenecks
Overlook

Sunset
Point

③

④

Cassidy
Arch

⑤

Orientation
Pullout

Behunin
Cabin

River
ford

Notom

24

Fruita
Gifford
House

Ferns
Nipple

Golden
Throne

Grand Wash

Visitor Center

WATERPOCKET FOLD

👍 **Goosenecks & Sunset Point**

FISHLAKE
NATIONAL FOREST

👍 **Fruita**

Singletree

B O U L D E R

M O U N T A I N

Larb Hollow
Overlook

Pleasant
Creek ▲

Oak Creek ▲

▲

12

Steep Creek
Overlook

Homestead
Overlook

Capito Gorge

⑥

Extremely rough
unmaintained
4WD road

⑧

📷 **Cassidy Arch**

👣 **Burro Wash**

To Henry Mountains
Extremely rough
4WD roads

DIXIE NATIONAL
FOREST

🚙 **Burr Trail Road**

Anasazi
Boulder ▪ State Park

Deer
Creek ▲

12

Cedar
Mesa

Surprise Canyon
Headquarters Canyon

W A T E R P O C K E T

Muley Twist Canyon

Strike
Valley
Overlook

Post
Corral

F O L D

Muley Twist Canyon

Calf Creek
▲

12

To Escalante and
Bryce Canyon NP

GRAND STAIRCASE-ESCALANTE
NATIONAL MONUMENT

Eggnog
Junction

Brimhall
Bridge

⑨

Halls Creek
Overlook

To Bullfrog
Marina, Glen
Canyon NRA

👣 **Halls Creek Narrows**

GLEN CANYON
NATIONAL
RECREATION AREA

Halls Creek
Narrows

CHIMNEY ROCK/SPRING CANYON

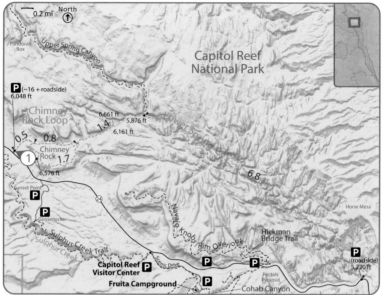

Chimney Rock | Moderate | 3.5 miles | 700 feet | Lollipop
Spring Canyon | Moderate | 9.5 miles | 300 feet | Point-to-point
Trailhead: Chimney Rock (1)

Chimney Rock is an okay trail. Views from atop the rock stretch across Sunset Point to Fruita and beyond. The trailhead is close to the park's west entrance on SR-24 and far from the much busier Scenic Drive (and Hickman Bridge), so it's not a bad idea to stop here, but if you do, don't hike Chimney Rock and leave, explore Spring Canyon too.

Spring Canyon is great! You'll see signs along Chimney Rock Loop for "River Ford," and that phrase probably gets people to skip it. Obviously, if it's raining, a narrow canyon is not a good place to be. But this is arid country, and most days you should not have any issues. So, at the northeast corner of Chimney Rock Loop, you'll find a trail leading into Chimney Rock Canyon. Take it. Eventually you'll hit Spring Canyon. Upper Spring Canyon leads to some wild rock features where people fool around (a trail beginning just outside the park boundary comes at Spring Canyon from above—route-finding and technical skills required). Lower Spring Canyon is the choice for most of us. It's a long, winding thoroughfare ending at a river ford to SR-24, between Grand Wash and Hickman Bridge trailheads. It's a great hike and a wonderful idea if you can arrange a ride at the other end. At the Fremont River crossing, you'll find a network of social trails from people trying to pick the best spot to cross. High water levels aren't common, but if you want to be extra cautious, scout it out or call to inquire about conditions.

FRUITA AREA

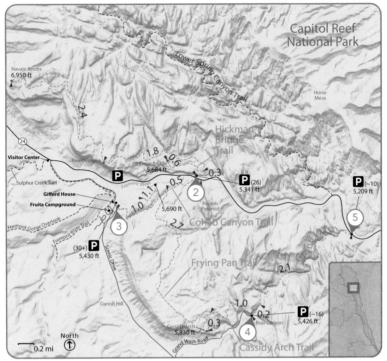

There's maybe room for a dozen vehicles around the paved loop at Chimney Rock trailhead. And there's a pullout on the opposite side of SR-24 that can be used for additional parking.

Hickman Bridge | Moderate | 1.7 miles | 360 feet | Out-and-back
Navajo Knobs | Strenuous | 8.9 miles | 2,900 feet | Out-and-back
Trailhead: Hickman Bridge (2)

Hickman Bridge is one of the most popular hikes in the park. And it's cool. Definitely worth checking out, especially if you aren't going to see other Arches around Utah on this visit. With that said, Cassidy should be the top arch on your Capitol Reef arch checklist.

As you're climbing up to Hickman Bridge, you'll quickly reach a trail junction. Left leads to Hickman. Continuing north leads to Rim Overlook and Navajo Knobs, following the cliff's edge around the Castle, and then a final scramble up to the knobs. SR-24 is awesome, and this is even better!

The trailhead has one of the park's largest parking areas with room for about two dozen vehicles. Still, arrive early to assure a spot.

Cohab Canyon | Moderate | 3.1 miles | 500 feet | Out-and-back
Trailhead: Cohab Canyon, Scenic Drive (3)

Cohab Canyon is like the hike to Rim Overlook/Navajo Knobs but with less impressive viewpoints. It's just on the other side of SR-24. The trailhead is located in Fruita, at the south end of the large parking area, opposite the barn and pasture. Hiking begins with a steep ascent, then it's moderate ups and downs to a pair of overlooks looking back to Fruita and SR-24. Aerial views are great, but I think you'll have more fun in the park's narrow canyons (especially in summer when shade is a welcome bonus). But Cohab Canyon Trail offers an alternative route to Cassidy Arch. Grand Wash gets real busy during peak season. Frying Pan Trail is usually peaceful. Taking it to Cassidy Arch is a longer haul, but not a bad idea. And that idea gets even better if you can arrange a pick up on Grand Wash Road or SR-24 to do it as a point-to-point.

Grand Wash | Easy | 4.5 miles | 220 feet | Out-and-back
Cassidy Arch | Strenuous | 3.1 miles | 800 feet | Out-and-back
Trailhead: Grand Wash Road (4), SR-24 (5)

Grand Wash isn't the kind of slot canyon that'll have you turning your hips to squeeze through tight spaces. You drive right into it (when dry, the road is accessible to most vehicles—big rigs and trailers are a bad idea). Things get narrowest toward the outlet near SR-24, so if you only have time for a very short walk, do an out-and-back beginning from the highway trailhead. Narrow or not, the sheer walls remain impressive. I think my preference of the two drive-in canyons is Capitol Gorge, but they're both fun.

Less than a quarter mile into the hike through Grand Wash you'll reach a trail junction leading steeply up to Cassidy Arch and Frying Pan trails. There is a canyon floor-level viewing point for Cassidy Arch, but this trail leads to the top of the rock, which has become a popular photo-op.

Flash Floods

There are a lot of sheer rock walls at Capitol Reef so it's imperative you pay attention to the weather. Be disciplined watching weather forecasts, but also continuously watch the sky while you're out exploring the park. I know, you don't see much of the sky from the bottom of a narrow slot canyon. This is a problem. If rain looks eminent, stay the heck away from any narrow canyons. Overall, this isn't much of a concern. The climate is arid, and rain/snow is infrequent, but when it does come, it's often intense. In 2022, a storm washed a bunch of vehicles out of Capitol Gorge. Don't let that scare you from visiting. As mentioned, it's uncommon, and if you pay attention (not only to the forecast but to what you're seeing while there), you have absolutely nothing to worry about. Summer is typically the wettest time of year, but again, still infrequent and unpredictable.

GOLDEN THRONE/CAPITOL GORGE

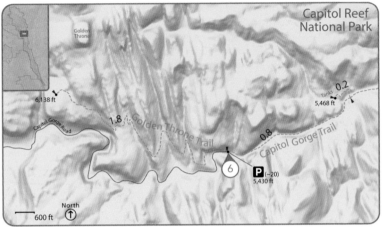

Capitol Gorge | Easy | 1.9 miles | 200 feet | Out-and-back
Golden Throne | Moderate | 3.6 miles | 720 feet | Out-and-back
Trailhead: Capitol Gorge Road (6)

Like Grand Wash, Capitol Gorge is another gravelly road winding its way between towering walls of rock. Also like Grand Wash, it's very cool! Also Also like Grand Wash, it's not a good place to tow a trailer or drive an over-sized rig. Small cars will be just fine as long as it's dry. Final also, the trail crosses the Waterpocket Fold, but it exits to a 4WD road near Notom-Bullfrog Road. Most people go to the Tanks and back. Opposite the Tanks is Waterpocket Canyon. And, of course, you can continue walking to the 4WD roads.

A very small fraction of the Capitol Gorge crowd heads in the opposite direction up to Golden Throne. Views of the throne are a bit underwhelming (it's more of a Golden Highchair), but the walk along the rim is quite enjoyable. You'll have an aerial view of visitors driving in through the gorge.

Lower Cathedral Valley Overlooks | Moderate | 2.4 miles | 310 feet | Out-and-back | **Trailhead:** Hartnet Road (7)

This trail leads to a pair of saddles overlooking Temple of the Sun and Temple of the Moon. If you make the drive here, you may as well hike to both saddles. But mornings are better at the east saddle. Evenings are better at the west saddle. Both are outstanding. Feel free to get a little curious. There's no reason you need to turn around right at the saddle. Just use common sense and don't do anything that makes you uncomfortable.

The trailhead has room for two vehicles inside a little wooden car corral. Whichever way you come at it, you're going to run into some complications.

LOWER CATHEDRAL VALLEY OVERLOOKS

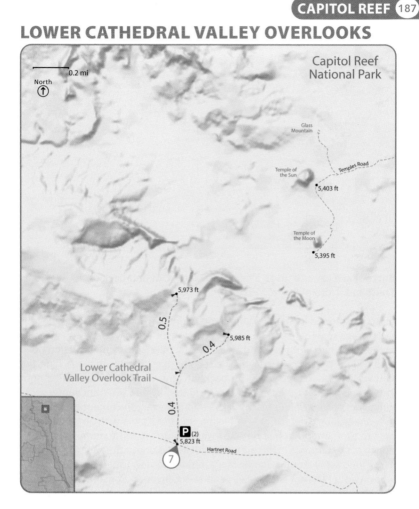

Capitol Reef
National Park

North

0.2 mi

Glass Mountain

Temples Road

Temple of
the Sun
• 5,403 ft

Temple of
the Moon
• 5,395 ft

• 5,973 ft

0.5

5,985 ft

0.4

Lower Cathedral
Valley Overlook Trail

0.4

P (2)
5,823 ft

Hartnet Road

7

The first is you'll need a 4x4. From the south, there are a couple options to access Hartnet Road. One is a maze of sandy roads. The other is an unmarked road directly south of the river ford. It's steep and rugged but it's way better than taking the sandy route. Almost immediately you'll be at the river ford. The river isn't much of a problem under typical conditions. A bigger problem is sand. On the other side you'll find more deep sand (having a pump so you can lower your tire pressure is a good idea). It's a terrible place to encounter traffic. Once you're out of the sandy flats, it's relatively smooth sailing (with a couple sandy stretches) all the way to the trailhead. From the north, there's no sand, but the road is considerably more rugged, and things get steep near Cathedral Valley Campground. With that said, doing the Hartnet–Cathedral Loop is a great idea! Then you can see Temple of the Sun/Moon from above and below, and it's pretty much non-stop mesmerizing scenery.

BURRO WASH

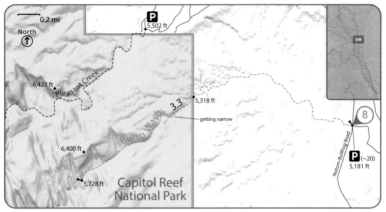

Burro Wash | Strenuous | 6.5 miles | 600 feet | Out-and-back
Trailhead: Notom–Bullfrog Road (8)

Burro Wash takes some navigating and cairn-spotting skills. The trailhead is located at a small BLM parking area with a sign for 'Burro Wash.' The trail begins at the south end of the parking area. The first mile is wash/trail crossing open land. Things begin to narrow by the second mile. Shortly after reaching the Capitol Reef boundary, you drop back into the wash and then take a right into a sandy, narrow canyon. Now you're in the slot and you'll encounter some difficult obstacles before reaching the end (for everyone except experienced canyoneers). Be careful. If you're feeling uncomfortable with an obstacle, it's best to turn around before getting yourself into a bad situation. There are a bunch of slot canyons in this area. (Capitol Reef is one of the best parks to take a nice long scroll around Google Maps in satellite view.) Sheets Gulch, Cottonwood Wash, Pleasant Creek, Headquarters Canyon, Surprise Canyon, Upper and Lower Muley Twist. They're all here. Some go straight through the waterpocket fold to South Draw (unpaved, 4x4 road continuing from Scenic Drive).

Halls Creek Narrows | Strenuous | 23.1 miles | 1,400 feet | Lollipop
Trailhead: Halls Creek Overlook (9)

I haven't done this yet, but I keep mentioning it as a reminder for the next trip. It's also a better backpacking (or horse) trip. You're going to get wet in the narrows. That will slow you down. But, on a long and hot summer day (maybe with a full moon?), it's not completely crazy to think about dayhiking it.

More Trails

There are many more trails. Headquarters Canyon, Surprise Canyon, and Sheets Gulch are all slot canyons on the east side of the Waterpocket Fold, accessed from Notom–Bullfrog Road (unpaved). Muley Twist provides some point-to-point or loop options. There are a few more trails along Hartnet road, like Jailhouse & Temple Rock (moderate, 4.5 miles). And this is an extremely fun part of the country to bring a little curiosity! Go explore.

HALLS CREEK NARROWS

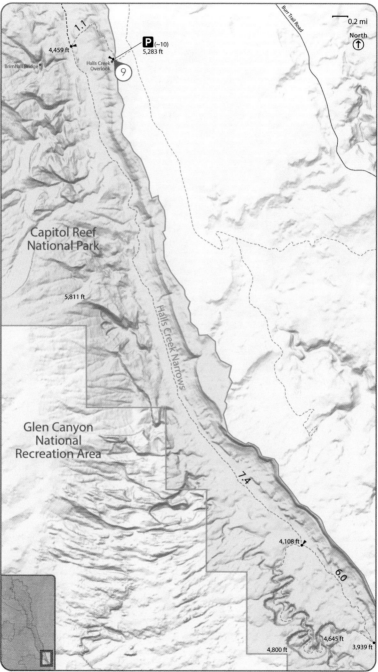

Capitol Reef
National Park

Glen Canyon
National
Recreation Area

Halls Creek Narrows

Burr Trail Road

0.2 mi

North

P (~10)
5,283 ft

9

Halls Creek
Overlook

1.1

4,459 ft

BrimHall Bridge

5,811 ft

7.4

4,108 ft

6.0

4,645 ft

4,800 ft

3,939 ft

Bryce Canyon
Hiking Trails: 50+ miles

Navajo Loop

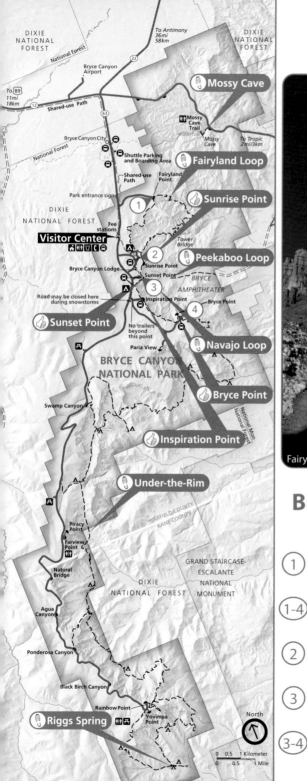

DIXIE NATIONAL FOREST

National Forest

To Antimony 36mi 58km

DIXIE NATIONAL FOREST

Bryce Canyon Airport

To 89 11mi 18km

Shared-use Path

22

63

12

National Forest

Bryce Canyon City

Shuttle Parking and Boarding Area

Shared-use Path

Park entrance sign

Fairyland Point

1

DIXIE NATIONAL FOREST

Fee stations

Visitor Center

Bryce Canyon Lodge

Sunrise Point

Sunset Point

Road may be closed here during snowstorms

2

Tower Bridge

3

Inspiration Point

BRYCE AMPHITHEATER

Bryce Point

4

Paria View

No trailers beyond this point

Sunset Point

BRYCE CANYON NATIONAL PARK

Swamp Canyon

Piracy Point

Farview Point

Natural Bridge

GARFIELD COUNTY KANE COUNTY

GRAND STAIRCASE-ESCALANTE NATIONAL MONUMENT

DIXIE NATIONAL FOREST

Agua Canyon

Ponderosa Canyon

Black Birch Canyon

Rainbow Point

Yovimpa Point

Riggs Spring

North

0   0.5   1 Kilometer
0   0.5   1 Mile

Mossy Cave

Mossy Cave Trail waterfall

Mossy Cave

To Tropic 2mi/3km

Fairyland Loop

Sunrise Point

Peekaboo Loop

National Mon National Forest

Navajo Loop

Bryce Point

Inspiration Point

Under-the-Rim

Fairyland

Bryce Canyon Favorites

1 Fairyland Loop
Strenuous | 8.3 miles | 2,300 ft

1-4 Rim
Moderate | 5.5 miles | 800 feet

2 Queens Garden
Moderate | 2.6 miles | 650 feet

3 Navajo/Wall Street
Moderate | 1.1 miles | 500 feet

3-4 Peekaboo
Strenuous | 4.5–6.0 mi | 1,600 ft

BRYCE AMPHITHEATER

Bryce Canyon
National Park

State Rte 63 · Old Bryce Town Loop
Great Western Trail
Park Road
Park Road

Ruby's Rim A. Loop

① (~22) P 7,771 ft Fairyland Point

Fairyland

Fairyland Loop

Rim Trail

Boat Mesa

2.5

Visitor Center

North Campground

Park Road

Park Road

0.3

The Lodge at Bryce Canyon

(100+) P 8,000 ft

Sunset Campground

0.5

Horse Corral
Sunrise Point 7,994 ft

② Queen Victoria

Bryce Amphitheater

Thors Hammer

0.8

Horse (only) Trail

Queen's Garden Loop

1.4

Chinese Wall 7,562 ft

0.3 Tower Bridge 7,148 ft

Tower Bridge Trail

3.9

Sunset Pt Loop

③ 0.7

Sunset Point 7,917 ft

Silent City

Wall Street

0.6

Two Bridges

0.6

0.8

0.2 7,452 ft

Tropic Trail

Bryce Canyon

Inspiration Pt Rd

8,133 ft
8,199 ft
Inspiration Point

(45) P 8,133 ft

8,211 ft

The Cathedral

Peekaboo Canyon

Peek A Boo Loop

1.7

1.3

Rim Trail

1.5

Wall of Windows

The Alligator

Bryce Point 8,169 ft

1.7

Under-the-Rim Trail

(50+) P 8,307 ft

④

North ↑

600 ft

Park Road

Under-the-Rim Trail

Fairyland | Strenuous | 8.3 miles | 2,300 feet | Loop
Trailhead: Fairyland (1) or Sunrise Point (2)

Fairyland is great! You can begin from the small parking area at Fairyland Point or by walking north along Rim Trail from Sunrise Point. Perhaps the best access is to camp at North Campground. Wake up, have breakfast, and walk on over to Rim Trail. It's a strenuous journey, but with nearly constant beautiful scenery, you likely won't mind all the ups and downs. I'd opt for a clockwise direction, to end with Tower Bridge and Chinese Wall closer to the conclusion but it's hardly imperative. The closest thing to an imperative for any Bryce Amphitheater hike is to get an early start. Morning light really makes the amphitheater's rocks dazzle. The hoodoos will be covered by the rim's shadow before you know it.

Rim | Moderate | 5.5 miles | 800 feet | Point-to-point
Trailhead: Fairyland (1), Sunrise Point (2), Sunset Point (3), Inspiration Point or Bryce Point (4)

Come to Bryce and you're going to spend at least some time on Rim Trail. Nothing complicated, just a trail following the rim of Bryce Amphitheater, serving up some of the best views on the planet. A half-mile of the trail around Sunset and Sunrise is paved and relatively flat. Other areas aren't as easy. The walk to Upper Inspiration Point is rugged and steep. Hiking up to Bryce Point from the south also traverses a bit of a grade. However, both those stops are very much worth the effort. While I most highly recommend walking among the hoodoos via any of the other listed trails, coming to Bryce and simply walking along the Rim can be an extremely rewarding experience.

Queens Garden | Moderate | 2.6 miles | 650 feet | Loop
Trailhead: Sunrise Point (2) or Sunset Point (3)

For the Queens Garden Loop, it's good to begin by descending into the amphitheater via Navajo or Wall Street. Both are steep and strenuous, featuring switchbacks. Both are also incredibly picturesque. If you won't have time to hike both, I'd choose the narrow walls of Wall Street. But note, Wall Street closes each winter. Once you reach the amphitheater's floor, hike north into the Queen's Garden. The trail is well-marked. It's also non-stop wonders of rock! If you're willing to risk the elements, being here after/during a snowstorm is a truly magical experience (but things get muddy/slippery). Exit the amphitheater at Sunrise Point and, if you parked at Sunset, return via Rim Trail.

Queen's Garden

Navajo | Moderate | 1.1 miles | 500 feet | Loop
Trailhead: Sunset Point (3)

The Navajo Loop simply combines Wall Street and Navajo Trails from Sunset Point. It's low on hoodoo content (so go deeper into the amphitheater if you can), but you'll see Thor's Hammer (popular sunrise photography feature). There's a spur to two bridges, and Wall Street is great. You'll have some steep and tiring switchbacks to negotiate, but once again, the scenery lures you deeper and deeper into the amphitheater.

Peekaboo | Strenuous | 4.5–6.0 miles | 1,600 feet | Lollipop
Trailhead: Sunrise Point (2), Sunset Point (3) or Bryce Point (4)

The park's long horseback ride heads into the amphitheater and over to Peekaboo Loop. Even if you aren't interested in that, you can still see what all these horses are fussing about. Turns out, the fuss is 100% legit thanks to a high density of hoodoos and non-stop colorful rock. There are quite a few ways to reach Peekaboo Loop. The most economical is to begin and end at Sunset. It only takes about 4.5 miles to complete the loop, and it gives you the opportunity to hike both Wall Street and Navajo trails. Now, Queens Garden Trail is awesome too, so you could begin there, complete Peekaboo Loop, and then return to the rim at Sunset Point. That loop is about six miles. The other option is to walk down into the Amphitheater from Bryce Point. Again, it's steep getting down to the loop, but so worth the energy required. Looping back to Bryce Point is roughly 5.1 miles.

> **Shuttles**
>
> A free shuttle service connects a few visitor hubs outside the park entrance with all the popular Bryce Amphitheater destinations. While I'd encourage you to wake up early and enter the park before the shuttles start running, it is a very useful (if not necessary) amenity. Shuttles run from spring through fall.

More Trails

There are a few more trails. Under-the-Rim runs nearly the length of the park. There are a few short access trails along the Main Park Road. And a few more at Yavimpa Point (the end of Main Park Road). There's a short trail to Paria View on the way to Bryce Point. Mossy Cave Trail (easy, 0.8 mile) leads to a lovely ephemeral waterfall (you can also head to Turret Arch and Little Windows) and the namesake attraction which is more of a grotto. Mossy Cave can be a good addition as the trailhead is located along Highway 12, not along the Main Park Road. With that said, priority should be given to properly exploring the relatively small Bryce Amphitheater area if you're in a hurry.

Slippery Trails

The trails here can be very slick and muddy after rain or snow. Traction devices are often useful in winter. Come prepared and you'll have a magnificent time in any conditions.

Mossy Cave

Zion
Hiking Trails: 100+ miles
Angel's Landing

Zion Favorites

1 **Canyon Overlook**
Moderate | 0.9 mile | 150 feet

2 **Angel's Landing**
Extreme | 4.3 miles | 1,500 feet

3 **Observation Point**
Strenuous | 7.2 miles | 2,200 feet

Hidden Canyon
Strenuous | 2.1 miles | 1,000 feet

4 **Mouth of the Narrows**
Moderate | up to 10.1 mi | 1,000 feet

5 **Zion Narrows**
Extreme | 14.7 miles | Downhill

6 **East Mesa**
Moderate | 6.9 miles | 700 feet

7 **Watchman**
Moderate | 3.3 miles | 400 feet

8 **Taylor Creek**
Moderate | 4.7 miles | 500 feet

9 **Kolob Arch**
Strenuous | 13.9 miles | 800 feet

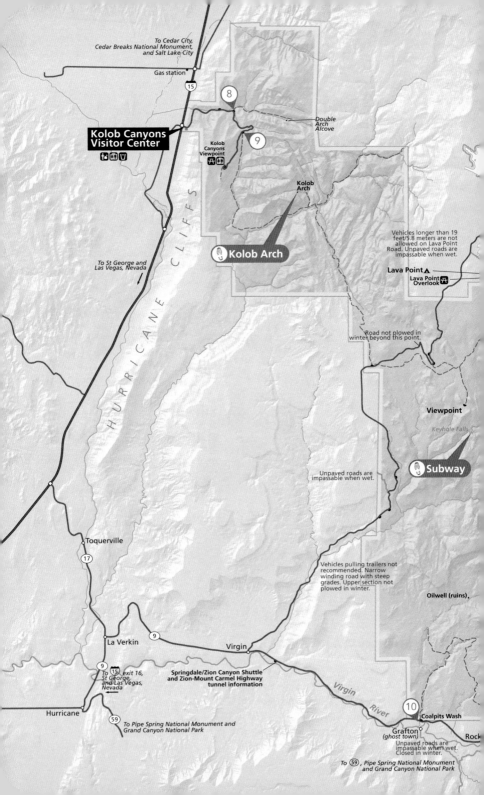

To Cedar City,
Cedar Breaks National Monument,
and Salt Lake City

Gas station

8

Double
Arch
Alcove

**Kolob Canyons
Visitor Center**

Kolob
Canyons
Viewpoint

9

Kolob
Arch

👣 **Kolob Arch**

To St George and
Las Vegas, Nevada

Vehicles longer than 19
feet/5.8 meters are not
allowed on Lava Point
Road. Unpaved roads are
impassable when wet.

Lava Point ⛺
Lava Point
Overlook 🏕

HURRICANE CLIFFS

Road not plowed in
winter beyond this point.

Viewpoint

Keyhole Falls

👣 **Subway**

Unpaved roads are
impassable when wet.

Toquerville

17

Vehicles pulling trailers not
recommended. Narrow
winding road with steep
grades. Upper section not
plowed in winter.

Oilwell (ruins)

La Verkin   **9**

Virgin

9
15 exit 16,
To St George,
and Las Vegas,
Nevada

Springdale/Zion Canyon Shuttle
and Zion-Mount Carmel Highway
tunnel information

Virgin River

10
Coalpits Wash

Hurricane

59
To Pipe Spring National Monument and
Grand Canyon National Park

Grafton
(ghost town)
Unpaved roads are
impassable when wet.
Closed in winter.

Rock

To **59**, Pipe Spring National Monument
and Grand Canyon National Park

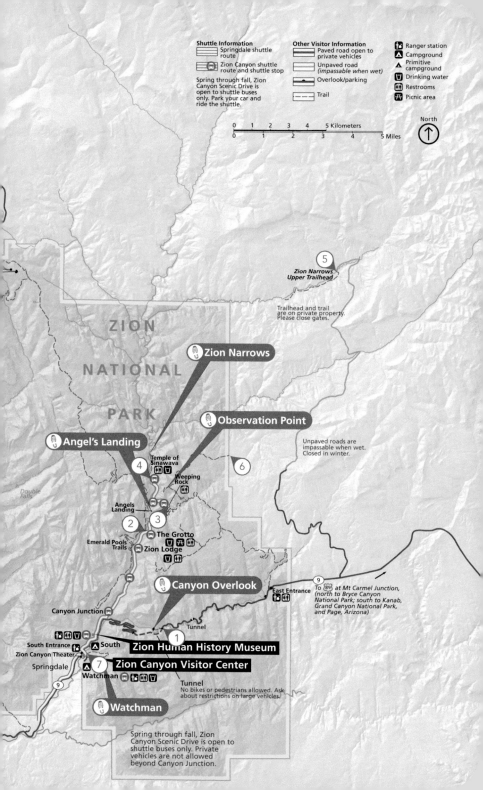

0 1 2 3 4 5 Kilometers
0 1 2 3 4 5 Miles

North

ZION

NATIONAL

PARK

Zion Narrows Upper Trailhead

5

Trailhead and trail are on private property. Please close gates.

Zion Narrows

Observation Point

Unpaved roads are impassable when wet. Closed in winter.

Angel's Landing

Temple of Sinawava

4

Weeping Rock

6

Double Falls

Angels Landing

3

2

The Grotto

Emerald Pools Trails

Zion Lodge

9

Canyon Overlook

East Entrance

To 89 at Mt Carmel Junction, (north to Bryce Canyon National Park; south to Kanab, Grand Canyon National Park, and Page, Arizona)

Canyon Junction

Tunnel

1

South Entrance

South

Zion Human History Museum

Zion Canyon Theater

Zion Canyon Visitor Center

Springdale

9

7

Watchman

Tunnel
No bikes or pedestrians allowed. Ask about restrictions on large vehicles.

Watchman

Spring through fall, Zion Canyon Scenic Drive is open to shuttle buses only. Private vehicles are not allowed beyond Canyon Junction.

CANYON OVERLOOK

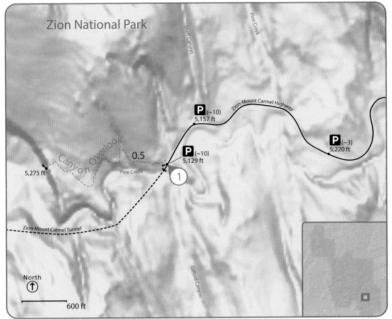

Canyon Overlook | Moderate | 0.9 mile | 150 feet | Out-and-back
Trailhead: Zion–Mount Carmel Highway (1)

Canyon Overlook is a short but exciting jaunt to where many visitors entering from the east catch their first glimpse of Zion Canyon. Along the way, you'll be able to peek into a slot canyon carved by Pine Creek. Pine Creek is a popular area for canyoneering, with some good rappelling locations. There's also a short slot canyon to the south, Gifford Canyon. And Shelf and Pine Creek are slot canyons to the north. The trailhead parking area has room for about twenty cars. There are more small parking areas to the east. It's a good idea to take a spot if you see one. With a mixture of long-term parkers playing in the slots and short-term hikers checking out Canyon Overlook, it's hard to say where/when spots will become available. And before you know it, you'll be at the point of no return, passing through Zion–Mount Carmel Tunnel, which is immediately west of the trail. Unfortunately, you need a car to reach the trailhead. The shuttle does not come this way.

Angel's Landing | Extreme | 4.3 miles | 1,500 feet | Out-and-back
Trailhead: The Grotto (2)

Angel's Landing is likely the first Zion trail you hear about. And if you aren't canyoneering, it'll likely be the most extreme thing you do. Aside from Walter's Wiggles (a series of tight switchbacks), the trail is somewhat ordinary

ANGEL'S LANDING/OBSERVATION POINT

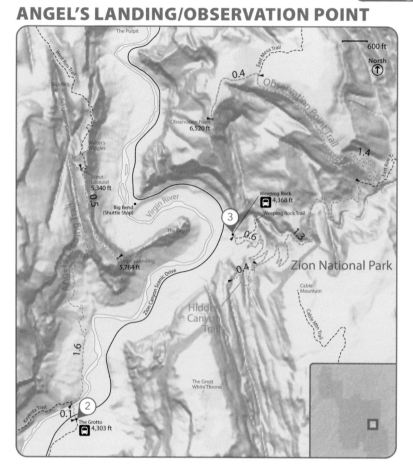

up until Scout Lookout. From there, it's a half-mile, hair-raising walk along a knife-edge ridgeline to reach the landing. A series of chains are there to assist you. The ridgeline invokes emotions ranging from exhilaration to panic. Fear has a limiting factor on who hikes the trail but it's still so popular the park needed to implement a lottery to help manage the crowds (only for the final half-mile). Lottery information is available at recreation.gov. Don't attempt the ridgeline if you are feeling considerable uneasiness. Uneasy or not, it's a good idea to hike a short distance along West Rim Trail, where you'll quickly be rewarded with outstanding views. It makes all of Walter's Wiggles worthwhile. Angel's Landing is not a great place for anyone with a fear of heights or young children. You can still make the trek in winter, but be sure to inquire about current conditions, and then come prepared for them.

The trailhead is located near the Grotto shuttle stop. A ranger is typically at Scout Lookout checking permits.

Observation Point | Strenuous | 7.2 miles | 2,200 feet | Out-and-back
Hidden Canyon | Strenuous | 2.1 miles | 1,000 feet | Out-and-back
Trailhead: Weeping Rock (3)

If you strike out on the lottery or rather not play it, Observation Point is a phe-nomenal Angel's Landing alternative. The most common route to this scenic vista is to get off the shuttle at Weeping Rock. From here, it's almost non-stop up, but when you reach the end and find yourself looking down on Angel's Landing, you'll be thankful you made the journey. You can also reach this point by East Rim and East Mesa trails. East Mesa is considerably shorter (6.9 miles) and with less elevation gain, but you'll have to exit the park to reach the trail-head. The full East Mesa Trail is visible on the Zion Narrows map (on the right).

Hidden Canyon is another fun one. It's a little like training for Angel's Landing, thanks to chains and exposure. Unfortunately, the trail was closed when we went to print. Hopefully it is reopened by the time you visit. Check the park website (nps.gov/zion) and/or socials for updates.

Riverside Walk/Mouth of the Narrows | Moderate | up to 10.1 miles | up to 1,000 feet | Out-and-back | **Trailhead:** Temple of Sinawava (4)

To begin Riverside Walk, take the park shuttle to its final stop, Temple of Sina-wava. From there you have about a mile of pavement before reaching the mouth of Zion Narrows. Continuing north in the shadow of the Narrows sheer red-rock walls, you'll spend most of the next four miles wading in the Virgin River. Hikers are free to go as far as Big Springs without a permit. You'll pass Mystery and Orderville Canyons along the way. The Narrows is completely dif-ferent from Zion's other iconic trail, Angel's Landing, but it's non-stop smiles as the rocks and shadows change throughout the day. It's easily one of the best hiking experiences in the national parks. Water shoes are a good idea. Wet-suit and boot rentals are available from local outfitters. In summer, it's usually plenty hot. The canyon's shade and Virgin River's cool water will feel refresh-ing. By October, you really need to think about renting some gear.

Zion Narrows (Top-Down) | Extreme | 14.7 miles | Downhill | Point-to-point
Trailhead: Upper Trailhead (5)

It's difficult to choose how to do Zion Narrows. The out-and-back from Tem-ple of Sinawava is fantastic because you have non-stop towering rock, and you can turn around whenever you feel like it and carry on to the next place. But then you can dayhike (or backpack) the full Narrows from the upper trail-head and you'll see an extra ten miles of canyon and have some fun water obstacles to negotiate. The cons to the thru hike are that you need a permit, you need to arrange a ride to the upper trailhead (available from several area outfitters), and, once you start, you must finish! If you are excited about a full day, spending most of your time in the Narrows wading in water, go for the full canyon! From the top down, it's nearly impossible to get lost. You'll pass a

ZION NARROWS/EAST MESA

0.2 mi

North

Zion National Park

Upper Trailhead
5,587 ft
5

9.1

Deep Creek Canyon

Amphitheater
Temple

Goose Creek Canyon

Big Spring
5,392 ft

Zion Narrows

Wynopits
Mountain

1.9

Imlay Canyon

Imlay Temple

Orderville Canyon

0.6

Elephant Temple
5,469 ft

Mountain of Mystery
6,565 ft

Mystery Canyon

2.5

6

P (~10)
6,520 ft

East Mesa Trail

3.1

Riverside
Walk

West Rim
Trail

Temple of
Sinawava
4,421 ft

4

0.4

Observation Pt Trail

East Rim Trail

Cathedral
Mountain

Observation Pt
6,520 ft

bunch of other canyons (Deep Creek, Kolob Creek, Goose Creek), but there's a good chance you won't notice them. You'll be too busy grinning as you follow the flow of the Virgin River through Zion's Narrows. It's a great deal of fun. If you have some hesitations, it's a good idea to sample the Narrows with an out-and-back from Temple of Sinawava. Love it and you'll have the full canyon to look forward to on your next visit or try to get a walk-up permit.

For what it's worth, I did the top-down on a beautiful October day without a wetsuit and it wasn't unbearable. But you better believe I was soaking up the sun at high noon and extremely thankful to board a shuttle at Temple of Sinawava. If you're doing it late/early in the year, it'd be fantastic to have friends/family waiting with dry clothes at the trailhead. If not, have a change of clothes ready in your car (or bring them with you in a dry bag).

East Mesa | Moderate | 6.9 miles | 700 feet | Out-and-back
Trailhead: East Mesa (6)

East Mesa is an alternative route to Observation Point, one of the best views in the park, where you're perched high above Angel's Landing. The trailhead is located near the park's eastern boundary, behind Zion Ponderosa Resort.

WATCHMAN

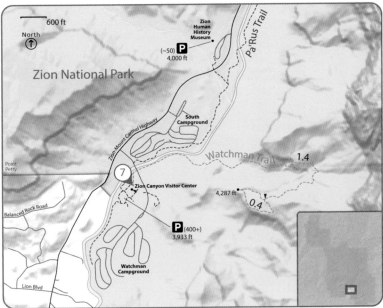

Watchman | Moderate | 3.3 miles | 400 feet | Lollipop
Trailhead: Zion Canyon Visitor Center (7)

Watchman Trail is convenient for anyone staying at Watchman or South campground or if you're waiting to meet with people at the Visitor Center. It's not that long and not that difficult. It's also not particularly glamorous at the beginning, passing employee housing. But it gets better. You don't hike to the top of Watchman (the summit is about a mile south of the final viewpoint), but you'll be treated to effort-affirming views toward Springdale. There's nothing tricky about this trail. Well-marked. Heavily used. I've seen plenty of

TAYLOR CREEK/KOLOB ARCH

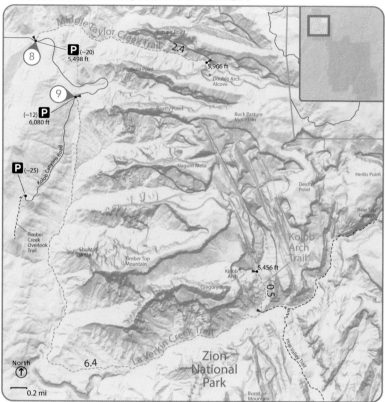

people take a morning jog on the trail to start off their day. (If you're looking for something without any grade, nearby Pa'Rus Trail is the one for you. It's the hiking/biking path to Zion Canyon.)

Taylor Creek | Moderate | 4.7 miles | 500 feet | Out-and-back
Trailhead: Taylor Creek (8)

Zion Canyon is busy almost all year long. If you'd like to enjoy a bit of that sublime Zion scenery with a fraction of the crowds, consider making the trip to Kolob Canyons. Taylor Creek leads to Double Arch Alcove, an incredible conclusion at a fraction of the mileage required to reach this corner's other highlight, Kolob Arch. The trail crosses Taylor Creek several times and leads past a couple historic homestead cabins.

Kolob Arch | Strenuous | 13.9 miles | 800 feet | Out-and-back
Trailhead: Lee Pass (9)

It's a haul but not excessively strenuous. La Verkin Creek Trail follows Timber Creek to La Verkin Creek and after nearly seven miles of tracing creeks, you'll reach a spur trail leading to one of the world's largest natural arches, Kolob Arch. It spans 287 feet and is 75 feet thick. If you're interested in doing this much mileage in a day, West Rim Trail is a better option (but you'll need to arrange a shuttle to get dropped off at the trailhead near Lava Point because it's a point-to-point hike, ending at Angel's Landing/The Grotto).

Permits & Lotteries

Utah National Park visitation decreased in 2022, but permit and lottery systems are likely here to stay. At press time, a permit was required for Angel's Landing (recreation.gov), The Subway, and Zion Narrows (thru-hikes, overnight trips, or anyone planning to head beyond Big Springs). These three trails are epic highlights of many guests' Zion adventures, but they are far from the only attractions you'll find in the park.

Safety

If you're thinking about the full Narrows, it's a good idea to scout it out. Feel the water's temperature, learn how much cooler it is under cover of the canyon's shadow. Winter hiking is becoming more popular. It's a great idea. Ephemeral waterfalls appear in a few places. You can freely drive Zion Canyon Scenic Drive. And whitecapped red rock is a feast for the eyes. Enjoy the snow while you can. It rarely sticks around (average high temperatures reach into the 50s°F in January.

Free Shuttles

The park runs shuttles transporting visitors up and down Zion Canyon Scenic Drive for most of the year. When shuttles are running, personal vehicles are not permitted on Zion Canyon Scenic Drive unless you're staying at Zion Lodge. A shuttle loop connects Springdale with Zion's South Entrance. The other runs between Zion Canyon Visitor Center and Temple of Sinawava. The park website (nps.gov/zion) posts current schedules. Try to catch the first shuttle of the day. The shuttle alternative is Pa'rus Trail. It's a paved multi-use path between South Campground and Canyon Junction.

More Trails

There are quite a few more trails. The most notable is Left Fork (strenuous, 9.0 miles), a non-technical route to The Subway from the bottom-up. It requires a permit. Find details at the park website (nps.gov/zion). If you can arrange a ride, hiking West Rim (strenuous, 14.2 miles, one-way) from point-to-point is a wonderful idea. Get dropped off at Lava Point, enjoy an uncommonly peaceful hike across a stunning plateau and you'll exit at Scout Lookout (near Angel's Landing), where you can walk down to the Grotto Shuttle Stop. You could tack Angel's Landing onto this hike (permit required), but you'll likely be tired, and the trail will be crowded. It's better to return another day, early in the morning. The nice thing about going from Lava Point to the Grotto is that the scenery continuously improves all the way to Angel's Landing. What's bad is you're hiking toward the sun, not away from it. Another way to shake the Zion Canyon crowds is to begin a hike outside the park, like Chinle Trail (moderate, 10.7 miles, point-to-point), which begins a few miles southwest of Springdale and heads up toward West Temple. Last but not least is Pa'rus Trail (easy, 3.5 miles, paved). It provides access to Zion Canyon for hikers and cyclers, an excellent alternative to the shuttle system. Beyond the hiking trails, if you are (or think you might be) interested in canyoneering, Zion is one of the best places on the planet. There are lots of narrow, deep canyons hidden within the park's interior.

Grand Canyon
Hiking Trails: 590+ miles

Mules descending Bright Angel

Grand Canyon Favorites

(1) **Bright Angel**
Strenuous | 18.2 mile | 4,500 feet

(2) **South Kaibab**
Strenuous | 13.1 miles | 4,700 feet

(3) **Grandview**
Strenuous | 8.3 miles | 3,300 feet

(1, 4) **West Rim**
Easy | up to 8.1 miles | 800 feet

(5) **Hermit**
Strenuous | 20.0 miles | 5,000 feet

(6) **Bright Angel Point**
Easy | 0.7 miles | 300 feet

(7) **North Kaibab**
Strenuous | up to 28.0 miles | 5,850 feet

(8) **Cape Final**
Easy | 4.1 miles | 250 feet

(9) **Cape Royal**
Easy | 0.8 miles | 30 feet

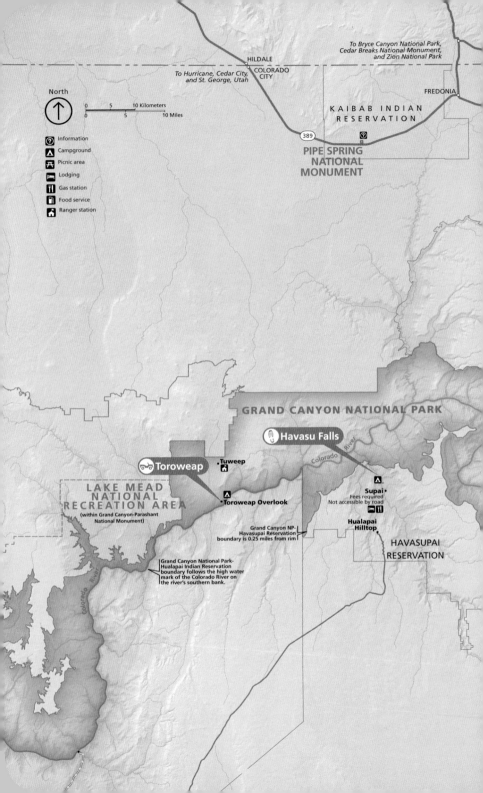

North

0   5   10 Kilometers
0   5   10 Miles

? Information
▲ Campground
⚘ Picnic area
🛏 Lodging
⛽ Gas station
🍴 Food service
⌂ Ranger station

To Hurricane, Cedar City,
and St. George, Utah

HILDALE

COLORADO
CITY

To Bryce Canyon National Park,
Cedar Breaks National Monument,
and Zion National Park

FREDONIA

KAIBAB INDIAN
RESERVATION

389

PIPE SPRING
NATIONAL
MONUMENT

GRAND CANYON NATIONAL PARK

Havasu Falls

Toroweap

▪Tuweep

LAKE MEAD
NATIONAL
RECREATION AREA
(within Grand Canyon-Parashant
National Monument)

▪Toroweap Overlook

▲
Supai▪
Fees required
Not accessible by road

Colorado River

Grand Canyon NP-
Havasupai Reservation
boundary is 0.25 miles from rim

**Hualapai
Hilltop**

HAVASUPAI
RESERVATION

Grand Canyon National Park-
Hualapai Indian Reservation
boundary follows the high water
mark of the Colorado River on
the river's southern bank.

Colorado River

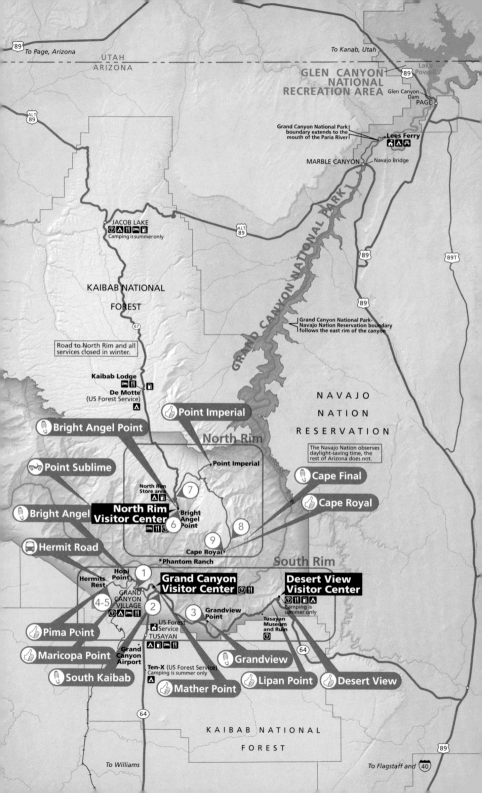

To Page, Arizona

To Kanab, Utah

UTAH
ARIZONA

GLEN CANYON
NATIONAL
RECREATION AREA

Lake Powell

Glen Canyon Dam

PAGE

Grand Canyon National Park
boundary extends to the
mouth of the Paria River

Lees Ferry

MARBLE CANYON

Navajo Bridge

JACOB LAKE
Camping is summer only

KAIBAB NATIONAL

FOREST

Grand Canyon National Park-
Navajo Nation Reservation boundary
follows the east rim of the canyon

Road to North Rim and all
services closed in winter.

Kaibab Lodge

De Motte
(US Forest Service)

NAVAJO

NATION

RESERVATION

GRAND CANYON NATIONAL PARK

Point Imperial

North Rim

The Navajo Nation observes
daylight-saving time, the
rest of Arizona does not.

Bright Angel Point

Point Imperial

Point Sublime

North Rim
Store area

Cape Final

**North Rim
Visitor Center**

7

Cape Royal

Bright Angel

6

Bright
Angel
Point

8

Hermit Road

9

Cape Royal

*Phantom Ranch

South Rim

Hopi
Point

1

Hermits
Rest

**Grand Canyon
Visitor Center**

**Desert View
Visitor Center**

Camping is
summer only

4-5

GRAND
CANYON
VILLAGE

2

3

Pima Point

US Forest
Service
TUSAYAN

Grandview
Point

Tusayan
Museum
and Ruin

Maricopa Point

Grand
Canyon
Airport

64

South Kaibab

Ten-X (US Forest Service)
Camping is summer only

Grandview

Mather Point

Lipan Point

Desert View

64

KAIBAB NATIONAL

FOREST

To Williams

To Flagstaff and

40

BRIGHT ANGEL/SOUTH KAIBAB (S. RIM)

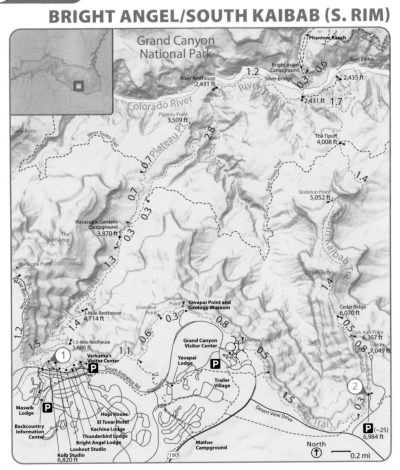

Bright Angel | Strenuous | 18.2 miles | 4,500 feet | Out-and-back
Trailhead: Bright Angel (1)

This is the most popular trail leading into Grand Canyon. You'll find two tunnels, a pair of resthouses (1.5 miles and 3 miles into the trail), and a couple bridges across the Colorado if you reach the canyon floor. With that said, a short out-and-back along Bright Angel Trail is a great introduction to inner-canyon hiking. Go as far as you like. Just remember you have to make it out of the canyon too, and that will take considerably more energy and time (usually twice as long out than in). Hiking to Plateau Point is 12 miles roundtrip with more than 3,000 feet of elevation change. So, for hiking to Plateau Point, you have an initial steep four-mile descent, followed by a relatively flat four miles to the viewpoint and back, concluding with the steep four-mile climb out of the canyon. Water is available at 1.5-Mile Resthouse, 3-Mile Resthouse, and Havasupai Gardens (but carry water in too). If you're fit, you may want to

South Kaibab (don't forget about the elevation change)

consider looping Bright Angel with South Kaibab (16.0 miles). There's camping at Havasupai Gardens and Bright Angel for backpackers. You can also hike or mule in and spend the night at Phantom Ranch. The perfect trip looks something like two nights at Phantom Ranch. A day hiking down to the ranch. Next day going out-and-back to Ribbon Falls (North Kaibab). And finally hiking out of the canyon on South Kaibab or Bright Angel (whichever one you didn't take in). A permit is required for all overnight trips.

South Kaibab | Strenuous | 13.1 miles | 4,700 feet | Out-and-back
Trailhead: South Kaibab (2)

South Kaibab doesn't have the amenities of Bright Angel, but its views are equally, if not more, appealing. Ooh Aah Point (1.7 miles) and Skeleton Point (5.6 miles) are both fantastic. Similarly, if you're doing an out-and-back, turn around with plenty of energy left in the tank. It's worth repeating, looping South Kaibab and Bright Angel is a very doable option for those with considerable stamina. There's very little shade and no water along the way. And it's about 15–20°F warmer at the canyon floor than the South Rim.

GRANDVIEW (SOUTH RIM)

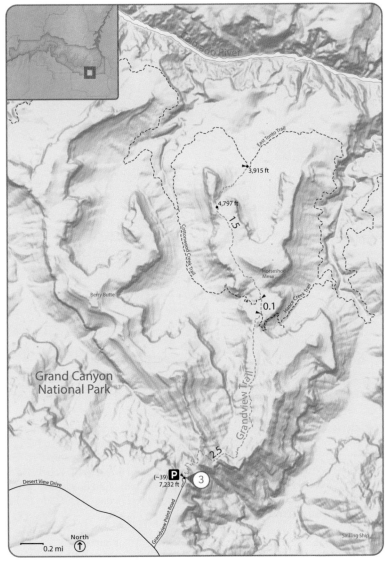

Grandview | Strenuous | 8.3 miles | 3,300 feet | Out-and-back
Trailhead: Grandview Point (3)

Grandview provides some of the grandest canyon views of all, but it also comes with an awful lot of elevation change without reaching the Colorado. The grade is steep and tricky right out of the gates. From then on things get

WEST RIM (SOUTH RIM)

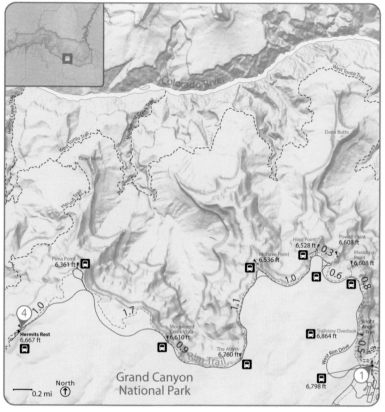

easier. The trail highlighted on the map makes a conservative out-and-back. But you can loop around, returning to Grandview via East Tonto and Hance Creek trails. This adds quite a bit of cliffside exposure and some steep climbs. And the total hiking distance bumps up to about 11 miles.

West Rim | Easy | up to 8.1 miles | up to 800 feet | Point-to-point
Trailhead: Bright Angel (1), Hermit (4), and many locations in between

Inner canyon trails are hard. If you want to take it easy, stick to the rims. Rim Trail from Bright Angel to Hermit's Rest offers up miles of jaw-dropping canyon views. It follows Hermit Road, which is accessed only by shuttles. Shuttles are a huge bonus, as you can hike to a few viewpoints, fill your scenery-admiring quota, and then hop on the shuttle to return to the shuttle stop near Bright Angel Trailhead. Hiking Rim Trail between viewpoints allows for a little more peaceful canyon experience. Still, don't skip the viewpoints. If forced to pick one, it'd probably be Mohave, but they're all great.

HERMIT (SOUTH RIM)

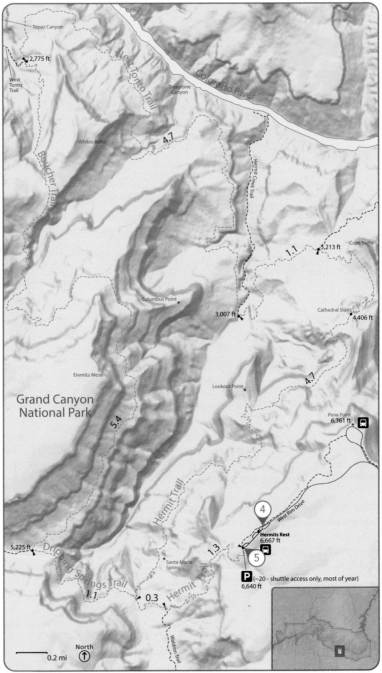

Topaz Canyon

2,775 ft

West Tonto Trail

West Tonto Trail

Colorado River

Travertine Canyon

Boucher Trail

Whites Butte

4.7

Hermit Creek Trail

1.1

3,213 ft

Cope Butte

Columbus Point

3,007 ft

Cathedral Stairs

4,406 ft

Eremita Mesa

Lookout Point

4.7

Grand Canyon National Park

5.4

Pima Point
6,361 ft

Hermit Trail

West Rim Drive

4

5,225 ft

Dripping Springs Trail

Santa Maria Spring

1.3

Hermits Rest
6,667 ft

5

1.1

0.3

Hermit Trail

P (~20 - shuttle access only, most of year)
6,640 ft

Waldron Trail

North

0.2 mi

A storm blowing in at Hermit's Rest

Hermit | Strenuous | 20.0 miles | 5,000 feet | Lollipop
Trailhead: Hermit's Rest (5)

First, the trailhead is located just west of Hermit's Rest. From spring through fall, you'll need to take a free shuttle to the final stop. In winter, you can drive directly to Hermit's Rest, but your hiking ambitions should decrease as days shorten and temperatures drop. Still, this is a great loop, with several miles of trail paralleling the Colorado River. The overall elevation gain is a lot. Comparable to Bright Angel, South Kaibab, and North Kaibab trails. And the trails aren't trafficked as heavily as the main corridor trails if you happened to get injured or exhausted. So, this isn't something you try on a whim. The whole loop is a major commitment and better to be done as an overnight trip or consider a shorter out-and-back as a dayhike. It's a beautiful area, rich with Grand Canyon history (it was heavily developed as a below-rim tourism destination, operating from 1910 until 1930).

BRIGHT ANGEL PT/NORTH KAIBAB (N. RIM)

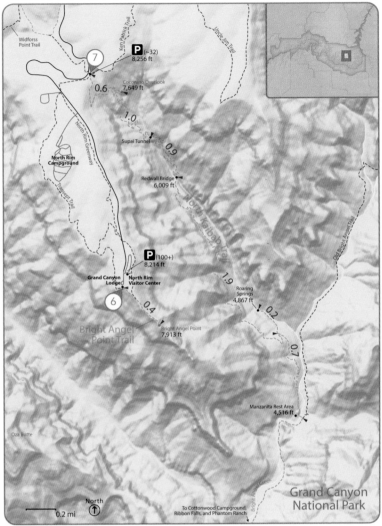

Bright Angel Point | Easy | 0.7 mile | 300 feet | Out-and-back
Trailhead: North Rim Visitor Center or Grand Canyon Lodge (6)

This short, narrow, paved path provides sweeping views of Grand Canyon. The trail loses elevation, but this is about as easy as things get at the North Rim. And scenery-to-effort ratio is very high. As always, if you can stay at the in-park lodge or campground without over-stressing your travel budget and planning, do it. The North Rim's relative uncrowdedness is a common talking point. Yes, it receives a tiny fraction of Grand Canyon's total visitors, but it also closes for winter and has considerably fewer amenities.

CAPE FINAL/CAPE ROYAL (NORTH RIM)

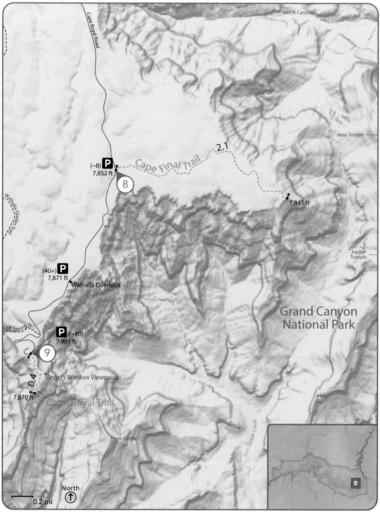

North Kaibab | Strenuous | up to 28.0 miles | up to 5,850 feet | Out-and-back or Point-to-point (with South Kaibab/Bright Angel) | **Trailhead:** North Kaibab (7)

North Kaibab is one of the least interesting hikes you can do at the North Rim. You might be tempted to hike in for Ribbon Falls or the trail-cred of going Rim-to-Rim, but I don't know, this is a long, tough hike with mostly similar scenery, walking through Bright Angel Canyon. There's a chance my memory is tainted because I did it as an out-and-back at the tail end of a cold, and the climb out kicked my butt. There are alternative inner canyon trails on this side, but I haven't checked them out yet. One thing to know is the North Rim is about 1,000 feet higher than the South Rim. More elevation change. Cooler temps.

Cape Final | Easy | 4.1 miles | 250 feet | Out-and-back
Trailhead: Cape Royal Road (8)

Cape Final provides dreamy canyon views. Pointing east, it's a good spot for sunrise or late in the day, when rays of sun remain above the canyon's rim. The trail begins meandering through forest before opening up to the massive canyon. The views, while very nice, are not as good as you'll find at Cape Royal. However, there is one lone campsite near the end of the trail if you're looking for an easy backpacking trip.

Cape Royal | Easy | 0.8 mile | 30 feet | Out-and-back
Trailhead: Cape Royal Road (9)

Cape Royal (paved) is a must-stop destination if you're visiting the North Rim.

Parking

There are four large parking lots at South Rim Visitor Center. From here you can explore the visitor center, walk to Mather Point and/or Rim Trail, or board a shuttle bus to get deeper into the park. Additional parking is available at Market Plaza and Village Historic District.

Free Shuttles

Free shuttles greatly simplify life on the South Rim. There are four separate loops, including a Hiker's Express Route between Bright Angel and South Kaibab. You should receive a pocket map with shuttle details at the park entrance or visit the park website (nps.gov/grca) for current information.

Safety

Safety is a major concern at Grand Canyon. Many visitors hike in, and then need assistance to get back out. Don't add to the statistics. Carry water. Wear a hat and apply sunscreen. Turn around long before you're tired. Summer can be unbearably hot, especially at the canyon floor (daytime highs above 100°F are common). There isn't much shade. Trails, especially anything into the canyon, become considerably more difficult when wet or snow-covered. The North Rim closes for winter, but the South Rim remains open year-round. Snow dramatically increases the canyon's beauty, but it also complicates exploration.

Mules

Mules frequent Bright Angel, South Kaibab and North Kaibab trails (overnight trips to Phantom Ranch). Expect to see them. Yield the right of way and listen to the wrangler's directions. Usually, it's expected for you to step off the trail to the uphill side of the canyon (away from the ledge). They also offer rim-top rides on both rims. It may sound like the easier way of getting into the canyon, but sitting in the saddle for a couple hours takes a toll on your body as well. I'd prepare for that too.

More Trails

There are several hundred more miles of trails. One of the Grand Canyon's most magical destinations is Havasu Falls. It can only be visited as a 3-night backpacking trip, with reservations booked through the Havasupai Tribe (havasupaireservations.com). If you really want to get away from things, you can look into a few other North Rim hiking trails like Widforss Point, Tiyo Point (4x4 required), or Powell Plateau (4x4 required). Also, with a 4x4, you can reach incredible North Rim viewpoints like Point Sublime or Toroweap.

Ancient trees and windswept summits

Great Basin
Hiking Trails: 65+ miles

Great Basin Favorites

1 **Bristlecone/Glacier**
Moderate | 4.6 mile | 1,100 feet

2 **Wheeler Peak**
Strenuous | 8.3 miles | 2,900 feet

Alpine Lakes
Easy | 2.7 miles | 500 feet

3 **Baker & Johnson Lakes**
Strenuous | 10.9 miles | 3,300 feet

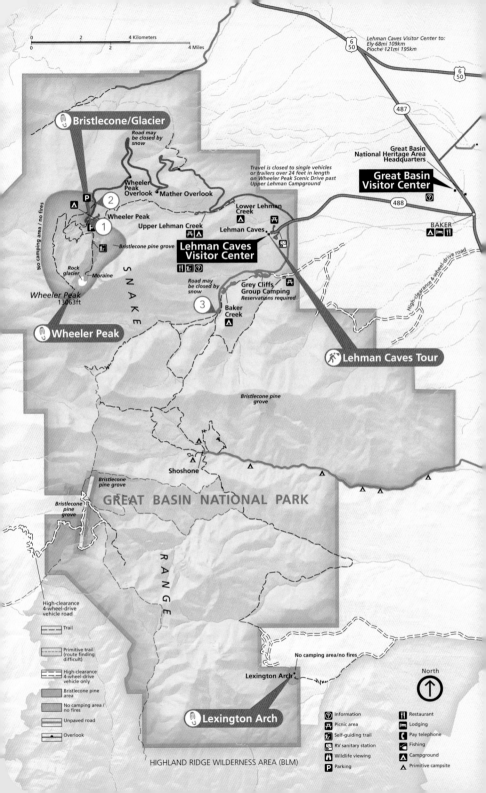

Great Basin National Park map

Scale: 0 to 4 Kilometers / 0 to 4 Miles

Lehman Caves Visitor Center to:
Ely 68mi 109km
Pioche 121mi 195km

Bristlecone/Glacier

Road may be closed by snow

Wheeler Peak Overlook

Mather Overlook

Travel is closed to single vehicles or trailers over 24 feet in length on Wheeler Peak Scenic Drive past Upper Lehman Campground

Great Basin National Heritage Area Headquarters

Great Basin Visitor Center

Lower Lehman Creek

Wheeler Peak

Upper Lehman Creek

Lehman Caves

BAKER

Lehman Caves Visitor Center

Bristlecone pine grove

Rock glacier

Moraine

Wheeler Peak 13063ft

Road may be closed by snow

Grey Cliffs Group Camping
Reservations required

Baker Creek

No camping area / no fires

Wheeler Peak

Lehman Caves Tour

S N A K E

Bristlecone pine grove

Bristlecone pine grove

GREAT BASIN NATIONAL PARK

Shoshone

High-clearance 4-wheel-drive road

Bristlecone pine grove

R A N G E

No camping area/no fires

Lexington Arch

Lexington Arch

North

↑

HIGHLAND RIDGE WILDERNESS AREA (BLM)

Legend

- High-clearance 4-wheel-drive vehicle road
- Trail
- Primitive trail (route finding difficult)
- High-clearance 4-wheel-drive vehicle only
- Bristlecone pine area
- No camping area / no fires
- Unpaved road
- Overlook

- Information
- Picnic area
- Self-guiding trail
- RV sanitary station
- Wildlife viewing
- Parking

- Restaurant
- Lodging
- Pay telephone
- Fishing
- Campground
- Primitive campsite

WHEELER PEAK/BRISTLECONE

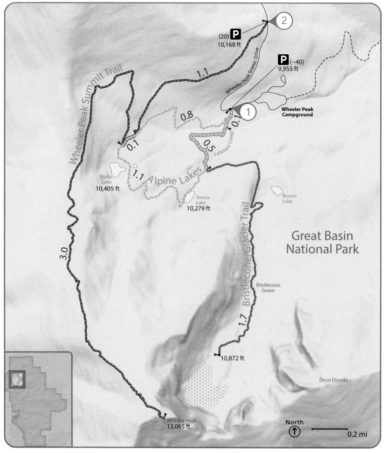

Bristlecone/Glacier | Moderate | 4.6 miles | 1,100 feet | Out-and-back
Alpine Lakes | Easy | 2.7 miles | 500 feet | Loop
Trailhead: Bristlecone (1)

Great Basin's bristlecone groves were one of the most pleasant surprises I've come across in our magnificent parks. And this grove, with Wheeler Peak looming in the background, is extremely pretty (especially in the morning light). The trail is not difficult, but plan on spending extra time browsing the ancient trees, some of them were alive when the pyramids were being built. You may as well continue on Glacier Trail since you're here. It provides more views of Wheeler Peak, which are nice, and you'll see Nevada's only glacier. It's a rock glacier (rocks cemented with ice). Now I'm no glacier expert so I won't comment on how glacier-y it is, but it wasn't all that interesting. Probably neater earlier in the year.

Alpine Lakes is short and easy. The rewards far outweigh the commitment.

Wheeler Peak | Strenuous | 8.3 miles | 2,900 feet | Out-and-back
Trailhead: Summit Trail (1)

This is the thigh burner. Up, up, and more up to the top of Wheeler Peak and it's 360-degree views. You'll be able to look across the vast Great Basin to the west. Be warned, it's often very windy along the ridge and at the summit. It's best to begin the hike from the Summit Trail parking area, but you can also access it from Alpine Lakes Loop.

BAKER LAKE

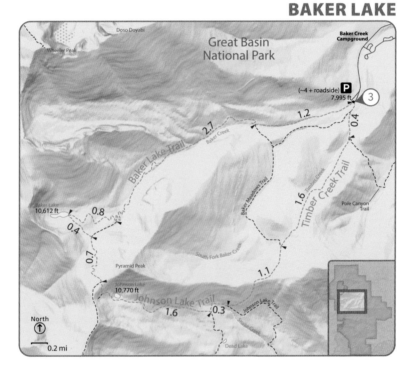

Baker & Johnson Lakes Loop | Strenuous | 10.9 miles | 3,300 feet | Loop
Trailhead: Baker Creek Road (3)

Combining Baker Lake and Johnson Lake makes for a challenging (longer and more elevation gain than Wheeler Peak) dayhike or a pretty casual backpacking trip (permit required).

More Trails

Be sure to tour the cave while you're here. Reservations are made through recreation.gov. Tours are short, inexpensive, and you'll see some unique cave formations. Back above the earth's surface there are more trails to hike. Lexington Arch (moderate, 5.4 miles) requires a high-clearance 4x4 to reach the trailhead. And, also with a high-clearance 4x4, you can reach a network of trails near the park's western boundary near Pole Canyon. The region features more 11,000-foot summits and 1,000-year-old trees.

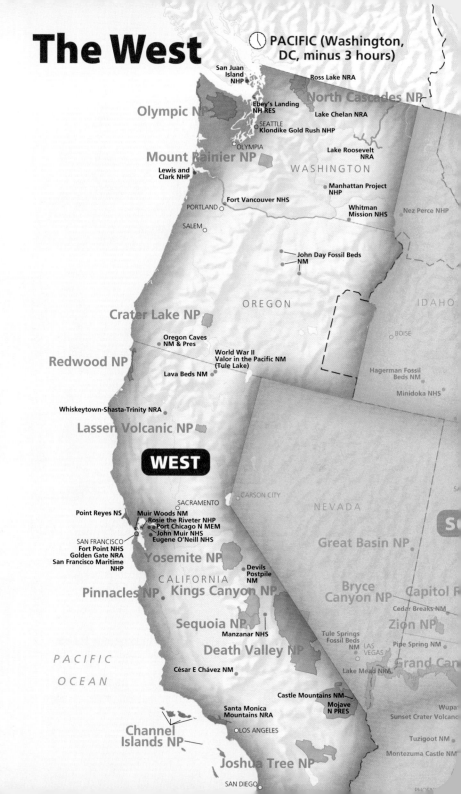

The West

🕐 PACIFIC (Washington, DC, minus 3 hours)

San Juan Island NHP
Ross Lake NRA
North Cascades NP
Olympic NP
Ebey's Landing NH RES
Lake Chelan NRA
SEATTLE
Klondike Gold Rush NHP
OLYMPIA
Mount Rainier NP
Lake Roosevelt NRA
WASHINGTON
Lewis and Clark NHP
Manhattan Project NHP
Fort Vancouver NHS
Whitman Mission NHS
Nez Perce NHP
PORTLAND
SALEM

John Day Fossil Beds NM

OREGON
IDAHO
BOISE

Crater Lake NP

Oregon Caves NM & Pres
World War II Valor in the Pacific NM (Tule Lake)
Redwood NP
Lava Beds NM
Hagerman Fossil Beds NM
Minidoka NHS

Whiskeytown-Shasta-Trinity NRA

Lassen Volcanic NP

WEST

CARSON CITY

SACRAMENTO

Point Reyes NS
Muir Woods NM
Rosie the Riveter NHP
Port Chicago N MEM
John Muir NHS
Eugene O'Neill NHS
SAN FRANCISCO
Fort Point NHS
Golden Gate NRA
San Francisco Maritime NHP

NEVADA

Great Basin NP

Yosemite NP
Devils Postpile NM

CALIFORNIA
Bryce Canyon NP
Capitol R

Pinnacles NP
Kings Canyon NP
Cedar Breaks NM
Zion NP

Sequoia NP
Manzanar NHS
Tule Springs Fossil Beds NM
Pipe Spring NM

Death Valley NP
LAS VEGAS
Lake Mead NRA
Grand Can

PACIFIC OCEAN

César E Chávez NM

Castle Mountains NM
Mojave N PRES

Wupa

Santa Monica Mountains NRA
Sunset Crater Volcano

Channel Islands NP
Tuzigoot NM

OLOS ANGELES
Montezuma Castle NM

Joshua Tree NP

SAN DIEGO
PHOEN

Boy Scout Trail

Joshua Tree
Hiking Trails: 65+ miles

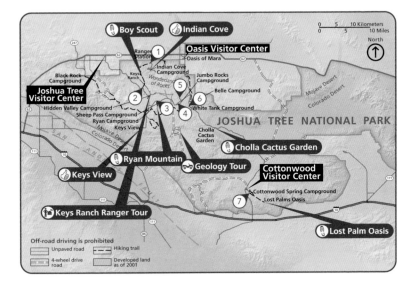

Boy Scout

Indian Cove

Oasis Visitor Center
Oasis of Mara

Ranger Station

Indian Cove Campground

Jumbo Rocks Campground

Keys Ranch

Wonderland of Rocks

Belle Campground

Black Rock Campground

Joshua Tree Visitor Center

Hidden Valley Campground

White Tank Campground

JOSHUA TREE NATIONAL PARK

Mojave Desert
Colorado Desert

Sheep Pass Campground
Ryan Campground
Keys View

Mojave Desert
Colorado Desert

Cholla Cactus Garden

Cholla Cactus Garden

Ryan Mountain

Geology Tour

Cottonwood Visitor Center

Keys View

Cottonwood Spring Campground
Lost Palms Oasis

Keys Ranch Ranger Tour

Lost Palm Oasis

Off-road driving is prohibited

Unpaved road
4-wheel drive road
Hiking trail
Developed land as of 2001

0   5   10 Kilometers
0   5   10 Miles

North

Joshua Tree Favorites

1-2 Boy Scout
Moderate | 6.9–12.4 miles | 250+ ft

3 Ryan Mountain
Strenuous | 2.9 miles | 1.050 feet

4 Skull Rock
Easy | 1.6 miles | 120 feet

5 Split Rock
Easy | 2.4 miles | 150 feet

6 Arch Rock
Easy | 1.4 miles | 40 feet

7 Mastodon Peak
Moderate | 2.4 miles | 380 feet

Lost Palm Oasis
Strenuous | 7.1 miles | 400 feet

BOY SCOUT

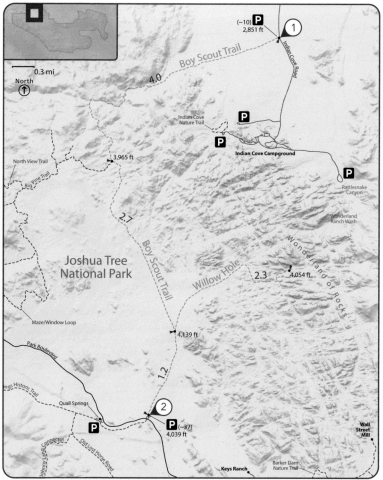

0.3 mi
North

Boy Scout Trail

(~10) P 2,851 ft

1

Indian Cove Road

4.0

Indian Cove Nature Trail

P

P

Indian Cove Campground

P

Rattlesnake Canyon

North View Trail

Big Pine Trail

3,965 ft

2.7

Wonderland Ranch Wash

Joshua Tree National Park

Boy Scout Trail

Willow Hole

2.3

4,054 ft

Wonderland of Rocks

Maze/Window Loop

4,139 ft

Park Boulevard

1.2

ings Historic Trail

Quail Springs

2

P (~37) 4,039 ft

P

Johnny Lang Canyon Connector

Old Lost Horse Road

Keys Ranch

Barker Dam Nature Trail

Wall Street Mill

Boy Scout/Willow Hole | Moderate–Strenuous | 6.9–12.4 miles | 250–1,500 feet | Out-and-back or Point-to-point
Trailhead: Indian Cove (1) or Park Boulevard (2)

Moderately long, minimally steep, and maximally fun is a suitable description for the seven-mile trek to Willow Hole, beginning from the large Boy Scout Trail parking area on Park Boulevard. The first two-and-a-half miles feature standard Joshua Tree scenery. Funky rocks. Funkier trees. But things really start to get interesting around Willow Hole and Wonderland of Rocks. Joshua Tree is without a doubt one of the best parks to bring a little curiosity to, because there are curiosities all over the place. Wonderland of Rocks isn't the only wonder in the area. Boy Scout Trail north of the Willow Hole junction is pretty darn

RYAN MOUNTAIN

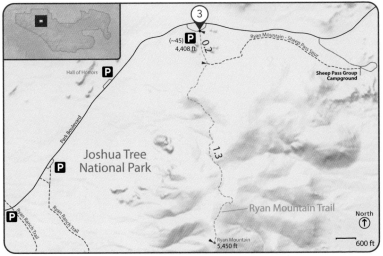

cool too. If you can cache a car, or arrange a ride, hiking from the trailhead at Indian Cove, completing the spur to Willow Hole/Wonderland of Rocks, and ending at Park Boulevard would be a nearly perfect hike clocking in at 12.4 miles. The northern portion of Boy Scout Trail is short on Joshua Trees and long on goofy rock piles. The trail is well marked, with signs at the junction with Big Pine and Willow Hole. Willow Hole is pretty obvious. Wonderland of Rocks is beyond Willow Hole, and let's just say you'll know it when you see it. It's accurately named but be warned, it can get confusing in the rock jumble. Track your hike or make mental notes of identifiable landmarks.

Ryan Mountain | Strenuous | 2.9 miles | 1,050 feet | Out-and-back
Trailhead: Ryan Mountain (3)

Ryan Mountain is a very popular trail. Who doesn't like an aerial view of a beautiful place? Well, not everyone is up for a 1,000-foot climb. While it's good, I'd hold off on this trail until after you've had your fill of whacky rocks and Joshua trees. They're the true stars of this park.

Skull Rock | Easy | 1.6 miles | 120 feet | Loop
Trailhead: Skull Rock (4)

Skull Rock is incredibly popular. But the thing is, most visitors park, take a photo with the skull-shaped rock located a few feet from the road, and get in their cars and carry on down Park Boulevard. However, there's more fun to be had goofing around in the rocks. Spend a few extra minutes (or more) here, and I believe you'll be happy to meet some less-skeletal rocks. Another thing to note about this place is there's no right or wrong way to enjoy the rocks and trees (as long as you're giving them the respect they deserve). Trust your gut and let the rocks show you the way!

SKULL ROCK/SPLIT ROCK

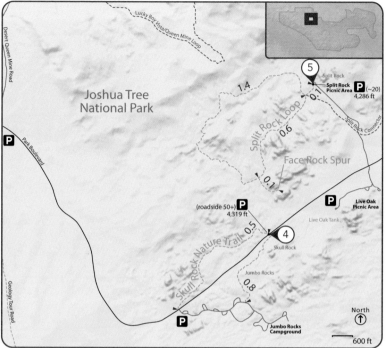

Split Rock | Easy | 2.4 miles | 150 feet | Loop
Trailhead: Split Rock (5)

Like Skull Rock, Split Rock is right next to the parking area. The loop is filled with rocks too! Maybe the thing to say here, is "if you aren't a rock person, this park might not be for you." But if any place has the power to turn an anti-rock individual pro-rock, it's Joshua Tree. Plus, cool trees!

Split Rock

ARCH ROCK

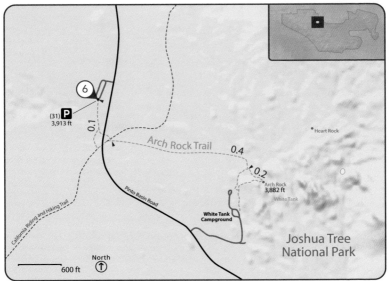

Arch Rock | Easy | 1.4 miles | 40 feet | Lollipop
Trailhead: Twin Tanks (6)

The most convenient way to get a good look at Arch Rock is from White Tank Campground. It's quite literally a short stroll from your campsite. (And Joshua Tree has some of the best campgrounds in the National Park System.) But you can also park on the west side of Pinto Basin Road at Twin Tanks parking area and complete the short trail. The Arch opens up to the west, so evening light is typically best, but it's standing in fairly tight confines with lots of rocky obstacles, so your best bet for fun photos is low and close with a wide angle lens. A popular Heart-shaped Rock is just northeast of the loop.

Mastodon Peak | Moderate | 2.4 miles | 380 feet | Loop
Lost Palm Oasis | Strenuous | 7.1 miles | 400 feet | Out-and-back
Trailhead: Cottonwood Spring (7)

If you're pressed on time, you might want to forget about the entire southern half of the park and focus on all the sights along Park Boulevard between the West Entrance and Split Rock. If you do plan on entering/exiting here, hiking these trails is a good idea. You'll begin in a refreshing palm oasis at Cottonwood Spring. The Mastodon Peak loop leads to Mastodon Mine, just below Mastodon Peak (which is accessible via an unmaintained trail).

Lost Palm Oasis crosses desert scrubland concluding with a tricky descent into Lost Palm Canyon, where you'll find a couple dozen palm trees.

MASTODON PEAK/LOST PALM OASIS

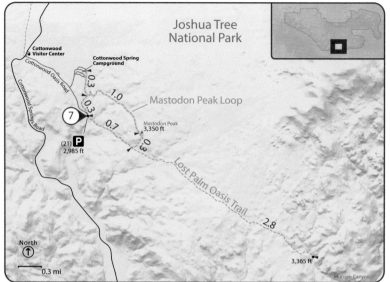

Weather

This is desert country. Actually it's two, the Mojave meets the Colorado Desert within Joshua Tree. But that's not the point. The point is it's uncomfortably hot here in summer. Fall through spring is usually fantastic.

Popularity

Being relatively close to a large population center, Joshua Tree is especially busy on weekends and holidays, fall through spring.

More Trails

There's so much going on at Joshua Tree. People always cite Cholla Cactus Garden (easy, 0.3 mile) as The Place for sunset. That isn't exactly right. It's a cool place a couple hours before sunset and an hour or two after sunrise. The sun needs to be above the surrounding mountains for the cactus to glow. And that's a fantastic feature, because it allows enough time to hustle up to Park Boulevard and find your favorite Joshua trees or rock pile to admire while things begin to get colorful during sunrise/sunset. Up at Indian Cove you'll find Rattlesnake Canyon. It's a free-for-all rock scramble. The name of the game is follow the water. It's tricky, but you should find some interesting things. It's also close to Wonderland of Rocks, but don't get yourself into a jam. Scrambling rocks isn't for everyone. Barker Dam (easy, 1.1 miles) is very popular, giving a glimpse into ranching life. It also is close to Wonderland of Rocks. I haven't gone off trail here, but my guess is things are far more interesting beyond Barker Dam. A better way to peek into Joshua Tree living is to join a ranger on a Keys Ranch tour (permit required, recreation.gov). There are tons of cool rocks found along or near Park Boulevard at Hidden Valley, Cap Rock, Hall of Horrors (it's a little tricky to find the hall), Jumbo Rocks, White Tank, and Indian Cove. There's another palm tree oasis accessed from the park's northern boundary, Fortynine Palms Oasis. And there are a couple more mine trails: Lost Horse Mine (moderate, 4.0 miles) and Contact Mine (moderate, 4.0 miles). Remember to pack some curiosity. Oddities extend beyond the maintained trails. Samuelson Rocks and Eagle Cliff Mine are two sites people like to hunt.

Along the way to Pelican Bay

Channel Islands
Hiking Trails: 50+ miles

OUTDOORS SANTA BARBARA VISITOR CENTER

Santa Barbara Harbor

Kayaking

Painted Cave

VISITOR CENTER

Ventura

Ventura Harbor

CHANNEL ISLANDS NATIONAL PARK

Channel Islands Harbor

SAN MIGUEL ISLAND

SANTA ROSA ISLAND

SANTA CRUZ ISLAND

Arch Rock

ANACAPA ISLAND

Point Bennett - Seals/Sea Lions

PACIFIC OCEAN

Hike/Backpack

Do Not Use This Map For Navigation
For safe boating, National Ocean Survey charts are indispensable.

Authorized park boundary
The Channel Islands National Park boundary extends 1.8 km (1 nautical mile) from the shore of each island.

Authorized marine sanctuary boundary
The Channel Islands National Marine Sanctuary boundary extends 10.8 km (6 nautical miles) from the shore of each island.

North

SANTA BARBARA ISLAND

0   5   10 Kilometers
0   5   10 Miles

Channel Islands Favorites

(1) Anacapa
Easy | 2.2 miles | 260 feet

(2) Potato Harbor
Moderate | 4.7 | 600 feet

(3) Pelican Bay
Moderate | 4.2 | 900 feet

ANACAPA ISLAND

Anacapa Island | Easy | 2.2 miles | 260 feet | Out-and-back
Trailhead: Landing Cove (1)

Anacapa is the closest island to the mainland and it's a popular destination. You know who else loves this destination? Seagulls, that's who! Seagulls can be a nuisance, but I'm not sure they should scare you away from Anacapa, especially if your time is extremely limited. Guests are only permitted to hike on East Anacapa. From Landing Cove, you'll ascend a stairway, providing access to a figure-8-ish trail network. It's about 2.2 miles to hike the figure 8 and take a quick stroll to the lighthouse. The sinuous spine of rocks is cool to see from on top, but let's be honest, the best part of this trip is the sea life you'll (hopefully) spot traveling to and from the island.

POTATO HARBOR (SANTA CRUZ)

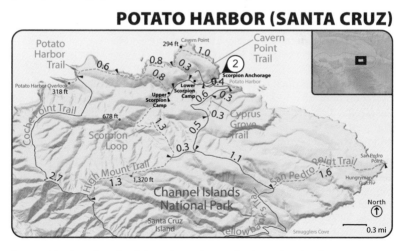

Potato Harbor Overlook | Moderate | 4.7 miles | 600 feet | Lollipop
Trailhead: Scorpion Anchorage, Santa Cruz (2)

Santa Cruz is the other island with year-round transportation services. If you arrive like most people—by boat with Island Packers—you'll have the chance

PELICAN BAY (SANTA CRUZ)

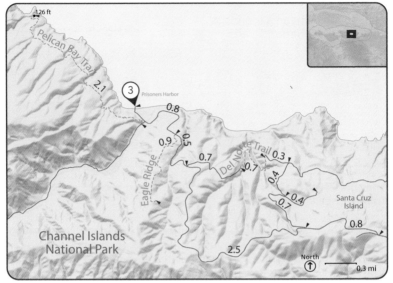

to join a naturalist on a short hike (likely Cavern Point Trail). You may have enough time to reach Potato Harbor Overlook, which is great. It's just under five miles to Potato Harbor Overlook and back to the dock. The network of trails is substantial. Further exploration requires your own water transportation or an overnight stay.

Pelican Bay | Moderate | 4.2 miles | 900 feet | Out-and-back
Trailhead: Prisoner's Harbor, Santa Cruz (3)

Santa Cruz's other dock is located at Prisoner's Harbor. Similarly, with transportation from Island Packers, you'll have a chance to join a guided hike on Pelican Bay Trail. What's different is you could not do this hike on your own. The west end of Santa Cruz is Nature Conservancy Property and cannot be entered without permission.

Camping

If you want to get to know the Channel Islands, spend the night. Each island has at least one campground. It's really backpacking. And there are some complications. You must pack in water for every campground except Water Canyon Campground on Santa Rosa and Scorpion Canyon Campground on Santa Cruz. And you'll also want to pack your food in an animal-proof container to keep the rodents out. Book your island transportation from Island Packers first, as it typically fills before campsites (but campsites book to capacity too).

San Miguel

Island Packers makes seasonal trips to San Miguel. Point Bennett is a gathering spot for seals and sea lions (usually beginning in spring). Caliche Forest is a peculiar collection of fossilized vegetation. Hiking here requires the presence of a park ranger. Visiting the island requires a permit.

Hiking's great but the park's stars are in the water

Santa Barbara

Santa Barbara is the smallest and most disconnected of the five islands. Here you'll find about five miles of hiking trails. Island Packers' Santa Barbara excursions are infrequent, resulting in a long (3+ day) camping trip if you're thinking about spending the night.

Santa Rosa

Santa Rosa has a large network of trails and it's up there on the list of things I need to take a look at yet.

Other Activities

Kayaking is popular at Santa Cruz's Scorpion Beach. There are sea caves nearby. Santa Rosa and San Miguel are good kayaking options too, but favorable water conditions are not as reliable. In summer, snorkel equipment is available for rent at Scorpion Anchorage. Arrive by boat, and you may spot marine life along the way.

Pinnacles
Hiking Trails: 35 miles

High Peaks

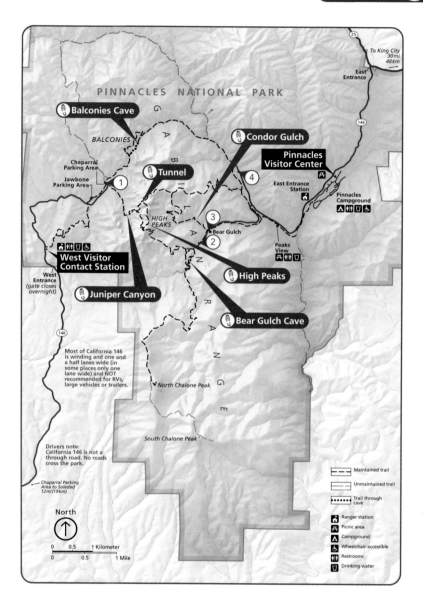

Pinnacles Favorites

(1) Balconies Cave
Moderate | 2.6 miles | 400 feet

(2-4) Bear Gulch Cave
Moderate | 0.8 mile | 300 feet

Juniper Canyon
Strenuous | 4.1 miles | 1,200 feet

High Peaks
Strenuous | 7.7 miles | 1,500 feet

HIGH PEAKS

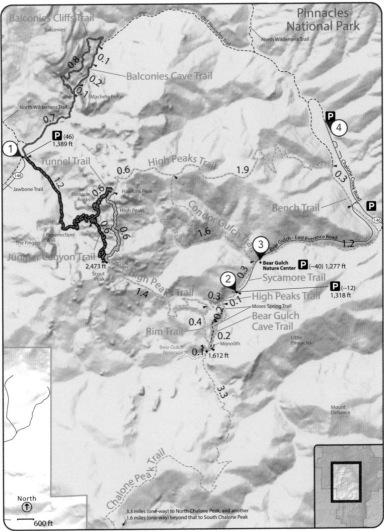

Balconies Cave | Moderate | 2.6 miles | 400 feet | Loop
Trailhead: Chaparral (1)

Pinnacles' two talus caves are a riot. Balconies (orange loop) is on the west side of the park, beginning at Chaparral trailhead. Heading toward Balconies, you'll notice a metal gate at the cave entrance (it's always a good idea to check if the cave is open prior to arrival). Follow the arrows through the dark passages. Upon exiting, return to Chaparral Parking Area via Balconies Cliffs Trail for 2.6 miles. Or you can extend it by taking Old Pinnacles to get into the High Peaks.

Juniper Canyon | Strenuous | 4.1 miles | 1,200 feet | Loop
Trailhead: Chaparral (1)

This is a great High Peaks Loop (red loop) including two trails most eastside visitors don't see, Juniper Canyon and Tunnel! If you're expecting a tunnel on Tunnel Trail, you will not be disappointed. It's a decent tunnel.

Bear Gulch Cave | Moderate | 0.8 mile | 300 feet | Loop
Trailhead: Bear Gulch (2)

Of the two caves, this is the one I would prioritize. Again, check with the park to see if the upper section is open (call them). Unfortunately, it's typically only open a few weeks each year (usually in March and October), but that changes.

High Peaks | Strenuous | 7.7 miles | 1,500 feet | Loop
Trailhead: Bear Gulch (2), Bear Gulch (3) or Old Pinnacles (4)

High Peaks is fun, but it's also very popular. This is a park best visited mid-week. If Bear Gulch is open, start with the cave, pass the reservoir, and then follow Rim Trail into High Peaks. Crossing High Peaks requires traversing rocky stairs and dealing with some exposure aided by rails. The 7.7-mile (yellow) loop returns via Bench and Sycamore trails. You can cut it short via Condor Gulch Trail, which is also nice. If you don't plan on going to the west side, consider doing an extra loop around the High Peaks by going down Tunnel and back up Juniper Canyon. It adds about a mile and it's good fun.

Shuttle
A free shuttle runs on the east side for busy weekends and holidays. During these times, parking areas fill extremely early and long queues form for the shuttle by mid-day. Arrive early or pack some patience.

Bear Gulch

Caves

Not your traditional caves, these talus caves formed as rocks fell on top of one another, blocking out the sun. You'll need a light source. A headlamp is best, as you'll have to do some scrambling. Crawling is likely. The caves are one-way. Enter Balconies from the south, Bear Gulch from the north. White arrows painted on rocks show you the way. They're short, fun, and not-too-claustrophobic.

More Trails

Pinnacles is a small park and almost all visitors congregate in and around High Peaks. If you'd like to get away from all that, take Chalone Peak Trail (strenuous), leading to North and South Chalone peaks. It's 3.3 miles (one-way) to the north summit and another 1.6 miles to the south summit. In all, you're looking at a little more than ten miles. You can also reach Balconies Trail via Old Pinnacles Road from the east side of the park, bypassing High Peaks.

Titus Canyon

Death Valley
Hiking Trails: 100+ miles

Death Valley Favorites

(1) Golden Canyon
Moderate | 6.9 miles | 1,100 feet

(2) Mesquite Flat Dunes
Moderate | 1.9+ miles | Varies

(3) Mosaic Canyon
Moderate | 1.9–3.4 miles | 1,070 feet

(4) Wildrose Peak
Strenuous | 8.0 miles | 2,200 feet

(5) Telescope Peak
Strenuous | 12.0 miles | 2,950 feet

(6) Darwin Falls
Easy | 2.0 miles | 200 feet

(7) Titus Canyon
Moderate | up to 7.8 miles | Varies

Fall Canyon
Moderate | 6.8 miles | 1,700 feet

(8) Ubehebe Peak
Strenuous | 3.9 miles | 2,300 feet

To Dyer

168

To Big Pine

In winter carry chains. Road may be closed.

👍 **Warm Springs**

To Manzanar, Bishop, and Yosemite

INYO

NATIONAL

FOREST

Warm Springs Campground

Saline Valley Dunes

Road conditions require experienced 4-wheel drivers.

Lone Pine

136

395

Keeler

🚙 **The Racetrack**

190

Olancha

🥾 **Darwin Falls**

395

To Lake Isabella

178

14

178

To Sequoia and Los Angeles

To San Bernardino

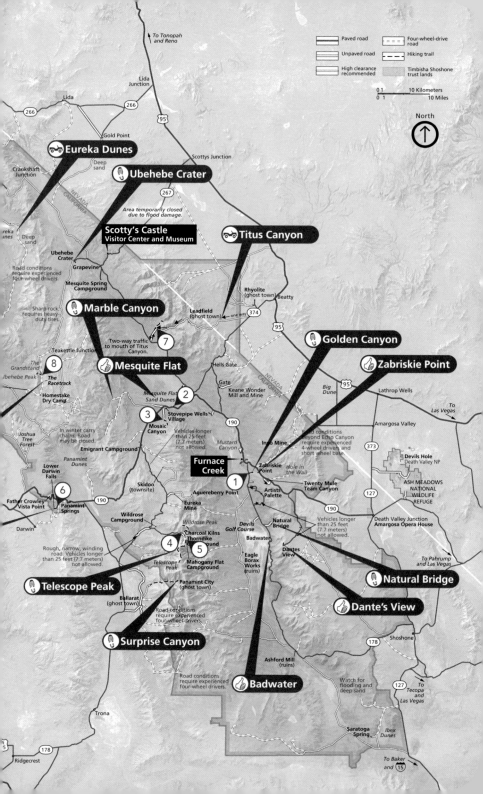

Paved road
Unpaved road
High clearance recommended
Four-wheel-drive road
Hiking trail
Timbisha Shoshone trust lands

0 1   10 Kilometers
0 1   10 Miles

North

To Tonopah and Reno

Lida Junction

Lida

266

266

95

Gold Point

Deep sand

Eureka Dunes

Crankshaft Junction

NEVADA
CALIFORNIA

Scottys Junction

Ubehebe Crater

267

Deep sand

Area temporarily closed due to flood damage.

Scotty's Castle
Visitor Center and Museum

eka nes

Deep sand

Ubehebe Crater

Grapevine

Road conditions require experienced four-wheel drivers.

Mesquite Spring Campground

Titus Canyon

Rhyolite (ghost town)

Beatty

Sharp rock, requires heavy duty tires.

Marble Canyon

Leadfield (ghost town)

one way

374

95

Golden Canyon

7

Two-way traffic to mouth of Titus Canyon.

Teakettle Junction

The Grandstand

8

Ibehebe Peak

The Racetrack

Homestake Dry Camp

Mesquite Flat

Hells Gate

Gate

Keane Wonder Mill and Mine

NEVADA
CALIFORNIA

Big Dune

Zabriskie Point

Lathrop Wells

95

To Las Vegas

Amargosa Valley

In winter carry chains. Road may be closed.

Joshua Tree Forest

Panamint Dunes

Emigrant Campground

Mesquite Flat Sand Dunes

2

3

Mosaic Canyon

Stovepipe Wells Village

Vehicles longer than 25 feet (7.7 meters) not allowed.

190

Mustard Canyon

Road conditions beyond Echo Canyon require experienced 4-wheel drivers and short wheel base.

373

Devils Hole
Death Valley NP

ASH MEADOWS
NATIONAL
WILDLIFE
REFUGE

127

Lower Darwin Falls

6

Father Crowley Vista Point

Panamint Springs

190

Darwin

Skidoo (townsite)

Aguereberry Point

Eureka Mine

Furnace Creek

1

Inyo Mine

Zabriskie Point

Hole in the Wall

Twenty Mule Team Canyon

Devils Golf Course

Artists Palette

190

Death Valley Junction
Amargosa Opera House

To Pahrump and Las Vegas

Rough, narrow, winding road. Vehicles longer than 25 feet (7.7 meters) not allowed.

Wildrose Campground

Wildrose Peak

Charcoal Kilns
Thorndike Campground

4

5

Telescope Peak

Mahogany Flat Campground

Natural Bridge

Badwater

Eagle Borax Works (ruins)

Dantes View

Vehicles longer than 25 feet (7.7 meters) not allowed.

Natural Bridge

Dante's View

Telescope Peak

Ballarat (ghost town)

Panamint City (ghost town)

Road conditions require experienced four-wheel drivers.

Surprise Canyon

Trona

Ashford Mill (ruins)

Road conditions require experienced four-wheel drivers.

Badwater

Watch for flooding and deep sand.

178

Shoshone

127

To Tecopa and Las Vegas

Saratoga Spring

Ibex Dunes

Ridgecrest

178

To Baker and

15

GOLDEN CANYON

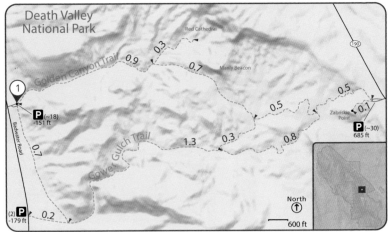

Golden Canyon | Moderate | 6.9 miles | 1,100 feet | Loop
Trailhead: Golden Canyon (1)

Golden Canyon is awesome, but it comes with a few options. You can begin from Zabriskie Point (CA-190) or Golden Canyon (1). There are a variety of loop or out-and-back options. At a minimum, you should walk by Manly Beacon and pay a visit to the Red Cathedral. Doing the full loop through Golden Canyon/Gower Gulch and going up to Zabriskie Overlook (a great sunrise location) is just under seven miles. The spur to Zabriskie Point has a pretty good grade. You could skip it and drive there another time, bringing the loop mileage under six miles. There isn't an official parking area or trail at the end of Gower Gulch but there is enough room for a couple cars alongside the road if the Golden Canyon Trailhead lot is full.

Mesquite Flat Dunes | Moderate | 1.9+ miles | Varies | Follow the Ridges
Trailhead: Mesquite Flat Sand Dunes (2)

There's no right or wrong way to explore Mesquite Flat Sand Dunes. Being the most easily accessible dunes in the park it's also the most popular. Personally, humans make sand dunes more fun, adding an element of scale to such an unusual sight. Morning or evening light is best. Just make sure the sun is still above the surrounding mountains, allowing shadows to dance across the dunes. It's about two miles to the top of the tallest dune from the parking lot but there are a ton of interesting crests to explore. Go where you want. Climb a few ridges then bound down their slopes. Have fun! Just be warned, it's a workout going up and down these things and the dunes are not a particularly pleasant place to be when it's windy.

MESQUITE FLAT/MOSAIC CANYON

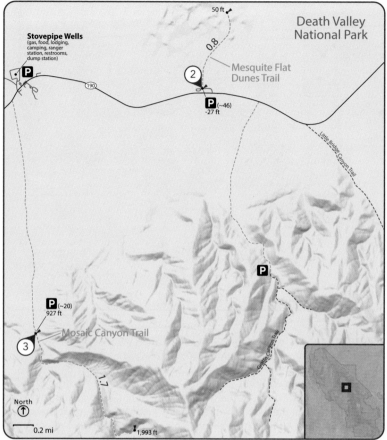

Mosaic Canyon | Moderate | 1.9–3.4 miles | 1,070 feet | Out-and-back
Trailhead: Mosaic Canyon (3)

Mosaic Canyon begins simple enough, following a gravelly wash into a soon-to-be-narrowing canyon. Just about a mile into your hike you'll encounter a rock jumble. If you aren't comfortable scrambling around, this is the turn-around point. If you'd like to continue, look to the east side of the jumble for an access point to the alcove beyond. Back on track, you'll quickly reach a dry waterfall chute. Backtrack and scan the western wall for a faint bypass trail. This is the route. Cross the dryfall and get back into the wash. Continue south, where a few short scrambles lead into another alcove at the base of an impassable dryfall. Return the way you came, carefully scrambling down the smooth boulders. It's nice to carry very little on any hike involving scrambling. And Mosaic Canyon isn't particularly long or difficult so a minimalist approach should be fine. However, that might not be the best idea if it's deathly hot outside. You know your body. Do what works for you.

WILDROSE PEAK

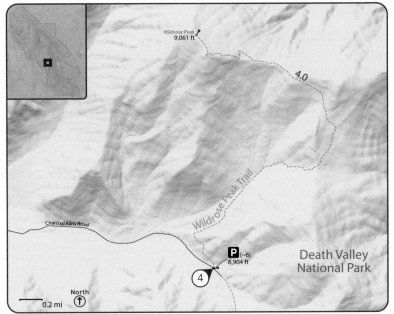

Wildrose Peak
9,061 ft

4.0

Wildrose Peak Trail

Charcoal Kilns Road

🅿 (~6)
6,904 ft

Death Valley
National Park

④

North ↑
0.2 mi

Wildrose Peak | Strenuous | 8.0 miles | 2,200 feet | Out-and-back
Trailhead: Charcoal Kilns, Emigrant Canyon Road (4)

The trailhead is located along Emigrant Canyon Road at the Wildrose Charcoal Kilns parking area. This is the less-strenuous alternative to hiking Telescope Peak, the park's highest point, which begins just to the south at Mahogany Flat Campground. Along this well-worn path, you're treated to nearly-continuous, far-reaching views. A set of switchbacks quickly ascend to a more gradual final approach to the summit, where on a clear day you'll have 360-degree views spanning from the highest point in the Lower 48 (Mount Whitney) to the west, and the lowest point in the Americas (Badwater) to the east. It's a tremendous vantage point, enjoy it, and then return the way you came. You shouldn't have to worry about snow or ice summer through October, but it's always a good idea to check conditions when hiking at elevation.

Telescope Peak | Strenuous | 12.0 miles | 2,950 feet | Out-and-back
Trailhead: Telescope Peak (5)

Stepping things up a notch from Wildrose Peak is the trek to its neighboring summit, Telescope Peak. To reach the trailhead, take Emigrant Canyon Road past Charcoal Kilns, and Thorndike and Mahogany Flat Campgrounds. At a gaited intersection, you'll see the trailhead on your left. The road beyond the gait continues to Rogers Peak. Road conditions change, and the park suggests a high-clearance vehicle beyond Thorndike, but ordinary cars regularly make the trip to Telescope Trailhead. Although this is a serious

TELESCOPE PEAK

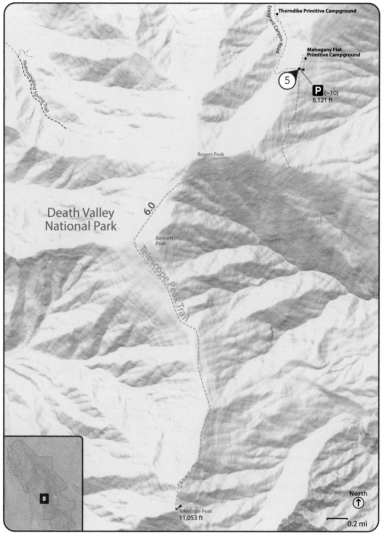

Emigrant Canyon Road

Thorndike Primitive Campground

Humboldt Spring Trail

Mahogany Flat
Primitive Campground

5

P (~10)
8,121 ft

Rogers Peak

Death Valley
National Park

6.0

Bennett
Peak

Telescope Peak Trail

North

Telescope Peak
11,053 ft

0.2 mi

hike at high elevation, the grade is not terrible. It isn't even relentless, with a long mostly flat stretch sandwiched between two steady grades. There's one set of switchbacks before the final summit, and then you're free to relax and enjoy the views across Nevada and California. On a clear day, the view ends at the Sierra Nevada, including the tallest point in the Lower 48, Mount Whitney. To the east, you'll look across Badwater and Death Valley, over the Amargosa Range all the way to the Spring Mountains near Las Vegas. Return as you came and take your time to appreciate the ancient bristlecone pines you'll pass along the way.

DARWIN FALLS

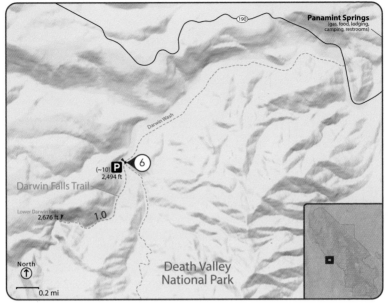

Darwin Falls | Easy | 2.0 miles | 200 feet | Out-and-back
Trailhead: Darwin Falls (6)

Just east of Panamint Springs, there's a short, unpaved road (Old Toll Road) leading visitors on the path to a peculiar desert oasis. The trailhead quickly appears on the righthand side of the road. From here, it's an easy walk back to Lower Darwin Falls. It's a real treat to see water flowing in such a vast, seemingly-uninhabitable region. Although only about 20-feet tall, the lower falls is pretty, and seeing water and trees in such a harsh environment is a very enjoyable experience.

Titus Canyon | Moderate | 0–7.8 miles | Varies | Out-and-back
Fall Canyon | Moderate | 6.8 miles | 1,700 feet | Out-and-back
Trailhead: Titus Canyon Mouth (7)

Titus Canyon is good fun (in a car or on your feet). The caveat here is Titus Canyon is a (mostly) one-way road driven by all kinds of vehicles and motorbikes. High-clearance will provide peace of mind. The rugged road is 26.8 miles, driven east to west. It's slow-going but 100% worth the time commitment. Not sure about it? Consider driving to the mouth of Titus Canyon (the lone stretch of road open to two-way traffic) to see what you think. Rambling along this stretch provides a good indicator if you can endure a couple hours of bouncing around in your vehicle to see some cool, colorful rocks. If the drive's a bad idea, stop at the trailhead and hike into the canyon as far as you care to go. This is the narrowest section, just barely wider than a large vehicle at several points.

TITUS CANYON/FALL CANYON

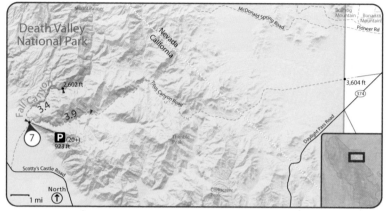

You can also hike up Fall Canyon from the Titus Canyon parking area. It's not as beautiful, but it also doesn't have a regular stream of cars and motorbikes flowing through it. The most difficult part of this hike is the initial climb and descent before reaching the wash you'll follow the rest of the way. The wash is mostly flat and easy going. There's a short side trail to a waterfall chute. After about three miles, the canyon narrows before reaching its conclusion at another dry waterfall chute. It didn't look insurmountable, but I wasn't willing to take an unnecessary risk trying to climb it. Note that Fall Canyon was closed when this book went to print.

Conditions

Death Valley's weather extremes receive a disproportionate amount of the media's attention. For most of the year, it's a fantastic place to be. Even in summer, you can find a comfortable perch (like Telescope Peak) to enjoy unbelievable views. But don't completely ignore the weather. Exploring anything on (or near) the valley floor mid-day in summer is not a good idea. Temperature exceeded 130°F at Furnace Creek in August 2022. However, mornings can be bearable (80s°F) and it's usually about a 40°F temperature difference from the lowest point in the park (Badwater) to the highest (Telescope Peak). A more realistic approach to making the most of a Death Valley trip is to visit between fall and spring.

Off-Roading

Death Valley is an off-roader's paradise! The entry point is probably Titus Canyon Road. If you enjoyed that, it's time to consider heading to the Racetrack or some of the canyons accessed via West Side Road. If you'd like to take it easier and want to enjoy a less popular sand dune than Mesquite Flat, check out Ibex dunes in the park's southeast corner, Panamint Dunes (just north of Panamint Springs), or Eureka Dunes (at the northern end of the park). Unpaved roads explore nearly every corner of this massive park. Just come prepared. Off-roading Death Valley is not something to take lightly. Full-sized spare, jerry cans, compressor, tow strap, traction boards, and even an emergency beacon are good ideas, just in case. Self-recovery is much better than waiting for a tow or rescue.

UBEHEBE PEAK

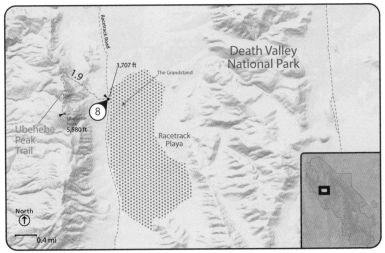

Ubehebe Peak | Strenuous | 3.9 miles | 2,300 feet | Out-and-back
Trailhead: Grandstand Parking Area, Racetrack Road (8)

Ubehebe is a nice perk for anyone who makes the long off-road drive to The Racetrack. You gain quite a bit of elevation in a short amount of distance. It's rocky and kind of dangerous toward the top. But the 360-degree views from Racetrack Playa to Saline Valley are excellent. It's a long (and bumpy) journey to The Racetrack, whichever way you're coming from. The access road from the north is heavily washboarded. And the road from the south occasionally closes in winter due to snow. A summer visit? That's usually not a good idea. But it is a great idea to take your time once you arrive, get a little workout summiting Ubehebe Peak, and then hop back in your 4x4 and begin the journey to your next Death Valley destination.

More Trails

There are several trails that weren't mentioned because they're short and easy to access. At the top of the list is Badwater Salt Flat (easy, 1+ miles), where you can walk out to a perfectly flat basin and play with perspective. The crusty salt formations are fun to photograph as well. While it isn't exactly a hike, you also shouldn't skip a quick stop at Zabriskie Point, preferably for sunrise. Golden Canyon walks right past the prominent pinnacle, but the viewpoint is excellent too. Artist Palette (easy) is Instagram popular but still worth a stop to see the cool colorful rocks. And then there's Natural Bridge (easy, 1–2 miles), a short and fun hike to a massive stone bridge. But there's much more of everything. There are more canyons: Grotto, Sidewinder, Desolation, Marble, Star Wars. There are more dunes: Panamint, Eureka, Ibex, Saline Valley. And I'm sure there are plenty of things I don't know about. The park is more than 3 million acres! Death Valley is one of my all-time favorite places and it makes me sad whenever someone trashes it, probably because they went to the valley in summer or had the bad luck of showing up in the middle of a sandstorm. Or maybe something else? I don't know. What I do know is, it's like no other place on earth. And as testament to the park's otherworldly nature, it's been used as a setting for many space-based movies, including the original *Star Wars*.

Mesquite Flat Sand Dunes

Sequoia–Kings Canyon
Hiking Trails: 800+ miles

Mist Falls

Sequoia–Kings Canyon Favorites

(1) Mosquito Lakes
Strenuous | 6.6 miles | 2,000 feet

Eagle Lake
Strenuous | 6.2 miles | 2,400 feet

(2) Moro Rock
Moderate | 0.4 mile | 300 feet

(3) Big Trees
Easy | 1.3 miles | 50 feet

(4) General Sherman
Moderate | 1.0 mile | 220 feet

(5) Lakes
Strenuous | 11.2 miles | 2,800 feet

Alta Peak
Strenuous | 13.0 miles | 4,000 feet

(6) Tokopah Falls
Easy | 3.8 miles | 900 feet

(7) Little Baldy
Moderate | 3.2 miles | 800 feet

(8) Big Stump
Easy | 1.9 miles | 200 feet

(9) General Grant
Easy | 1.6 miles | 40 feet

(10) Mist Falls
Moderate | 8.7 miles | 800 feet

(11) Kearsarge Pass
Strenuous | 9.3 miles | 2,650 feet

(12) Mount Whitney
Extreme | 21.0 miles | 6,120 feet

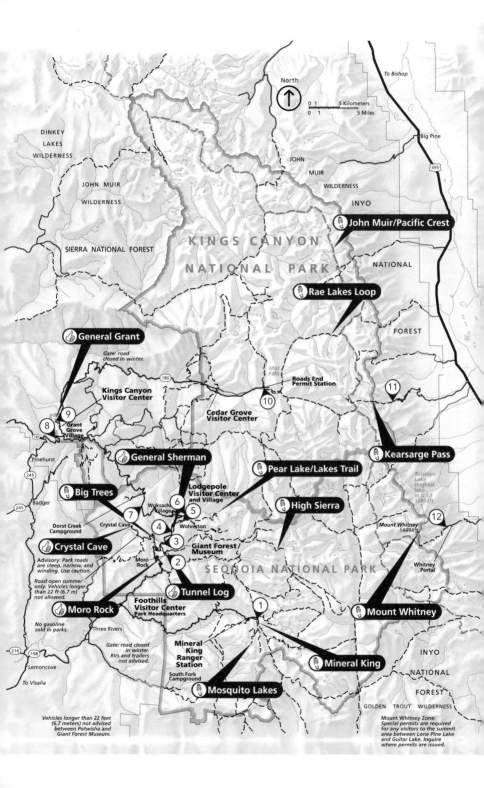

North

0 1   5 Kilometers
0 1   5 Miles

To Bishop

DINKEY
LAKES
WILDERNESS

JOHN
MUIR
WILDERNESS

395

Big Pine

JOHN MUIR

WILDERNESS

INYO

SIERRA NATIONAL FOREST

KINGS CANYON

NATIONAL PARK

NATIONAL

John Muir/Pacific Crest

Rae Lakes Loop

FOREST

General Grant

Gate: road
closed in winter.

180

Kings Canyon
Visitor Center

Mist
Falls

Roads End
Permit Station

9

8

Grant
Grove
Village

180

Pinehurst

245

Cedar Grove
Visitor Center

10

11

Kearsarge Pass

Tulainyo
Lake
(highest
lake
in U.S.)
12802ft

General Sherman

Badger

245

Big Trees

Lodgepole
Visitor Center
and Village

Pear Lake/Lakes Trail

Dorst Creek
Campground

7

Wuksachi
Village

6

5

High Sierra

Crystal Cave

Crystal Cave

4

3

Wolverton

Giant Forest/
Museum

Mount Whitney
14494ft

12

Whitney
Portal

Advisory: Park roads
are steep, narrow, and
winding. Use caution.

2

Moro
Rock

SEQUOIA NATIONAL PARK

Road open summer
only. Vehicles longer
than 22 ft (6.7 m)
not allowed.

Tunnel Log

Moro Rock

Foothills
Visitor Center
Park Headquarters

1

Mount Whitney

No gasoline
sold in parks.

Three Rivers

Gate: road closed
in winter.
RVs and trailers
not advised.

Mineral
King
Ranger
Station

INYO

216

198

South Fork
Campground

Mineral King

NATIONAL

Lemoncove

Mosquito Lakes

FOREST

To Visalia

GOLDEN TROUT WILDERNESS

Vehicles longer than 22 feet
(6.7 meters) not advised
between Potwisha and
Giant Forest Museum.

Mount Whitney Zone:
Special permits are required
for any visitors to the summit
area between Lone Pine Lake
and Guitar Lake. Inquire
where permits are issued.

MOSQUITO LAKES/EAGLE LAKE

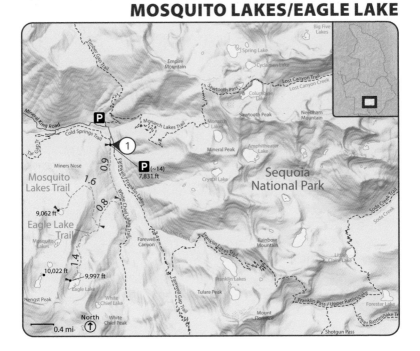

Mosquito Lakes | Strenuous | 6.6 miles | 2,000 feet | Out-and-back
Eagle Lake | Strenuous | 6.2 miles | 2,400 feet | Out-and-back
Trailhead: White Chief, Mineral King Road (1)

The easiest way to get some of Sequoia's famous High Sierra scenery is to make the long, narrow, and (occasionally) rough drive to Mineral King. 2WD cars can make the journey (RVs and trailers are not a good idea). The road closes in winter near Lookout Point entrance. From the trailhead, these trails are easy to follow. It's a straight, relatively flat (but constantly gaining elevation) walk to White Chief Junction, where you head west toward Eagle/Mosquito Lakes and the grade begins to increase. In under a mile, you'll be at the Eagle Lake junction. Following the path to the south leads to a relentless climb to Eagle Lake. Continuing to the north leads up, over, and down a ridge before the final ascent to Mosquito Lakes. If you're loving life back here, you can navigate to three more Mosquito Lakes. It takes some trail finding. The social path is difficult to follow but cairns mark the way. Scenery improves with each successive lake. Strong hikers with an early start shouldn't have too much difficulty exploring all five lakes in a day.

There's maybe room for twenty vehicles at the trailhead. It's a good idea to camp at Cold Springs if you'd like to hike this area. Recently, rangers have warned visitors about famished marmots ravaging visitors' vehicles, eating tasty tubing, seals, and wiring. Now, the cynic in me imagines people in the

MORO ROCK/BIG TREES

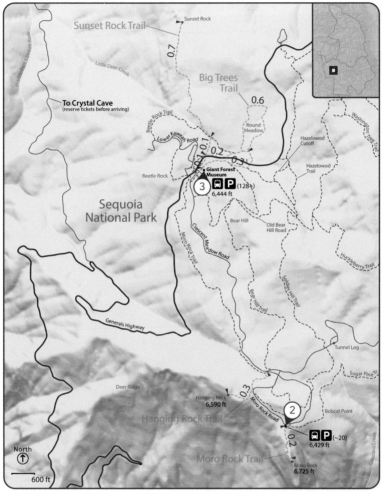

know pointing and laughing at "tourists" as they marmot-proof their cars (typically wrapping with tarp), but I'm not sure what's the truth. Maybe marmots are disabling cars. Maybe they aren't. Anyway, the park says, marmot malfeasance is worst early in the hiking season, so there's less to worry about during prime hiking time (August–October).

Moro Rock | Moderate | 0.4 mile | 300 feet | Out-and-back
Trailhead: Moro Rock, Crescent Meadow Road (2)

Short, difficult, with a little bit of fear factor, Moro Rock is near the top of many activity wish lists due to its location, length, and views. While in the area, it's a

GENERAL SHERMAN

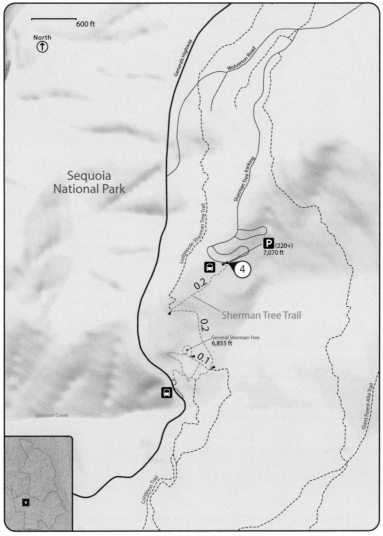

good idea to check out Tunnel Log, Hanging Rock, and Crescent Meadow (a good place to spot bears). Crescent Meadow is also where you can access the High Sierra Trail. It's largely traversed by backpackers, but you can hike 11.5 miles to Bearpaw Camp (meals, beds, showers, flush toilets). From the camp, you can easily reach places like Precipice Lake (if you can get a reservation).

This is an extremely busy area. The park runs four shuttle routes during peak season to help alleviate congestion. Use them or get an early start.

LAKES/ALTA PEAK

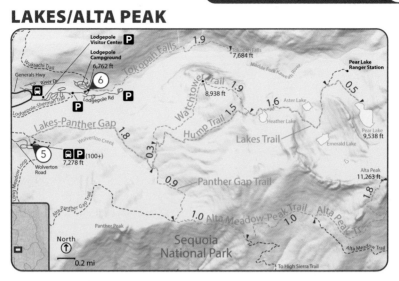

Big Trees | Easy | 1.3 miles | 50 feet | Loop
Trailhead: Giant Forest Museum, Generals Highway (3)

Big Trees is a pleasant loop among towering trees. If you'd like a little longer lollipop with equally impressive trees, consider taking Congress Trail to General Sherman and back. It's great too!

General Sherman | Moderate | 1.0 mile | 220 feet | Out-and-back
Trailhead: General Sherman Tree, Wolverton Road (4)

If you're visiting Sequoia, chances are you're going to make the short (but moderately steep) hike to General Sherman, the world's most massive single living organism. It's worth seeing, but if you're visiting during peak season, especially on a weekend, you may want to think about doing a longer hike or visiting a less-popular region like Muir Grove (near Dorst Creek Campground).

Lakes | Strenuous | 11.2 miles | 2,800 feet | Out-and-back
Alta Peak | Strenuous | 13.0 miles | 4,000 feet | Out-and-back
Trailhead: Lakes, Wolverton Road (5)

Lakes Trail is your direct route to sublime Sierra scenery, featuring four rock-rimmed lakes (Heather, Aster, Emerald, and Pear). Pear Lake is the highlight but each one is worth the effort you'll expend hiking up to 9,500-feet elevation. Getting there, you'll have to choose between Hump or Watchtower trails to Heather Lake Basin. Hump is shorter but less scenic. Watchtower is longer, more scenic, and has some exposure. If you have a fear of heights, you'll want to Hump it. If not, take Watchtower. Don't dip your toes in Heather Lake and turn around. If you're doing this as a dayhike, make sure you have enough

LITTLE BALDY

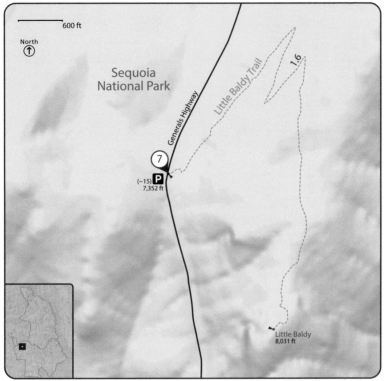

Sequoia
National Park

600 ft

North

Generals Highway

Little Baldy Trail

1.6

7

(~15) P
7,352 ft

Little Baldy
8,031 ft

time to reach Pear Lake. If you'd like to slow the pace down a bit, this is also a popular backpacking destination (permit required).

Alta Trail leads hikers to Alta Peak, towering high above Pear Lake. Hike to Pear. If you loved it, come back and hike to Alta Peak!

These are popular trails but there's quite a bit of parking at the trailhead and nearby picnic area. It's also a shuttle stop, but an early start is ideal.

Tokopah Falls | Easy | 3.8 miles | 900 feet | Out-and-back
Trailhead: Lodgepole Campground (6)

A nice easy walk to enjoy right from your campsite. The falls will be more impressive in spring/early summer, but don't scratch it off your list because the waterfall won't be near maximum volume. It's still nice.

Shuttles
The park operates four free shuttle routes during peak summer season. During winter holidays, free shuttles are usually available in the Giant Forest and Lodgepole areas. You'll want to check the park website (nps.gov/seki) for current routes and schedules.

BIG STUMP

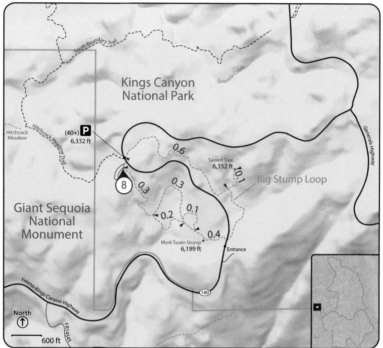

Little Baldy | Moderate | 3.2 miles | 800 feet | Out-and-back
Trailhead: Little Baldy, Generals Highway (7)

It's a steady climb to scenic views atop Little Baldy. The trail is a lightly trafficked trail and it's easy to access as you're transitioning between Sequoia and
Kings Canyon. If you have some time, pull over and take a hike!

Big Stump | Easy | 1.9 miles | 200 feet | Loop
Trailhead: Big Stump Picnic Area, Generals Highway (8)

This is a more peaceful version of Grant Grove. The Army cut down Mark Twain
Tree in 1891. Its cross sections were used to amaze audiences in New York and
London (and one's still on display at the British Museum). Sawed Tree proved
to be too much tree for a couple loggers.

Weather

With elevation ranging from 1,700 feet in the foothills to 14,494 feet at the top
of Mount Whitney, weather has a huge degree of variance. Know where you're
headed. Watch the weather. Come prepared. Massive slabs of wide-open
granite are not good places to be during a thunderstorm.

GENERAL GRANT

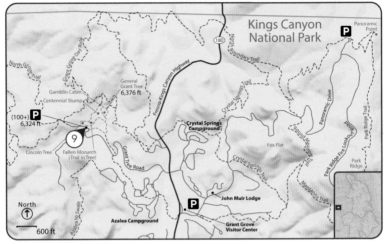

Kings Canyon National Park

180

North Grove Trail

Grant Grove Day Hikes

North Grove Trail

Gamblin Cabin
Centennial Stump

General Grant Tree
6,376 ft

(100+)
6,324 ft

9

Lincoln Tree

Fallen Monarch
(Trail in Tree)

Grant Tree Road

Fresno-Kings Canyon Highway

North Boundary Trail

Crystal Springs Trail

Crystal Springs Campground

Fox Flat

Crystal Springs Trail

Jenny Meadow Trail

Panoramic Point

P Panoramic Point

Park Ridge Trail

Park Ridge Fire Lookout

Panoramic Drive

Dead Road

Park Ridge

Manzanita Trail

John Muir Lodge

P

Grant Grove Visitor Center

Azalea Campground

North
↑

600 ft

MIST FALLS

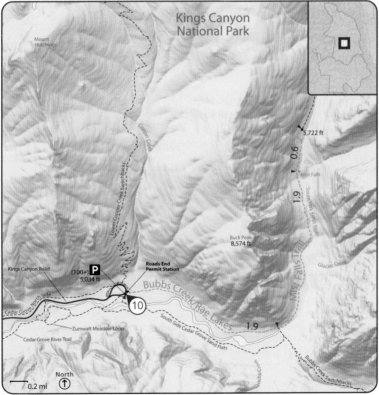

Kings Canyon National Park

Mount Hutchings

Gardiner Creek

Lower Copper Creek Switchbacks

Kings Canyon Road

(100+)
5,034 ft

P

Roads End Permit Station

Cedar Grove North Side

Zumwalt Meadow Loop

Cedar Grove River Trail

10

Bubbs Creek/Rae Lakes

South Side Cedar Grove Sand Flats

Buck Peak
8,574 ft

5,722 ft

0.6

Mist Falls

1.9

South Fork Kings River

Mist Falls Trail

Glacier Creek

1.9

Bubbs Creek Switchbacks

North
↑

0.2 mi

General Grant | Easy | 1.6 miles | 40 feet | Out-and-back
Trailhead: Grant Tree Road (9)

Short, easy, impressive trees, and a tree (Fallen Monarch) you can walk through are all quality traits. If you want more big trees, Grant Grove is home to some very impressive specimens.

Mist Falls | Moderate | 8.7 miles | 800 feet | Out-and-back
Trailhead: Roads End, Kings Canyon Scenic Byway (10)

Roads End at Kings Canyon is more about backpacking than dayhiking. If you will not be denied, your best bet is to follow the South Fork Kings River up to Mist Falls. The trail's a modest incline until the last mile. Be careful on the rocks near the waterfall. They're often slippery. If you still have some energy left in your tank, keep hiking toward Paradise Valley. The grade remains steep, but distant views begin to open up and they're, well, paradise. Kings Canyon Scenic Byway closes for winter. Even though it's nice, you get better views for your effort on Lakes Trail or from trailheads on the east side of the Sierra Range. That's where you'll find all kinds of jaw-dropping scenery.

KEARSARGE PASS

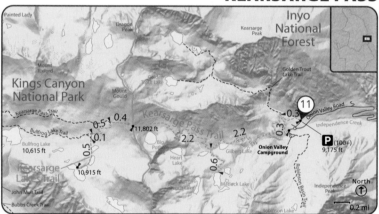

Kearsarge Pass | Strenuous | 9.3 miles | 2,650 feet | Out-and-back
Trailhead: Kearsarge Pass, Onion Valley Road (11)

The trail doesn't begin in the park but it's good to know about the Eastern Sierra and many wonders along US-395. The journey begins in Inyo National Forest (John Muir Wilderness). And from there, after less than five miles, you can get a good peek into Kings Canyon from Kearsarge Pass. With an early start, a strong hiker could make it to Kearsarge Lakes and back. If you can get up to the pass with the sun still behind you, the views down toward Kearsarge

Lakes will be amazing. Enjoy the lakes for a while, then climb back up to the pass, and the sun should be behind you for brilliant views back into Onion Valley. Early start! Get to the pass! You still don't want to rush. Heading over to Matlock Lake in the morning is another fantastic decision. Golden Trout Lakes sound nice but it's steep scree, with tracts of taillessness. Try it at your own risk.

MOUNT WHITNEY

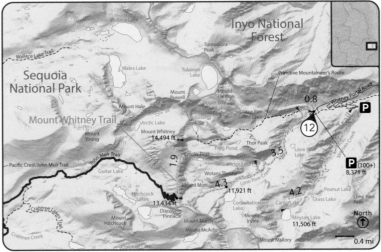

Mount Whitney | Extreme | 21.0 miles | 6,120 feet | Out-and-back
Trailhead: Lone Pine, Whitney Portal Road (12)

Mount Whitney, the tallest peak in the Lower 48 lies within Sequoia National Park, but, like Kearsarge Pass, the "dayhiking" option begins in Inyo National Forest. First, let me tell you, unless you're some sort of superhuman with unbelievable lungs willing to begin the trek before the sun rises, this is (most likely) not a dayhike. But it is a phenomenally beautiful area, with some far-less-extreme dayhiking options. If you're one of those superhumans looking to dayhike Whitney, you'll need to win a permit lottery (recreation.gov). Mirror Lake. Meysan Lake. Those are more realistic dayhiking options for us commoners. If you want Whitney, you're talking about more than 6,000 feet of elevation gain, and nearly 100 switchbacks. Start training! Realistically, it's a 2-night backpacking trip, to take it easy and acclimate to the elevation.

Coming over here, it's a good idea to spend the night at Whitney Portal or Lone Pine campgrounds. Make reservations through recreation.gov. Even though you're at the foot of the tallest mountain in the Lower 48, weather at its base can be reasonably comfortable even in winter if you'd like to sit back and admire this mighty mountain.

Yosemite
Hiking Trails: 750+ miles

Half Dome

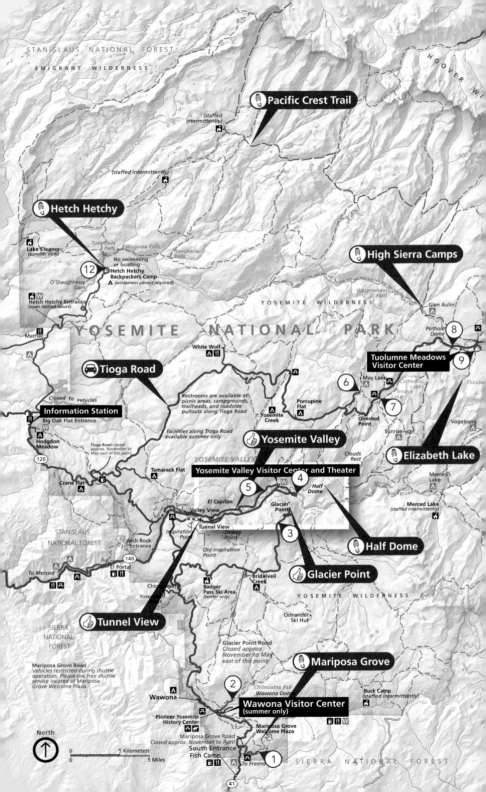

Pacific Crest Trail

(staffed intermittently)

HOOVER WI

STANISLAUS NATIONAL FOREST

EMIGRANT WILDERNESS

(staffed intermittently)

Hetch Hetchy

Tueeolala Falls · Wapama Falls

Lake Eleanor *(summer only)*

Rancheria Falls

No swimming or boating

Hetch Hetchy Backpackers Camp
▲ *(wilderness permit required)*

O'Shaughnessy Dam

12

Waterwheel Falls

High Sierra Camps

YOSEMITE WILDERNESS

Glen Aulin

Hetch Hetchy Entrance *(open limited hours)*

Mather

YOSEMITE NATIONAL PARK

Pothole Dome

8

Tioga Road

White Wolf ▲ ⊞

Restrooms are available at picnic areas, campgrounds, trailheads, and roadside pullouts along Tioga Road

Porcupine Flat

Yosemite Creek

Tuolumne Meadows Visitor Center

May Lake **6**

Cathedral Lakes

Tenaya Lake

9

Elizabeth

Information Station

Big Oak Flat Entrance

Hodgdon Meadow

Tioga Road closed approx. November to May east of this point

Facilities along Tioga Road available summer only

7

Olmsted Point

Sunrise

Vogelsang

120

Crane Flat

Tamarack Flat

YOSEMITE VALLEY

Yosemite Valley

Clouds Rest

Elizabeth Lake

Merced Lake

STANISLAUS NATIONAL FOREST

Tunnel

El Capitan

Yosemite Valley Visitor Center and Theater

5 ⊞ Valley View

4

Glacier Point

Half Dome

Merced River

Merced Lake *(staffed intermittently)*

Arch Rock Entrance

Inspiration Point

Tunnel View

Dewey Point

3

140

El Portal

Old Inspiration Point

Half Dome

To Merced ⊞ ▲

Chinquapin

Badger Pass Ski Area *(winter only)*

Bridalveil Creek

Glacier Point

YOSEMITE WILDERNESS

Yosemite West

Tunnel View

SIERRA NATIONAL FOREST

Ostrander Ski Hut

Glacier Point Road Closed approx. November to May east of this point

Mariposa Grove

Chilnualna Fall

Wawona Dome

Buck Camp *(staffed intermittently)*

Mariposa Grove Road *Vehicles restricted during shuttle operation. Please use free shuttle service located at Mariposa Grove Welcome Plaza.*

2

Wawona Visitor Center *(summer only)*

Wawona ▲

Pioneer Yosemite History Center

Mariposa Grove Welcome Plaza

North

Mariposa Grove Road Closed approx. November to April

South Entrance Fish Camp

1

0 5 Kilometers
0 5 Miles

To Fresno

SIERRA NATIONAL FOREST

41

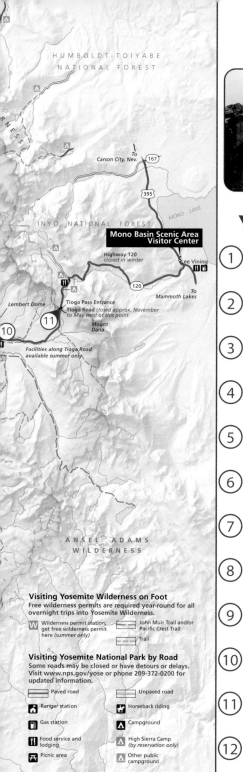

HUMBOLDT-TOIYABE
NATIONAL FOREST

To Carson City, Nev. (167)

395

MONO LAKE

INYO NATIONAL FOREST

Mono Basin Scenic Area Visitor Center

Lee Vining

Highway 120
closed in winter

120

To Mammoth Lakes

Lembert Dome

Tioga Pass Entrance
Tioga Road closed approx. November
to May west of this point

Mount Dana

10

11

Facilities along Tioga Road
available summer only

ANSEL ADAMS
WILDERNESS

Visiting Yosemite Wilderness on Foot
Free wilderness permits are required year-round for all
overnight trips into Yosemite Wilderness.

W Wilderness permit station;
get free wilderness permit
here (summer only)

— John Muir Trail and/or
Pacific Crest Trail

— Trail

Visiting Yosemite National Park by Road
Some roads may be closed or have detours or delays.
Visit www.nps.gov/yose or phone 209-372-0200 for
updated information.

Paved road

Unpaved road

Ranger station

Horseback riding

Gas station

Campground

Food service and
lodging

High Sierra Camp
(by reservation only)

Picnic area

Other public
campground

Taft Point

Yosemite Favorites

(1) Grizzly Giant
Moderate | 2.1 miles | 300 feet

(2) Chilnualna Falls
Strenuous | 7.4 miles | 2,200 feet

(3) Sentinel Dome & Taft Point
Moderate | 4.8 miles | 1,100 feet

(4) Vernal Falls/Half Dome
Moderate/Extreme | 3.0/15.4 miles | 4,900 feet

(5) Yosemite Falls
Strenuous | 5.6 miles | 3,000 feet

(6) May Lake
Easy | 2.7 miles | 500 feet

(7) Clouds Rest
Strenuous | 11.9 miles | 2,000 feet

(8) Cathedral Lakes
Moderate | 7.8 miles | 1,000 feet

(9) Elizabeth Lake
Moderate | 4.2 miles | 900 feet

(10) Lembert Dome
Moderate | 1.8 miles | 800 feet

(11) Gaylor Lakes
Moderate | 3.6 miles | 850 feet

(12) Wapama Falls/Rancheria Falls
Moderate/Strenuous | 4.6/12.2 miles | 850 feet

GRIZZLY GIANT

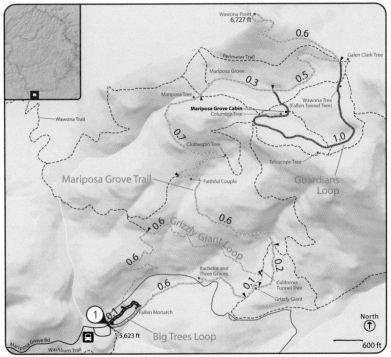

Grizzly Giant | Moderate | 2.1 miles | 300 feet | Loop
Trailhead: Mariposa Grove Road (1)

Grizzly Giant Loop offers a nice sampling of Mariposa Grove's famous sequoia trees. Among the many ancient sentinels, you'll witness Grizzly Giant and California Tunnel Tree. Tunnel Tree was cut in 1895 to allow carriages through. It's still standing. Still living!

As you can see, there are quite a few hiking options at Mariposa Grove. You can take the short (0.3 mile) Big Trees Loop or the long (7.0 miles) and strenuous Mariposa Grove Trail, which concludes at Wawona Point. On the way back from Wawona Point, you can take a detour on Guardians Loop, passing by Wawona Tree. Wawona Tree was made famous for its tunnel, cut in 1881. The mighty tunneled tree stood for nearly a century, falling in 1969.

Mariposa Grove Road is typically closed to vehicles from December through March. You can still access the grove by hiking, snowshoeing, or cross-country skiing two miles up Mariposa Grove Road or Washburn Trail. Another winter perk is camping is allowed in the grove (when there's snow and the road is closed). When Mariposa Grove Road is open, it is only accessible via shuttle from the Mariposa Grove Welcome Plaza (located near the South Entrance

CHILNUALNA FALLS

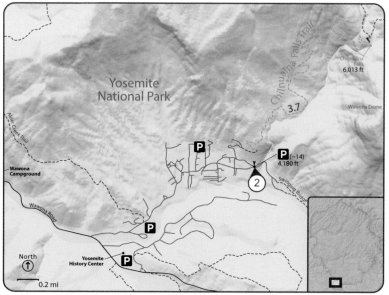

Yosemite National Park

Chilnualna Falls Trail

Chilnualna Falls 6,013 ft

Wawona Dome

3.7

Alder Creek Trail

Wawona Campground

P

P (~14) 4,180 ft

2

Swinging Bridge

Wawona Road

P

North ↑

Yosemite History Center

P

0.2 mi

roundabout). Things change so it's always a good idea to get an up-to-date shuttle schedule from the park (nps.gov/yose) prior to arrival. The Welcome Plaza has roughly 300 parking spaces. That may sound like a lot but expect them to fill by mid-morning during peak season. Mariposa Grove is great but if you're short on time, spend most of it exploring Yosemite Valley.

Chilnualna Falls | Strenuous | 7.4 miles | 2,200 feet | Out-and-back
Trailhead: Chilnualna Falls Road (2)

Looking to escape the foot traffic found at Yosemite Valley's waterfall trails? Chilnualna is a pretty darn good alternative. Yes, it's fairly long. Yes, the incline is unrelenting. Yes, it isn't quite as beautiful as those Yosemite Valley waterfalls. But it is more secluded, and it features a bunch of swimming holes along the way as well as a variety of views of impressive Wawona Dome. Just note, even though this trail features a massive granite dome, this is not the Yosemite many visitors come to expect. You'll be in the lower elevations, so it's pretty thick pine forest until you get close to the main waterfall. Once you've reached Chilnualna Falls, take a break, have a snack, and then spend a little time exploring the area.

Sentinel Dome & Taft Point | Moderate | 4.8 miles | 1,100 feet | Loop
Trailhead: Pohono, Glacier Point Road (3)

While Taft Point and Sentinel Dome are popular destinations, they'll feel like forgotten wonders compared to nearby Glacier Point and Yosemite Valley.

SENTINEL DOME/TAFT POINT

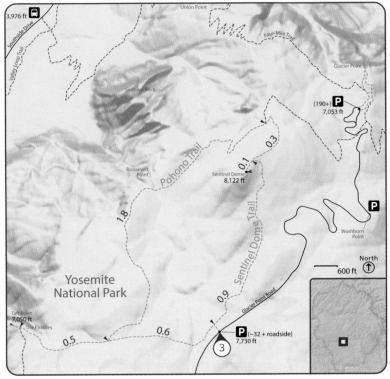

And they're awesome! Taft Point overlooks Yosemite Valley with great views of El Capitan and Yosemite Falls. It's a great place for sunrise or sunset. Sentinel Dome is just one of Yosemite's many famous granite domes and it serves up stunning views of the most famous dome of them all, Half Dome.

There's only room for about two dozen vehicles at the trailhead and spaces fill early during peak season. After morning, finding a spot is left to luck. You can also reach the loop from Glacier Point, adding about two miles to the trek.

Vernal Falls/Half Dome | Moderate/Extreme | 3.0/15.4 miles | 1,000/4,900 feet | Loop/Lollipop
Trailhead: Happy Isles (Shuttle Stop #16), Yosemite Valley (4)

This corridor is one of the most beautiful sections of one of the most beautiful places on the planet, Yosemite Valley. The hike to Vernal Falls gets congested. It's also a lot of stairs. Still, if you go to Vernal, love it and have more time/energy, keep going up to Nevada Falls, and then return via John Muir Trail. You'll enjoy the view from Clark Point (looking back to Nevada Fall), which is spectacular (especially in the late afternoon light). If you're fit, can get an

MIST/HALF DOME/MIRROR LAKE

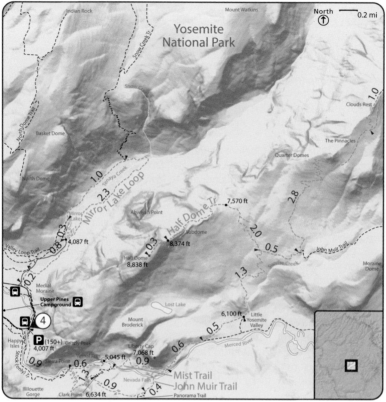

early start (first light), and want a more adventurous hike, then you should start thinking about going for Half Dome. Without checking those boxes, it's probably not worth the effort/expense to try and win the Half Dome Lottery (recreation.gov). Half Dome is accessible to non-rock climbers thanks to two steel cables and a ladder of wooden slats. It's a long, difficult-but-doable day. If you think you have what it takes, the first step is entering the permit lottery through recreation.gov. No permit. No hike. Even if you're backpacking in Little Yosemite Valley. You know your typical hiking pace best. If 15.4 miles and nearly 5,000-feet elevation gain sound like a lot but you're confident you can get it done, you probably want to start before sunrise. The last thing you want to do is feel rushed on the cables. A mistake could be deadly. Make sure you're wearing shoes with good grip (and are broken in!) and pack a pair of gloves (there's usually a pile of gloves at the start of the cables, but it'd be much better if everyone brought their own and carried them out). Grippy shoes and gloves are essential for ascending the cables. While the trail is long, it'll likely go by quickly, thanks to distractions like Vernal and Nevada Falls. But then time slows down a bit at subdome. Its switchbacks are where the difficulty cranks up a few levels. But make it to the top of Subdome and you'll be staring Half Dome right in the back! Take a break. Drink some water. Have a snack. And then queue up for the cables. Climbing up Half Dome is a grind. Go at your own pace but try to remain cognizant of faster hikers behind you, and, if at all possible, allow them to pass. Before you know it, you'll be on top of the rock! Walk around. Have a snack. And then it's back down the cables. It's important to listen to your body. I've been up there when a guy cramped up mid-cables. Not good. Like with Vernal and Nevada Falls, return via John Muir Trail for some wonderful evening views back toward Nevada Falls.

Cables are usually put up before Memorial Day and taken down in the middle of October. Do not attempt the climb if Half Dome is wet or storm clouds are present. Like any High Sierra hiking, get to lower (and preferably less rocky) ground during a storm. It's a good idea to pack a headlamp, just in case you're late getting back. And before you depart, know when the sun sets and give yourself a firm turn around time. It should be a quicker hike on the return trip, going downhill nearly the entire way, but if you think you'll be dead tired from 15 miles and 5,000 feet of elevation gain, don't be too optimistic. Be honest with yourself, and then choose your turn around time conservatively (and adjust it along the way). You may cruise on the trail but spend too much time at Vernal and Nevada Falls and daylight could slip away from you. Backpacking is a great option. Not only will you have more time to enjoy some superlative scenery, but you can wake up and climb Subdome and Half Dome before the dayhikers arrive. And, if you like downhills, you can begin from Tioga Road, hike to Clouds Rest, camp at Little Yosemite Valley, climb Half Dome, and exit at Happy Isles. A perfect trip! The only problem is you'll have to win not one but two lotteries. How lucky do you feel?

Happy Isles is the northern terminus of the John Muir Trail. The bonus of starting with the sun is you should be able to get a parking space. Happy Isles is a shuttle stop but you probably want to begin before the shuttles. Camping at one of the Pines (Upper, Lower, North) campgrounds or spending the night at Curry Village are good options if you can get a reservation.

Yosemite Falls | Strenuous | 5.6 miles | 3,000 feet | Out-and-back
Trailhead: Yosemite Falls, Yosemite Valley (5)

Most visitors are satisfied seeing Yosemite Falls, the tallest waterfall in North America, from the valley floor, but you can hike to the top of it via Yosemite Falls Trail. It's a workout. With an early start and unlimited energy, you could make it to the top of Yosemite Falls and North Dome in a day. North Dome is about five more miles (one-way) from the top of Yosemite Falls.

YOSEMITE FALLS

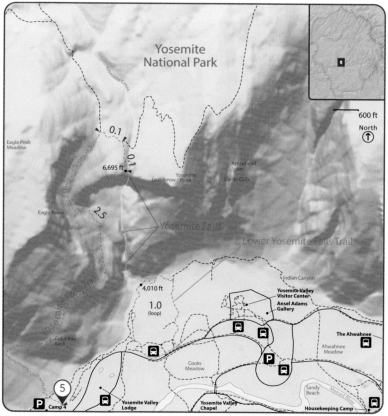

600 ft

North

Yosemite National Park

Yosemite Creek

Eagle Peak Meadow

0.1

0.1

6,695 ft

Lost Arrow

Yosemite Point

Arrowhead Spire

Castle Cliffs

Eagle Tower

2.5

Yosemite Falls Trail

Yosemite Falls

Lower Yosemite Falls Trail

Indian Canyon

4,010 ft

1.0 (loop)

Yosemite Valley Visitor Center

Ansel Adams Gallery

The Ahwahnee

Ahwahnee Meadow

Columbia Rock

P

Cooks Meadow

Sandy Beach

Merced River

5 Camp 4

P

Yosemite Valley Lodge

Yosemite Valley Chapel

Housekeeping Camp

MAY LAKE

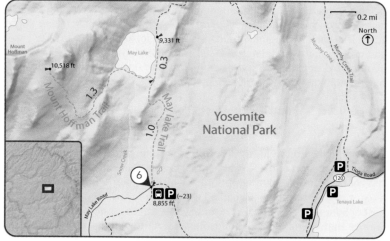

0.2 mi

North

Mount Hoffman

10,518 ft

Mount Hoffman Trail

May Lake

9,331 ft

0.3

1.3

May Lake Trail

1.0

Snow Creek

Yosemite National Park

Murphy Creek

Murphy Creek Trail

6

P (~23)

8,855 ft

May Lake Road

P

Tioga Road

120

P

Tenaya Lake

P

CLOUDS REST

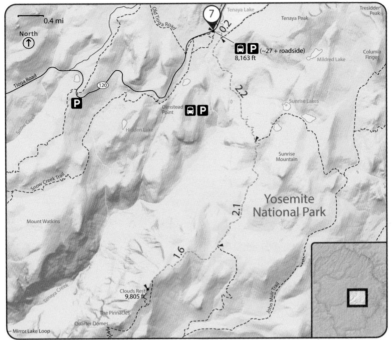

May Lake | Easy | 2.7 miles | 500 feet | Out-and-back
Trailhead: May Lake Road (6)

This is about as easy as it gets for High Sierra hikes. A quick out-and-back leads through forest to a High Sierra Camp. (Check out travelyosemite.com if you'd like to know about High Sierra Camps and their lottery reservation system.) Being so close to the road, spending the night at camp is hardly required. In fact, dayhiking May Lake, enjoying it for a few hours, and then hiking about 2.5 miles to nearby Mount Hoffman (you'll be looking at it from May Lake) and back is only a moderately difficult Yosemite high-country hike. There are about two dozen parking spaces at the trailhead. Many of them will be used by overnight guests of the High Sierra Camp.

Clouds Rest | Strenuous | 11.9 miles | 2,000 feet | Out-and-back
Trailhead: Sunrise Lakes, Tioga Pass Road (7)

You could hike up to Clouds Rest from Yosemite Valley, but it'd take a near superhuman effort to make that happen in a day. Hiking in from Tioga Road is a much more reasonable option. You'll pass quite a few trail junctions along the way, but it's well-marked. Be sure to follow the signs for Clouds Rest or Sunrise High Sierra Camp (until you reach the spur for Sunrise Lakes/ Sunrise High Sierra Camp). Clouds Rest is a narrow ridgeline with views of

CATHEDRAL LAKES/ELIZABETH LAKE

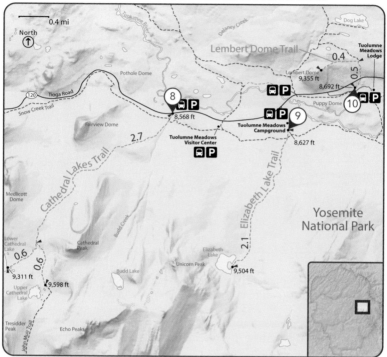

Yosemite Valley to the west (best experienced in the morning when the sun is to the east). The view of Half Dome is wondrous. The ridgeline exposure is no joke. While not as extreme as Zion's Angel's Landing, there aren't any aids to help navigate the knife-edge. If you have a strong fear of heights, sit this one out. If you don't have a problem with exposure, it's one of the more thrilling maintained trails in the park.

Cathedral Lakes | Moderate | 7.8 miles | 1,000 feet | Out-and-back
Trailhead: Cathedral Lakes, Tioga Pass Road (8)

Cathedral Lakes provides some classic High Sierra scenery while requiring relatively low intensity. This makes it a very popular destination. Plus, it has the notoriety of being part of the famed John Muir Trail. Most hikers are satisfied turning around at Upper Cathedral Lake, but the trail continues to Sunrise High Sierra Camp and eventually Yosemite Valley (at Happy Isles). Parking is alongside the road. You can also take the Tuolumne Meadows Shuttle.

GAYLOR LAKES

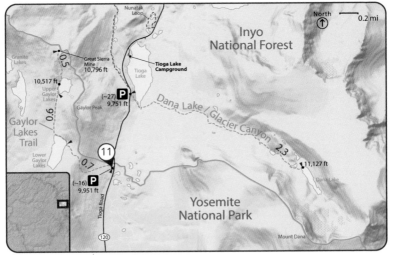

Elizabeth Lake | Moderate | 4.2 miles | 900 feet | Out-and-back
Trailhead: B Loop, Tuolumne Meadows Campground (9)

This trail is a very pleasant surprise for anyone staying at Tuolumne Meadows Campground. An easy hike (by Yosemite standards) leads to a picturesque lake at the base of Unicorn Peak.

Lembert Dome | Moderate | 1.8 miles | 800 feet | Out-and-back
Trailhead: Rafferty Creek/Lyell Canyon (10)

It's not the most spectacular dome in the park, but it's a pretty minor commitment to reach the top of this granite rock overlooking Tuolumne Meadows. If friends/family want to spend time at the visitor center or restaurant and you'd rather hike, this is a good choice, or you can't go wrong hanging around Tenaya Lake.

Gaylor Lakes | Moderate | 3.6 miles | 850 feet | Out-and-back
Trailhead: Gaylor Lakes, Tioga Road (11)

This trail offers something a little different than all the classic High Sierra lakes and granite. You'll find the Great Sierra Mine Historic Site at the end of the trail. Apparently there were a lot of shepherds running around the Sierras back in the day. John Muir is a famous shepherd turned conservationist. Another shepherd, Thomas Brusky, Jr., staked several claims around the area, later selling them to a mining company. It's a fun area to explore, not only for the old stone mining cabins, but the surrounding lakes.

The trailhead parking area is on the north side of Tioga Road immediately west of Tioga Pass Entrance Station.

WAPAMA FALLS/RANCHERIA FALLS

Wapama Falls/Rancheria Falls | Moderate/Strenuous | 4.6/12.2 miles | 200/850 feet | Out-and-back
Trailhead: O'Shaughnessy Dam, Hetch Hetchy (12)

Yosemite Valley starts to get crowded in spring, when swollen streams power thunderous waterfalls. Hetch Hetchy also has tall granite walls and roaring falls. A dayhike to Wapama is very reasonable. The trail is obvious and elevation gain is minimal. Rancheria Falls is a stretch to do in a day. Not because it's so long or hard, but because Hetch Hetchy is only open from 8am until 5pm each day. Start at 8am and you shouldn't have a problem, but if it looks like you're cutting it close, you better turn around or be prepared to get locked in. Being at lower elevation, this is not a particularly good summer destination. You're way better off exploring sites along Tioga Road.

Shuttles

The park operates several free shuttle routes running from Toulumne Meadows to Mariposa Grove. The only year-round shuttle is in Yosemite Valley. And, when you're in the valley, the best approach is to park your car and use the shuttle. Check out the park website (nps.gov/yose) for current details.

When to Visit?

There's no such thing as a bad time to visit (unless it's closed due to ridiculous snowfall or flooding like in 2023!). The busiest season (summer) is probably the worst. Crowds. Highest likelihood of forest fires/smoke. Heat. The benefit is Tioga Road opens, adding hiking opportunities to your itinerary. Spring is waterfall season. Fall is hiking season. And in winter, Yosemite is truly a wonderland.

More Trails

There are a lot more trails at Yosemite, but plan at least a day to explore Yosemite Valley. Admiring Half Dome from Mirror Lake, El Capitan from the shores of the Merced River, and Yosemite Falls through a window of trees are often guest's most magical moments. Don't miss out on them. It's so much better to explore Yosemite Valley by foot/shuttle in the middle of the day as opposed to crossing your fingers hoping to find a parking space at a popular trailhead.

Lassen Volcanic
Hiking Trails: 150+ miles

Lassen Peak

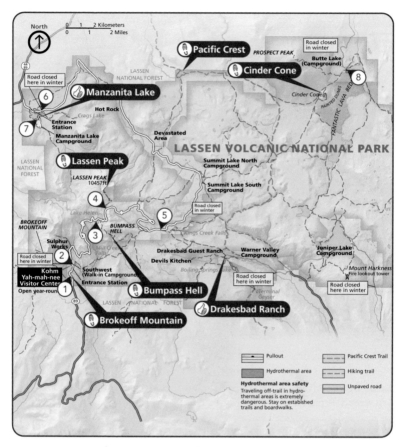

Lassen Volcanic Favorites

(1) Brokeoff Mountain
Strenuous | 7.3 miles | 2,500 feet

(2) Mill Creek Falls
Moderate | 3.3 miles | 300 feet

(3) Bumpass Hell
Moderate | 2.7 mile | 400 feet

(4) Lassen Peak
Strenuous | 5.0 miles | 2,000 feet

(5) Kings Creek Falls
Moderate | 2.8 mile | 500 feet

(6) Manzanita Lake
Easy | 2.2 miles | 50 feet

(7) Chaos Crags
Moderate | 4.0 miles | 800+ feet

(8) Cinder Cone
Moderate | 3.2 miles | 1,000 feet

Prospect Peak
Strenuous | 7.0 miles | 2,300 feet

BROKEOFF MOUNTAIN

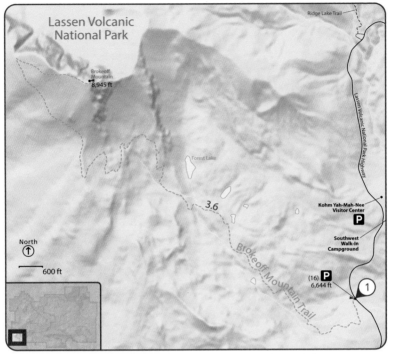

Brokeoff Mountain | Strenuous | 7.3 miles | 2,500 feet | Out-and-back
Trailhead: Brokeoff Mountain, CA-89 (1)

Lassen Peak gets all the social media likes, but Brokeoff Mountain is quite the hike. You'll have views of Mount Shasta, Lassen Peak, and Brokeoff's caldera! Length, elevation gain, and conditions (snow usually hangs around in a few places into August) make it a challenge, but the rewards easily outweigh the effort. Wildflowers are common from July (low elevations) through August (high elevations). This is a good trail to put near the top of your Lassen Volcanic National Park hiking wish list. There's only room for about 16 vehicles at the trailhead parking area (on the east side of CA-89), located about a half-mile south of the park's entrance station, but it isn't especially popular.

Mill Creek Falls | Moderate | 3.3 miles | 300 feet | Out-and-back
Trailhead: Behind Southwest Campground Amphitheater (2)

Like most of the park, this area was affected by the 2021 Dixie Fire. Downed trees are abundant. Bridges at the falls were lost and have not been rebuilt as of 2023. It's possible to cross the creek at the falls by traveling off-trail upstream. At 75 feet, Mill Creek is the tallest waterfall in the park. It drops into a deep-cut valley, creating very few decent viewing angles. If you can arrange

MILL CREEK FALLS

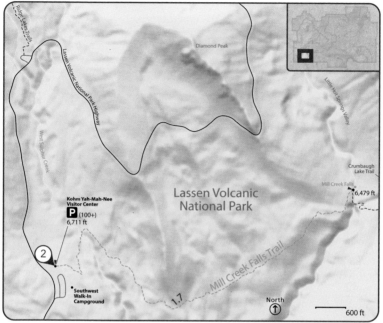

a ride, cache a car, or hitch, this is a good area for point-to-point hiking. From Mill Creek Falls, you can continue to Crumbaugh Lake and Cold Boiling Lake (2.5 miles). From there you can return to CA-89 at Kings Creek Picnic Area (0.7 miles) or by walking through Bumpass Hell (3.2 miles). Look at the Lassen Peak/Bumpass Hell map to get a better idea of the trail network.

Bumpass Hell | Moderate | 2.7 miles | 400 feet | Out-and-back
Trailhead: Bumpass Hell, CA-89 (3)

Bumpass Hell is the largest hydrothermal area in the park. It has the look and smell associated with parts of Yellowstone, but it isn't nearly as boisterous or otherworldly as its more renowned kin. The path is heavily used and well-marked and dirt turns to boardwalk once you enter the hydrothermal setting. It's a nice change of pace from mountains and lakes and volcanoes, plus it's not particularly long or strenuous. If you're looking for a unique and relatively easy trail along CA-89, this is the one to pick. Even if you don't hike the trail, the view of Lassen Peak from Helen Lake is worth a quick stop. Lassen Peak looks tremendous from here, all day long, whenever the sky is clear and the sun is out. The trailhead parking area is large, but it fills during peak season, especially on weekends.

BUMPASS HELL/LASSEN PEAK

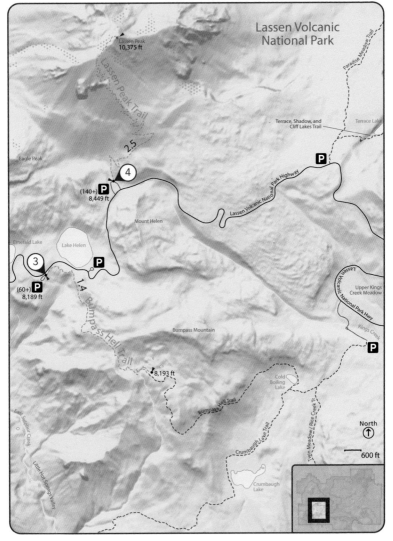

Lassen Peak | Strenuous | 5.0 miles | 2,000 feet | Out-and-back
Trailhead: Lassen Peak, CA-89 (4)

This is the hike most national park adventurers are excited to do, and with good reason, you're climbing to the top of one of the world's largest plug dome volcanoes. It's not too long (five miles). It's not too steep (2,000 feet elevation gain). But the grade is relentless, there are a bunch of switchbacks, and you're exposed to the sun and wind. Still, if you're prepared for the workout, you'll

KINGS CREEK FALLS

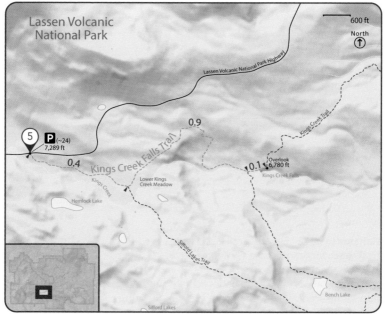

be very pleased with the scenic gains. The maintained trail concludes with a few interpretive signs. A few social trails continue to explore the area around the summit and volcanic crater. Volcanoes always sound a little scary. Should you be worried? Probably not. It last erupted back in 1921, so it's unlikely (but not impossible) to blow while you're visiting. And, for further peace of mind, USGS scientists continually monitor Lassen Volcano, hoping to predict potentially hazardous conditions. There's a large parking area at the trailhead and it fills up in summer, especially on weekends. So, this isn't one of those trails you'll have to yourself. It's a good idea to arrive early. You can hike up in the cooler morning air and guarantee you'll get a parking space. While snow sticks around well into summer, the trail can be hiked late spring/early summer. Just be sure to check on trail conditions and come prepared for them.

Kings Creek Falls | Moderate | 2.8 miles | 500 feet | Out-and-back
Trailhead: Kings Creek Falls, CA-89 (5)

Not the most interesting trail in the park, but its moderate distance and difficulty make this walk to a 30-foot waterfall one of the more popular attractions. The falls are commonly viewed from a fenced off overlook, but you'll also notice an obvious social trail down to the creek bed. Trailhead parking is available on either side of the road. There's extensive fire damage throughout this entire area. If you'd like to see rejuvenation of a razed forest, this is a pretty good choice.

MANZANITA LAKE/CHAOS CRAGS

Manzanita Lake | Easy | 2.2 miles | 50 feet | Loop
Trailhead: Manzanita Lake Campground (6)

Manzanita Lake is one of the park's activity hubs. A short and easy trail loops around the scenic lake with decent views of the surrounding setting, including Lassen Peak and Chaos Crags. If you're spending the night at the campground or camping cabins, it's a great place for a casual stroll. And don't forget to go across the road to explore Reflection Lake and Lily Pond as well.

Chaos Crags | Moderate | 4.0 miles | 800+ feet | Out-and-back
Trailhead: Manzanita Lake Campground Road (7)

Crags Lake isn't anything special, in fact it often isn't there. But the formation of Chaos Crags and Chaos Jumbles, remanence of a massive rock avalanche extending nearly all the way to Reflection Lake, is a wild event to think about. You can get good views of it from the road. The trail passes through forest but officially stops short of the crags and shoulder of Lassen Peak.

Cinder Cone | Moderate | 3.2 miles | 1,000 feet | Out-and-back
Prospect Peak | Strenuous | 7.0 miles | 2,300 feet | Out-and-back
Trailhead: Butte Lake (8)

This is a great area of the park, but it takes some commitment to reach. It's almost a two-hour drive from Lassen Peak Trailhead to Butte Lake Campground. The access road is unpaved but it's usually accessible to 2WD vehicles. It's worth the trip. These are two of the best trails in the park.

Cinder Cone is short and kind of tough, especially the final push up to the cone. From its summit you'll have wide-ranging views of the painted dunes and fantastic lava beds. Enjoy them, then continue into the cinder cone's crater or return the way you came. The trail is loose rock and sandy, so it'll likely be more challenging than you expect.

CINDER CONE/PROSPECT PEAK

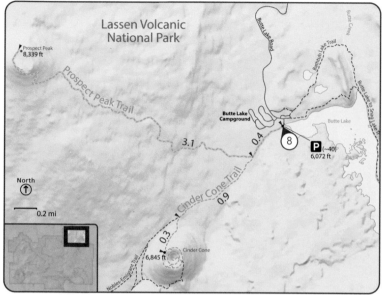

Prospect Peak is a less popular and longer alternative. On a clear day you'll be at a wonderful vantage point to survey damage from the Dixie Fire with views clear across the park to Lassen Peak and beyond to Mount Shasta.

The trailhead is located near the Butte Lake boat ramp.

More Trails

More importantly than more trails, there are more regions of the park. Unpaved roads lead to Warner Valley and Juniper Lake, both located near the park's southern boundary. From Warner Valley you can hike into the Devil's Kitchen (moderate, 4.4 miles) or follow the Pacific Crest Trail to Boiling Springs Lake (easy, 3.0 miles) and Terminal Geyser (moderate, 5.8 miles). From Juniper Lake you can hike up to Mount Harkness Lookout (strenuous, 3.8 miles) or it could serve as a great departure point for a few point-to-point backpacking routes up to Butte Lake.

King's Creek

Redwood
Hiking Trails: 200+ miles

Boy Scout Tree Trail

Redwood Favorites

(1) Tall Trees
Moderate | 3.7 miles | 800 feet

(2) Lady Bird Johnson
Easy | 1.3 miles | 200 feet

(3) Fern Canyon
Easy | 1.1 miles | 50 feet

(4) James Irvine/Miner's Ridge
Strenuous | 7.4 miles | 1,200 feet

(4-5) Foothills/Rhododendron
Strenuous | 9.2 miles | 1,000 feet

(6) Hidden Beach
Easy | 1.2 miles | 50 feet

(7) Damnation Creek
Strenuous | 4.1 miles | 1,100 feet

(8) Nickel Creek
Moderate | 1.4 miles | 230 feet

(9) Boy Scout Tree
Moderate | 4.9 miles | 700 feet

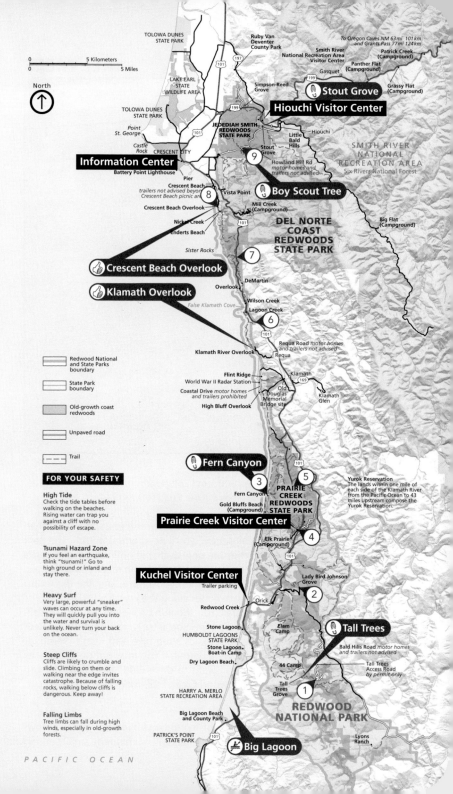

TOLOWA DUNES
STATE PARK

Ruby Van
Deventer
County Park

To Oregon Caves NM 63 mi / 101 km
and Grants Pass 77 mi / 124 km

Smith River
National Recreation Area
Visitor Center

Patrick Creek
(Campground)

Panther Flat
(Campground)

Gasquet

Simpson-Reed
Grove

Stout Grove

Grassy Flat
(Campground)

LAKE EARL
STATE
WILDLIFE AREA

Hiouchi Visitor Center

TOLOWA DUNES
STATE PARK

JEDEDIAH SMITH
REDWOODS
STATE PARK

Little
Bald
Hills

Hiouchi

SMITH RIVER
NATIONAL
RECREATION
AREA

Point
St. George

Castle
Rock

Stout
Grove

9

CRESCENT CITY

Six Rivers National Forest

Information Center

Battery Point Lighthouse

Howland Hill Rd
motor homes and
trailers not advised

Pier

Crescent Beach
trailers not advised beyond
Crescent Beach picnic area

8

Vista Point

Boy Scout Tree

Big Flat
(Campground)

Crescent Beach Overlook

Mill Creek
(Campground)

Nickel Creek

Enderts Beach

**DEL NORTE
COAST
REDWOODS
STATE PARK**

Sister Rocks

7

👍 **Crescent Beach Overlook**

DeMartin

Overlook

👍 **Klamath Overlook**

Wilson Creek

Lagoon Creek

False Klamath Cove

6

Klamath River Overlook

Requa Road motor homes
and trailers not advised
Requa

Flint Ridge

Klamath

World War II Radar Station

Coastal Drive motor homes
and trailers prohibited

Old
Douglas
Memorial
Bridge site

Klamath
Glen

High Bluff Overlook

North

↑

0   5 Kilometers
0   5 Miles

🚶 **Fern Canyon**

3

5

Yurok Reservation
The lands within one mile of
each side of the Klamath River
from the Pacific Ocean to 43
miles upstream compose the
Yurok Reservation.

Fern Canyon

**PRAIRIE
CREEK
REDWOODS
STATE PARK**

Gold Bluffs Beach
(Campground)

Prairie Creek Visitor Center

Elk Prairie
(Campground)

4

**Redwood National and State Parks
boundary**

**State Park
boundary**

**Old-growth coast
redwoods**

Unpaved road

Trail

Kuchel Visitor Center

Lady Bird Johnson
Grove

2

Trailer parking

Orick

Redwood Creek

Elam
Camp

🌲 **Tall Trees**

FOR YOUR SAFETY

High Tide
Check the tide tables before
walking on the beaches.
Rising water can trap you
against a cliff with no
possibility of escape.

Stone Lagoon

HUMBOLDT LAGOONS
STATE PARK

Stone Lagoon
Boat-in Camp

Dry Lagoon Beach

Bald Hills Road motor homes
and trailers not advised

Tall Trees
Access Road
by permit only

44 Camp

Tall
Trees
Grove

1

**REDWOOD
NATIONAL
PARK**

Tsunami Hazard Zone
If you feel an earthquake,
think "tsunami!" Go to
high ground or inland and
stay there.

Heavy Surf
Very large, powerful "sneaker"
waves can occur at any time.
They will quickly pull you into
the water and survival is
unlikely. Never turn your back
on the ocean.

Steep Cliffs
Cliffs are likely to crumble and
slide. Climbing on them or
walking near the edge invites
catastrophe. Because of falling
rocks, walking below cliffs is
dangerous. Keep away!

HARRY A. MERLO
STATE RECREATION AREA

Big Lagoon Beach
and County Park

Lyons
Ranch

Falling Limbs
Tree limbs can fall during high
winds, especially in old-growth
forests.

PATRICK'S POINT
STATE PARK

🛶 **Big Lagoon**

PACIFIC OCEAN

TALL TREES

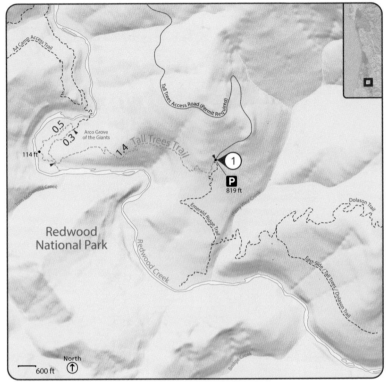

Tall Trees | Moderate | 3.7 miles | 800 feet | Lollipop
Trailhead: Tall Trees Grove, Tall Trees Access Road (1)

Tall Trees Grove is home to some of the world's tallest trees, some taller than the Statue of Liberty. To see it in person, you'll need a free permit. The park issues 50 permits per day and they are only available online from the park's non-profit, Redwood Parks Conservancy. The trail is by no means an easy walk. It's all downhill to Redwood Creek, and then you'll have to make the return trip, all uphill. But you'll find a few benches along the way, if you'd like to take a break. As far as staying on the trail. You shouldn't have any issues. It's well-worn and well-marked. But there are a few social trails leading down to Redwood Creek (to look at some tall trees!). It's a fun hike and worth the minor inconvenience of needing to procure a permit. If you miss out on permits, or want to take a longer hike, or don't want to drive Bald Hills Road, you can also hike to Tall Trees Grove via Redwood Creek Trail (moderate, 16 miles, two stream crossings).

The access road is dirt, but it shouldn't be a problem for regular vehicles. However, RVs over 21 feet or vehicles towing trailers will not fit in the small parking

LADYBIRD JOHNSON

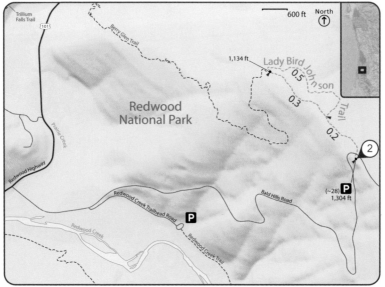

area. Expect it to take about one hour to reach the trailhead from Kuchel Visitor Center. A locked gate controls visitation. You'll receive the combination (as well as instructions) via email 24 hours before your scheduled visit.

Lady Bird Johnson | Easy | 1.3 miles | 200 feet | Lollipop
Trailhead: Bald Hills Road (2)

Lady Bird Johnson is your easy option for a peaceful stroll through old-growth redwood forest. President Nixon dedicated the grove to former First Lady, Lady Bird Johnson, in recognition of all the conservation and environmental work she accomplished. A plaque is on display in the grove. Only about 40,000 acres of old-growth redwood forest remain today, and nearly half of that is protected by Redwood National and State Parks. The parking area is surrounded by second-growth Douglas fir trees, but once you cross the hiker's bridge you'll be walking beneath the canopy of towering old-growth redwoods. Pay attention to the differences when you visit. In summer, this is the site of daily ranger-led hikes. Check online (nps.gov/redw) or at a visitor center for a schedule and join one if you can. It's also an interpretive trail. You can download the brochure online from the park app.

The road is narrow and winding, not a particularly good place for RVs or trailers, and parking spaces are sized for ordinary vehicles. You'll know you're approaching the trailhead parking area when you see the elevated walkway crossing above Bald Hills Road.

FERN CANYON/JAMES IRVINE

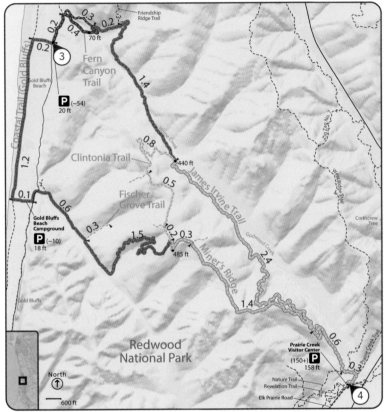

Fern Canyon | Easy | 1.1 miles | 50 feet | Loop
Trailhead: Fern Canyon, End of Gold Bluffs Road (3)

Fern Canyon sounds cool, doesn't it? A lush wall of ferns transports imaginative visitors to the jungles of the Jurassic period from the concrete jungles we're living in today. And it's a short, highly-rewarding trail. But there is a catch. In summer (May through September), you'll need to secure a free Gold Bluffs Beach/Fern Canyon parking permit. Permits are issued from Redwood Parks Conservancy, but you can find all pertinent information at the park website (nps.gov/redw). It's a pilot program, installed in 2022, so it could get scrapped, or it could exist in perpetuity. It's just one of those things you need to keep track of in order to have better (on average) user experiences. As for the trail, it's short and easy. Wooden footbridges are typically installed in summer, but, regardless of when you visit, it's a good idea to arrive expecting to get your feet wet. So, have a spare set of shoes and towel in your car. If you're looking for a longer hike or were unable to get a parking permit, you can hike into Fern Canyon via James Irvine/Friendship Ridge trails (see the next trail description).

CATHEDRAL TREES/RHODODENDRON

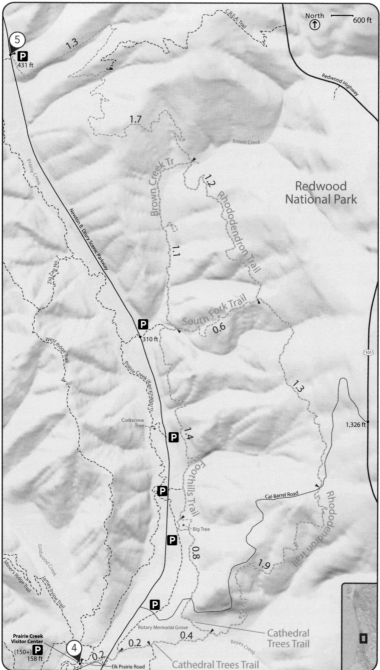

North

600 ft

5

P
431 ft

1.3

C.R.E.A. Trail

Redwood Highway

1.7

Brown Creek

Brown Creek Tr

1.2

Redwood
National Park

Rhododendron Trail

1.1

Prairie Creek

Newton B. Drury Scenic Parkway

Zig Zag No. 2

South Fork Trail

0.6

101

West Ridge Trail

Prairie Creek Trail

P
310 ft

Corkscrew Tree

1.3

1,326 ft

1.4

Foothills Trail

Cal-Barrel Road

Rhododendron Trail

P

Big Tree

0.8

P

1.9

Godwood Creek

Miner's Ridge Trail

James Irvine Trail

P

Rotary Memorial Grove

0.4

Cathedral
Trees Trail

Prairie Creek
Visitor Center

(150+) P
158 ft

4

0.2

0.2

0.2

Boyes Creek

Elk Prairie Road

Cathedral Trees Trail

The dirt access road (Davison Road) is not a good place for RVs or trailers, and at times it can be impassable. Before heading out, you'll want to inquire about road conditions, either online, over the phone, or in person at a visitor center.

James Irvine/Miner's Ridge | Strenuous | 7.4 miles | 1,200 feet | Loop
Trailhead: Prairie Creek Visitor Center (4)

You can do the yellow loop through old-growth redwood forest or it's a reasonable, albeit considerably longer, alternative to reach Fern Canyon and Gold Bluffs Beach (two of the park's best non-tree-centric highlights) following the orange loop all the way to the Pacific Ocean. The James Irvine/Miner's Ridge loop, shortened via Clintonia Trail, is less than eight miles. Continuing along James Irvine Trail to Fern Canyon and Gold Bluffs Beach, you're looking at roughly 12.0 miles (1,500 feet climbing) from Prairie Creek Visitor Center. Miner's Ridge is slightly shorter than James Irvine, but it has more elevation change. If you have the time, energy, and fitness level (or didn't score a Fern Canyon parking permit), this is the way to visit Gold Bluffs Beach and Fern Canyon, providing a wide range of environments on one scenery-filled hike. With that said, there are some really fun hiking alternatives right from Prairie Creek Visitor Center, like Prairie Creek, Foothills, and Rhododendron trails.

Parking is limited at Prairie Creek Visitor Center, but you'll find more space along Newton B. Drury Scenic Parkway.

Foothills/Rhododendron | Strenuous | 9.2 miles | 1,000 feet | Lollipop
Trailhead: Prairie Creek Visitor Center (4), Newton B. Drury Scenic Parkway (5)

From Prairie Creek Visitor Center, you'll find several more loop options on the east side of Newton B. Drury Scenic Parkway. And they're much less popular than James Irvine/Miner's Ridge (or Prairie Creek). Loops come in a variety of distances using Rhododendron, South Fork, Brown Creek, and Foothills trails, heck, you could even use Cal-Barrel Road, which is extremely scenic. If you have about ten miles left in your hiking boots, the peaceful loop up Rhododendron Trail and back via Brown Creek, Foothills, and Cathedral Trees trails is a pretty good choice. Arrange a ride or cache a car and you could enjoy a very peaceful walk along the lightly used Rhododendron Trail (8.2 miles), but you'll miss some big trees and an exciting creek crossing found on the loop.

Hidden Beach | Easy | 1.2 miles | 50 feet | Out-and-back
Trailhead: US-101 (6)

You can reach Hidden Beach via an out-and-back on the Klamath section of Coastal Trail or from a short trail beginning just north of Trees of Mystery. There's quite a bit of parking at Lagoon Creek and Wilson Creek, where you can get on Coastal Trail. Or there's a tiny pullout on each side of US-101 just north of Trees of Mystery. You cannot miss Trees of Mystery. But the pullouts, they're easy to zip past. Where to start is your choice. The map shows the short

HIDDEN BEACH

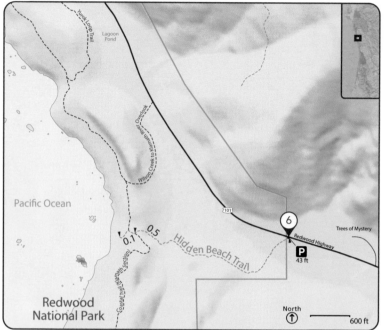

route from Trees of Mystery. The beach is very nice, with plenty of driftwood and sea stacks to admire.

Damnation Creek | Strenuous | 4.1 miles | 1,100 feet | Out-and-back
Trailhead: US-101 (7)

Damnation Creek is a wonderful spot for a foggy redwood hike AND spectacular coastal views. The trees get smaller as you approach the ocean, but you won't be complaining about that when you reach the rocky beach with some tidepooling potential. The trail isn't difficult to follow. Just make sure you don't find yourself cruising down the Coastal Trail when you intersect it. If you don't start descending shortly after that, you screwed up. The trail begins at an unmarked gravel pullout.

*When we went to print, the final footbridge remained in a state of disrepair. Visitors are not supposed to continue beyond this point (1.7 miles into the hike). Check in to see if it's fixed before you arrive.

Nickel Creek | Moderate | 1.4 miles | 230 feet | Out-and-back
Trailhead: Last Chance, Enderts Beach Road (8)

This is really the Last Chance Section of Coastal Trail, but from the end of Enderts Beach Road, it's just a half-mile to Nickel Creek, where a spur trail leads

DAMNATION CREEK

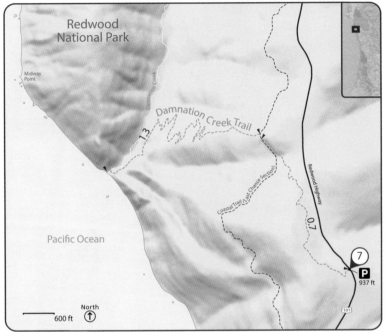

down from the bluff to Enderts Beach. It's great but also very popular. Tide-pooling and wildlife sightings are possible.

Boy Scout Tree | Moderate | 4.9 miles | 700 feet | Out-and-back
Trailhead: Boy Scout Tree, Howland Hill Road (9)

Oddly, the most wonderful element of Boy Scout Tree Trail isn't the mighty redwoods you'll encounter along the way or even the namesake double redwood, it's what you won't notice in this corner of the park ...the constant buzz of traffic. Boy Scout Tree Trail is gloriously peaceful. The access road is unpaved, narrow, and winding, but the drive to the trailhead is its own adventure. On the trail, it's pretty straightforward walking, except Boy Scout Tree is reached via an unmarked spur less than a quarter-mile from the underwhelming waterfall conclusion (Fern Falls is often just a trickle). It's a nice, peaceful trail and without question worth your time when you're exploring the north end of the park.

NICKEL CREEK/ENDERTS BEACH

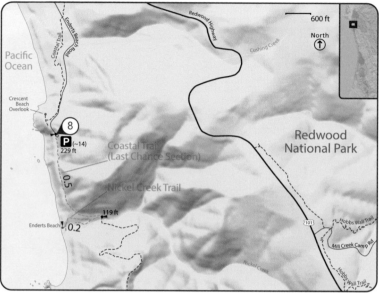

BOY SCOUT TREE

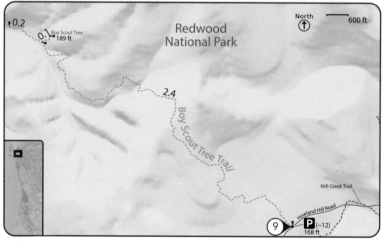

If you're looking for a short and easy redwood trail on the park's north end, consider heading to Stout Grove (just down Howland Hill Road from Boy Scout Tree Trailhead). Mill Creek (moderate, 7.2 miles) and Little Bald Hills (strenuous, 7+ miles) are nearby. Little Bald Hills is uniquely open to mountain bikers. On the south end, if you can't get enough redwoods and creeks, make another great loop by combining Prairie Creek (Karl Knapp) and West Ridge trails. The Coastal Trail is 35 miles long. Nickel Creek and Fern Canyon are already discussed but there are several more sections with backcountry campsites sprinkled along the way. There are more, but these should keep you busy for a while.

More Trails

Crater Lake
Hiking Trails: 100+ miles

Wizard Island

Crater Lake Favorites

① **Garfield Peak**
Strenuous | 2.4 miles | 1,000 feet

② **Watchman Peak**
Moderate | 1.6 miles | 300 feet

③ **Wizard Summit**
Moderate | 2.4 miles | 700 feet

④ **Cleetwood Cove**
Strenuous | 1.9 miles | 700 feet

⑤ **Mount Scott**
Strenuous | 4.0 miles | 1,300 feet

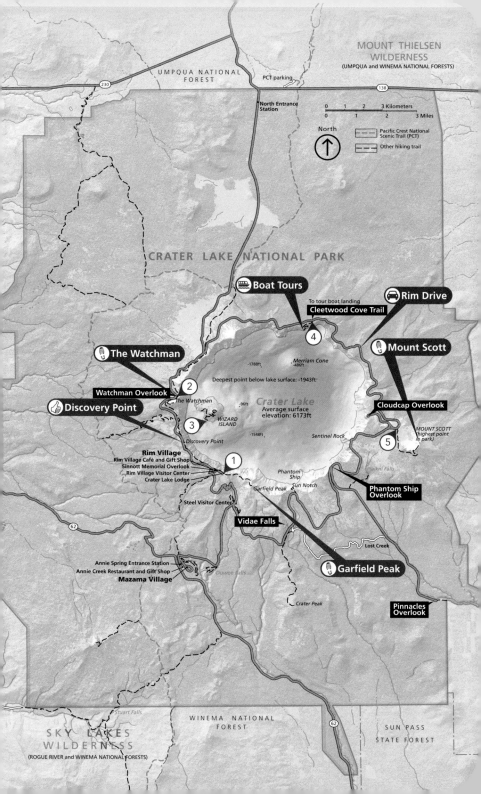

MOUNT THIELSEN
WILDERNESS
(UMPQUA and WINEMA NATIONAL FORESTS)

UMPQUA NATIONAL
FOREST

230

138

PCT parking

North Entrance
Station

0   1   2   3 Kilometers
0   1   2   3 Miles

North

Pacific Crest National
Scenic Trail (PCT)
Other hiking trail

CRATER LAKE NATIONAL PARK

🚤 Boat Tours

To tour boat landing
Cleetwood Cove Trail

🚗 Rim Drive

4

👟 The Watchman

Merriam Cone
486ft

-1788ft

👟 Mount Scott

Watchman Overlook

2

Deepest point below lake surface: -1943ft

The Watchman

-96ft

Crater Lake
Average surface
elevation: 6173ft

Cloudcap Overlook

👍 Discovery Point

3

WIZARD
ISLAND

MOUNT SCOTT
(highest point
in park)

Discovery Point

-1548ft

Sentinel Rock

5

Rim Village
Rim Village Café and Gift Shop
Sinnott Memorial Overlook
Rim Village Visitor Center
Crater Lake Lodge

1

Phantom
Ship

Hakni Falls

Sun Notch

Garfield Peak

Phantom Ship
Overlook

Steel Visitor Center

Vidae Falls

Lost Creek

Annie Spring Entrance Station
Annie Creek Restaurant and Gift Shop
Mazama Village

Duwee Falls

👟 Garfield Peak

Crater Peak

Pinnacles
Overlook

62

62

Stuart Falls

WINEMA NATIONAL
FOREST

SUN PASS
STATE FOREST

SKY LAKES
WILDERNESS
(ROGUE RIVER and WINEMA NATIONAL FORESTS)

GARFIELD PEAK

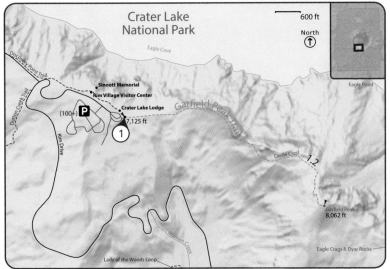

Garfield Peak | Strenuous | 2.4 miles | 1,000 feet | Out-and-back
Trailhead: Crater Lake Lodge (1)

Rim Drive provides something of an aerial view of this one-of-a-kind deep blue lake, but making the short and gratifying trek to the top of Garfield Peak moves things up a few levels, quite literally. There's no bad time as long as it's a clear day, but morning is better, as you'll avoid the afternoon crowds and Wizard Island will be basking in soft morning light. Feasting on the fantastic views from the summit, you'll see Mount Shasta to the south and Thielsen Peak to the north. Enjoy them before returning the way you came.

WATCHMAN PEAK/WIZARD SUMMIT

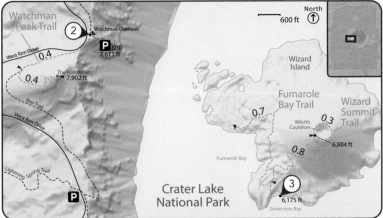

Watchman Peak | Moderate | 1.6 miles | 300 feet | Out-and-back
Trailhead: Watchman Overlook, Rim Drive (2)

The park is all about Crater Lake. It is a little bit of a one-trick pony, but there's a wide variety of views to enjoy along Rim Drive's 33 miles of pavement. One of the best spots to sit in awe of this treasured setting is Watchman Peak. The trail begins at the south end of Watchman Overlook. You'll notice a spur trail heading up the back of Watchman Peak. Take it, and soon you'll be basking in the picturesque panorama from Watchman Fire Lookout perched high above Wizard Island.

Wizard Summit | Moderate | 2.4 miles | 700 feet | Out-and-back
Trailhead: Governors Bay, Wizard Island (3)

Wherever you are on the rim, it's hard not to notice Wizard Island. And while you're looking at it, it's even harder not to want to visit that big cinder cone peeking out of this 1,943-foot-deep volcano-top lake. And you can! Boat tours drop guests off at Governors Bay, and from there you can hike to Fumarole Bay and/or the island's cinder-y summit, where you can peer into the Witch's Cauldron. Visit travelcraterlake.com for boat tour information. Reaching the boats is no easy task. You'll have to hike Cleetwood Cove Trail (next) to get there.

CLEETWOOD COVE

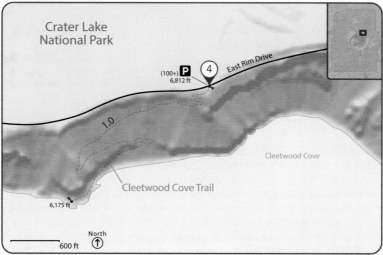

Cleetwood Cove | Strenuous | 1.9 miles | 700 feet | Out-and-back
Trailhead: Cleetwood Cove, Rim Drive (4)

Looking at photos, you might assume there's no way to reach the water. Not so. Cleetwood Cove descends steeply via a few switchbacks to the water's edge. Some guests make the trip just to confirm it's ordinary water filling this caldera and not a few trillion gallons of blue paint. Others make the trek to go for a swim (water temperature usually tops out around 55°F). Last but not least, if you would like to join a boat tour, you'll have to make the descent (and ascent when you return to shore). It isn't crazy difficult. It's steep. But it's short and there are benches along the way if you'd like to catch your breath. Still, you need to be honest about your fitness. Most park rescues happen right here. If you plan on taking a dip, wear your swimsuit, and bring a towel and warm dry clothes. Swimming is only allowed within 100 yards of Cleetwood Cove and Wizard Island (and at least 50 feet away from any boat, boat dock or buoy). Wetsuits, snorkel gear, inflatables, life jackets, and pretty much anything that isn't a basic swimsuit are not permitted.

MOUNT SCOTT

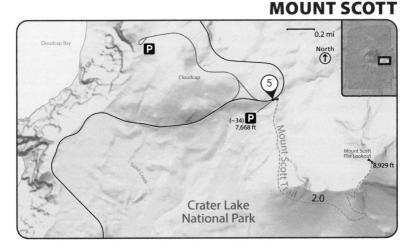

Mount Scott | Strenuous | 4.0 miles | 1,300 feet | Out-and-back
Trailhead: Mount Scott, Rim Drive (5)

Mount Scott is the highest point in the park (8,929 feet). There's a fire lookout at the summit. It's a pretty good spot to look down at a lake worthy of being one of the world's wonders. The trail's grade increases gradually until you reach a set of switchbacks near the summit and its fire lookout. Morning is my preference, as you can enjoy the whole lake in the soft light. However, coming up here for sunset isn't a bad idea either. Bring extra layers and a headlamp, and the hike down shouldn't be too much trouble (especially if there's a full moon). Parking is limited. There's room for maybe 20 vehicles in a roadside pullout just east of the turnoff for Cloudcap.

Winter
The park is always open, but Rim Drive usually closes from mid-October until mid-July (weather dependent). It's still possible to visit in winter. Even though the park receives a few hundred inches of snow each year, they keep the road to Rim Village plowed. During this time, you can snowshoe or cross-country ski (and camp) along the rim.

Mount Rainier
Hiking Trails: 260+ miles

Shriner Peak

Mount Rainier Favorites

(1) Gobbler's Knob
Moderate | 11.2 miles | 2,600 feet

(2) Comet Falls
Strenuous | 6.0 miles | 1,300 feet

(3) Skyline
Strenuous | 5.7 miles | 1,800 feet

(4) Pinnacle Peak
Strenuous | 2.5 miles | 1,200 feet

(5) Snow & Bench Lakes
Moderate | 2.4 miles | 700 feet

(7) Shriner Peak Lookout
Strenuous | 7.9 miles | 3,400 feet

(6, 8) Summerland
Strenuous | 15.0 miles | 4,500 feet

(9) Glacier Basin
Moderate | 5.0 miles | 1,300 feet

(10) Burroughs Mountains
Strenuous | 6.2–8.8 miles | 2,500 feet

Mount Fremont Lookout
Moderate | 5.7 miles | 1,100 feet

(11) Tolmie Peak Lookout
Strenuous | 4.8 miles | 1,100 feet

(12) Spray Falls
Moderate | 4.0 miles | 300 feet

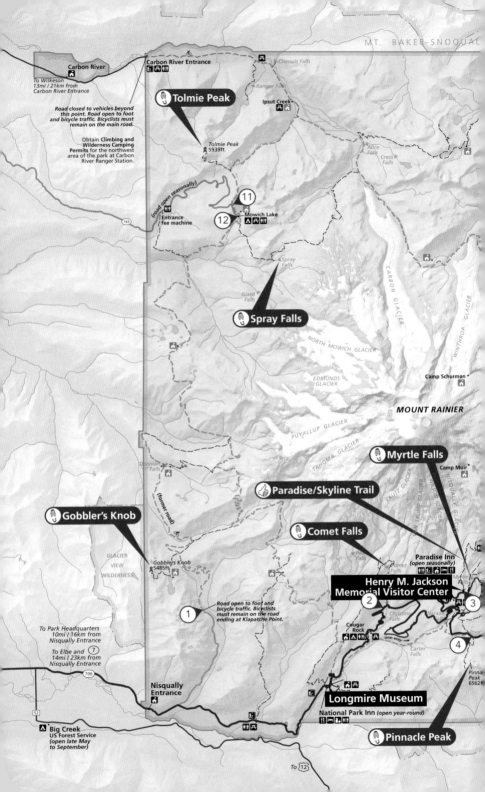

Carbon River
To Wilkeson
13mi / 21km from
Carbon River Entrance

Carbon River Entrance

Chenuis Falls

Road closed to vehicles beyond
this point. Road open to foot
and bicycle traffic. Bicyclists must
remain on the main road.

Obtain **Climbing and
Wilderness Camping
Permits** for the northwest
area of the park at Carbon
River Ranger Station.

Ranger Falls

Ipsut Creek

Tolmie Peak

Tolmie Peak
5939ft

Alice
Falls

Cress
Falls

(road open seasonally)

165

Entrance
fee machine

11

12

Mowich Lake

Spray
Falls

CARBON GLACIER

Spray Falls

Giant
Falls

NORTH MOWICH GLACIER

EDMUNDS
GLACIER

Camp Schurman

WINTHROP GLACIER

MOUNT RAINIER

PUYALLUP GLACIER

Denman
Falls

(former road)

TAHOMA GLACIER

Myrtle Falls

Camp Muir

Paradise/Skyline Trail

Gobbler's Knob

GLACIER
VIEW
WILDERNESS

Gobblers Knob
5485ft

Comet Falls

Comet
Falls

Paradise Inn
(open seasonally)

**Henry M. Jackson
Memorial Visitor Center**

Myrtle
Falls

KAUTZ GLACIER

NISQUALLY GLACIER

WILSON GLACIER

N TRUMP GLACIER

1

Road open to foot and
bicycle traffic. Bicyclists
must remain on the road
ending at Klapatche Point.

To Park Headquarters
10mi / 16km from
Nisqually Entrance

To Elbe and
14mi / 23km from
Nisqually Entrance

7

52

706

2

Cougar
Rock

Christine
Falls

Narada
Falls

3

one-way

Carter
Falls

4

Pinnacle
Peak
6562ft

Nisqually
Entrance

Longmire Museum

National Park Inn (open year-round)

Big Creek
US Forest Service
(open late May
to September)

Pinnacle Peak

To 12

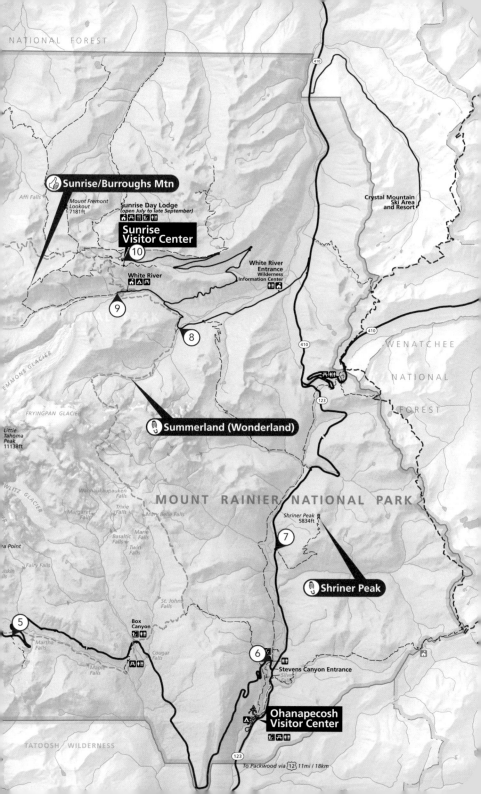

NATIONAL FOREST

Crystal Mountain
Ski Area
and Resort

410

Affi Falls

🥾 **Sunrise/Burroughs Mtn**

Mount Fremont
Lookout
7181ft

Sunrise Day Lodge
(open July to late September)
🏠 ⛺ 🍴 🚻 ♿ 🅿️

**Sunrise
Visitor Center**

⑩

White River
Entrance
Wilderness
Information Center
♿ 🅿️

White River
⛺ 🅿️

⑨

EMMONS GLACIER

410

⑧

WENATCHEE

FRYINGPAN GLACIER

🚻 🅿️

NATIONAL

123

Little
Tahoma
Peak
11138ft

🥾 **Summerland (Wonderland)**

FOREST

WLITZ GLACIER

Wahhaukaupauken
Falls

MOUNT RAINIER NATIONAL PARK

Margaret
Falls

Trixie
Falls

Mary Belle Falls

Shriner Peak
5834ft

a Point

Basaltic
Falls

Marie
Falls

⑦

Twin
Falls

🥾 **Shriner Peak**

nskin
s

Fairy Falls

St. John
Falls

⑤

Martha
Falls

Box
Canyon
🚻 🅿️

Cougar
Falls

🅿️ 🚻

Maple
Falls

⑥
🚻
♿ 🅿️

Stevens Canyon Entrance
Silver

⛺

**Ohanapecosh
Visitor Center**

🅿️ 🚻 ♿ 🅿️

TATOOSH WILDERNESS

123

To Packwood via 12 11mi / 18km

GOBBLERS KNOB

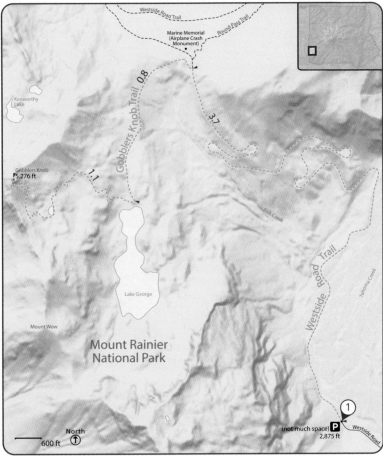

Westside Road Trail
Round Pass Trail
Marine Memorial
(Airplane Crash
Monument)
Gobblers Knob Trail 0.8
Kenworthy Lake
3.7
Gobblers Knob
5,276 ft
1.1
Fish Creek
Lake George
Westside Road Trail
Taboma Creek
Mount Wow
**Mount Rainier
National Park**
1
(not much space)
2,875 ft
Westside Road
North
600 ft

Gobbler's Knob | Moderate | 11.2 miles | 2,600 feet | Out-and-back
Trailhead: Westside Road (1)

Back in the early 1900s there was talk of building "Wonder Road" around Mount Rainier. It never happened, but Westside Road remains a vestige of that plan. Today, a gate prevents motorists from driving beyond Dry Creek (where parking is extremely limited). Mountain bikers can continue beyond this point all the way to Klapatche Point. In between, you'll find a bike rack at the Gobbler's Knob Trailhead. Gobbler's Knob Trail passes Lake George and concludes at a fire lookout with real nice Rainier views, especially in the evening. You don't need to bike. You can hike, cross-country ski, or snowshoe Westside Road too. It's also a great place to backpack (permit required), allowing more time to explore the area. There are five sites at Lake George. Rockfalls and

COMET FALLS/VAN TRUMP PARK

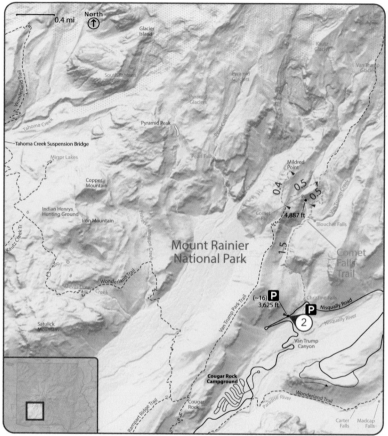

floods have damaged the roadway, so it's always a good idea to check road/trail conditions before arriving. There's some room to park alongside the road near Nisqually Entrance, but then you're looking at least another three miles hiking or biking down Westside Road each way.

Comet Falls/Van Trump | Strenuous | 6.0 miles | 1,300 feet | Out-and-back
Trailhead: Comet Falls, Paradise Road (2)

It's a relatively ordinary (by Mount Rainier standards) uphill, forested hike to a far-from-ordinary 380-foot, two-tiered waterfall! Make it to the waterfall with energy to spare and it's highly advisable to continue up to Van Trump Park and Mildred Point. It's a mini-Paradise up there.

There's only room for about 20 vehicles at the trailhead. Get an early start or cross your fingers and have a backup plan ready. Some people park at Christine Falls and walk back to the trailhead.

SKYLINE

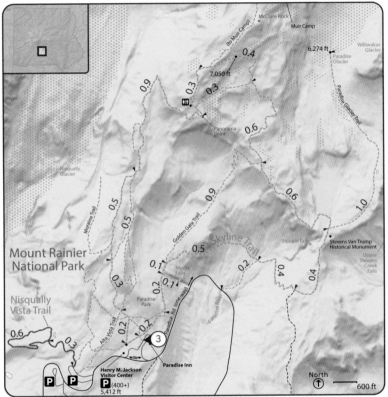

Skyline | Strenuous | 5.7 miles | 1,800 feet | Loop
Trailhead: Paradise (3)

Skyline is one of the best trails on the planet. If you're getting an early start (a great idea because Paradise is extremely popular), do it counterclockwise. You'll get to Myrtle Falls with nice light on the waterfall and Mount Rainier and you'll come to the spur to Paradise Glacier early (do it if you're confident you'll have enough water, snacks, and energy to complete the High Skyline Loop). And then you can fool around in the snow along High Skyline as long as you like before returning to Paradise. With an afternoon start, the direction is less important. Most people go clockwise, many turning around at Panorama Point. Panorama Point is a fine spot looking out to the south. Mount St. Helens, Mount Adams, and Mount Hood all come into view on a clear day. But Rainier is the star of this hike, and that's where your focus should be. Of course, you'll have outstanding views of this mesmerizing mountain from almost anywhere you are. Enjoy them!

PINNACLE PEAK/SNOW & BENCH LAKES

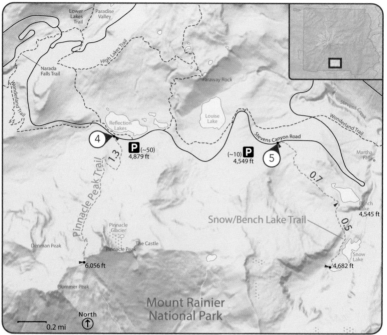

Paradise is mostly parking spaces. And they fill up ... early on weekends. Plan on arriving before 8am on beautiful summer weekends/holidays. It's a good idea to take a spot if you see one. This way you won't have any chance of accidentally driving past Paradise Inn, where the road becomes one-way, forcing you to circle back, resetting your hunt for parking space.

Pinnacle Peak | Strenuous | 2.5 miles | 1,200 feet | Out-and-back
Trailhead: Reflection Lakes, Stevens Canyon Road (4)

Even when you aren't hiking the slopes of Rainier, trails are still about its commanding presence. Pinnacle Peak leads to a saddle between Pinnacle and Plummer Peaks. With incredible views from the saddle as well as along the short but steep trail, this is the turnaround for most hikers. Others scramble around the back of Pinnacle Peak or take the less treacherous alternative route to Plummer Peak.

The trailhead is directly across from Reflection Lakes, where you'll find space for about 30 vehicles. There's another small pullout with room for a few more cars just to the west. Reflection Lakes is a popular sunrise destination, so the lot can fill up early in the morning. Fortunately, Snow & Bench Lakes or Shriner Peak are wonderful nearby alternatives for an early morning hike.

SHRINER PEAK LOOKOUT

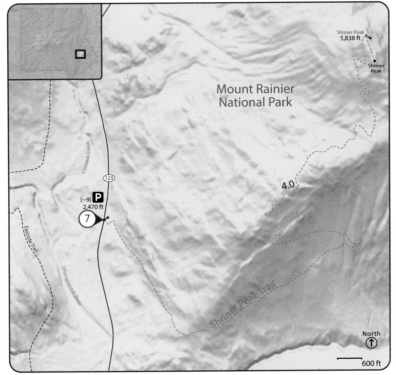

Snow & Bench Lakes | Moderate | 2.4 miles | 700 feet | Out-and-back
Trailhead: Snow Lake, Stevens Canyon Road (5)

You'll get some Rainier views here. That isn't unique. The fact you'll find two backcountry campsites at Snow Lake is something of an oddity. It's one of the shortest and easiest backpacking trails in the park, and a great location to start exploring when you wake up. There's room for about 14 cars at the trailhead.

Shriner Peak Lookout | Strenuous | 7.9 miles | 3,400 feet | Out-and-back
Trailhead: Shriner Peak, Route 123 (7)

Shriner Peak is all about the destination, not the journey. The journey is all uphill and heavily forested, except a break or two in the trees where you'll be treated to views of Rainier looming in the west. But the destination is most assuredly worth the effort. And it's another fun backpacking destination, with two sites near the lookout. Similar to Sunrise, you'll get that nice morning light on Mount Rainier with an early start to your day.

SUMMERLAND/WONDERLAND

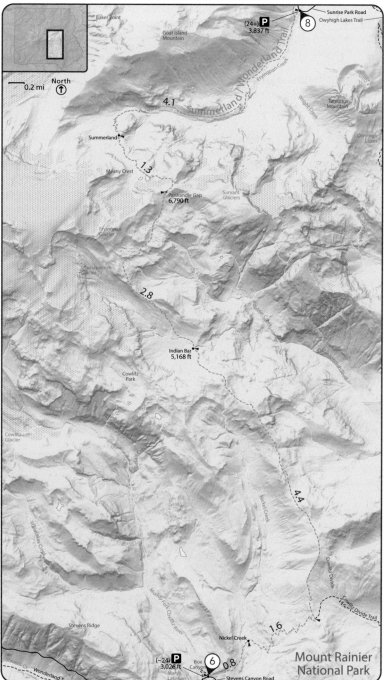

Baker Point

Goat Island Mountain

Sunrise Park Road

(24+) **P** 3,837 ft

⑧ Owyhigh Lakes Trail

Fryingpan Creek

Summerland/Wonderland Trail

Wright Creek

Tamanos Mountain

0.2 mi

North ↑

4.1

Summerland

Owyhigh Lakes

Meany Crest

1.3

Panhandle Gap 6,790 ft

Sarvant Glaciers

Fryingpan Glacier

Ohanapecosh Glacier

2.8

Baldwin Creek

Indian Bar 5,168 ft

Cowlitz Park

4.4

Cowlitz Glacier

Nickel Creek

Gowlitz Divide

Cowlitz Divide Trail

1.6

Williwakas Creek

Muddy Fork Cowlitz River

Stevens Ridge

Nickel Creek

(~24) **P** 3,026 ft

Box Canyon

⑥ 0.8

Marsh Lake

Wonderland Trail

Stevens Canyon Road

Mount Rainier National Park

Access is a little strange. There's no parking directly near the trailhead. However, there is a pullout on the opposite (west) side of the road (WA-123) about 800 feet to the north. It has room for maybe ten cars. You'll have to walk alongside WA-123 to reach the trailhead.

Summerland (Wonderland) | Strenuous | 15.0 miles | 4,500 ft | Point-to-point
Trailhead: Box Canyon, Stevens Canyon Road (6), Summerland, Sunrise Park Road (8)

This one's a haul with some serious logistical considerations. If you do it as a point-to-point (or out-and-back from Summerland) you can visit the highest point on Wonderland Trail, Panhandle Gap. Along the way you'll be treated to Mount Rainier views (while catching your breath on switchbacks), waterfalls, wildflowers, and you'll end at a beautiful box canyon (if you go for the point-to-point). It's really a backpacking trip (permit required), but dayhiking is possible. You'll need to arrange a ride or cache a car to do it as a point-to-point. No matter what, you'll want to check on trail conditions (and come prepared for them). It's named Summerland for a reason. Snow persists well into summer around here, and if you're trying to complete a long, strenuous hike, there isn't a whole lot of extra time for getting slowed down by snow or difficult/treacherous grades. Start at Summerland. The early morning light will treat you right with wonderful Rainier views and you'll appreciate the cool morning air as you climb up to Panhandle Gap. Summerland is getting a lot of buzz these days, but I still think the mainstays—Skyline, Comet Falls, Burroughs Mountain, and Tolmie Peak—are superior Rainier hikes.

As for parking, there's quite a bit at Summerland, although it fills up through summer. On the other side of the trail, Box Canyon is one of the easier places to find parking, and there's additional space at Box Canyon Picnic Area just to the west. If you're getting picked up, you don't want to rely on cell coverage. For more reasons than communication, it's a good idea to carry a rescue beacon with satellite text messaging for trails this length.

Mount Fremont

Glacier Basin | Moderate | 5.0 miles | 1,300 feet | Out-and-back
Trailhead: White River Campground (9)

Glacier Basin is a convenient choice for anyone camping at White River. Compared to Sunrise hikes, this trail's a ghost-town, primarily used by mountaineers approaching Rainier from the west (Camp Curtis, Camp Schurman). But there are nice Rainier views, and you

BURROUGHS/MOUNT FREMONT LOOKOUT

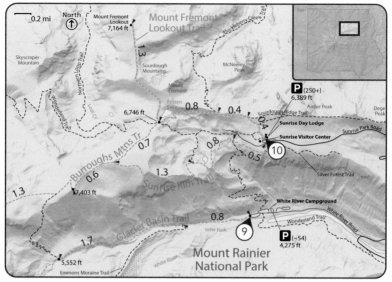

can often hear the White River rearranging its bed of boulders. There's also a mile-long (one-way) spur trail to Emmon's Glacier, the largest glacier in the Lower 48. It's worth checking out.

Burroughs Mtns | Strenuous | 6.2–8.8 miles | up to 2,500 ft | Out-and-back
Mount Fremont Lookout | Moderate | 5.7 miles | 1,100 feet | Out-and-back
Trailhead: Sourdough Ridge, Sunrise (10)

These two trails begin at Sourdough Ridge Trailhead, located between Sunrise Visitor Center and Day Lodge. The trail starts with a gradual climb, past a picnic area, to a t-intersection. Sourdough Ridge goes to the right (a great place to watch the first rays of sun hitting Mount Rainier). Taking a left sets you on the path to Mount Fremont Lookout and Burroughs Mountains. Just beyond Frozen Lake, you'll arrive at the nexus of Sunrise hiking trails. Mount Fremont Lookout is to the north. I'd rank it fourth on the list of best Mount Rainier fire lookouts, but they're all fun. If you have to choose between Fremont or Burroughs, I'd pick Burroughs seven times out of ten. Burroughs is a little tougher, but it's just steady climbing, nothing scary. Chances are you'll be distracted by Mount Rainier anyway. It'll be staring you in the face. As a bonus, you can make a reverse-lollipop, hiking back via Sunrise Rim Trail.

There's a large parking area at Sunrise but it fills, early on beautiful weekends. You'll want to be intentional about your visit. When the lot is full, the park typically closes the entrance and lets one car in as one car leaves. That's not what you want to be doing on your vacation when you could be hiking and enjoying the majesty of Mount Rainier.

TOLMIE PEAK LOOKOUT/SPRAY FALLS

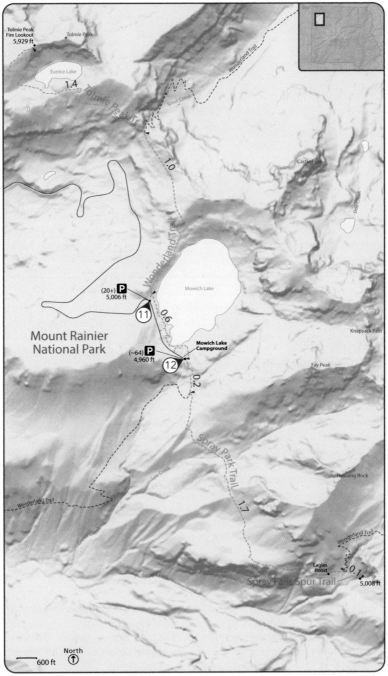

Tolmie Peak Fire Lookout
5,929 ft

Tolmie Peak

Eunice Lake

1.4

Tolmie Peak Tr

Ipsut Creek

Wonderland Trail

Castle Peak

Deer Creek

1.0

Wonderland Trail

Mowich Lake

(20+) P
5,006 ft

11

0.6

Knapsack Pass

Mount Rainier
National Park

Mowich Lake
Campground

(~64) P
4,960 ft

12

Fay Peak

0.2

Spray Park Trail

Lee Creek

Hessong Rock

1.7

Wonderland Trail

Wonderland Trail

Eagles
Roost

0.1

Spray Falls Spur Trail

5,008 ft

North

600 ft

Tolmie Peak Lookout | Strenuous | 4.8 miles | 1,100 feet | Out-and-back
Trailhead: Tolmie Peak, Mowich Lake Road (11)

The trail is steep and strenuous. The rewards are massive. Phenomenal Mount Rainier views overlooking Eunice Lake are what's in store for you from this scenic lookout. It's especially nice in evening light. the access road (SR-165) is a rough gravel road, but sedans can make the journey under typical conditions. Parking is alongside the road, and you can also park down at Mowich Lake Campground, walking along the west shore of Mowich Lake to get to Tolmie Peak Trail.

Spray Falls | Moderate | 4.0 miles | 300 feet | Out-and-back
Trailhead: Mowich Lake Campground (12)

Backpackers enjoy the Northern Loop, but you can easily dayhike to Spray Falls, a 300-foot cascade, and Spray Park. The journey begins on Wonderland Trail. After a quarter mile you'll reach Spray Park Trail. Take the short spur to Spray Falls and continue into Spray Park if you'd like to walk through a beautiful alpine meadow with more Mount Rainier views (it's a good spot for wildflowers). The trailhead is located at Mowich Lake Campground. It's walk-in, tent-only and a great place to spend the night if you can get a spot. Spray Park and Tolmie Peak are extraordinary, but if this is your first time to Mount Rainier, it's a good idea to focus on trails around Paradise and Sunrise.

Snow

Paradise remains paradise in winter, and it'll be the only region of the park open to motorists (typically late December through mid-March). You can also cross-country ski or snowshoe Westside Road. You must carry tire chains. Even hiking in summer, you might want traction devices for a few trails. The largest glacier in the Lower 48 is on Mount Rainier. Snow hangs around. It makes things more fun, and also slightly more dangerous.

More Trails

A few small sections of Wonderland Trail are covered already, but it's a 93-mile loop around the mountain. Particularly on the southern arc, you'll find many waterfalls, and these stretches are going to be considerably less crowded than popular sites like Paradise and Sunrise. Speaking of waterfalls, Silver Falls, located near Stevens Canyon Entrance, is worth a quick look. Tipsoo Lake is a great sunrise/sunset location near Chinook Pass. But on a clear day, any trail with a view of Mount Rainier is going to be wonderful.

Skyline

Myrtle Falls (Mount Rainier)

Second Beach

Olympic
Hiking Trails: 600+ miles

Olympic Favorites

① **Lake Angeles**
Strenuous | 11.8 miles | 5,000 feet

② **Grand Lake**
Strenuous | 8.2 miles | 1,400 feet

③ **Mount Storm King**
Strenuous | 3.9 miles | 2,000 feet

④ **Pyramid Peak**
Strenuous | 6.0 miles | 2,200 feet

⑤ **Seven Lakes Basin**
Strenuous | 18.5 miles | 4,000+ feet

⑥ **East Fork Quinault River**
Strenuous | 30.0 miles | 3,000 feet

⑦ **Second Beach**
Easy | 1.4 miles | 300 feet

⑧ **Shi Shi Beach**
Moderate | 4+ miles | 200+ feet

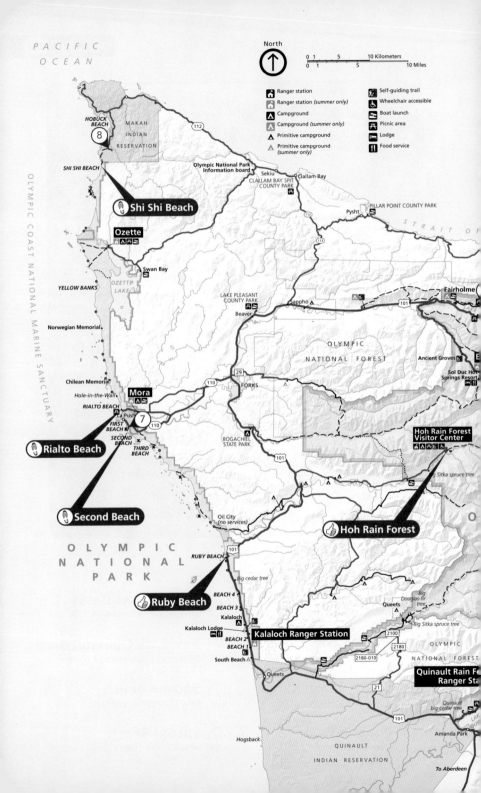

PACIFIC
OCEAN

North

| 0 | 1 | 5 | 10 Kilometers |
| 0 | 1 | 5 | 10 Miles |

♨ Ranger station
♨ Ranger station (summer only)
△ Campground
△ Campground (summer only)
△ Primitive campground
△ Primitive campground (summer only)
🚩 Olympic National Park Information board

♿ Self-guiding trail
♿ Wheelchair accessible
🚤 Boat launch
🅿 Picnic area
🛏 Lodge
🍴 Food service

HOBUCK BEACH

⑧

MAKAH INDIAN RESERVATION

112

SHI SHI BEACH

Sekiu
CLALLAM BAY SPIT COUNTY PARK
Clallam Bay

STRAIT OF

👣 Shi Shi Beach

Ozette

Swan Bay

YELLOW BANKS

OZETTE LAKE

LAKE PLEASANT COUNTY PARK
Beaver

Sappho

Pysht
PILLAR POINT COUNTY PARK

112

113

Fairholme

101

OLYMPIC
NATIONAL FOREST

Ancient Groves
Sol Duc Hot Springs Resort
E

Norwegian Memorial

Chilean Memorial

Hole-in-the-Wall
RIALTO BEACH
Mora
La Push
FIRST BEACH
⑦
SECOND BEACH
THIRD BEACH

29
FORKS

110

110

BOGACHIEL STATE PARK

Hoh Rain Forest Visitor Center

Big Sitka spruce tree

👣 Rialto Beach

👣 Second Beach

101

101

👍 Hoh Rain Forest

Oil City (no services)

OLYMPIC
NATIONAL
PARK

RUBY BEACH

Big cedar tree

👍 Ruby Beach

BEACH 4

BEACH 3

Kalaloch

Kalaloch Lodge

Kalaloch Ranger Station

BEACH 2

BEACH 1

South Beach

Queets

Big Douglas-fir tree

Queets

Big Sitka spruce tree

2100

2180

OLYMPIC
NATIONAL FOREST

2180-010

Quinault Rain Fo
Ranger Sta

21

Quinault big cedar tree

Hogsback

QUINAULT
INDIAN RESERVATION

101

Amanda Park

To Aberdeen

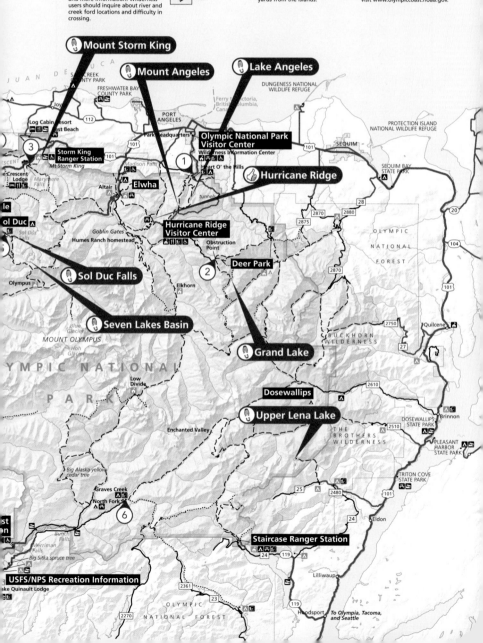

Not a Drive-through Park

No roads pass through the heart of the Olympics. US 101 provides the main access, with numerous spur roads leading into the park.

Paved road

Unpaved road

Hiking the Wilderness

Do not use this map for hiking. Get detailed topographic maps.

Permits required for all overnight wilderness stays. Obtain permits at the Wilderness Information Center (WIC). Call 360-565-3100 or visit the WIC to get *Wilderness Trip Planner* and more information. Wilderness users should inquire about river and creek ford locations and difficulty in crossing.

- - - Trail

········ Primitive trail

⚡ Pass

Visiting the Coast

Caution: Don't get trapped by high tides; get current tide chart at a ranger station. When hiking, watch for targets marking overland trails ●.

Sudden high waves can pick up beach logs and turn them into weapons; they kill.

Most reefs, rocks, islets, and islands (except the James Island group) are designated **wilderness** and **national wildlife refuges, CLOSED** to visitors to protect wildlife. Boats must remain 200 yards from the islands.

✕ Impassable headland; ALWAYS use overland trail

● Wait for low tide or use overland trail if available

Olympic Coast National Marine Sanctuary covers 3,310 square miles of marine waters. The sanctuary provides habitat for one of the most diverse populations of marine mammals in North America. It is a link in the Pacific flyway and provides critical habitat for nesting and migrating birds. To learn more, visit www.olympiccoast.noaa.gov.

LAKE ANGELES/MOUNT ANGELES

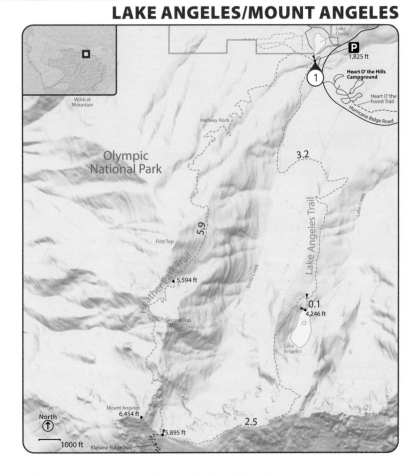

Lake Angeles | Strenuous | 11.8 miles | 5,000 feet | Loop
Trailhead: Lake Angeles, Heart O' the Hills (1)

With more than a dozen disconnected vehicle entry points, Olympic is a difficult park to navigate. What it lacks in road connectivity, it makes up in trail connectivity. There are many good loop options. This is one of them. Most people hike Lake Angeles as an out-and-back, but why do that when you can get above the trees for a while on a 12-mile loop. And you'll visit Mount Angeles, one of the park's most interesting peaks. Direction isn't too important. It'll be uphill going out, and downhill coming back no matter what. Going to Lake Angeles postpones the grade a little bit, but you're going to get it eventually. The lake is beautiful. The hike there is forested. And then, after gaining some elevation, you'll be treated to excellent views along Klahane Ridge all the way to the Switchbacks intersection. Mount Angeles is a funky rock. You can also reach it from Switchbacks Trail (beginning from Hurricane Ridge Road) or High Ridge/Sunrise Point/Klahane Ridge trails (beginning

GRAND LAKE/BADGER VALLEY

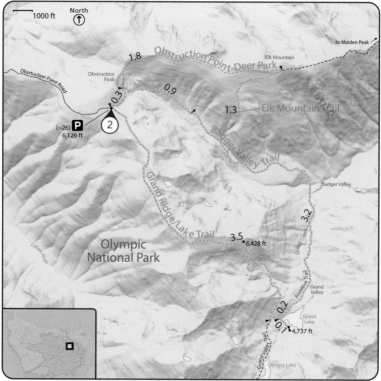

1000 ft   North

to Maiden Peak

Obsrtuction Point Road

Obstruction Peak

Obstruction Point-Deer Park

Elk Mountain

1.8

0.3

0.9

1.3

Elk Mountain Trail

(~26) P
6,126 ft

2

Badger Valley Trail

Grand Ridge Lake Trail

Badger Valley

Lillian River

Olympic National Park

3.5   •6,428 ft

3.2

Grand Creek

Primitive Trail

Grand Valley

0.2

Grand Lake
4,737 ft

Grand Valley Trail

0.1

Moose Lake

at the east end of Hurricane Ridge Visitor Center's parking lot). The former is short and steep. The latter is just over six miles but requires a little route finding and rock scrambling. Back to the loop. There's significant exposure coming around Second Top, and then it's mostly downhill back to Heart O' the Hills. Backpacking (permit required) is an option here with sites at Lake Angeles and Heather Park. The trailhead is located off a short spur road before Heart 'O the Hills Ranger Station.

Grand Lake-Badger Valley | Strenuous | 8.2 miles | 1,400 feet | Loop
Trailhead: Obstruction Point Road (2)

This is a good departure point for backpacking trips (permit required), but you can also have some fun dayhiking around the area. With an early start, you could loop to Grand Lake and back via Badger Valley. If you're moving at a pretty good clip, before reaching Grand Lake, you could head south to Moose Lake and all the way to Grand Pass, and then turn around to complete the loop back to the end of Obstruction Point Road. Grand Lake Trail is exposed. Expect wind and sun. There's more protection in the valley, but this is still a tough trek. Obstruction Point is a lightly traveled unpaved road that should be accessible to all vehicles.

MOUNT STORM KING

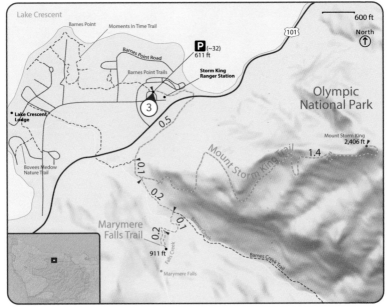

Mount Storm King | Strenuous | 3.9 miles | 2,000 feet | Out-and-back
Trailhead: Storm King Ranger Station, Lake Crescent Road (3)

Mount Storm King is a fun hike, featuring a steep rope-aided climb, some exposure, and a final scramble to a rocky promontory overlooking Lake Crescent. The cherry on top is a short detour to Marymere Falls. Even if you find rope-aided climbs fun, you're going to want to stay away from Storm King if the trail is wet. It's a dirt trail, and can be a little tricky in dry conditions.

The trail begins next to Storm King Ranger Station, where you'll find room for a few dozen vehicles.

Pyramid Peak | Strenuous | 6.0 miles | 2,200 feet | Out-and-back
Trailhead: North Shore Picnic Area, Camp David Jr. Road (4)

Pyramid Peak is the counterpoint to Mount Storm King. It's a continuous ascent through forests, with occasional views looking out across Lake Crescent and into the heart of Olympic National Park. There is a narrow section of cliffside trail that could give you a scare. But if you make it to the peak, you'll be treated to a mountaintop shelter and exceptional views. The trailhead is easy to find from the parking area at the end of Camp David Jr. Road. The road is unpaved, but any car should be able to manage it just fine. You'll also find a fun little dockside picnic area nearby.

PYRAMID PEAK

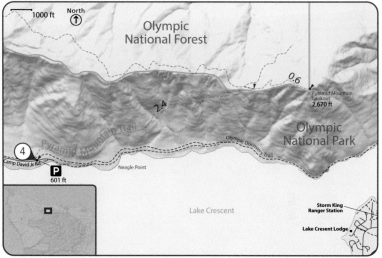

SEVEN LAKES BASIN/HIGH DIVIDE

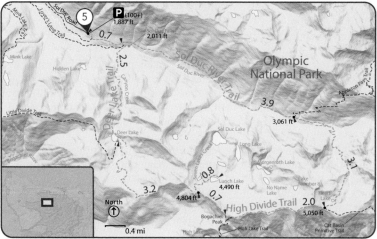

Seven Lakes Basin | Strenuous | 18.5 miles | 4,000+ feet | Loop
Trailhead: Sol Duc Road (5)

Seven Lakes Basin is another popular backpacking area (permit required). Quite frankly, it's not a good idea to do the loop in a day (even if you can without a problem). The elevation gain is considerable. Snow usually sticks around along High Divide Trail into July, and it can be real tricky getting around Bogachiel Peak (call to discuss trail conditions if you're going early in the season). There are also a few creek crossings along the way. But this

EAST FORK QUINAULT RIVER

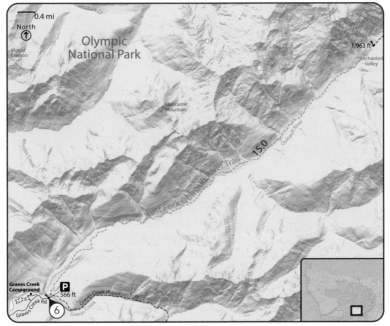

is one to put on your radar. (High Divide Trail in particular is fantastic.) And if you like to backpack, get online and try to reserve permits six months in advance. Even if you don't go to the backcountry, you should make a stop at Sol Duc to look at the falls, which is less than a two-mile walk. And now you'll know there's more interesting sights beyond the falls.

There's a lot of parking at the end of Sol Duc Road, but this is also one of the busiest destinations. Most visitors are making the short out-and-back to three-pronged Sol Duc Falls, so it turns over quickly.

East Fork Quinault River | Strenuous | 30.0 miles | 3,000 feet | Out-and-back
Trailhead: Graves Creek Campground (6)

If you're hardcore, it's within the realm of possibility to hike to Enchanted Valley and back in a day. But it's a better backpacking destination (permit required). The trail is long, sometimes muddy, and heavily forested until you reach Enchanted Valley's waterfall-accented mountains. You'll need rain or snowmelt for the waterfalls to charge up, making the trek out here tougher. Nestled in Enchanted Valley is a relic of tourism's past, a historic chalet originally built in 1930 and, since then, used as a lodge, ranger station, and emergency shelter. The park service has moved it around, saving it from the river's seasonal floods. Today, its fate remains uncertain. Move it. Leave it. Take

SECOND BEACH

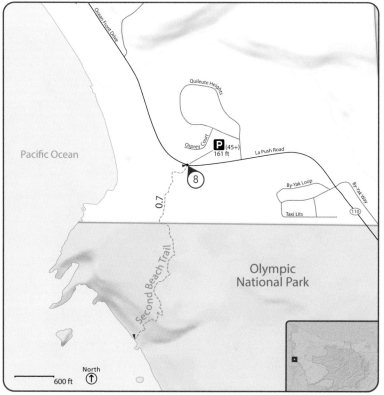

it apart. It'll provide lively discussion between interested parties for years to come. Regardless, the reason to visit Enchanted Valley isn't a nearly hundred-year-old weathered chalet. It's to enjoy a hike to a stunningly beautiful destination (most of the hike is somewhat ordinary forested river valley). Dayhiking isn't a great idea. Backpacking is better. And if it's enchanting backpacking you're looking for, look into The Enchantments instead.

Second Beach | Easy | 1.4 miles | 300 feet | Out-and-back
Trailhead: Second Beach, La Push Road (8)

Second Beach is a short and easy hike to a pristine beach with interesting tide-pooling and sea stacks. There's very little grade on this intuitive trail. The parking area is large, with room for more than 50 vehicles, but it'll fill up, especially on weekends. The beach is expansive, with plenty of room to do your own thing, so while you won't be alone, it never feels overly crowded.

SHI SHI BEACH

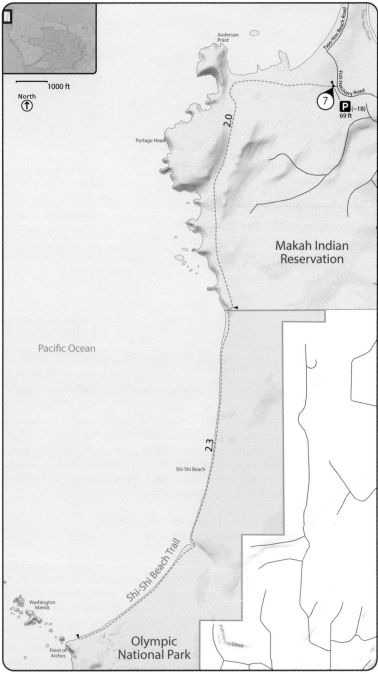

1000 ft

North

Anderson Point

Too-Yess Beach Road

Too-Yess River

Fish Hatchery Road

7 P (~18)
69 ft

Portage Head

2.0

Makah Indian
Reservation

Pacific Ocean

2.3

Shi-Shi Beach

Shi-Shi Beach Trail

Washington
Islands

Point of
Arches

Olympic
National Park

petroleum Creek

Shi Shi Beach | Moderate | 4+ miles | 200+ feet | Out-and-back
Trailhead: Shi Shi Beach, Hobuck (Fish Hatchery) Road (7)

Olympic's coast provides a wonderful contrast to its mountains a few miles away. Of the accessible coastal beaches, Shi Shi takes the biggest commitment. The trailhead is tucked away in the very northwest corner of Olympic Peninsula. And you'll need to purchase a Makah Recreation Pass to park at any trailheads on the Makah Reservation (Shi Shi Beach's trailhead is located on tribal land). Several places sell them in Neah Bay. Shi Shi Beach is also a popular backpacking site (permit required). The trail is well marked and easy, aside from a relatively steep descent from the trail to the beach. It's four miles to the beach and you could walk quite a few more miles to the south. It is a popular destination, especially on weekends, but you usually don't have to walk too far down the beach to have a more tranquil experience. As always with ocean hikes, you'll want to be aware of the tides.

Environment

Olympic National Park features remarkable environmental diversity. In winter, you can ski or tube at Hurricane Ridge, and then stroll along the Pacific in the evening as the sun sets. The west side of the park is some of the wettest/lushest land in the country. The east side can experience desert-like conditions. So, choosing the right time to visit depends on what you'd like to do and where you'd like to go. The coast can be great all year long. Hiking the mountains, that's best in late summer/early fall, but some lower elevation hikes will be exceptional in spring when snow is melting and the rivers run.

More Trails

There are plenty more great hiking trails. On the coast, Third Beach (easy, 2.8 miles), Rialto Beach's Hole-in-the-Wall (easy, 3.0 miles), and Ruby Beach (easy, varies) are worth a look. In the mountains, you could think about Royal Lake (strenuous, 16 miles) or a few short but very strenuous trails near Staircase or Lena Lake (there's also an Upper Lena Lake). And then there's the rainforests of the western Olympics. You'll find a bunch of big trees between Quinault and Hoh. Hall of Mosses (easy, 0.8 mile) at Hoh is pretty cool. I wouldn't quite put it in the must-visit category because it's a long drive to reach the trailhead, but if you're looking for short, easy, and green, with pretty high probability of wildlife sightings (elk!), this is the place. To me, Hoh is better suited as a departure point for backpacking trips to Blue Glacier/Mount Olympus. You could even make the steep climb up Hoh Lake Trail to Seven Lakes Basin/High Divide. There's an awful lot to see and do here, and then the National Park is largely surrounded by National Forest land with plenty of its own hiking opportunities.

Marymere Falls

Sol duc Falls (Olympic)

North Cascades
Hiking Trails: 400+ miles

Doubtful Lake (Sahale Arm)

North Cascades Favorites

(1) **Sahale Arm/Glacier**
Strenuous | 11.5 miles | 4,100 feet

(2) **Hidden Lake Lookout**
Strenuous | 7.2 miles | 3,200 feet

(3) **Lookout Mountain**
Strenuous | 8.2 miles | 4,500 feet

Monogram Lake
Strenuous | 8.7 miles | 4,600 feet

(4) **Thornton Lakes**
Strenuous | 10.0 miles | 2,800 feet

(5) **Maple Pass/Lake Ann**
Strenuous | 7.2 miles | 2,200 feet

(6) **Blue Lake**
Moderate | 4.4 miles | 900 feet

(7) **Rainbow Falls**
Easy | 0.3 mile | 30 feet

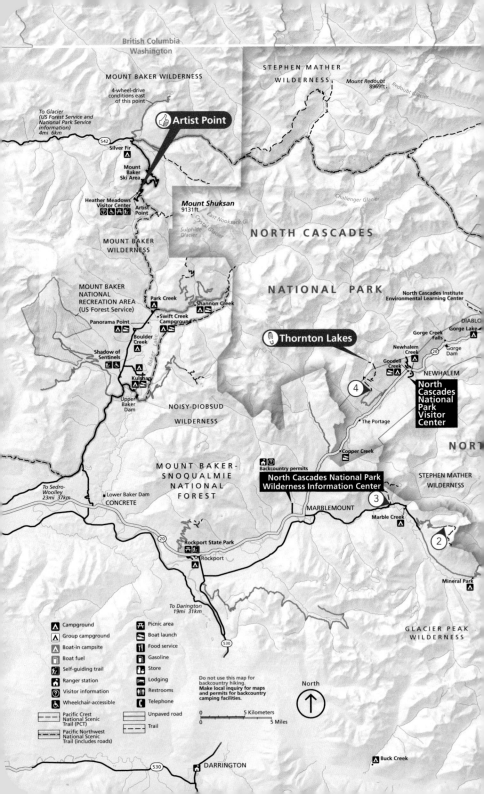

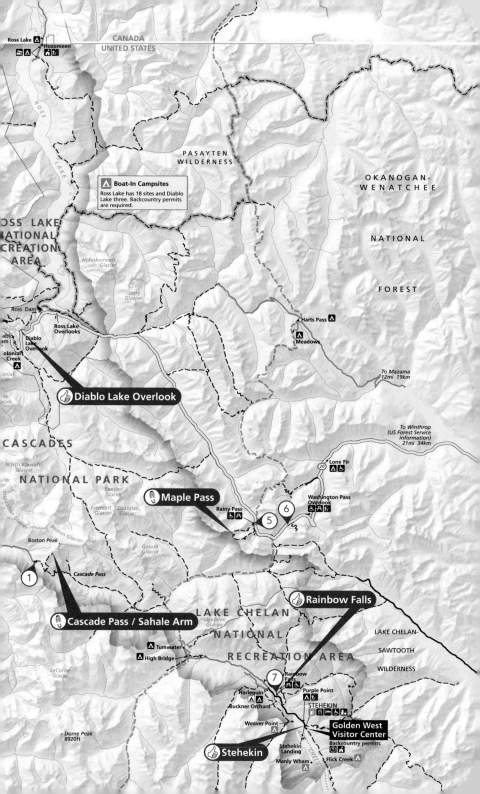

CANADA
UNITED STATES

Ross Lake

Hozomeen

ROSS LAKE NATIONAL RECREATION AREA

PASAYTEN
WILDERNESS

OKANOGAN-
WENATCHEE

NATIONAL

Boat-In Campsites
Ross Lake has 18 sites and Diablo
Lake three. Backcountry permits
are required.

FOREST

Nohokomeen
Glacier

Jerry
Glacier

Ross Dam

Harts Pass

Meadows

Ross Lake
Overlooks

Diablo
Lake
Overlook

Colonial
Creek

To Mazama
12mi 19km

Diablo Lake Overlook

CASCADES

To Winthrop
(US Forest Service
information)
21mi 34km

North Klawatti
Glacier

NATIONAL PARK

Lone Fir

20

Banded
Glacier

Fremont
Glacier

Douglas
Glacier

Maple Pass

Rainy Pass

Washington Pass
Overlook

5

6

Boston Glacier

Boston Peak

Goode
Glacier

1

Cascade Pass

Cascade Pass / Sahale Arm

LAKE CHELAN

Rainbow Falls

Sandalee
Glacier

NATIONAL

LeConte
Glacier

Tumwater

High Bridge

RECREATION AREA

LAKE CHELAN-
SAWTOOTH
WILDERNESS

Dome Peak
8920ft

Rainbow

7

Purple Point

Harlequin

Buckner Orchard

STEHEKIN

Weaver Point

**Golden West
Visitor Center**

Backcountry permits

Stehekin

Stehekin
Landing

Manly Wham

Flick Creek

SAHALE ARM/GLACIER

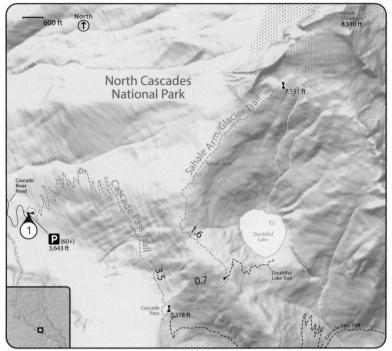

Sahale Arm/Glacier | Strenuous | 11.5 miles | 4,100 feet | Out-and-back
Trailhead: Cascade Pass, Cascade River Road (1)

It's a truly amazing hike but there are three distinct stages to this one. The first stage is up. A long tedious climb up a series of switchbacks, with no substantial views to make you feel like the effort couldn't possibly be worthwhile. The second stage is where this hike begins to prove its value. You'll reach Cascade Pass, with fine views looking down at Doubtful Lake and up at Sahale Arm. The grade is moderate, the views are much improved. The third stage is bliss. You head up Sahale Arm (snow hangs around well into summer, come prepared if you're hiking early in the season), where it ends with a very loud exclamation point, but it's a serious amount of effort to reach it.

The Trailhead is at the end of Cascade River Road, where you'll find room for about 70 vehicles, maybe a few more squeeze along the side of the road. The road is unpaved, but you shouldn't need high-clearance or 4WD to get out here when it's open (summer through fall). It's a beautiful drive, and you'll be energized to trudge up those switchbacks to a little slice of heaven. There are two campgrounds along Cascade River Road. They're outside the park, located in Mt. Baker-Snoqualmie National Forest. Camping at one of them is a good idea. Reservations are available at recreation.gov.

HIDDEN LAKE LOOKOUT

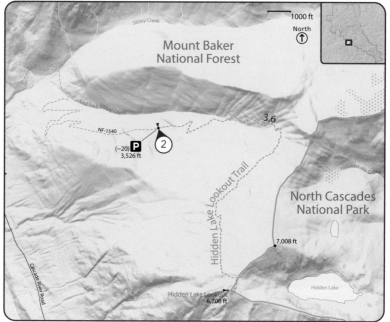

Hidden Lake Lookout | Strenuous | 7.2 miles | 3,200 feet | Out-and-back
Trailhead: Hidden Lake Lookout, NF-1540 (2)

The view from Hidden Lake Lookout is superlatively great. The road to reach the trailhead can be at the exact opposite end of the superlative spectrum. It's rough. It's narrow. It's rutted. There are switchbacks. It's not a particularly good place to drive and an awful place for traffic. These things are all filters for who you'll meet on the trail. You'll want a high-clearance vehicle for this one. Cascade River Road is an absolute dream by comparison. As for the trail. It's up, up, and up a tad more to a fire lookout with views looking out toward some of the park's most prominent and picturesque peaks. So, the question is, is the drive worth the views? Most certainly! For uncomfortable drives like this, I usually like to get an early start before anyone might be coming down from the trailhead. But, on clear days, you're going to have better mountain views later in the day, when Hidden Lake, Triad, and Eldorado Peak dazzle with the soft evening light at your back. But remember, you still have to hike back to your vehicle, and drive to wherever you're spending the night.

You get on NF-1540 from Cascade River Road. The turn is about 1.3 miles beyond Marble Creek Campground. NF-1540 is only 4.5 miles long, but it'll take you a while to reach the trailhead.

LOOKOUT MTN/MONOGRAM LAKE

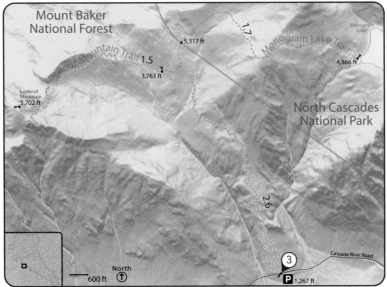

Mount Baker
National Forest

Monogram
Lake

5,317 ft

1.7

Monogram Lake Trail

Lookout Mountain Trail 1.5

4,866 ft

3,763 ft

Lookout
Mountain
5,702 ft

North Cascades
National Park

2.6

Cascade River Road

3

North

600 ft

P 1,267 ft

Lookout Mountain | Strenuous | 8.2 miles | 4,500 feet | Out-and-back
Monogram Lake | Strenuous | 8.7 miles | 4,600 feet | Out-and-back
Trailhead: Lookout Mountain, Cascade River Road (3)

On this hike you're going to gain a whole lot of elevation in a relatively short distance. Still, it's not ridiculous to think about hiking down to Monogram Lake and up to Lookout Mountain in the same day. It's about twelve miles to do them both. The fire lookout has your expected panoramic views, and you're in the midst of some very special mountains. As for Monogram Lake, views from above it are better than views from its shore. The lake is usually frozen into July. You can backpack (permit required) at the lake but remember that has you hauling more weight up this arduous climb. Unless you're stair-mastering regularly at home, I'd forget about trying to do this with an extra 30–40 pounds strapped to your back. So to recap, this trail is more difficult than Hidden Lake Lookout, the views aren't as impressive, and you're looking at a lot of the same peaks from this fire lookout. The big pros are it's much easier to reach compared to Hidden Lake Lookout, located right alongside Cascade River Road, and it's not nearly as popular as Sahale Arm. It's a trade-off. Regardless, it's another fun place to know about. If you're going to do it, there's a small pullout next to the trailhead seven miles down Cascade River Road. That might be the big perk, you won't have much company on this trail.

THORNTON LAKES

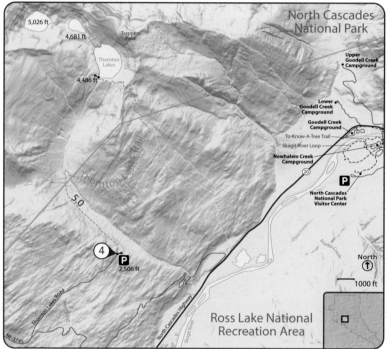

Thornton Lakes | Strenuous | 10.0 miles | 2,800 feet | Out-and-back
Trailhead: Thornton Lakes, Thornton Lakes Road (4)

This is an easier—albeit still strenuous—hike to scenic alpine lakes. The first two miles of trail are along an old logging road, then the grade picks up, before descending (steeply) to Thornton Lakes. It's ten miles roundtrip to the first lake. You have some opportunities to explore social trails to the other two. You can also scramble up toward Trappers Peak.

The trailhead is located at the end of the vehicle-accessible portion of Thornton Lakes Road. The park recommends a high-clearance vehicle due to its rough and steep nature.

MAPLE PASS/LAKE ANN/RAINY LAKE

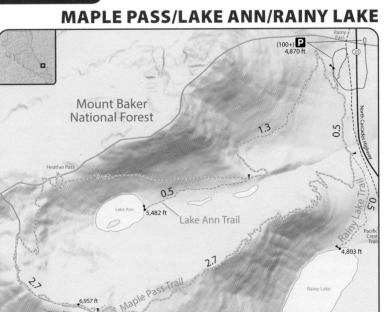

Maple Pass | Strenuous | 7.2 miles | 2,200 feet | Loop
Trailhead: Rainy Pass Picnic Area, North Cascades Highway (5)

You have some excellent options here. Rainy Lake and Ann Lake are short, easy, and stunning. And then you can take Maple Pass to hike above them, not only for views of the lakes, but for views into the North Cascades South Unit and Lake Chelan National Recreation Area. From Maple Pass #740 Trailhead, you climb steeply above Lake Ann. Effort pays off, clearing the trees and walking up to the National Park boundary. The return trip follows the ridgeline between Lake Ann and Rainy Lake. Along the way you'll have substantial views in every direction. Don't skip the spurs to Lake Ann and Rainy Lake. You'll like them. Rainy Lake is paved for anyone with disabilities. To do everything—Lake Ann, Rainy Lake, and Maple Pass Loop—it'll end up being about nine miles. Almost everyone hikes it in a counterclockwise direction, starting at the Maple Pass #740 Trailhead. If you're starting early, which you should, clockwise will give you that nice morning light looking down on Lake Ann, and then you'll have better light again looking down on it from Maple Pass (if you take your time around the loop). The bad thing is, you'll be going against the flow. And this is a very popular area. The parking lot is

BLUE LAKE

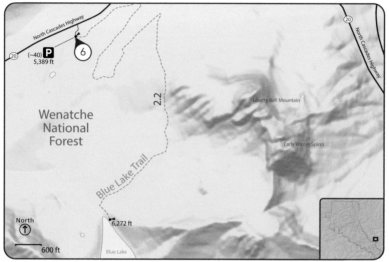

big, but it fills early, especially in fall when everyone's out for larch madness. If the lot is full, you can park along North Cascades Highway (WA-20). Speaking of WA-20, it closes for winter.

Blue Lake | Moderate | 4.4 miles | 900 feet | Out-and-back
Trailhead: Blue Lake, North Cascades Highway (6)

Similar to Maple Pass/Lake Ann/Rainy Lake, Blue Lake isn't within the National Park but it's one of the more easily accessible trails in the area, thanks to its location right off North Cascades Highway (WA-20). You're gaining some elevation on this trail and the treat at the end of the climb is a pristine mountain lake. There's room for about 40 cars at the trailhead, with more parking alongside WA-20.

Preparation

With more than 300 glaciers and many more snowfields, you need to be prepared to encounter snow/ice if you're arriving early in the year and/or hiking into the higher elevations. Peak and pass hikes also call for wind and sun prep. For the lakes and waterfalls, you'll want to be ready for bugs.

Sheep near Blue Lake

RAINBOW FALLS

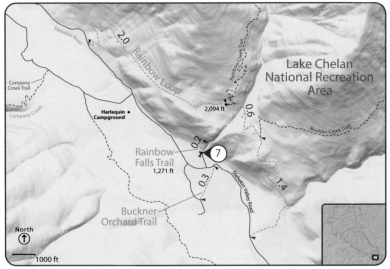

Rainbow Falls | Easy | 0.3 mile | 30 feet | Out-and-back
Trailhead: Rainbow Falls, Stehekin (7)

Rainbow Falls is probably the one destination every Stehekin visitor admires. Short, easy, and a beautiful waterfall. The trailhead is a little more than three miles from Stehekin Landing/Visitor Center. If you're coming and going on the same day via ferry, you won't have enough time to walk down Stehekin Valley Road to the trailhead. That's no problem, you can also bike or catch a ride on the shuttle. Spend the night and you'll have time for much more.

You cannot drive to Stehekin. Access is via ferry or plane. Taking the ferry for a daytrip only allows a couple hours to explore the region. It's enough time for an introduction to this small eclectic community but not nearly enough time for any significant hiking. Spend the night and you could do much more, like Rainbow Loop also highlighted on the map. Stehekin Valley extends all the way back to Cascade Pass. Cascade Pass to Stehekin is an interesting back-packing point-to-point (getting picked up by plane or ferry in Stehekin).

More Trails

This corner of the country is a hiker's/mountaineer's paradise. There are a lot of trails. Seemingly unlimited public land. The North and South Units of the actual National Park are difficult to access. To reach the North Unit you must hike into it. There's a lot of fun to be had trying to figure these things out. The South Unit is accessed via Cascade River Road. There are a few other easily accessible trails in Ross Lake National Recreation Area, which is bisected by WA-20 (North Cascades Highway). Ladder Creek Falls (easy, 0.4 mile), Gorge Creek Falls (easy, 0.5 mile), Pyramid Peak (moderate, 4.2 miles), and Thunder Knob (moderate, 3.6 miles) can be accessed from WA-20. Thunder Creek Trail leads to all sorts of interesting backcountry sites.

Alaska

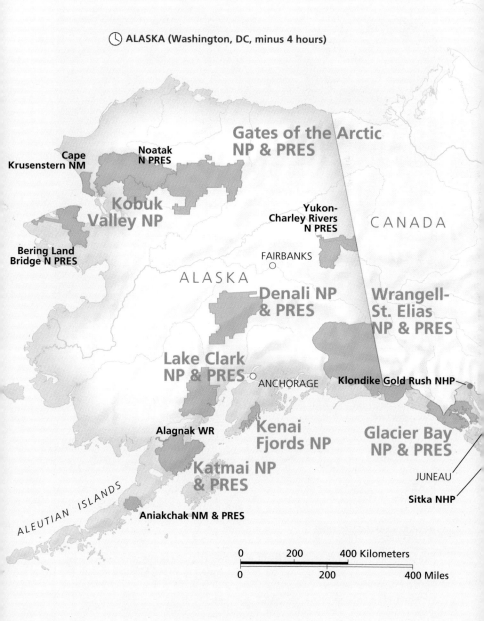

🕐 **ALASKA (Washington, DC, minus 4 hours)**

Cape Krusenstern NM

Noatak N PRES

Gates of the Arctic NP & PRES

Kobuk Valley NP

Bering Land Bridge N PRES

Yukon-Charley Rivers N PRES

CANADA

FAIRBANKS

ALASKA

Denali NP & PRES

Wrangell-St. Elias NP & PRES

Lake Clark NP & PRES

ANCHORAGE

Klondike Gold Rush NHP

Alagnak WR

Kenai Fjords NP

Glacier Bay NP & PRES

Katmai NP & PRES

JUNEAU

Sitka NHP

Aniakchak NM & PRES

ALEUTIAN ISLANDS

0   200   400 Kilometers

0   200   400 Miles

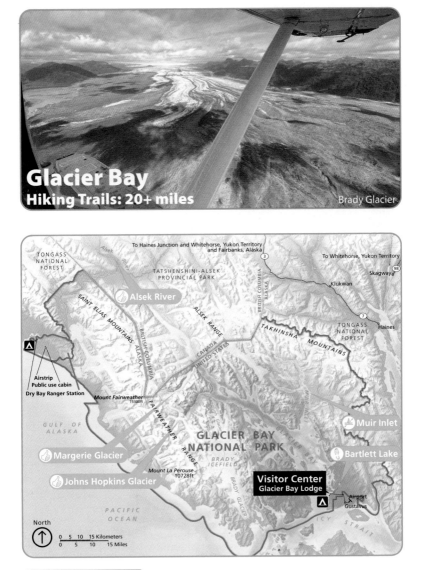

Glacier Bay
Hiking Trails: 20+ miles

Brady Glacier

Hiking Glacier Bay

Glacier Bay isn't about hiking but there are a few trails, all spanning out from the visitor center and campground. You can hike to Bartlett River (4.0 miles), Bartlett Lake (10.0 miles), and along the coast from Bartlett Cove to Point Gustavus. Hiking is all about the Bartletts. A very small minority of park visitors stay at the lodge or campground and hike the trails. Most arrive via cruise, enjoying up close views of Margerie and Johns Hopkins Glaciers.

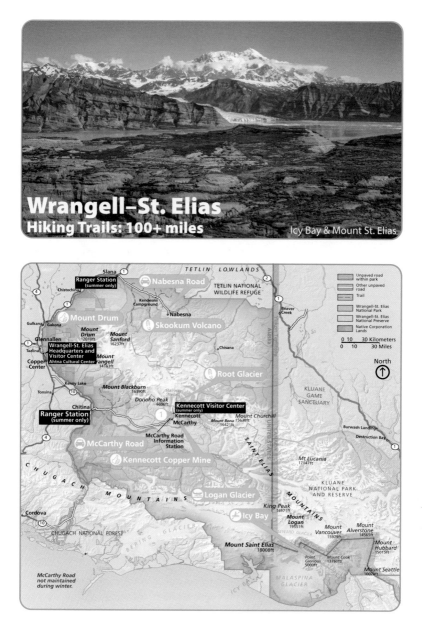

Wrangell–St. Elias
Hiking Trails: 100+ miles
Icy Bay & Mount St. Elias

Wrangell–St. Elias Favorites

(1) **Root Glacier**
Moderate | 2.7+ miles | 500 feet

ROOT GLACIER/KENNECOTT

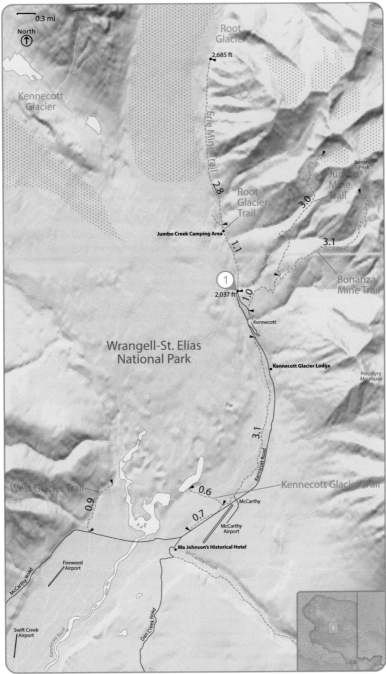

0.3 mi

North

Dorana Peak

Root
Glacier

2,685 ft

Kennecott
Glacier

Erie Mine Trail

2.8

Root
Glacier
Trail

Jumbo
Mine
Trail

Bonanza
Peak

3.0

Jumbo Creek Camping Area

1.1

3.1

1

2,037 ft

1.0

Bonanza
Mine Trail

Kennecott

Wrangell-St. Elias
National Park

Kennecott Glacier Lodge

Porphyry
Mountain

3.1

Kennecott Road

West Glacier Trail

0.9

0.6

Kennecott Glacier Trail

McCarthy

0.7

McCarthy
Airport

Ma Johnson's Historical Hotel

McCarthy Creek

Fireweed
Airport

McCarthy Road

Kennicott River

Dan Creek Road

Swift Creek
Airport

Root Glacier | Moderate | 2.7+ miles | 500 feet | Out-and-back
Trailhead: Kennecott (1)

It's a good idea to check out Root Glacier, but there's quite a bit of prerequisite information you need to know. First, McCarthy Road ends short of McCarthy and Kennecott. You'll have to walk or pay for a shuttle to McCarthy (one mile away) or Kennecott (five miles away). The extra five miles (each way) to Kennecott really stretches this hike out. Spending a night (or more) at McCarthy or Kennecott is a good idea (there are several options). Or, better yet, there's a primitive camp at Jumbo Creek. There are also designated backcountry camping sites on the far side of Root Glacier at Donoho Basin. Take your time and enjoy the scenery. These aren't things you do on a whim with no experience. To reach Donoho Basin, you must cross Root Glacier. If you have any significant doubts, it's best to hire a guide. There are many of those too.

More Trails

Wrangell–St. Elias is more than 13 million acres. Four times the size of Death Valley! There are a few short trails around the visitor center, where you'll have views looking into the Wrangell Mountains, beginning with the imposing Mount Drum.

The map on the previous page shows several more trails in the Kennecott/McCarthy area. Jumbo Mine (8 miles) and Bonanza Mine (7.3) climb into the nearby mountains, where you'll achieve an elevated view of Root Glacier and the Wrangell Mountains. It's a great place to head early in the morning.

There are more trails along McCarthy Road, but, if you're limited on time, you really don't want to spend too much of it exploring these side trails. Kennecott wasn't all about its minerals. Scenic beauty often plays a role in development. The drive down McCarthy Road takes most people about two hours. While there are no frontcountry campgrounds in the park, you can camp at pullouts along McCarthy and Nabesna roads. Camping/lodging or not, you absolutely must plan some time to explore McCarthy and Kennecott. However, if you aren't real keen on the long gravel road; jockeying for first-come, first-served pullouts; and managed access to McCarthy/Kennecott, this is arguably the best National Park to take a flightseeing trip. You'll be treated to a never-ending display of some of the planet's most beautiful snow-capped peaks and glaciers. And getting here by plane also opens opportunities for camping in the backcountry (there are several backcountry cabins). It's something worth thinking about when you're budgeting your vacation.

Back to dayhiking. Most of the trail mileage is around Nabesna Road. Skookum Volcano (5.2 miles) is a common destination among hikers, but it seems like this is an area more commonly explored by hunters (hunting is permitted in the preserve areas of Wrangell–St. Elias National Park and Preserve). And, once again, don't forget about the park's size. It's more than a 2.5-hour drive just to get from Chitina (where McCarthy Road begins) to Slana (where Nabesna Road begins). Each of those roads takes about two hours (each way). You don't want to spend your entire Alaskan holiday behind the wheel. Yes, days will be long if you're visiting in summer and there will be time to rest when you return home, but hiking/driving tired can lead to all kinds of serious problems.

Denali
Hiking Trails: 30+ miles

Denali

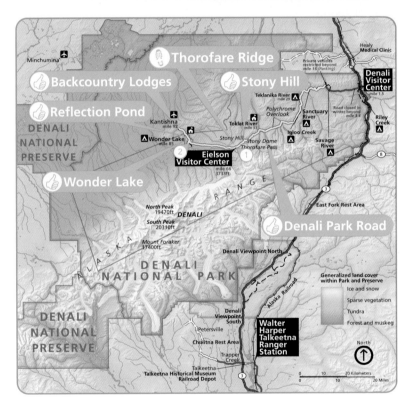

Minchumina

Thorofare Ridge

Backcountry Lodges

Stony Hill

Healy Medical Clinic

Private vehicles restricted beyond mile 15 (Parking)

Denali Visitor Center
mile 1.5

Reflection Pond

Teklanika River
mile 29

Polychrome Overlook

Kantishna
mile 92

Toklat River
mile 53

Sanctuary River

Road closed in winter beyond mile 3.4

Riley Creek

DENALI NATIONAL PRESERVE

Wonder Lake
mile 85

Stony Hill

Stony Dome
Thorofare Pass

Igloo Creek

Savage River

8

Eielson Visitor Center
mile 66
3733ft

2

1

Wonder Lake

RANGE

East Fork Rest Area

3

North Peak
19470ft
DENALI

South Peak
20310ft

Mount Foraker
17400ft

Denali Park Road

A L A S K A

DENALI
NATIONAL PARK

Denali Viewpoint North

Alaska Railroad

Generalized land cover within Park and Preserve

Ice and snow

Sparse vegetation

Tundra

Forest and muskeg

DENALI
NATIONAL
PRESERVE

Denali
Viewpoint
South

Petersville

Chulitna Rest Area

Trapper Creek

Talkeetna
Talkeetna Historical Museum
Railroad Depot

Walter
Harper
Talkeetna
Ranger
Station

North

3

0   10   20 Kilometers
0   10   20 Miles

Denali Favorites

① **Thorofare Ridge**
Strenuous | 2.7 miles | 1,000 feet

② **McKinley Bar**
Easy | 5.0 miles | 450 feet

THOROFARE RIDGE (EIELSON ALPINE)

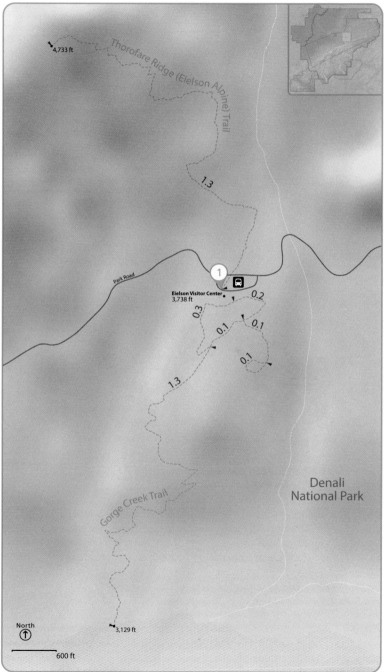

4,733 ft

Thorofare Ridge (Eielson Alpine) Trail

1.3

Park Road

1

Eielson Visitor Center
3,738 ft

0.2

0.3

0.1

0.1

0.1

1.3

Gorge Creek Trail

Denali
National Park

3,129 ft

North

600 ft

MCKINLEY BAR

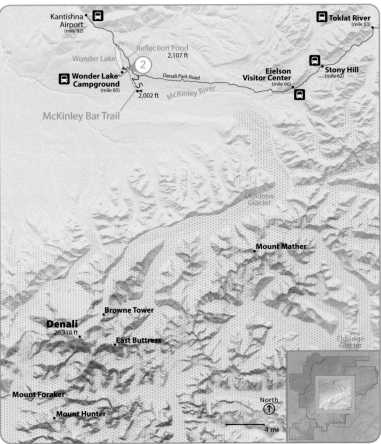

Thorofare Ridge (Eielson Alpine) | Strenuous | 2.7 miles | 1,000 feet | Out-and-back | **Trailhead:** Eielson Visitor Center (1)

Of all the maintained trails in the park, this is the one to do. It begins at Eielson Visitor Center (Mile 66) and climbs steeply to one of the best viewpoints along Denali Park Road. It rivals the view from Stony Hill a few miles east of Eielson Visitor Center. There's also a fun nature trail at the visitor center.

McKinley Bar | Easy | 5.0 miles | 450 feet | Out-and-back
Trailhead: Wonder Lake Campground (2)

Wonder Lake Campground or the park's backcountry lodges are where you want to spend the night to maximize your Denali views (or non-views—it's often shrouded in clouds, so cross your fingers and find a four-leaf clover, wishing for clear skies). The main reason this map is included is to make the park's scale crystal clear. Wonder Lake Campground is 85 miles down Denali

Park Road. Denali views are pretty darn good from Wonder Lake Campground, but you're still 27 miles (as the crow flies) from Denali's summit. If you're camping at Wonder Lake, it's a good idea to hike to McKinley Bar. It leads through spruce forest, to the gravel bars along the McKinley River. Crossing the river can be deadly, especially during summer run-off. Be careful once you're there.

*Denali Park Road is closed to all vehicle traffic beyond mile 43 until summer 2025 (if not later). You may be able to visit the park's interior by flying into Kantishna. That's something worth looking into, budget permitting. If you can't get beyond mile 43, it's a good idea to postpone Denali plans for another time.

Denali Park Road

Denali Park Road Closure

Denali Park Road is closed to all vehicle traffic beyond mile 43 until summer 2025 (or later) while a suspension bridge is constructed near Pretty Rocks. There is a chance you will be able to reach the park's interior by flying into Kantishna. That's something to look into if your heart's set on seeing the tallest mountain in North America.

Denali Park Road Buses

Most of the year, Denali Park Road can only be accessed via buses run by the park and its private backcountry lodges. There are three types of park buses: narrated, "non-narrated," and camper. Camper require a camping reservation. Narrated run a set itinerary. "Non-narrated" are typically narrated but you can hop off and on whenever you'd like as far into Denali Park Road as your ticket allows. Farther is better, but you're talking about a 13-hour bus ride to get to Kantishna and back.

More Trails

Denali is mostly trailless wilderness. However, there are a few trails near the park entrance (nearly 100 miles from Denali). Mount Healy (strenuous, 5.3 miles) begins near the Visitor Center and climbs to a scenic viewpoint where you can just barely see the tip of Denali on a clear day. Horseshoe Lake (moderate, 3.3 miles) is a pleasant lollipop to two nearby lakes. The trail also begins near the visitor center, but you can access it from a few other locations as well (like Taiga Trail). There are two short trails at Savage River, the farthest you can drive in your own vehicle during peak season. Savage Alpine Trail provides better views of Denali than you'll find at Mount Healy, but still nothing like you'll get deeper in the park. It's 1.5 miles up a moderate incline from the parking area to the viewpoint. You can also hike to the viewpoint from Savage River Campground, although it's slightly longer and steeper. That just about does it for trails. There are a few trails around the privately-run backcountry lodges near Kantishna. You pay a hefty premium to stay there but the location is impossible to beat.

Kenai Fjords
Hiking Trails: 30+ miles

Exit Glacier from Harding Icefield Trail

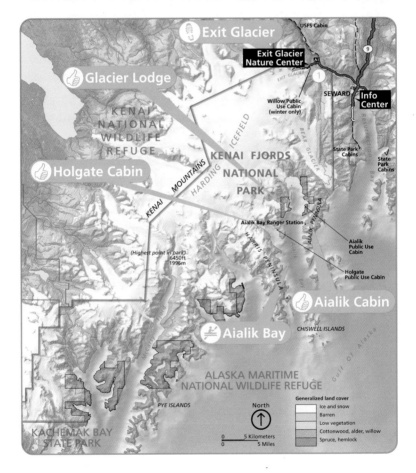

Exit Glacier

USFS Cabin

Exit Glacier
Nature Center

Glacier Lodge

SEWARD

Info
Center

KENAI
NATIONAL
WILDLIFE
REFUGE

Willow Public
Use Cabin
(winter only)

State Park
Cabins

State
Park
Cabins

KENAI FJORDS

NATIONAL

PARK

Holgate Cabin

KENAI MOUNTAINS

HARDING

ICEFIELD

BEAR GLACIER

Aialik Bay Ranger Station

AIALIK PENINSULA

Aialik
Public Use
Cabin

(Highest point in park)
6450ft
1996m

HARRIS PENINSULA

Holgate
Public Use Cabin

Aialik Cabin

Aialik Bay

CHISWELL ISLANDS

Gulf Of Alaska

ALASKA MARITIME
NATIONAL WILDLIFE REFUGE

PYE ISLANDS

North

KACHEMAK BAY
STATE PARK

Generalized land cover
- Ice and snow
- Barren
- Low vegetation
- Cottonwood, alder, willow
- Spruce, hemlock

0   5 Kilometers
0   5 Miles

Kenai Fjords Favorites

① **Glacier Overlook**
Moderate | 2.0+ miles | 400 feet

① **Harding Icefield**
Strenuous | 8.7 miles | 3,200 feet

HARDING ICEFIELD/EXIT GLACIER OVERLOOK

Glacier Overlook | Moderate | 2.0+ miles | 400 feet | Out-and-back
Trailhead: Exit Glacier Nature Center (1)

Kenai Fjord's only established hiking trails are found at Exit Glacier. Glacier View Loop is an accessible trail (paved/gravel) with clear views of Exit Glacier. Glacier Overlook is a little further, a little higher, and a little better view of Exit Glacier. Along the way you'll notice signs marking the glacier's terminus for several years dating back to the late 1800s. It's a powerful visualization of how our climate is changing. That's something to think about. What you don't need to think about is whether you should hike this trail. Just do it. (You can also explore around the outwash plain and Exit Creek.)

Parking is limited at Exit Glacier Nature Center. Instead of taking a shuttle or hoping to get lucky in the afternoon, it's a good idea to arrive early. That'll give you time to hike Harding Icefield (below) and lighting is better in the morning. Now if you just happen to be driving into Seward one evening and it's a clear day, get in the park and take a look. Fog and clouds are common.

Harding Icefield | Strenuous | 8.7 miles | 3,200 feet | Out-and-back
Trailhead: Exit Glacier Nature Center (1)

Harding Icefield is all uphill but it's also all awesome! On clear days you'll have unbelievable views of Exit Glacier along the way. If you're short on time or energy, don't feel like you have to do the whole trail. While the emergency shelter and getting a good look at the vastness of Harding Icefield is pretty cool, you'll be all smiles at Marmot Meadows or Top of the Cliffs (if fog isn't clogging the views). It's all downhill on the way back. Don't leave without a quick walk to Glacier Overlook as well.

Lake Clark
Hiking Trails: 6+ miles

Lake Clark

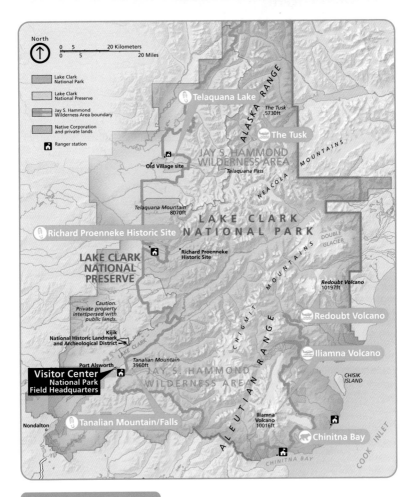

North

0	5	20 Kilometers	
0	5	20 Miles	

Lake Clark
National Park

Lake Clark
National Preserve

Jay S. Hammond
Wilderness Area boundary

Native Corporation
and private lands

Ranger station

Telaquana Lake

ALASKA RANGE

The Tusk
5730ft

The Tusk

JAY S. HAMMOND
WILDERNESS AREA

Old Village site

Telaquana Pass

NEACOLA MOUNTAINS

Telaquana Mountain
8070ft

LAKE CLARK
NATIONAL PARK

DOUBLE
GLACIER

Richard Proenneke Historic Site

Richard Proenneke
Historic Site

LAKE CLARK
NATIONAL
PRESERVE

CHIGMIT MOUNTAINS

Redoubt Volcano
10197ft

Redoubt Volcano

Caution.
Private property
interspersed with
public lands.

Kijik
National Historic Landmark
and Archeological District

LAKE CLARK

Iliamna Volcano

CHISIK
ISLAND

Tanalian Mountain
3960ft

Port Alsworth

Visitor Center
National Park
Field Headquarters

JAY S. HAMMOND
WILDERNESS AREA

ALEUTIAN RANGE

Iliamna
Volcano
10016ft

Nondalton

Tanalian Mountain/Falls

Chinitna Bay

CHINITNA BAY

COOK INLET

Hiking Lake Clark

From Port Alsworth, you can hike to Tanalian Mountain (strenuous, 8.1 miles), Tanalian Falls (moderate, 4.4 miles), and continue beyond the falls to Kontrashibuna Lake. Many visitors come to see Richard Proenneke's Cabin on Upper Twin Lake. Beyond that, Lake Clark is rugged wilderness, and with no roads penetrating its boundary, you'll have to get here by plane. Backcountry exploration requires finding your own route (with the help of the park rangers).

Brooks Falls

Katmai
Hiking Trails: 5 miles

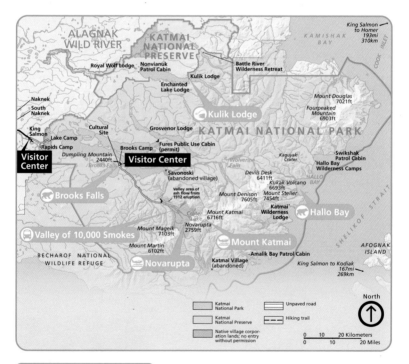

Hiking Katmai

From Brooks Camp Campground it's 3.2 miles (one-way) to the top of Dumpling Mountain and about 1.4 miles (one-way) to Brooks Falls Viewing Platform. There's also a short spur to a cultural site. That's it for maintained trails. However, if you take the Valley of 10,000 Smokes tour, you'll go on a short walk to a waterfall. The waterfall is nice, but the interesting thing is how the annual meltwater is eroding volcanic ash left here from the 1912 eruption.

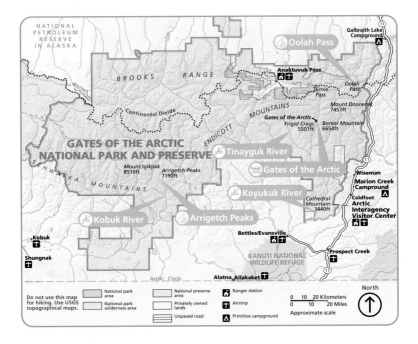

Oolah Pass

Anaktuvuk Pass

Galbraith Lake Campground

BROOKS RANGE

Ernie Pass

Oolah Pass

NATIONAL PETROLEUM RESERVE IN ALASKA

Mount Doonerak 7457ft

Continental Divide

MOUNTAINS

Gates of the Arctic Frigid Crags 5501ft

Boreal Mountain 6654ft

ENDICOTT

GATES OF THE ARCTIC NATIONAL PARK AND PRESERVE

Tinayguk River

Gates of the Arctic

Wiseman

Mount Igikpak 8510ft

Arrigetch Peaks 7190ft

Koyukuk River

Cathedral Mountain 3440ft

Marion Creek Campground

Coldfoot Arctic Interagency Visitor Center

SCHWATKA MOUNTAINS

Kobuk River

Arrigetch Peaks

Kobuk

Bettles/Evansville

Shungnak

KANUTI NATIONAL WILDLIFE REFUGE

Prospect Creek

Arctic Circle

Alatna Allakaket

North

Do not use this map for hiking. Use USGS topographical maps.

	National park area		National preserve area		Ranger station
National park wilderness area		Privately owned lands		Airstrip
	Unpaved road			Primitive campground

0 10 20 Kilometers
0 10 20 Miles
Approximate scale

DALTON HIGHWAY

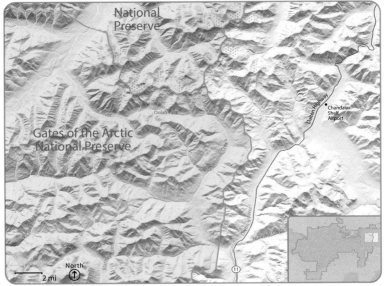

National Preserve

Oolah Pass

Dalton Highway

Chandalar Shelf Airport

Gates of the Arctic National Preserve

North

2 mi

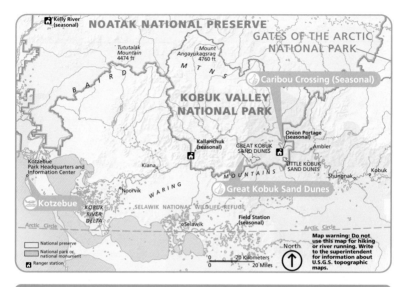

Hiking Gates of the Arctic and/or Kobuk Valley

You aren't dayhiking these two parks. While it is possible to walk into Gates of the Arctic from Dalton Highway, that's a backpacking trip. Most visitors' experiences take place in a plane. Another great way to explore them is by packraft. If you want to backpack or packraft, consult with the park or hire a guide. I included that detailed map on the left to show the terrain's ruggedness, which isn't obvious looking at elevation data or the maps above. It's also obvious in the picture below!

Arrigetch Peaks (Gates of the Arctic)

Hawaii Volcanoes

Remote Islands

HAWAII

🕐 **HAWAII (Washington, DC, minus 5 hours; minus 6 hours during daylight saving time)**

KAUA'I

NI'IHAU

O'AHU   **World War II Valor in the Pacific NM**

Honouliuli NM

HONOLULU

Kalaupapa NHP

MOLOKA'I

Haleakalä NP

HAWAII

MAUI

Pu'ukoholä Heiau NHS   *HAWAI'I*

Kaloko-Honoköhau NHP

Pu'uhonua o Hönaunau NHP

Hawai'i Volcanoes NP

AMERICAN SAMOA

🕐 **AMERICAN SAMOA (Washington, DC, minus 5 hours; minus 6 hours during daylight saving time)**

National Park of American Samoa

TUTUILA   *OFU*   *TA'Ü*

PAGO PAGO

AMERICAN SAMOA

U.S. VIRGIN ISLANDS

🕐 **PUERTO RICO and VIRGIN ISLANDS (Washington, DC, plus 1 hour; same time during daylight saving time)**

PUERTO RICO   VIRGIN ISLANDS

SAN JUAN
San Juan NHS

Virgin Islands NP

CHARLOTTE AMALIE   **Virgin Islands Coral Reef NM**

Buck Island Reef NM

Salt River Bay NHP and Ecological Preserve   **Christiansted NHS**

Salomon Beach

U.S. Virgin Islands
Hiking Trails: 40+ miles

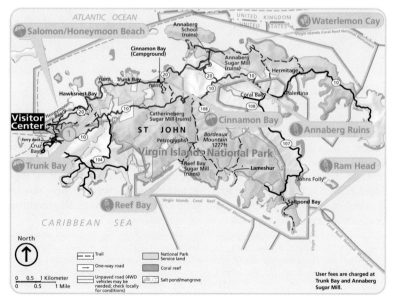

ATLANTIC OCEAN

UNITED KINGDOM

Salomon/Honeymoon Beach

Waterlemon Cay

Virgin Islands Coral Reef National Monument

Annaberg School (ruins)

Cinnamon Bay (Campground)

Annaberg Sugar Mill (ruins)

ruins   Trunk Bay   ruins

Hermitage

Hawksnest Bay

Trunk Bay

Coral Bay   Palestina

Visitor Center

Honeymoon Beach

Catherineberg Sugar Mill (ruins)

Cinnamon Bay

Annaberg Ruins

ferry dock
Cruz
Bay

ST   JOHN

Petroglyphs

Bordeaux Mountain 1277ft

Trunk Bay

Virgin Islands National Park

Reef Bay Sugar Mill (ruins)

Lameshur

Ram Head

Johns Folly

Reef Bay

Virgin Islands Coral Reef National Monument

Saltpond Bay

CARIBBEAN   SEA

North

↑

0   0.5   1 Kilometer
0   0.5   1 Mile

- - - Trail

→ One-way road

Unpaved road (4WD vehicles may be needed; check locally for conditions)

National Park Service land

Coral reef

Salt pond/mangrove

User fees are charged at Trunk Bay and Annaberg Sugar Mill.

U.S. Virgin Islands Favorites

(1) **Lind Point**
Easy | 2.4 miles | 160 feet

LIND POINT

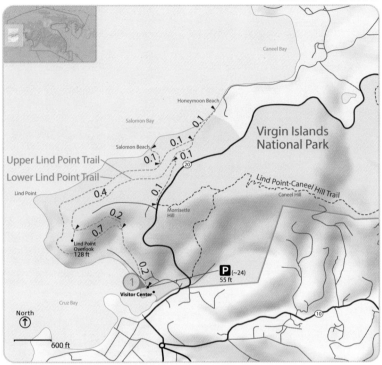

Lind Point | Easy | 2.4 miles | 160 feet | Out-and-back
Trailhead: Visitor Center (1)

Salomon and Honeymoon are two of the island's most picture-perfect beaches. It's a good idea to check them out. You can hike there via Upper or Lower Lind Point trails. The trailhead is located behind the visitor center. Both trails are somewhat rugged, with an abundance of rocks (not great for flip-flops). Lower, as the name suggests, has less elevation change. Upper has an overlook of Cruz Bay. Looping it is a good idea. Still, this one's all about the destination, not the journey. Go to enjoy the beaches.

> **More Trails**
>
> There are quite a few more trails. Reef Bay (4.5 miles) is popular, primarily because the park non-profit leads snorkeling trips where you hike down and (usually) boat out. There's a short spur to some petroglyphs. It's kind of neat. On the island's east end, you'll find short and easy trails to Ram Head (0.7 mile) and Drunk Bay (2.2 miles). Also in this area is Bordeaux Mountain Trail (0.8 mile, one-way). Bordeaux Mountain is the highest point in the park and the trail connects Bordeaux Mountain Road with Little Lameshur Bay. It's forested with occasional views. Nothing real exciting. Little Lameshur is probably the best part. There are also trails on the north shore to Brown Bay, Leinster Bay, and Francis Bay. They're worth a look, especially if you're interested in peaceful snorkeling.

Haleakala
Hiking Trails: 30+ miles

Sliding Sands

Haleakala Favorites

1-2 Sliding Sands
Strenuous | 11.0 miles | 1,600 feet

3 Pipiwai Falls
Moderate | 3.3 miles | 800 feet

SLIDING SANDS/HALEMAUU

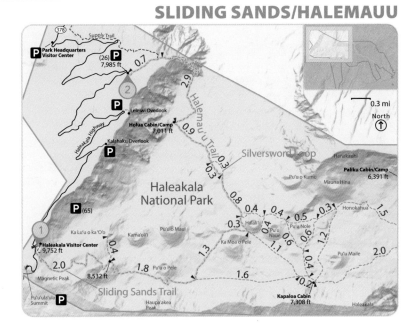

Sliding Sands | Strenuous | 11.0 miles | 1,600–3,100 feet | Point-to-point
Trailhead: Haleakala Visitor Center (1) or Halemauu (2), Haleakala Highway

Sliding Sands (AKA Keoneheehee) is incredible. It feels like you've been transported to another planet. The mileage sounds a little intimidating. So does the name. But even if you only walk a short way down the sliding sands to the first bench, it'll be a worthwhile journey. With that said, if you can make the point-to-point from Haleakala Visitor Center to Halemauu Trailhead (or reverse), you're in for a real treat. Just note, you'll probably put on a few more miles because once you're down by the cinder cones, it'll be hard to resist further exploration. And you must plan for a slower exit pace. It's all uphill. Even cutting down on the total elevation gain by starting at the Visitor Center, Halemauu is a very steep exit from the volcano's floor.

Sliding Sands begins at the southwest corner of the visitor center parking lot. You should start early. Come here for sunrise and you'll need to get a permit from recreation.gov. Sunrise is popular, but Sliding Sands is the real star. It's all about cinder cones, sliverswords, and a colorful otherworldly environment. There are even a couple cabins down there, if you'd like to spend the night. Even though you're in Hawaii, it gets cold at 10,000 feet. Come prepared for it. Layers and a good windbreaker are key. Parking is abundant at the Summit Visitor Center. There's room for about two dozen vehicles at Halemauu Trailhead. If doing a point-to-point, you'll need to arrange a ride or hitch. Hitching shouldn't take long, as there's a steady stream of visitors making their way up the volcano (it's likely easier to catch a ride ending at the summit, since almost everyone stops there, but that's only an educated guess).

PIPIWAI FALLS

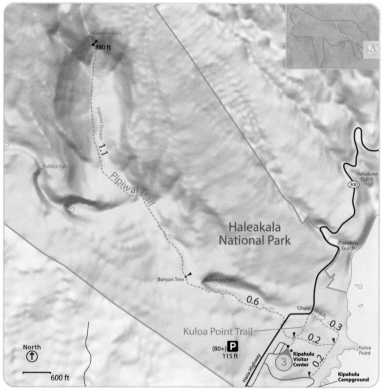

Pipiwai | Moderate | 3.3 miles | 800 feet | Out-and-back
Trailhead: Kipahulu Visitor Center (3)

Pipiwai is the other must-hike Haleakala Trail. Kipahulu Visitor Center is only 14 miles from Haleakala Summit as the bird flies. But the problem with having a massive volcano in between you and your desired destination is you probably can't drive there directly. Maybe it's a good problem. We don't need pavement across volcanoes, do we? It's about a 2.5-hour drive to Kipahulu from Haleakala Summit, arriving from the south via Piilani Highway (mass-marketed as a rough and terrible roadway that will wreck your rental and void the agreement—it may void your rental agreement, but it is not a terrible road, in fact, if all you're doing is driving, it's far more enjoyable than the infinitely-more-popular Hana Highway). Pipiwai explores a lush jungle, an extreme contrast to the summit's barren Marscape. Along the way, you'll pass a viewpoint of Makahiku Falls, a huge banyan tree, a bamboo forest, trickling cascades, and its conclusion, 300 feet of falling water known as Pipiwai Falls. It's understandable if you don't want to lug a ton of gear to Hawaii, but if you can, camping at Kipahulu or booking a night (or two) in Hana is a good idea to get to the falls early and have an enjoyable experience on the Hana Highway.

Hawaii Volcanoes
Hiking Trails: 100+ miles

Kilauea Iki

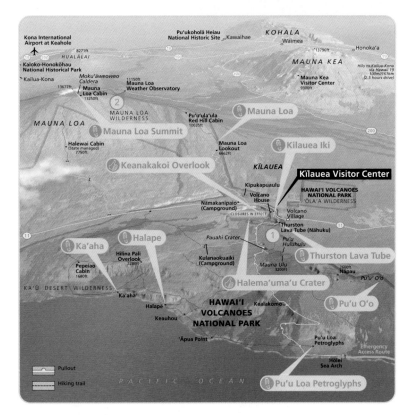

Hawaii Volcanoes Favorites

(1) **Kilauea Iki**
Moderate | 3.2 miles | 600 feet

(2) **Mauna Loa Summit**
Strenuous | 12.7 miles | 2,700 feet

KILAUEA IKI/THURSTON LAVA TUBE

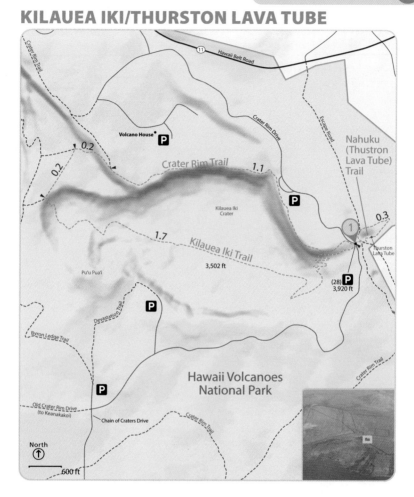

Kilauea Iki | Moderate | 3.2 miles | 600 feet | Loop
Trailhead: Kilauea Iki Overlook (1)

Kilauea Iki is a fun look into the park's volcanic past. From the overlook you can see the old lava lake's "bathtub ring" and a well-worn path across the crater. Make your way around the crater's rim and it's down to the crater you go. The trail is easy to follow. Almost every single person goes in a counterclockwise fashion, saving the steep climb back up to the overlook for the end. I prefer ending with the easy Crater Rim Trail, looking back into the crater you just crossed along the way. But it hardly matters. If you have a preference, do it.

Be sure to spare a few minutes and hike the short loop through Thurston Lava Tube (Nahuku). It'll probably be busy here, as this is a coach bus stop, but it's a unique, easy hike.

MAUNA LOA SUMMIT

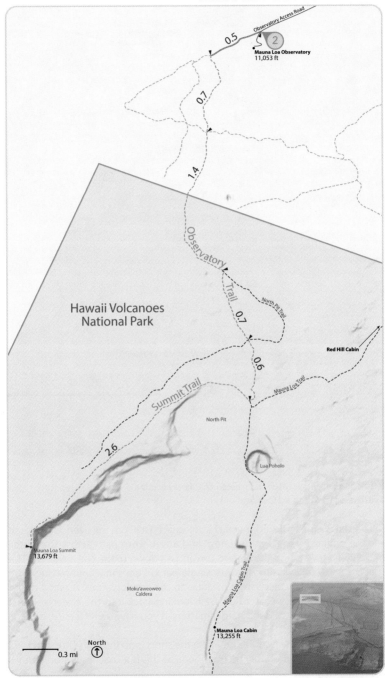

Observatory Access Road

0.5

2

Mauna Loa Observatory
11,053 ft

0.7

1.4

Observatory Trail

0.7

North Pit Trail

Red Hill Cabin

0.6

Mauna Loa Trail

Hawaii Volcanoes
National Park

Summit Trail

2.6

North Pit

Lua Poholo

Mauna Loa Summit
13,679 ft

Moku'aweoweo
Caldera

Mauna Loa Cabin Trail

Mauna Loa Cabin
13,255 ft

North

0.3 mi

Mauna Loa Summit | Strenuous | 12.7 miles | 2,700 feet | Out-and-back
Trailhead: Mauna Loa Observatory Road (2)

Dayhiking is possible but you better get acclimated for the elevation. There's a campground along Saddle Road, sleep in your car at the trailhead (if allowed), find a high-elevation vacation rental, do something. Thinking my body's more resilient than it is, I woke up early at sea level, drove to the trailhead and started strolling up the world's most massive volcano (mountain if you measure from its base below the water's surface). The altitude kicked my butt, and I ended up averaging about one mph. Fortunately, I was staying at the cabin on the caldera's eastern rim, but it was a miserable experience. Learn from my mistakes. You do not want to feel miserable because views of Mauna Kea and looking into the summit's caldera are out of this world. Plus, it's going to look like a completely new volcano after the 2022 eruption!

The trail begins from a small parking lot at the end of Mauna Loa Observatory Road. You'll need a permit if you plan on spending the night. Fortunately, you can phone (808.985.6178) in your request. This trail was closed when we went to print. However, on the other side of the mountain, the trail to Red Hill Cabin just reopened, so things change. Check with the park about current status.

There are quite a few more trails, but the only thing I'd consider a mandatory activity is to hike to Keanakakoi Overlook if there's a lava lake at Halemaumau Crater. When filled with lava it lights up the night sky, creating a very doomsday-type feeling. It's super awesome. The view, not the feeling. I'm not one of these people hoping for the end of days.

Lava should be priority one. If the volcano is active, you do what's necessary to see some lava. After you've filled your lava quota (if that's possible), then start looking at past volcanic activity (Devestation Trail or Napau Trail to Mauna Ulu). It's also worth noting, you can reach Mauna Loa Summit from the south as well. It's a longer trek, but you'll find cabins along the way. Hiking the coast to Keauhou, Halape, or Kaaha makes for a fun (but hot) backpacking trip, too. There's an awful lot of unique adventures waiting for you on this island, so do some research and budget your time wisely.

More Trails

Safety

Many of the park's trails cross open lava fields. Particularly if you're hiking along the coast, be prepared for considerable sun exposure and hot conditions. Temperature at the visitor center is often cool, prompting many guests to buy a sweatshirt from the gift shop.

If you're looking for lava. It's always a good idea to contact the visitor center for current activity and safe-viewing locations (if active). With that said, it's also a good idea to search the internet and social media for up-to-date imagery.

Halemaumau

American Samoa
Hiking Trails: 15+ miles

Ofu Beach

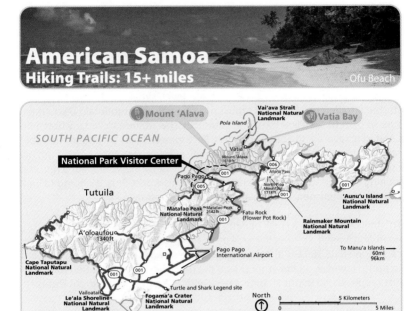

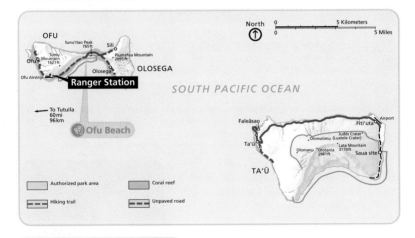

Hiking American Samoa

On Tutuila Island, you can get good views of Pola Island via Pola Island Trail (easy, 0.1 mile) or the steep, rope-aided Tuafanua Trail (strenuous, 2.2 miles). On Tau, you can hike to Siu Point (moderate, 5.7 miles). On Olosega, there's a trail to Oge Beach (easy, 2.7 miles). On Ofu, you can gain spectacular views from the top of Tumu Mountain (strenuous, 5.5 miles).

We Hope You Enjoyed
Your National Parks

And The Dayhiker's Guide
to the National Parks

You Might Also Like...

Your Guide to the National Parks

By Michael Joseph Oswald

Printed in the USA

The Complete Guide to All
63 National Parks
A Stone Road Press Title

This is the everything book. Lodging & camping info, hiking tables, all park activities, history, logistics, maps, flora & fauna, accessibility, weather, and tips & recommendations for all 63 parks.

7.5" x 9" | 724 pages | $28

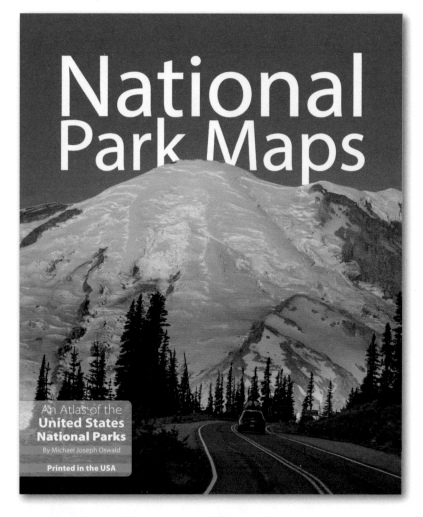

An atlas-sized title that's much more than just maps. It includes driving distances, favorite lists, itinerary suggestions, need-to-know info, and why you should visit each of the 63 U.S. National Parks. And there's more than 100 photos to help you preview each park before setting foot in them.

10.75" x 13.5" | 187 pages | $20

**America's Best Ideas
My National Parks Journal**

Park-specific checklists, illustrations, and plenty of space to document your National Park travels!

5" x 7" | 284 pages | $15

Photo Credits

Michael J. Oswald: Cover, Intro Images, 9, 10, 16, 23, 24, 28, 30, 31, 35, 37, 38, 43, 44, 45, 55, 56, 57, 59, 61, 64, 67, 68, 69, 70, 71, 73, 74, 76, 78, 79, 84, 85, 87, 99, 100, 105, 108, 112, 113, 116, 117, 123, 125, 128, 130, 132, 133, 134, 135, 142, 144, 152, 153, 158, 159, 161, 164, 165, 172, 173, 175, 180, 181, 190, 191, 193, 194, 195, 205, 209, 213, 217, 222, 225, 228, 231, 232, 236, 245, 257, 259, 270, 277, 278, 288, 293, 305, 306, 307, 317, 318, 319, 327, 334, 337, 338, 341, 344, 345, 347, 350, 353, Closing Images, Back Cover

Rebecca Latson: National Parks Traveler Recommendation

NPS: 330, 331, 340, 343, 354